# The Descent of the Soul and the Archaic

*The Descent of the Soul and the Archaic* explores the motif of *kátabasis* (a "descent" into an imaginal underworld) and the importance it held for writers from antiquity to the present, with an emphasis on its place in psychoanalytic theory.

This collection of chapters builds on Jung's insights into *katabasis* and *nekyia* as models for deep self-descent and the healing process which follows. The contributors explore ancient and modern notions of the self, as obtained through a "descent" to a deeper level of imaginal experience. With an awareness of the difficulties of applying contemporary psychological precepts to ancient times, the contributors explore various modes of self-formation as a process of discovery. Presented in three parts, the chapters assess contexts and texts, goddesses, and theoretical alternatives.

This book will be of interest to scholars and analysts working in wide-ranging fields, including classical studies; all schools of psychoanalysis, especially Jung's; and postmodern thought, especially the philosophy of Deleuze.

**Paul Bishop** is William Jacks Chair of Modern Languages in the School of Modern Languages and Cultures at the University of Glasgow, UK.

**Terence Dawson** is an independent scholar, following a career of teaching in the UK and Singapore. He has a special interest in the relation between literature, music, and the visual arts.

**Leslie Gardner** is the Director of the international literary agency Artellus Limited, based in London, UK. She is a founding member of the International Association of Jungian Studies and is currently a Fellow in the Department of Psychosocial and Psychoanalytic Studies at the University of Essex.

# The Descent of the Soul and the Archaic

## Katábasis and Depth Psychology

Edited by Paul Bishop,
Terence Dawson and
Leslie Gardner

Routledge
Taylor & Francis Group

LONDON AND NEW YORK

Cover image: *"The Architecture of Katabasis"*, Chirag Jindal, M.Arch Thesis, 2016

First published 2023
by Routledge
4 Park Square, Milton Park, Abingdon, Oxon OX14 4RN

and by Routledge
605 Third Avenue, New York, NY 10158

*Routledge is an imprint of the Taylor & Francis Group, an informa business*

*British Library Cataloguing-in-Publication Data*
A catalogue record for this book is available from the British Library

ISBN: 978-0-367-51498-3 (hbk)
ISBN: 978-0-367-51501-0 (pbk)
ISBN: 978-1-003-05413-9 (ebk)

DOI: 10.4324/9781003054139

Typeset in Times New Roman
by SPi Technologies India Pvt Ltd (Straive)

# Contents

# Preface

The motif of a *descent* into a realm associated with death is one of the oldest motifs in world mythology, and one of the oldest in Western literature. It featured in stories told in the fertile crescent of Mesopotamia from about 2100 BCE. It was a key motif in a Sumerian myth about the goddess Innana. Some eight hundred years later, it formed part of a dream in the Babylonian *Epic of Gilgamesh* (Tablet VII), and several hundred years later, in a new story about Enkidu descending into the underworld (Tablet XII).[1] The motif is also found in the mythology of ancient Egypt, most obviously in the various stories about Osiris.

In Greek mythology, accounts of a physical descent into the underworld are relatively rare. They include three stories about Herakles: his 'twelfth' labour (to bring Cerberus up from the underworld), his rescue of Theseus (usually tagged onto this myth), and his rescue of Alcestis.[2] They also include the failed attempt by Theseus and Pirithous to recover Persephone (who had been abducted by Hades), the more successful descent of Hermes to do the same, and the descent of Orpheus into the underworld to recover his wife.[3] Although often referred to as such, the episode in the *Odyssey* in which the wily hero *summons* up Teiresias and other shades is not strictly a descent: it is a *nekyia* (book 11). The most frequently cited example of the *descent* motif in classical literature is not Greek but Roman. It appears in Virgil's *Aeneid* (written 29–19 BCE), in which the protagonist descends into the underworld (his *descensus ad inferos*). He passes personifications of human ailments and vices, then monsters, then the unburied dead clamouring for burial, then those who died for love (including Dido), then heroes, and then those guilty of monstrous crimes before he finally meets his father's shade, who foretells both his fate and that of Rome.

All descent stories invite the question: How do we define the figure who makes the descent? This question is complicated in the Greek archaic and classical ages by new ways of thinking about individual identity. An important aspect of this development can be illustrated by the evolution of the meaning attributed to the word *psyche* (from *psýchein* = to breathe).[4] In Homer, there is no indication that the psyche represents a significant aspect of a living person: the soul is merely something which departs at death (that is, when a person stops breathing).[5] During the next two centuries, how-ever, the soul gradually came to mean the quality of being *alive* (= *empsychos*, lit. 'en-souled'). Empedocles refers to the soul as that which animates all liv-ing things. Heraclitus may have been the first to intuit the implications of this when he writes: 'You would not find out the boundaries of soul, even by trav-elling along every path: so deep [βαθὺν] a measure does it have'.[6] Pythagoreans and Orphics believed that the soul was immortal. Herodotus uses the word to indicate moral character (describing Telines); so, too, does Thucydides (in Pericles' funeral oration).[7] In his final days, Socrates re-affirms that the soul is immortal, imperishable, and can be classified as either pure *or* polluted (*Phaedo*). The psyche was associated with deeply felt pleasure *and* pain.[8] By the end of the fifth century BCE, it had become possible not only to distin-guish between body and soul but also to associate a person's behaviour with their soul.

Aristotle preferred to privilege sense impressions, and he doubted whether the soul influenced thought. Epicurus tried to ally sense impressions with his theory of atoms, and yet he subscribed to the theory of a divided soul. Lucretius distinguishes between two aspects of the soul. One is the soul proper, the *anima*, which is composed of sense impressions, which are non-rational and stem from all parts of the body. The other describes intellectual processes, which are rational and which he refers to as the *animus*, the mind, which he locates in the middle of the breast.[9] The stoics insisted that only humans have a soul, that all psychological and intellectual activity stems from the soul, and that all its activities are rational: in other words, not only thought but even the emotions are 'rational'.[10]

The evolution of the different meanings ascribed to the *soul* was to have a considerable impact on religious and philosophical thought. The Greek word *katábasis* (lit. a 'going down') applies to any kind of *descent*. In geography, it describes a move from higher ground to lower ground. In military terms, it designates a retreat.[11] But most importantly, it came to be associated with the central experience in the mystery traditions, not only those identified with specific cult centres (such as Eleusis) but also those associated with Dionysus and Orpheus, which were practised throughout most of Greece. In reference to these traditions, a *katábasis* refers to the 'descent into oneself' in search of spiritual enlightenment. It is for this reason that in later depth psychology (Freudian and Jungian), the word came to refer to a descent both into oneself and into the deeper implications of a dream or waking fantasy.

In myth, the figure that 'descends' is a metaphor related to the *society* in which the story arose rather than to any specific individual. But in the mys-tery religions, the *katábasis* refers to the *initiate* 'descending' into themselves from a deliberate desire to obtain a life-transforming experience. In psycho-analysis, the 'descent' might refer to a dream motif, which would be regarded as either largely or entirely unconscious, or to the analysand deliberately pro-voking a dream-like state.

The ancient Greeks *buried* their dead. There is no need to speculate why they thought of the underworld as a place 'below' ground level. But this does not explain the combination of fascination and fear that the 'underworld' exercises on the imaginations of the mythmakers of Sumerian, Babylonian, Greek, and Roman culture. A possible reason is provided by Seneca in one of his moral essays, when he suggests that it is natural to become dizzy when one stands at the edge of a high precipice and looks down.[12] Might this memory of vertigo help to explain why the human imagination has long been fascinated by the idea of an *abyss*? Recently, James I. Porter has suggested that the late Roman self was not fashioned 'as a conduit to self-knowledge or to some non-illusory truth about oneself, but only as an abyssal problem'.[13] That is, in his view, to refer to the soul is to *suggest* a descent into an abyss.

In our post-Romantic age, we take it for granted that to explore the self is to stare into the depths. In 'The Imp of the Perverse' (1845), the narrator describes the temptation to behave in an unaccustomed fashion in metaphorical terms: 'We stand upon the brink of a precipice. We peer into the abyss – we grow sick and dizzy'. Hegel regarded the abyss as 'the materiality of Nature from which the soul struggles to free itself'.[14] In *Thus Spoke Zarathustra*, the Wanderer realises that his every experience reflects himself.[15] He is hit by an 'abyss-deep thought', which is *his* thought.[16] To self-reflect is to stare into the depths, and to expose oneself to the risks that such inquiry entails.

Nevertheless, it must be insisted that every descent – especially a descent into one's authentic self or soul – implies a need to re-*ascend*, that is, to re-connect with the social world.

On being told that he must return with Cerberus, Herakles descends into the underworld as if he were taking a walk to the nearest gym. Writing in the early fourth century BCE, Xenophon describes the extraordinarily well-managed retreat (*katábasis*) of the large army of mercenaries of which he was part. But he gave his work the title *Anábasis* (ascent, goal) to indicate the *success* of the endeavour, which is epitomised in the soldiers' cry 'The sea! The sea!' They have been through an ordeal; they are now safe. And yet, it is not until the time of Virgil that the challenge implicit in the ascent is explicitly formulated. Shortly before Aeneas makes his descent into the underworld, the Sibyl warns him:

> From Avernus, the descent is easy.
> Night and day, the doors of gloomy Dis stand open.
> But to recall your steps and return to the world above,
> There is the task, and there the challenge.[17]

This emphasis on the difficulty of the 'ascent' or return is equally important in psychoanalysis. An individual can quickly be overwhelmed by their own nightmares. C.G. Jung built his theories on his own experience of a series of vivid waking fantasies. He recorded them and spent considerable time trying to make sense of them.[18] He described this both as his 'descent into the unconscious' and his 'confrontation with the unconscious'. Later, he came to be fascinated by alchemy, which he understood as a psychological *katábasis*. But his attention was always on the outcome: the *rebirth* – that is, the *anábasis*: the need to re-ascend, or return to reality.

This collection of essays began life as papers delivered at 'Descent of the Soul: Katábasis and Depth Psychology', a conference held at the Freud Museum, London, in the summer of 2019. Its purpose was to explore how depth psychology can illuminate ancient texts which involve a descent or *katábasis*, either because they express an important aspect of a culture or because they reveal an important tendency pertinent to a character. Although the theme was expected to appeal to scholars and analysts working from a post-Jungian perspective, the organisers were particularly glad to receive proposals from scholars and analysts working from other theoretical perspectives.

The study has an introduction, three parts, and an epilogue. In the introduction, Paul Bishop outlines the importance that *kátabasis* held for writers from antiquity to the present, with an emphasis on its place in psychoanalytic theory and, especially, in the work of C.G. Jung. The first part explores the motif of katábasis in a selection of texts written between the Homeric age and the late Hellenistic period.

It begins with two articles on ancient Greek culture. It should be noted that contributors have been encouraged to use their preferred system of transliteration. In 'Psycho-cosmic Descent in Ancient Greece: From Abyss to Self-containment', Richard Seaford explores Jung's debt to ancient Greek culture. Referencing the *Homeric Hymn to Demeter* and texts by Herakleitos, Parmenides, and Plato, he outlines the evolution of Greek ideas and practices about a ritual descent to the underworld, the experience there of cosmic unity, and the bottomless inner self. He then traces how these lead to the construction of a new conception of a self-contained inner self with access to universal Being.

In '*Katabasis* in Reverse: Heraclitus, the Archaic, and the Abyss', Paul Bishop reflects on Jung's reading of Heraclitus in the light of two texts from the Christian mystical tradition: the fifth-century Pseudo-Dionysus the Areopagite's claim about the soul's knowledge of God, and the exhortation of the fourteenth-century German theologian, Johannes Tauler, to 'sink into thy inmost soul, into thy nothingness'. His purpose is to explore how both these texts illuminate the implications of the relation between the archaic and the abyss in the work of Heraclitus.

The following essay is on Roman literature. In 'Virgil, Epicureanism, and unseemly behaviour', Terence Dawson examines the tension between a quasi-social and a mythic reality in each of the three *katábases* at the heart of the epyllion in *Georgics* IV. His purpose is to offer a fresh interpretation of the myth of Orpheus and Eurydice, to suggest that it illustrates the need to cultivate a peace of mind (*ataraxia*) that cannot be shaken by the vicissitudes of either social or political life, and to propose that it may represent the first emphatically personal interpretation of a myth.

The last two essays in this part focus on the importance of language. In 'The Neoplatonic *Katábasis* of the Soul to the World of the Senses: Language as a Tool for Regaining Self-Consciousness', Maria Chriti analyses views of the soul by commentators on Aristotle, from the School of Alexandria, who held that the deepest, most authentic aspect of the soul must be recovered. The soul's *katábasis* from the One to the earth thus also requires the soul to aspire to the heights. The essay offers a Jungian perspective on Neoplatonic claims about the fall of the soul from the One to the world of the senses.

In 'Acting Out, Science Fiction and Lucian's *True History*', Leslie Gardner proposes that Lucian was consciously exploring the question why people like to read what they know is not true. Foregrounding his use of defamiliarisation, she argues that the imagination is a mirror which becomes both an 'influencing machine' (Victor Tausk) and a 'projection' (C.G. Jung) of the writer's 'acting out' of their own defensive strategies, whether in relation to society or to their own sexual anxieties. Her purpose is to suggest that every fiction is both a katábasis and an acting out of the author's own 'tissue of lies'.

The second part explores the motif of *katábasis* as it refers either to goddesses from different cultures (ancient Sumer, ancient India) or to saints (in the Greek Byzantine tradition). All three essays seek to recover the importance of a female tradition and a feminist perspective on traditions that have been subsumed by patriarchal assumptions. The first two explore the relevance in myth of Jung's concept of the transcendent function.

In 'Inanna's Descent to the Netherworld and Analytical Psychology: What Has the Mistress of All the Lands Done?', Catriona Miller presents an intriguing new reading of the myth of Inanna. Drawing upon the latest scholarly work, she presents an intriguing Jungian reading of the story of the goddess's descent to the underworld. In contrast to Brinton Perera (1981) and de Shong Meador (1992), she argues that Enki represents socially adapted consciousness; that Ereshkigal represents the neglected unconscious; and that Inanna personifies what Jung called the transcendent function, the fusion of opposites: that is, Enki becomes better grounded; Ereshkigal is consoled.

In '*Katabasis* in an Ancient Indian Myth: Savitri Encounters Yama', Sulagna Sengupta explores the Indian myth of Savitri and Yama. In contrast to both traditional readings, which foreground devotion and sacrifice, and 'colonialist' readings, which distort Indian sensibility, she argues that the story can be usefully read through a Jungian lens. Savitri's descent underscores the dual nature of consciousness and illustrates the importance of the reconciling third. Savitri emerges deepened and darkened through privation and longing, and Yama is touched by a feminine luminescence coming from another world: the sacred temenos of hell.

In 'Katabasis in Middle Eastern Female Hagiography: A Post-Jungian Perspective', Roula-Maria Dib offers a fresh perspective on the stories of several Byzantine Greek Orthodox female saints who sought refuge in 'maternal' environments. Whereas the hagiographic literature on these saints focuses on the motif of ascension and reflects a 'worldly' patriarchy, her purpose is to explore the heroism of female 'sainthood' and to highlight the psychically nourishing aspects of a descent into nature and the self.

The third part brings the study into modern times. It explores the importance of katabatic metaphors for psychoanalysis, the relation between classical myth and contemporary tendencies, the intersection of Freudian, Jungian, and Deleuzian theories.

'Raising Hell: Freud's Katabatic Metaphors in *The Interpretation of Dreams*', by Jonathan Shann, takes a fresh look at the katabatic metaphors in Freud's masterpiece, which include images of underworld rivers, royal roads, furies, Titans, and Tartarus. It illustrates how metaphors of easy descent (*'facilis descensus Averno'*) and tangled paths (the mycelium of dream-wishes) shape analytic practice, and how the related metaphors of conquistador and outsider are at once constitutive and subversive of his theory-building.

In 'Orestes, *Katabasis*, and Aggrieved Masculine Entitlement', Kurt Lampe explores the significance of the myth of Orestes for the polis of Rhegium, the implications of the visit of Orestes to Athens in the *Oresteia*, and the importance of the myth for understanding aggrieved masculine entitlement. His purpose is to shift the discussion from the character of Orestes to the individuals and communities who tell his story and thereby to show how repetitive and destructive stupidity can be prevented by better understanding what needs to be integrated.

In 'Regression, *Nekyia*, and Involution in the Thought of Jung and Deleuze', Christian McMillan revisits conceptual affinities between the work of Jung and Deleuze, both of whom were interested in 're-birth', and the myth of the hero who embarked on a 'night-sea journey' (*nekyia*), which Jung associated with katábasis, and Deleuze, with 'involution'. He proposes a Deleuzian adoption of a 'Jungian reading' of Freud's death instinct, and a theory of both psychological and biological-vitalistic transformation.

The Epilogue features a poem which illustrates how psychoanalytic theory enriches a profound personal experience. In 'Salon Noir', classical scholar and poet Ruth Padel describes her 'descent' into the limestone Grotte de Niaux (near Ariège in the French Pyrenees), and her thoughts on coming face to face with the 13,000-year-old rock paintings in its most famous recess. As she gazes at the images of bison and goats, and the wall of horses 'like a page of Leonardo's sketch-book', she is reminded of all that her mother taught her about the need to be curious, the gift of wonder about the natural world, and the importance of time and transformation.

Leslie Gardner and Terence Dawson

# Notes

1 See *The Epic of Gilgamesh*, tr. Andrew George. London: Allen Lane/Penguin, 1999; on the problems of Tablet XII, see N. Vulpe, 'Irony and the Unity of the Gilgamesh Epic', *Journal of Near Eastern Studies*, October 1994, vol. 53, no. 4, 275–283.

2 References to the story about Herakles and Cerberus appear in both the *Iliad* (8.362–369) and the *Odyssey* (11.617–626), although its description as the 'twelfth' labour is much later. For the myth about his rescue of Theseus, see Euripides, *The Madness of Herakles*; as well as Apollodorus, *The Library*, tr. J.G. Frazer, Cambridge, MA: Harvard University Press, 1921, vol. 1, pp. 234–237, and vol. 2, pp. 152–153. For the myth about his rescue of Alcestis, see Euripides, *Alcestis*.

3 Of the Greek myth of Orpheus and Eurydice, only fragmentary references survive; the earliest extant account of the myth is found in Virgil's *Georgics*.

4 See H. Lorenz, 'Ancient Theories of Soul', *Stanford Encyclopedia of Philosophy* (Summer 2009 Edition), ed. E.N. Zalta (ed.). Available online HTTP <https://plato.stanford.edu/archives/sum2009/entries/ancient-soul/>.

5 For example, Achilles says: '[I am] constantly staking my life [*psuchèn*] in fight' (see *Iliad*, 9.322); cf. J.N. Bremmer, *The Early Greek Concept of the Soul*, Princeton: Princeton University Press, 1983.

6 Diels-Kranz fragment B45; cited in G.S. Kirk, J.E. Raven and M. Schofield (eds), *The Presocratic Philosophers*, 2nd edn, Cambridge: Cambridge University Press, 1983, p. 205.

7 Herodotus, 7.153; Thucydides, 2.40.3.

8 For example, at the outset of *Oedipus the King*, the protagonist tells the elders: 'My soul [*psuchè*] mourns equally for the city and for myself and for you' (*Oedipus Tyrannus*, 64).

9 Lucretius, *De Rerum Natura*, tr. W.H.D. Rouse, rev. M.F. Smith, Cambridge, MA: Harvard University Press, 1992, pp. 94–95 (3.94–96).

10 This anticipates Pascal's famous aphorism, *Le cœur a ses raisons que la raison ne connaît point* (the heart has its reasons of which reason knows nothing); see B. Pascal, *Pensées*, #397, in *Oeuvres complètes II*, ed. M. Le Guern, Paris: Gallimard, 2000, p. 679.

11 As, for example, in the greater part of Xenophon's *Anábasis*.

12 Seneca, 'On the Trials of Travel', in Seneca, *Epistles 1-65*, tr. R.M. Gummere, Cambridge, MA: Harvard University Press, 1917, pp. 384–385.

13 J.I. Porter, 'Time for Foucault? Reflections on the Roman Self from Seneca to Augustine', *Foucault Studies*, 2017, vol. 22, 113–133.

14 See J. Mills, *The Unconscious Abyss: Hegel's Anticipation of Psychoanalysis*, New York: State University of New York Press, 2002, p. xiv.

15 See F. Nietzsche, *Thus Spoke Zarathustra*, tr. G. Parkes, Oxford: Oxford University Press, 2005, p. 131, using an idea he borrowed from Emerson (see note on p. 307).

16 Nietzsche, *Zarathustra*, p. 140.

17 *Aeneid* VI, 126–129 (my translation), see Virgil, *Eclogues, Georgics, Aeneid I-VI*, tr. H. Rushton Fairclough, rev. G.P. Goold, Cambridge MA: Harvard University Press, 1999, pp. 540–541.

18 C.G. Jung, *The Red Book: Liber Novus*, ed. S. Shamdasani, tr. M. Kyburz, J. Peck, and S. Shamdasani, New York and London: Norton, 2009.

# Contributors

**Paul Bishop** holds the William Jacks Chair of Modern Languages in the School of Modern Languages and Cultures at the University of Glasgow. For Routledge, he has edited *The Archaic: The Past in the Present* (2012), co-edited (with Leslie Gardner) *The Ecstatic and the Archaic: An Analytical Psychological Inquiry* (2018), and has recently published *On the Blissful Islands: With Nietzsche & Jung in the Shadow of the Superman* (2016) and *Ludwig Klages and the Philosophy of Life: A Vitalist Toolkit* (2017).

**Dr Maria Chriti** is at the Aristotle University of Thessaloniki, School of Modern Greek Language. Her fields of interest include Aristotelian logic, ancient linguistics, philosophy of language, and Neoplatonism. She has done her post-doctorate research at Center for Hellenic Studies, University of Harvard, and her work includes 'Aristotle as a Name-giver: The Cognitive Aspect of his Theory and Practice'. Among her published works are (with A.-F. Christidis & M. Arapopoulou), *A History of Ancient Greek: From the Beginnings to Late Antiquity* (Cambridge UP, 2007) and (with P. Kotzia) 'Ancient Philosophers on Language', in G. Giannakis et al. (eds), *The Encyclopedia of Ancient Greek Language and Linguistics* (2014), vol. 1, 124–133.

**Terence Dawson** is an independent scholar, following a career of teaching in Brazil, the UK, and Singapore. He has a special interest in both music and the visual arts. With Polly Young-Eisendrath, he co-edited *The Cambridge Companion to Jung* (1997; 2nd edn, 2008). He is the author of *The Effective Protagonist in the Nineteenth-Century British Novel: Scott, Brontë, Eliot, Wilde* (2004), and articles mostly on English and European literature.

**Roula-Maria Dib** obtained her PhD degree at the University of Leeds and is presently Assistant Professor of English at the American University in Dubai and editor-in-chief of *Indelible*, the university's literary journal. She teaches courses in composition, literature, creative writing, and world mythology. Her doctoral dissertation focuses on the role of Carl Jung's alchemy and individuation theories in Modernist poetics. She has a forthcoming book, *Jungian Metaphor in Modernist Literature* (Routledge), and writes poems, essays, and articles in several journals. The themes that pervade her work usually revolve around different aspects of human nature, ekphrasis, surrealism, alchemy, and mythology. She is a member of the International Association for Jungian Studies (IAJS), the Jungian Society for Scholarly Studies (JSSS), and the British Association for Modernist Studies (BAMS).

**Leslie Gardner**, PhD, is the Director of the international literary agency Artellus Limited, based in London, and the founding member of the International Association for Jungian Studies. She is the author of *Rhetorical Investigations: G.B. Vico and C.G. Jung* (Routledge, 2013), co-editor (with Luke Hockley) of *House: The Wounded Healer on Television* (Routledge, 2010), co-editor (with Fran Gray) of *Feminist Views from Somewhere* (Routledge, 2017), co-editor (with Raya Jones) of and contributor of two chapters to *Narratives of Individuation* (Routledge, 2019), author of a chapter on Cocteau and archetypal theories in *Routledge International Handbook of Jungian Film Studies* (Routledge, 2018), as well as author of articles and reviews. She is presently Fellow in the Department of Psychosocial and Psychoanalytic Studies, University of Essex. Previous IAJS regional conferences in London include '(Dis)enchantment' with Mark Saban and Kevin Lu, 'Feminist Views from Somewhere' with co-convenor Fran Gray, and 'Ecstasy and Archaic Thought' in London in Summer 2018, the first in a series of classics and depth psychology gatherings, and a subsequent book including papers (edited with Paul Bishop) as *The Ecstatic and the Archaic* (Routledge, 2018).

**Kurt Lampe**'s doctoral work was in ancient philosophical hedonism, leading to *The Birth of Hedonism* in 2015 (Princeton UP). After that, he moved into modern continental philosophy with a 2016 AHRC Networking Grant, from which the primary outputs are two forthcoming collections on Stoicism in modern French and German philosophy (Bloomsbury). Most recently, he has become fascinated by ancient Greek religious practices and their bearing on philosophy of mind and the cultivation of mental wellbeing. Throughout 2018–2019, he has been running workshops with psychotherapists, academics from various subjects, and modern pagans from various backgrounds in order to think about the interface of 'pagan' polytheism and mental wellbeing (see https://aesculapiads.com).

**Christian McMillan** was Senior Research Officer in the Department for Psychosocial and Psychoanalytic Studies at the University of Essex working on an AHRC funded project '"One World": Logical and Ethical Implications of Holism' (2016–2018). His doctoral thesis, 'The Image of Thought in Jung's Whole-Self: A Critical study' (2014), focused on similarities and differences in the thought of the depth psychologist C.G. Jung and the French post-structuralist philosopher Gilles Deleuze. Forthcoming publications include (co-edited with Roderick Main and

David Henderson) *Jung, Deleuze, and the Problematic Whole* (Routledge, 2019); 'Jung, Literature, and Aesthetics', in Jon Mills (ed.), *Jung and Philosophy* (Routledge, 2019); and 'The "image of thought" and the State-form in Jung's "The Undiscovered Self" and Deleuze and Guattari's "Treatise on Nomadology" in *Jung, Deleuze, and the Problematic Whole*. Previous publications include 'Archetypal Intuition: Beyond the Human' in David Henderson (ed.), *Psychoanalysis, Culture and Society* (Cambridge Scholars, 2012); and 'Jung and Deleuze: Enchanted Openings to the Other', *International Journal of Jungian Studies*, special issue (Dec, 2018).

**Dr Catriona Miller** is Senior Lecturer in Media at Glasgow Caledonian University with a particular interest in feminism and mythology from a Jungian perspective. Recent publications include 'Enki at Eridu: God of Directed Thinking', in L. Gardner and P. Bishop (eds), *The Ecstatic and the Archaic: An Analytical Psychological Inquiry* (Routledge, 2018), and 'A Jungian Textual Terroir' in L. Hockley (ed), *The Routledge International Handbook of Jungian Film Studies* (Routledge, 2018). She has a monograph titled *Cult TV Heroines: Angels, Aliens and Amazons* forthcoming with Bloomsbury.

**Ruth Padel** is a London poet, author, and conservationist, Professor of Poetry at King's College London, Fellow of the Royal Society of Literature. Recent poetry includes *Darwin – A Life in Poems*, a verse biography of her great-great-grandfather Charles Darwin; *The Mara Crossing*, on migration and immigration from cells to souls, trees, sharks, and human beings; *Learning to Make an Oud in Nazareth*, shortlisted for the T.S. Eliot Prize, on harmony and fission in ourselves and in the Middle East, and most recently *Emerald*, a lyrical exploration of the search for value in the mourning process. She started out as a classical Greek scholar, and her prose includes *In and Out of the Mind: Greek Images of the Tragic Self* and *Whom Gods Destroy: Elements of Greek and Tragic Madness*, as well as *Tigers in Red Weather*, a personal prose account of wild tiger conservation. She was Chair of Judges for the 2016 T.S. Eliot Prize and Judge for the 2016 International Man Booker Prize. Her poems have been published in *The New Yorker*, *Harvard Review*, *Kenyon Review*, *Times Literary Supplement*, *London Review of Books*, and *The White Review*. Awards include First Prize in the National Poetry Competition and a British Council 'Darwin Now' Fellowship. See www.ruthpadel.com.

**Sulagna Sengupta** is a Jungian scholar and the author of *Jung in India* (Spring Journal Books, 2013). She is a member of the International Association of Jungian Studies (IAJS) and has presented at IAJS conferences since 2014. Her paper, 'Indeterminate States: Cultural Other in Jung's India', presented at the 2018 IAJS–IAAP conference in Frankfurt, is planned for publication in the *International Journal of Jungian Studies* in 2020; and her paper 'Earth, Ecology and the Feminine' is to be published in *Feminist*

*Views from Somewhere* (Routledge, 2020). Sulagna is currently initiating her PhD in Jungian Studies at the University of Essex, UK, working on the Indian epic, Ramayana. She has actively supported and been part of India's environmental initiatives and lives in an ecological commune in Bangalore, South India.

**Jonathan Shann** read English at Cambridge (1979–1982), then worked as a secondary school teacher for three years before attending the College of Law. He was admitted as a solicitor in 1989 and worked in private practice until 2016. He took an MSc in Theoretical Psychoanalytic Studies (with Distinction) at UCL (2016–2017) and is now a PhD candidate in UCL's Psychoanalysis Unit (2017–). His research area is Freud and Metaphor.

**Richard Seaford** is Emeritus Professor of Ancient Greek at the University of Exeter. He is the author of numerous books and articles on ancient Greek drama, poetry, religion, society, and philosophy. In 2009, he was Honorary President of the UK Classical Association. His most recent books are *Cosmology and the Polis: The Social Construction of Space and Time in the Tragedies of Aeschylus* (2012), *Tragedy, Ritual and Money in Ancient Greece: Selected Essays*, edited by Robert Bostock (2018), and *The Origins of Philosophy in Ancient Greece and Ancient India: A Historical Comparison* (2020), all published by Cambridge University Press.

# Introduction

## Is the Only Way Up?

*Paul Bishop*

According to the words of a song written by George Jackson and Johnny Henderson (which, originally released in 1980 by Otis Clay, became in 1988 a chart-topping single for Yazz and the Plastic Population), *the only way is up, baby*. But is it? What about the way *down*? What about *katabasis*, or *nekyia*, or the descent of the soul? After all, Nietzsche described the modern age as precisely one of *descent* rather than ascent, telling his reader that 'it is true you climb upon the sunbeams of knowledge up to heaven, but you also climb down to chaos', and warning:

> Your manner of moving, that of climbing upon knowledge, is your fatality; the ground sinks away from you into the unknown; there is no longer any support for your life, only spider's threads which every grasp of new knowledge tears apart.[1]

Can we, as Nietzsche nevertheless suggested, view this matter 'more cheerfully' and, as Slavoj Žižek proposed, enjoy our symptom? What are the archaic dimensions that open up when the soul embarks on its descent?

Now the term *katabasis* is a transliteration from the ancient Greek κατάβασις, derived from κατὰ (= 'down') and βαίνω (= 'to go'), and thus indicates some kind of descent, some sort of journey or voyage to the depths.[2] There exist numerous literary-cum-mythical prototypes for this moment of descent: in Homer's *Odyssey*, for example, Odysseus follows the instructions of Circe and sails with his crew across the ocean until he reaches a harbour at the Western edge of the world. Here he sacrifices to the dead and descends to the underworld (and so, technically speaking, Odysseus performs not so much a *katabasis* as a *nekyia*, driving from the ancient Greek νέκυια ἡ νέκυα, i.e., consulting the dead – whilst the terms are not strictly interchangeable, in this volume the distinction is not central to its argument.)

In turn Odysseus encounters Elpenor, a former crewman; the prophet Tiresias, who advises Odysseus on how to appease Poseidon and thus return home; the spirit of his grief-stricken mother, Anticlea; and the two great heroes, Agamemnon and Achilles. The richness of the significance of this

DOI: 10.4324/9781003054139-1

account may be gauged by, for instance, Plato's decision for Socrates to refer to the lament of Achilles in the course of the allegory of the cave: 'And if they' – i.e., the prisoners in the cave – 'were in the habit of conferring honours among themselves on those who were quickest to observe the passing shadows and to remark which of them went before, and which followed after, and which were together; and who were therefore best able to draw conclusions as to the future, do you think that he' – i.e., the man who finds the way out of the cave – 'would care for such honours and glories, or envy the possessors of them? Would he not say with Homer', and here this quotation follows:

> Better to be the poor servant of a poor master, and to endure anything, rather than think as they do and live after their manner?[3]
> (*Republic*, 515e-516c)

What the *Odyssey* was to the Greeks, the *Aeneid* was to the Romans, and the *katabasis* in Virgil's epic occurs in book 6. Rather than conjuring up the spirits of the dead through sacrifice, Aeneas descends into the underworld and goes to Lethe to meet the spirit of his father, beginning his journey with a visit to Deiphobe, the Sibyl of Cumae (and a priestess of Apollo), to ask for her assistance in this journey. This is the background to the motif of the golden bough – something which Aeneas is told he must obtain and present to Proserpina, the queen of Pluto, the king of the underworld. When, aided by two doves sent by Venus, his mother, Aneas finds the bough and pulls it from the tree, another golden bough immediately springs up to replace it, and the Glasgow-born classical scholar, James George Frazer (1854–1941), made this legend central to his famous study of anthropology, *The Golden Bough* (2 vols, 1890; 2nd edn, 3 vols, 1900).[4]

Virgil lived and wrote in the Augustan period, and one of his younger contemporaries was Ovid, who reworked the legends of classical mythology in his *Metamorphoses*.[5] As such this long narrative poem (which pushes at the boundaries of the genre of epic) features several accounts of *katabasis*. In book 4, Ovid recounts the descent to Hades of Juno, where she asks one of the three Furies to help her in her quest for revenge against the family of Cadmus and sends Tisiphone to inflict madness on Ino and her husband so that they would destroy their children and themselves. In book 5, he tells us of how Proserpina, the daughter of Ceres, is kidnapped by Dis and taken to the underworld. And central to book 10 is the *katabasis* of Orpheus when, distraught at the death of his wife, Eurydice, Orpheus enters the underworld through the Spartan Gates to visit Dis and Proserpina in order to beg for the release of his bride. Moved by the song of Orpheus, Proserpina bids Eurydice to leave with her husband – but on the condition that he does not look back until he had left the underworld. But he does look back: and so Eurydice is lost a second time, and now forever.

The German medievalist Hugo Kuhn (1909–1978) suggested that such great medieval epics as Chrétien de Troyes's *Erec*, *Yvain*, and *Perceval*,

Hartmann von Aue's *Erec* and *Iwein*, and Wolfram von Eschenbach's *Parzival* were underpinned by 'a general myth and fairytale scheme', that he described as '*descensus – ascensus*, the return of a god, of a *heros*, or a fairytale hero from death, from the Other World, from animal metamorphosis, etc.'; accordingly, he designated this category of epic as *Descensusmärchen*.[6] Subsequently, the concept of *katabasis* has been applied more systematically to Wolfram's *Parzival* by the Kansas Germanist Ernst S. Dick (1929–2014), who has argued that 'the organizing principle' of Parzival's progress as Grail hero, from 'entering the world as a fool to his ascent to the grail kingdom', is 'the journey to the Other World' – and, more specifically, *katabasis* as the descent to the underworld.[7] Subsequently, Winder McConnell has placed Wolfram's *Parzival* in the category of those works C.G. Jung described as 'visionary', i.e., based on 'primordial experiences' that 'rend from top to bottom the curtain upon which is painted the picture of an ordered world, and allow a glimpse into the unfathomable abyss of the unborn and things yet to be',[8] and argued that the otherworldly, alchemical, and Pythagorean symbols in *Parzival* reveal how 'the entry into or sojourn of the hero in the physical otherworld corresponds to a psychic transformation of great significance for his process of individuation'.[9]

Even such a brief survey reveals the powerful moments associated with *katabasis*: loss, grief, mourning, distress, and fidelity even unto death.[10] In the case of Odysseus, the *katabasis* or *nekyia* relates to the very core of life itself: how to find one's way home.[11] Small wonder, then, that the motif has proved to be of such importance to psychoanalysis, beginning with Freud. In *The Interpretation of Dreams* (1900), Freud describes 'wishes of the past which have been abandoned, overlaid and repressed, and to which we have to attribute some sort of continued existence only because of their-re-emergence in a dream' as 'not dead in our sense of the word but only like the shades in the *Odyssey*, which awoke to some sort of life as soon as they had tasted blood'.[12] Further on in this work, he suggests that 'if the "unconscious", as an element in the subject's waking thoughts, has to be represented in a dream, it may be replaced very appropriately by subterranean regions'.[13] Thus, as Freud remarks in his *New Introductory Lectures on Psycho-Analysis* (1933), if what the Greeks and the Romans called 'the underworld' is what psychoanalysts call 'the unconscious', then psychoanalysis itself can be defined as 'a depth-psychology or psychology of the unconscious'.[14]

Precisely these expressions, 'depth psychology' and 'psychology of the unconscious', were chosen by Jung as synonyms for his own psychoanalytic project of *analytical psychology*. In his correspondence with Freud, Jung repeatedly remarks on the common ground between psychoanalysis and mythology, telling Freud on 13 August 1908 that 'one thing and another have turned my thoughts to mythology and I am beginning to suspect that myth and neurosis have a common core'; on 8 November 1909 that 'I was immersed every evening in the history of symbols, i.e., in mythology and archaeology, reading Herodotus and Friedrich Creuzer's *Symbolik und Mythologie der alten Völker* (1810–1823) – rich lodes open up for the phylogenetic basis of the theory of neurosis'; on 15 November 1909 that 'for me there is no longer anydoubt what the oldest and most natural myths are trying to say' and that 'they speak quite "naturally" of the nuclear complex of neurosis', adding: 'Although the philologists moan about it, Greek syncretism, by creating a hopeless mishmash of theogony, can nevertheless do us a service', since 'it permits reductions and the recognition of similarities, *as in dream analysis*' (my emphasis), so that 'if A is put in place of C, then one may conjecture a connection from C to A'.[15] For his part, Freud responded with a typical mixture of enthusiasm and pointed remarks: he responded on 17 October 1909 that he was 'glad' that Jung shared his belief that they must 'conquer the whole field of psychology', adding: 'Thus far we have only two pioneers: Abraham and Rank. We need men for more far-reaching campaigns. Such men are rare'; on 11 November 1909 that he was 'delighted' that Jung was 'going into mythology', adding: 'A little less loneliness. I can't wait to hear of your discoveries'.[16]

Moreover, in *Memories, Dreams, Reflections* we are told that Jung's research into mythology and his subsequent break with Freud were followed by the release of 'an incessant stream of fantasies' and that, in order to 'grasp the fantasies that were stirring in [him] "underground"', Jung knew that he was going to have to let himself 'plummet down into them, as it were'.[17] This moment is recorded in *Memories, Dreams, Reflections* with a reference to how, during Advent of the year 1913 (in fact, on 12 December 1913), Jung 'resolved upon the decisive step' while he was sitting at his desk, and with the lapidary remark, 'Then I let myself drop'.[18] Exactly what this might have involved for Jung has become clearer only in recent years with the publication of Jung's *Red Book* (and, more recently, his *Black Books*).[19]

After all, in the *Red Book*, Jung followed in the footsteps of Gilgamesh, Orpheus, Odysseus, Hercules, and Aeneas, descending into the abyss of the underworld where he encountered a beautiful young woman called Salome and an old man with a white beard called Elijah, who developed into the figure of Philemon, an old man with the horns of a bull and the wings of a kingfisher. Looking back on his experiences, Jung regarded himself as having gained access to 'the matrix of a mythopœic imagination which has vanished from our rational age'.[20] The mysterious figure of Philemon represented for Jung 'superior insight' and acquired a startlingly reality of his own, 'as if he were a living personality'; in effect, he became for Jung a kind of guru.[21] Over time, Philemon became relativized by the emergence of a Ka, a figure depicted by Jung as a herm with a base of stone, an upper torso of bronze, and 'a daimonic – one might also say, Mephistophelian – expression'.[22] These visions, experiences, and dialogues were described in retrospect by Jung as 'primal stuff', as 'incandescent matter', and as 'the *prima mayeria* for a lifetime's work'.[23]

Curiously, a reference in the original German text of *Erinnerungen, Träume, Gedanken* to Jung's own *katabasis* experienced in the years of the

*Red Book* has been cut from the Anglo-American translation. This passage relates how, in 1910, Jung had gone on a sailing tour with his friends Albert Oeri (1875–1950) and Andreas Vischer (1877–1930) from Zurich to Walendstadt and back, during which Oeri had read aloud – in the iconic translation by Johann Heinrich Voß (1751–1826) – from book 11 of the *Odyssey* with its account of the story of Circe and Odysseus's *nekyia* which, Jung suggested, seemed to have anticipated his own *nekyia* or 'the descent into dark Hades' (*den Abstieg in den finsteren Hades*).[24] This loss is a real shame: not least because, inspired by the lines in Voß's Homer, 'Up our sails, we went, / May wayward fellows mourning now th' event. / A good companion yet, a foreright wind, / Circe (the excellent utt'rer of her mind) /Supplied our murmuring consorts with, that was / Both speed and guide to our adventurous pass' (book 11, ll. 6–8; translated Chapman), Jung transposes this Homeric vision to his native Switzerland, describing how 'a shimmer lay over the glinting lake and the banks shrouded in silvery mists'.[25] In a note also included in the German edition (but again omitted from the Anglo-American), Aniela Jaffé recalls that 'the strong excitement Jung underwent still reverberates when he tells of these matters', adding that Jung had proposed as the epigraph for the chapter about his 'confrontation with the unconscious' this quotation from the *Odyssey*, "Happily escaped from death"'.[26] As Sonu Shamdasani has put it, the omission of these statements from the English edition of *Memories, Dreams, Reflections* has led to 'the Homeric echoes of Jung's confrontation with the unconscious [being] lost, together with the connection to his numerous references to Odysseus's *nekyia* in the *Collected Works*'.[27] And as Peter Kingsley has remarked, 'the suppression of Jung's strong desire to express a parallelism between his own destiny and the fate of Odysseus in descending to the underworld is, itself, a sorry story'.[28]

Along with his reading of Herodotus, Creuzer, and Richard Payne Knight (1751–1824), and Oeri's performative reading of Voß's translation of book 11 of the *Odyssey*, Jung was also familiar with more contemporary work in the field of philology, anthropology, and comparative religion that was investigating the ancient phenomenon of *katabasis*. These include the German classical philologist and religious scholar Albrecht Dieterich (1866–1908), whose study of Abraxas, a central figure in the part of the *Red Book* published privately by Jung as the *VII Sermones ad mortuos* or *Seven Sermons to the Dead*, has been published in 1891 as *Abraxas: Studien zur Religionsgeschichte des späteren Altertums*; whose analysis of lines from ancient magical papyri as constituting a liturgical text of the Mithras cult had been published in 1903 as *Eine Mithrasliturgie*; and whose study (of central relevance of out topic here) of the recently discovered text of the Apocalypse of Peter had been published in 1893 as *Nekyia: Beiträge zur Erklärung der neuentdeckten Petrusapokalypse*. Nor should one overlook the significance for Jung of the work of Leo Frobenius (1873–1938), whose *Das Zeitalter des Sonnengottes* was published in 1904 and contained a diagram of the 'night sea-journey' of mythological solar figures that Jung himself reproduced in his own writings:[29]

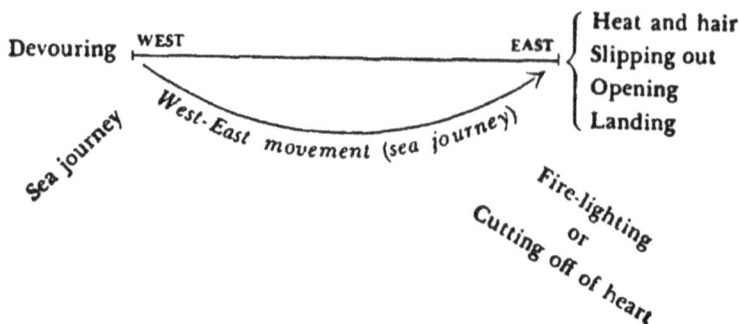

This reliance on ancient and contemporary authorities on myth tends to confirm the thesis put forward by Sonu Shamdasani in *Jung: A Life in Books* that Jung derives his ideas about the collective unconscious from his library. Indeed, Shamdasani describes the collective unconscious as 'the library within', and he observes in relation to an episode described in the *Red Book* that 'while Jung's self-investigation marked a turn away from scholarship, his fantasies and his reflections were marked by and indebted to his extensive scholarly readings' and '[his] self-experimentation was largely undertaken while seated in his library'.[30]

So the same question applies to Jung's own experience of *katabasis* (or *nekyia* or the night sea journey) as it does in Peter Kingsley's estimation to the *Red Book*: are we talking here (to use the terms of the Swiss classicist, Maria Laura Gemelli Marciano) about 'literary concepts' or 'attitudes', or are we talking about 'hard inner experience'?[31] Or is this itself a false binary? After all, does Shamdasani's thesis about the collective unconscious as 'the library within' in itself refute Jung's ideas about the collective unconscious? Or could it rather be said to modify our understanding of the transmission of those ideas, perhaps helping us change our idea of the collective unconscious from something *metaphysical* to something *cultural*, albeit no less *real*?

For the Homeric motif of the *nekyia* or *katabasis* is not just of anecdotal interest but constitutes one of the great structuring motives of the *Red Book*. In 'Mysterium. Encounter', Jung finds himself in 'a high hall with glittering walls'; as he sees images of Eve, the tree, and the serpent in the reflection of a bright stone the colour of water, he 'catch[es] sight of Odysseus and his journey on the high seas'.[32] Later in this episode, Jung recounts how Eve and the serpent show him how his next step 'leads to pleasure and from there again on lengthy wanderings like Odysseus' who 'went away when he played his trick at Troy'.[33] (The *Draft* of the *Red Book* continues by asking, 'What would Odysseus have been without his wandering?', while the *Corrected Drafts* adds, 'There would have been no odyssey'.) And so Jung comes to 'the bright garden' which is 'the space of pleasure', and whoever lives there 'needs no vision' (*bedarf des Sehens nicht*).

(In the text reproduced in Appendix B, Jung explains in relation to this episode against the distinction he makes between two principles, Eros and Logos, that 'temptation brings about a further movement toward the side of Eros', and 'this in turn forebodes many adventurous possibilities, for which the wandering of Odysseus is the fitting image', an image that in turn 'stimulates and invites adventurousness'; it is 'as if a door opened to a new opportunity *to free the gaze from the dark confinement and depths in which it was held fast*' (my emphasis).[34] If the red blooming trees represent a development of erotic feeling, the cool water of the well indicates the presence of Logos, suggesting that 'the development of Eros also means a source of knowledge' – and so 'Elijah begins to speak').[35]

Then again, in 'Nox Quarta', Jung alludes to the blood libation of the dead made by Odysseus, among others, when he rhetorically asks: 'Which fire has not been put out and which embers are still ablaze? We sacrificed innumerable victims to the dark depth, and yet it still demands more'. And: 'What is this crazy desire craving satisfaction? Whose mad cries are these? Who among the dead suffers thus? Come here and drink blood, so that you can speak'.[36] This same motif is used by Jung in a metaphorical sense in 1912/1913 in *Transformations and Symbols of the Libido* when he writes that, because of 'the absence of any personal relation' with Miss Frank Miller,

> the person of the author is on that account just as shadowy to me as are her phantasies; and, like Odysseus, I have tried to let this phantom drink only enough blood to enable it to speak, and in so doing betray some of the secrets of the inner life.[37]

There can certainly be no doubt that *katabasis* is Jung's central problem as it was reflected in his earliest major work, *Transformations and Symbols of the Libido* (1911–1912), and in its discussion of the figure of Peirithoos. Now according to mythology, Peirithoos (whose name derives from the ancient Greek περιθεῖν, i.e., *peritheein* = 'to run around') was the King of an Aeolian tribe located in the city of Larissa in Thessaly, in the valley of the Peneus and on the mountain Pelion. Peirithoos was a son of 'heavenly' Dia, the Perrhaebian daughter of Deioneus or Eioneus, and fathered either by Xion (who killed her father so as to not pay the bride price) or (according to Homer) by Zeus (disguised as a stallion) (and hence the folk etymology attaching to his name, since Zeus 'ran around' Dia in order to seduce her). It was the marriage of Peirithoos to Hippodamia, daughter of Atrax or Butes, that was the occasion of the famous Battle of the Lapiths and the Centaurs. Peirithoos was the father of Polypoetes, one of the Greek leaders in the Trojan War.

According to legend, Achilles was born in Larissa, and Peirithoos became his best friend, so much so that together they engage on a *katabasis* and descend to Hades to carry off Persephone from the underworld. At Athens Peirithoos was worshipped, along with Theseus, as a hero; and, in the first

Canto of the *Iliad*, Nestor includes Theseus and Peirithoos in his tribute to the heroes of an earlier generation:

> A godlike race of heroes once I knew,
> Such as no more these aged eyes shall view!
> Lives there a chief to match Pirithous' fame,
> Dryas the bold, or Ceneus' deathless name;
> Theseus, endued with more than mortal might,
> Or Polyphemus, like the gods in fight?
> [...]
> Fired with the thirst which virtuous envy breeds,
> And smit with love of honourable deeds,
> Strongest of men, they pierced the mountain boar,
> Ranged the wild deserts red with monsters' gore,
> And from their hills the shaggy Centaurs tore.[38]

Now shortly after giving birth to Polypoetes, Hippodomia died; going to visit Theseus at Athens, Peirithoos discovered that Theseus's own wife, Phaedra, was also dead. Both men pledge to gain revenge through kidnapping the daughters of Zeus: Theseus opts to kidnap the youthful Helen of Sparta, while Peirithoos chooses no less a figure than Persephone herself, Zeus's wife. Leaving the thirteen-year-old Helen at Aphidnae with Aethra (Theseus's mother), Theseus and Peirithoos undertake their journey to the underworld. But when they stop to rest, they find they have become bound to the stones on which they have sat down.

Although Heracles succeeds in freeing Theseus from the stone, the earth shakes when he attempts to do the same and free Peirithoos, for his crime in wanting to carry off the wife of a god as his bride was so great. By the time that Theseus returns to Athens, the Dioscuri (the twin brothers Castor and Pollux) have taken their sister, Helen, back to Sparta, but they have also captured Aethra and Peirithoos's sister, Physadeia, who subsequently become hand-maidens of Helen and follow her to Troy. As for Peirithoos, he must remain where he is; he must literally sit out his punishment in the underworld.

For Jung, the rescue of Theseus by Heracles and the fate of Peirithoos in remaining is a powerful symbol. For 'if, like Peirithoos, [the individual] tarries too long in this place of rest and peace', Jung writes, '[h]e is overcome by tor-por, and the poison of the serpent paralyzes him for all time'; and 'if he is to live he must fight and *sacrifice his longing for the past*, in order to rise to his own heights'.[39] In terms of the life of the individual, this means that, 'having reached the noonday heights, he must also *sacrifice the love for his own achievement*, for he may not loiter', and in this respect a cosmic pattern may be discerned:

> The sun also sacrifices its greatest strength in order to hasten onwards to the fruits of autumn, which are the seeds of immortality; fulfilled in children, in work, in posthumous fame, in a new order of things, all of which in their turn begin and complete the sun's course over again.[40]

Two decades later, in an essay written in November 1932 for the *Neue Zürcher Zeitung* on the occasion of a major exhibition in the Kunsthaus in Zurich of works by Picasso, Jung returned to the theme of descent, *katabasis*, or *nekyia*. Jung discerned a similarity between certain motifs in the work of Picasso material from his clients' dreams. 'The Nekyia', Jung wrote, 'is no aimless and purely destructive fall into the abyss, but a meaningful *katabasis eis antron*, a descent into the cave of initiation and secret knowledge' (CW 15, §213), and he went on to describe the entire process of therapy in terms of *katabasis* and *katalysis* (with, it should be noted, a significant nod in the direction of Goethe):

> The journey through the psychic history of humankind has as its object the restoration of the whole individual, by awakening the memories in the blood. The descent to the Mothers enabled Faust to raise up the sinfully whole human being – Paris united with Helen – that *homo totus* who was forgotten when the contemporary human individual lost themselves in one-sidedness. It is they who at all times of upheaval have caused the tremor of the upper world, and always will. This individual stands opposed to the individual of the present, since they are an individual who ever was as they are, whereas the other is what they are only for the present. With my patients, accordingly, the *katabasis* and *katalysis* are followed by a recognition of the bipolarity of human nature and of the necessity of the conflicting pairs of opposites.[41]

Not the least of the reasons why the allusion to Goethe's *Faust* is significant is because what is arguably the central scene of *Faust*, Part Two, involves a *katabasis* that is less mythological (and more aesthetic?), and a descent to a location that is, in a sense, beyond all space and time. This is the famous Mothers' Scene, which is set in Act 1 in a dark gallery in the imperial residence. Drawing in large part on sources found in Plutarch,[42] Goethe has Mephistopheles present Faust with 'a lofty mystery' (l. 6212):

> In solitude throne Goddesses sublime,
> Round them no place is, and still less a time,
> Only to speak of them the brain doth swim.
> The *Mothers* are they! [...] (ll. 6213–6216)[43]

These Mothers, says Mephisto, are 'Goddesses of you men / Unknown, whom we to name are none too fain. / To the uttermost Profound, wherein they tarry / Mayst burrow' (ll. 6218–20), and when Faust asks for more precise directions as to how to find them, he is told:

> No way! To the unexplorable
> Aye unexploréd; a way to the unimplorable,
> Aye unimploréd! Art thou in the mood?

No locks are there, no bolts to shoot asunder!
Through solitudes wilt thou be drifted yonder.
Dost know what desert is and solitude?

(ll. 6222–27)[44]

And Mephisto is at pains to underscore the utter isolation, desolation, and vacuity of this realm beyond all space and time:

And hadst thou swum through Ocean's vasty hollow,
And there beheld the boundless room,
Yet wouldst thou see on billow billow follow.
Aye, even shuddering at threatened doom
Something thou still wouldst see. The emerald gulf in
Of tranquil seas, wouldst spy the gliding dolphin,
Wouldst see the clouds drift by, sun, moon and star;
Naught wilt thou see i' the ever-empty Far,
Not hear thy footstep where 'tis prest,
Nor find firm ground whereon to rest.

(ll. 6239–6246)[45]

How seriously should we take this scene? After all, Faust himself says to Mephisto, 'Like the first mystagogue thou speak'st, that ever / Proved him the first neophyte's deceiver' (ll. 6249–50), and it is true that this scene is imbued with the ironic, even satirical tone that characterizes much of Goethe's writing in general and *Faust*, Part Two in particular. (This has not, however, prevented such commentators as the anthroposophist Rudolf Steiner from taking Goethe's text at face value.)[46]

Strangely, though, the Mothers' scene is paralleled later on in Act 2, in a scene set on the Lower Peneios where Faust encounters Chiron, a centaur. Just as, in Act 1, Faust descends (but one could just as well say: ascend, cf. l. 6275) to the Mothers to fulfil the Emperor's bidding to recover the souls of Helen and Paris, so, in Act 2, he sets off in search of Helen a second time, and is taken by Chiron to see Manto, a famous sibyl or soothsayer. Manto was the daughter of the prophet Tiresias, and her prophetic abilities are said to have exceeded those of her father; in the case of Goethe's *Faust*, her healing skills are emphasized by describing her as the daughter of Asclepius, the Greek god of medicine. Having conceived the desire to bring back Helen (cf. ll. 7434–7445), Faust is hailed by Manto as someone 'whom the impossible doth lure' (l. 7488); as someone who says, in the words inscribed above Jung's fireplace in Bollingen, *quaero quod impossibile* ('I seek what is impossible').[47] Manto invites Faust to follow her to the realm of Persephone, the queen of Hades, and Faust – like Orpheus before him – embarks on a descent to the underworld:

Enter, thou shalt be glad, audacious mortal!
Leads to Persephone the gloomy portal.
Within Olympus' hollow foot

She hears by stealth the banned salute.
Here did I smuggle Orpheus in of old.
Use thou it better! In, be bold!

[*They descend.*] (ll. 7439–94)[48]

Despite making plans for it, Goethe never wrote the scene where Faust encounters Persephone in the underworld and brings back Helena.

Finally, one might note the presence of this motif in a thinker whose influence on Jung was almost as great as Goethe's – namely, in Nietzsche. Nietzsche brings the first of the second volume of *Human, All Too Human* to a close with an aphorism titled 'The Journey to Hades' (§408):

> I too have been in the underworld, even as Odysseus, and I shall often be there again. Not sheep alone have I sacrificed, that I might be able to converse with a few dead souls, but not even my own blood have I spared. There were four pairs who responded to me in my sacrifice: Epicurus and Montaigne, Goethe and Spinoza, Plato and Rousseau, Pascal and Schopenhauer. With them I have to come to terms. When I have long wandered alone, I will let them prove me right or wrong; to them will I listen, if they prove each other right or wrong. In all that I say, conclude, or think out for myself and others, I fasten my eyes on those eight and see their eyes fastened on mine. – May the living forgive me if I look upon them at times as shadows, so pale and fretful, so restless and, alas! so eager for life. Those eight, on the other hand, seem to me so living that I feel as if even now, after their death, they could never become weary of life. But eternal vigour of life is the important point: what matters "eternal life," or indeed life at all?[49]

This whole tone of this passage points to the difficulty in disentangling esoteric content from parody; if indeed it is possible to make this distinction at all.[50] With reference to Nietzsche's discussion of this work (and its dedication to Voltaire) in *Ecce homo* and his statement, 'With a torch in hand which gives no trembling light I illuminate with piercing brightness this *underworld* of the ideal',[51] Nicholas D. More has suggested that 'by characterizing his earlier book as such a journey, and dedicating it to Voltaire, Nietzsche seems to locate *Human, All Too Human* in a satiric tradition', inasmuch as 'traveling to the underworld on a polemical mission is common in the genre', for 'the protagonist can engage the past directly and, if you like, kill it again'.[52]

Now it is true that, in the unpublished writings from the period of the *Untimely Meditations*, one of Nietzsche's notes reads as follows: 'Preface dedicated to Schopenhauer – entrance to the underworld – I have sacrificed many a black sheep to you – which has caused the other sheep to complain', an allusion to the passage in Homer's *Odyssey* (book 11, 23–50) where Odysseus, before descending to the underworld, sacrifices a black sheep to the gods in order to be certain of a safe return to Ithaca, as well as an anticipation of *Human All Too Human*, vol. 2, §408.[53] Yet here, the tone is surely different: the eight writers whom Nietzsche mentions are, after all, ones with whom he was in serious dialogue; the sacrifice being made is not a sheep, but Nietzsche himself, much as his Zarathustra will later declare, 'Of all weitings I love only that which is written with blood. Write with blood: and you will discover that blood is spirit';[54] and these eight thinkers are emblematic not just of life but of the 'eternal vigour' of life.

In short, perhaps we should take seriously Peter Kingsley's recent admonition that one pay attention to Aniela Jaffé when, in her initial transcript of the biographical material noted down in shorthand during her interviews with Jung between September 1956 and October 1958 (known as the Jaffé Protocols), Jung is recorded, immediately after being invited to speak openly about the whole scope of his life's work, as quoting the Homeric saying, 'Glad to have escaped from death', and as noting that 'in its original Greek wording it would make the most perfect epigram or motto if it could be printed right at the beginning of his autobiography'.[55] Kingsley points us to the original Homeric context of this saying (namely, *Odyssey*, 9.63; 9.566; and 10.134), and he places the entire concept of *katabasis* in the context of the ancient background to the traditions about Pythagoras's descent to the underworld,[56] while steering the reader away from what are called 'persistent attempts by "rational" scholars to keep suppressing any traces of these traditions'.[57] At which point, the entire question about the literal, figurative, metaphorical, or some other kind of reality of *katabasis* explodes into the open.

It does so, not simply because, in James Hillman's words, it is evidently the case that, topographically speaking, for psychoanalysis (and *a fortiori* for analytical psychology) 'the unconscious is a region below consciousness', but also because, as he further reminds us, it is essential to realize that 'to know the psyche at its basic depths, for a true depth psychology, one must go to the underworld'.[58] And it also does so because of the perennial significance of the theme and motif of *katabasis*, as the papers collected in this volume, taken together, powerfully evidence.

## Notes

1  F. Nietzsche, 'On the Uses and Disadvantages of History for Life', §9, in *Untimely Meditation*, tr. R.J. Hollingdale, Cambridge: Cambridge University Press, 1983, p. 108.

2  For previous studies of the phenomenon of *katabasis*, see A. Dieterich, *Nékyia: Beiträge zur Erklärung der neuentdeckten Petrusapokalypse*, Leipzig: Teubner, 1893, ²1913; R. Ganschinietz, 'Katabasis', in Pauly-Wissowa, *Realencyclopädie der classischen Altertumswissenschaft*, 85 vols, Stuttgart: Metzler, 1890–1980, vol. 10, cols 2359–2449; J. Kroll, *Beiträge zum Descensus ad Inferos*, Königsberg: Hartung, 1922; J. Kroll, *Gott und Hölle: Der Mythos vom Descensuskampfe*, Leipzig and Berlin: Teubner, 1932 (reprinted 1963); W. Fauch, 'Katabasis', in K. Ziegler and W. Sontheimer (eds), *Der kleine Pauly: Lexikon der Antike*, 5 vols, Stuttgart: Metzler, 1964–1975, vol. 3, pp. 152–153; and P. Bonnechere and G. Cursaru, 'Katábasis', *Cahiers des études anciennes*, 2016, vol. 53, 7–14.

3 This citation from Homer – to be precise, from the lament of Achilles in the *Odyssey*, book 11, ll. 489–491 – has already been quoted in full by Socrates at the beginning of book 3 of the *Republic* (386c). Its significance has been discerned by Allan Bloom in his edition of the *Republic* (*The Republic of Plato*, ed. and tr. A. Bloom, New York: BasicBooks, 1991, pp. 427–428 and 435–436). In his lament, Achilles bewails his fate, expressed in his preference for being alive as a serf instead of ruling over the dead. This sentiment is used by Socrates to support his argument for censorship in books 2 and 3 and in the allegory of the cave in book 7. In book 10, Socrates relates the myth of Er, an account of a visit to the other world based on the account of Odysseus's visit to dead in book 11 of the *Odyssey*. Er relates that, in the underworld, he met the shade of Ajax but not the shade of Achilles: why not? According to Bloom, the passages cited in book 3 serve as examples of what is unacceptable in art and hence what should be banned, since his complaint about Hades is a critique of the order of the world. So when Er mentions Ajax, whom Odysseus saw on his descent to the underworld as the twentieth shade of the dead, as the twentieth soul whom *he* saw, we are to conclude that 'Achilles no longer exists, alive or dead, in the new poetry or the new Socratic world' (*The Republic*, 'Interpretive Essay', 436). For a discussion of the myth of the underworld journey in Plato's *Phaedo* as a parallel case to the *Republic*, see R. G. Edmonds III, *Myths of the Underworld Journey: Plato, Aristophanes, and the "Orphic" Gold Tablets*, New York: Cambridge University Press, 2004.

4 For further discussion, see R.J. Clark, *Catabasis: Vergil and the Wisdom Tradition*, Amsterdam: Grüner, 1979; and C. Weber, 'The Allegory of the Golden Bough', *Vergilius*, 1995, vol. 41, 3–34.

5 For further discussion, see W.C. Stephens, 'Descent to the Underworld in Ovid's *Metamorphoses*', *The Classical Journal*, 1958, vol. 53, no. 4, 177–183.

6 H. Kuhn, *Tristan, Nibelungenlied, Artusstruktur* = *Bayerische Akademie der Wissenschaften, Philosophisch-historische Klasse, Sitzungsberichte*, vol. 5 (1973), Munich: Verlag der Bayerischen Akademie der Wissenschaften, 1973, p. 16.

7 E.S. Dick, '*Katabasis* and the Grail Epic: Wolfram von Eschenbach's *Parzival*', *Res publica litterarum: Studies in the Classical Tradition*, 1978, vol. 1, 57–87 (pp. 57–58).

8 Jung, 'Psychology and Literature' (1930), in C.G. Jung, *The Spirit in Man, Art, and Literature Collected Works of C.G. Jung*, vol. 15], trans. R.F.C. Hull, London: Routledge & Kegan Paul, 1966, §133–§162 (§141).

9 W. McConnell, 'Otherworlds, Alchemy, Pythagoras, and Jung: Symbols of Transformation in *Parzival*', in W. Hasty (ed.), *A Companion to Wolfram's "Parzival"*, Rochester, NY, and Suffolk: Camden House, 1999, pp. 203–222 (p. 204).

10 For further discussion, see M. V. Adams, 'War, Emotional Possession, and the Underworld: Affects in the Mythological Unconscious' [presentation delivered at the conference of the Association for the Psychoanalysis of Culture and Society, Philadelphia, 25 October 2002]. Available HTTP http://www.jungnewyork.com/war-emotional-possession-underworld.shtml; consulted 29.06.2020.

11 For further discussion, see D. A. Beardsley, *The Journey Back To Where You Are: Homer's "Odyssey" as Spiritual Quest*, Highland Park, NJ: Ideograph Media, 2014.

12 S. Freud, *Standard Edition of the Complete Works of Sigmund Freud*, ed. J. Strachey et al., 24 vols, London: Hogarth Press; Institute of Psycho-Analysis, 1953–1974, vol. 4, p. 249. On the use of a libation of blood to enable the dead to speak, see Walter Burkert's remark: 'The dead drink the pourings and indeed the blood – they are invited to come to the banquet, to the satiation with blood; as the libations seep into the earth, so the dead will send good things up above' (*Greek Religion*, tr. J. Raffan, Oxford: Blackwell, 1987, pp. 194–195).

13 Freud, *Standard Edition*, vol. 5, p. 410. 'Where they occur *without* reference to analytic treatment', Freud adds, these subterranean regions 'stands for the female body or the womb', explaining that '"down below" in dreams often relates to the genitals, "up above", on the contrary, to the face, mouth or breast' (p. 410).

14 Freud, *New Introductory Lectures on Psycho-Analysis*, in *Standard Edition*, ed. Strachey, vol. 22, pp. 3–182 (p. 158).

15 S. Freud and C.G. Jung. *The Freud/Jung Letters: The Correspondence between Sigmund Freud and C.G. Jung*, ed. William McGuire, tr. R. Manheim and R.F.C. Hull, Cambridge, MA: Harvard University Press, 1988, pp. 169, 258, 262–264.

16 Freud and Jung, *Freud/Jung Letters*, pp. 255 and 260.

17 C.G. Jung, *Memories, Dreams, Reflections*, ed. A. Jaffé, tr. R. and C. Winston, London: Collins; Routledge & Kegan Paul, 1963, p. 203.

18 Jung, *Memories, Dreams, Reflections*, ed. Jaffé, p. 203.

19 C.G. Jung, *The Black Books of C.G. Jung (1913–1932)*, 7 vols, ed. S. Shamdasani, tr. M. Liebscher and J. Peck, New York and London: Norton, 2020.

20 Jung, *Memories, Dreams, Reflections*, ed. Jaffé, p. 213.

21 Jung, *Memories, Dreams, Reflections*, ed. Jaffé, p. 208.

22 Jung, *Memories, Dreams, Reflections*, ed. Jaffé, p. 209.

23 Jung, *Memories, Dreams, Reflections*, ed. Jaffé, p. 225.

24 C.G. Jung, *Erinnerungen, Träume, Gedanken*, ed. A. Jaffé, Olten und Freiburg im Breisgau: Walter, 1990, pp. 103–104.

25 Jung, *Erinnerungen, Träume, Gedanken*, p. 103.

26 Jung, *Erinnerungen, Träume, Gedanken*, p. 180.

27 S. Shamdasani, 'Misunderstanding Jung: The Afterlife of legends', *Journal of Analytical Psychology*, 2000, vol. 45, 459–472 (pp. 465 and 470, n. 5).

28 P. Kingsley, *Catafalque: Carl Jung and the End of Humanity*, 2 vols, London: Catafalque Press, 2018, vol. 2, p. 497.

29 See L. Frobenius, *Das Zeitalter des Sonnengottes*, Berlin: Reimer, 1904, p. 30; cf. CW 5, §309.

30 See S. Shamdasani, *C.G. Jung: A Biography in Books*, New York and London: Norton, 2012, pp. 49 and 90.

31 Kingsley, *Catafalque*, vol. 2, pp. 493–494, n. 52; citing M. Laura Gemelli Marciano et al, *Parmenide: suoni, immagini, esperienza* (Sankt Augustin: Academia Verlag, 2013), pp. 231–233 and 280.

32 C.G. Jung, *The Red Book: Liber Novus [Reader's Edition]*, ed. S. Shamdasani, tr. M. Kyburz, J. Peck, and S. Shamdasani, New York and London: Norton, 2012, p. 174.

33 Jung, *Red Book*, pp. 181–182.

34 Jung, *Red Book*, p. 565.

35 Jung, *Red Book*, p. 565.

36 Jung, *Red Book*, p. 367.

37 Jung, *Psychology of the Unconscious: A Study of the Transformations and Symbolisms of the Libido: A Contribution to the History of the Evolution of Thought*, tr. B.M. Hinkle, London: Routledge, 1991, §57, n. 43.

38 Homer, *Iliad*, Canto 1; translated Alexander Pope.

39 Jung, *Psychology of the Unconscious*, tr. Hinkle, §566.

40 Jung, *Psychology of the Unconscious*, §566.

41 C.G. Jung, 'Picasso' [1932], in *The Spirit in Man, Arts, and Literature*, trans. R.F.C. Hull, London: Routledge and Kegan Paul, 1966, §204–§214 (here: §213, translation amended).

42 See Goethe's conversation with Eckermann of 10 January 1830; the Plutarch sources in question are his *Life of Marcellus*, §20, or *On the Decline of Oracles*, §22. For further discussion, see H. Jantz, *The Mothers in Faust: The Myth of*

*Time and Creativity*, Baltimore: Johns Hopkins Press, 1969; and J.R. Williams, 'The Problem in the Mothers', in P. Bishop (ed.), *A Companion to Goethe's "Faust": Parts I and II* (Rochester, NY, and Woodbridge: Camden House, 2001), pp. 122–143.

43  Goethe, *Faust: Parts I and II*, tr. A.G. Latham, London; New York: Dent; Dutton, 1908. p. 75.

44  Goethe, *Faust*, tr. Latham, p. 76.

45  Goethe, *Faust*, tr. Latham, p. 76.

46  See R. Steiner, 'Faust and the Mothers', in *Geisteswissenschaftliche Erläuterungen zu Goethes "Faust*, 2 vols (Dornach: Rudolf Steiner Verlag, 1982), which groups together lectures given by Steiner in Dornach at various dates from 1916 through 1919. In 'Faust and the Mothers' (a lecture given in Dornach on 2 November 1917), Steiner comments as follows: '[Faust] has descended to the Mothers: he has gone through some kind of transformation. Leaving aside what one otherwise knows of the matter and what has been said by us in the course of years, we need reflect only upon how the Greek poets, in speaking of the Mysteries, refer to those who were initiated as having learnt to know the three world-Mothers – Rhea, Demeter and Proserpina. These three Mothers, their being, what they essentially are – all this was said to be learnt through direct perception by those initiated into the Mysteries in Greece. When we dwell upon the significant manner in which Goethe speaks in this scene, and also upon what takes place in the next, we shall no longer be in any doubt that in reality Faust has been led into regions, into kingdoms, that Goethe thought to be like that kingdom of the Mothers into which the initiate into the Greek Mysteries was led. By this we are shown how full of import Goethe's meaning is' (vol. 2, *Das Faust Problem; Die romantische und die klassische Walpurgisnacht*, pp. 81–93 [pp. 81–82]; tr. G. Kaufmann). While such a reading neglects the parodic tone of Goethe's text, or of what he called in his letter to Wilhelm von Humboldt of 17 March 1832 'these very serious jokes' (*diese sehr ernsten Scherze*) (see Goethe, *Briefe*, ed. K.R. Mandelkow, 4 vols (Hamburg: Wegner, 1962–1967), vol. 4, p. 481) – assuming that one can make such an easy distinction between parody and esoteric content (see footnote 40 below).

47  As Peter Kingsley has pointed out, this text is the inspiration behind the inscription Jung had carved over the stone fireplace of his retreat at Bollingen, *Quaero quod impossibile* (Kingsley, *Catafalque*, vol. 1, p. 104 and vol. 2, pp. 528–529).

48  Goethe, *Faust*, tr. Latham, pp. 136–137.

49  F. Nietzsche, *Human, All-Too-Human*, vol. 2, trans. P.V. Cohn, New York: Macmillan, 1913, p. 178.

50  How legitimate is it to distinguish between 'serious' and 'parodic' texts? Or is such a distinction a projection of our own contemporary dilemmas and dichotomies onto previous times and ages? Might it be the case that, in the end, our modern ideas of 'seriousness' versus 'parody' (satire, humour …) say a lot about us, but not about history? (personal email exchange with Peter Kingsley, 18 June 2018).

51  F. Nietzsche, *Ecce Homo*, tr. R.J. Hollingdale, Harmondsworth: Penguin, 1992, p. 59.

52  N. D. More, *Nietzsche's Last Laugh: "Ecce Homo" as Satire*, New York: Cambridge University Press, 2014, p. 129; cf. *KSA* [*Kritische Studienausgabe*], vol. 7, 19[4], p. 418.

53  Nietzsche, *Unpublished Writings from the Period of "Unfashionable Observations"*, tr. R.T. Gray [*Complete Works of Friedrich Nietzsche*, vol. 11], Stanford, CA: Stanford University Press, 1995, pp. 4 and 394.

54  'Of Reading and Writing', in F. Nietzsche, *Thus Spoke Zarathustra*, tr. R.J. Hollingdale, Harmondsworth: Penguin, 1969, p. 67.

55  Kingsley, *Catafalque*, vol. 2, p. 498.

56 W. Burkert, 'Das Proömium des Parmenides und die Katabasis des Pythagoras', *Phronesis*, 1969, vol. 14, 1–30; Walter Burkert, *Lore and Science in Ancient Pythagoreanism*, tr. E.L. Minar, Jr., Cambridge, MA; Harvard University Press, 1972, pp. 151–161; P. Kingsley, *Ancient Philosophy, Mystery and Magic*, Oxford: Oxford University Press, 1995; and S. Schorn, 'Pythagoras in the Historical Tradition: From Herodotus to Diodorus Siculus', in C.A. Huffman (ed.), *A History of Pythagoreanism*, Cambridge Cambridge University Press, 2014, pp. 296–314 (esp. pp. 300–301).

57 Kingsley, *Catafalque*, vol. 2, pp. 498–499. As an example of such scholarship, Kingsley cites L. Zhmud, *Pythagoras and the Early Pythagoreans*. Oxford: Oxford University Press, 2012, pp. 216–218.

58 J. Hillman, *The Dream and the Underworld*, New York: Harper & Row, 1979, pp. 17 and 46.

# Part I

# Katábasis in Greek and Latin Literature

# Chapter 1

# Psycho-Cosmic Descent in Ancient Greece

## From Abyss to Self-Containment

*Richard Seaford*

On 12 December 1913 Carl Jung 'let myself drop. Suddenly it was as though the ground literally gave way beneath my feet, and I plunged down into the dark depths'.[1] Jung's awareness of ancient Greek precedents in his repeated descents into the depths (notably of the Homeric Odysseus in Hades) has been recently illuminated, with scholarly detail, by Peter Kingsley.[2] What I will add here is the development of certain Greek ideas and practices that did not exercise a direct influence on Jung's conception of his descent, but nevertheless converge with it: ritual descent to the underworld, the experience there of cosmic unity, and the bottomless inner self. The development leads to something different, the construction by Parmenides and Plato, of a new kind of self-contained inner self with non-spatial (philosophical) access to universal Being. The descent of Jung, as of many others, was an experience both psychic and cosmic: it is on this combination that I will focus.

## 1 Descent to the Underworld in Mystic Initiation

'The ground literally gave way beneath my feet'. This is not what happened to Odysseus, whose access to the dead was carefully achieved by sacrificial ritual. But there is an early Greek text that is in this respect closer to the sudden involuntary experience of Jung. This is the so-called *Homeric Hymn to Demeter*, which I will call the *Demeter* Hymn: it is certainly not by Homer and is probably of the sixth century BCE. Persephone is picking a flower when suddenly 'the earth gaped open', to emit a chariot in which Hades abducted Persephone down to the underworld. Her distraught mother Demeter sought for her, while refusing to allow the crops to emerge from the earth, with the result that the Olympian gods were deprived of offerings from mortals. Each of the three cosmic spheres (the underworld, the surface of the earth, the gods above) were isolated. This crisis of cosmic separation is eventually overcome by compromise in which the crops and offerings are restored, along with a new kind of interconnection between the underworld and the surface of the earth: Persephone returns joyfully from Hades to be reunited with her mother at Eleusis (and will spend only part of every year in Hades), and mortals are – if initiated into the mysteries – granted a happy eternity in Hades.

DOI: 10.4324/9781003054139-3

This last detail is a result of Demeter founding the mysteries at Eleusis. The *Demeter Hymn* is the earliest textual evidence for Greek mystic initiation. It narrates the aetiological myth of the Eleusinian mysteries: actions in the narrative prefigure details of the mystic ritual[3] founded at the end of the narrative. Mystic initiands participated in the fearful descent and joyful return of Persephone: we are told by Christian authors that 'Demeter and Kore (the Eleusinian name for Persephone) have become a mystic drama, and Eleusis celebrates with torches the wandering (of Demeter) and abduction (of Kore) and the grief of both', and that 'Persephone is sought with lighted torches, and when she is found the whole rite concludes with celebration and tossing of torches'.[4]

Mystic initiation was a rehearsal of death. Plato infers the nature of the descent to the underworld from 'rituals and ceremonies here on earth', which must refer to mystic initiations (*Phaedo*, 108a). The most detailed report of the experience of Eleusinian initiation is preserved in Plutarch. It compares the experience of the soul on the point of death to initiation into 'the great mysteries'[5] and includes journeys through darkness, people trampling on each other, fear and trembling: all dispelled by a wonderful light. It would not require much suggestibility for such darkness to be imagined as the underworld into which the initiands had descended[6] and were wandering in search of Kore.[7] But we also hear of actual subterranean spaces in cult places and of ritual descents into the earth.[8] Bacchic initiands were said by a Roman author to have been bound to machines that swept them into hidden caves.[9]

The abruptness of Hades abducting Persephone down to the underworld may have been felt as prefiguring the feared abruptness of death. But it results in *marriage*. What relation does the abduction of the bride have to death? The most complete transition regularly imposed by Greek society on an individual was the irreversible enforced departure of the bride from the enclosed security of her home and family to the control and bed of an unknown male. It was therefore regularly imagined as death-in-life,[10] and so might be conflated with the death-in-life of mystic initiation[11]: so it is for example in the *Demeter Hymn*, in which the fearful abruptness of death acquires objective and familiar form by being implicitly assimilated to the fearful abruptness of the male taking control of the bride. The mystic initiand, like Persephone, descends to the underworld. But in both cases the ritual will – as all ritual *qua* ritual must – end well: the bride will be reconciled to marriage, and the mystic initiand will pass through death to the permanent happiness associated with the return of Persephone.

Eleusinian initiation was into a *group*. Demeter in the *Hymn* founds the mysteries for humankind in general (480), and in fact any adult Greek speaker (except those polluted by bloodguilt) could be initiated. In Aristophanes' *Frogs* the initiates, continuing in the underworld their Eleusinian celebrations, form a joyful *chorus*. Experience of initiation as described by Plutarch implies a transition from anxious individual isolation in the darkness ('a mob [...] trampled and constrained by itself') to a wonderful light and joyful state that includes choruses and being 'with holy and pure men'.

The joyful chorus of initiates in the underworld in *Frogs* honours Iakchos, who is the Eleusinian Dionysos. As for Dionysiac mystic initiation, Plutarch (*Moralia*, 565e-f) describes a deep chasm extending downwards, shaped like 'Bacchic caves', the route taken by Dionysos in his ascent from the underworld. The souls encircling it are affected by rising scents to become friendly with each other, and 'the place was full of bacchic revelry and laughter and all kinds of festivity and delight'. The region, Plutarch adds, was called the place of *lethe*, forgetfulness. Of the famous gold leaves (found in tombs) that preserve formulae used in Dionysiac initiation, the earliest (c. 400 BCE), from Hipponion in southern Italy, gives instructions to someone about to die and go to the house of Hades, to which the souls are said to descend (κατερχόμεναι).[12]

The Greek word for 'souls' in both the Plutarch and the gold leaf is ψυχαί (singular ψυχή, *psuchē*). What exactly are these ψυχαί that descend to the underworld? This requires a new section.

## 2 The Inner Abyss

In Homer the only role of the ψυχή in the living person was to leave the body at loss of consciousness – in particular at death, whereupon it departed for Hades. Mystic initiation, inasmuch as it ensures the initiate a happy hereafter, has to be concerned with that part of her that survives bodily death, namely the soul (ψυχή). But because it *pre-enacts* death and the hereafter, it provides a focus on the ψυχή in the *living* person. Accordingly various texts of the fifth century BCE, besides the Hipponion gold leaf, associate the ψυχή with mystic initiation.[13]

In Homer there is no trace of mystic initiation. And (as in some cultures documented by anthropologists) there is no word for – and so no concept of – a single organ of comprehensive consciousness (comprising sensations, feelings, thoughts, etc.), such as we may call an inner self.[14] The closest to it, in a sense, is ψυχή. This is paradoxical, because in the *living* person the Homeric ψυχή is dormant. But accordingly it does not (like, e.g., the heart) refer to a specific part of the living body, and after death it refers to something like the whole person, who is insubstantial but conscious: a ghost. For instance, the ψυχή of the dead Patroklos appears and speaks to Achilles while he sleeps, looking and sounding like Patroklos (*Iliad*, 23. 62-8): in a sense it *is* Patroklos.

Some such sense of the wholeness of the ψυχή was likely to be present in the death-in-life of mystic initiation. Indeed, after Homer the word ψυχή came to be one of the words used for the new concept (whatever caused its emergence)[15] of a single organ of comprehensive consciousness, something like an inner self. Other words used with roughly the same meaning were νοὺς and φρήν, which will reappear in our discussion. All three words refer to an organ of consciousness: what distinguishes ψυχή is its general association with immortality.

The most influential proponent of this concept of ψυχή will be Plato. But the first extant writer to focus on it is Herakleitos of Ephesos (*floruit* circa 500 BCE).[16] The doctrines of Herakleitos and Plato were, despite being in various ways diametrically opposed to each other, influenced by mystic initiation not only in the manner of their presentation but also in their content.[17] In Homeric epic the inner self is not unitary, nor is the universe. The broadest account of the universe in Homer is *Iliad*, 15.184–211, where Poseidon, faced with a potential conflict with Zeus, declares that sky, sea, and underworld were inherited by the three brothers Zeus, Poseidon, and Hades, with earth and Olympos common to all three. He regards Zeus as no more than his equal and tells him to stay in his share (though in the end he acknowledges his greater power).

In the fragments of Xenophanes, by contrast, an Ionian contemporary of Herakleitos, there is both a single organ of consciousness and a unitary cosmos, which are moreover co-extensive with each other, or even identical. There is one god who, without moving from where he is, exercises power over everything by thought alone. 'All of him sees, all of him thinks, all of him hears'. He is 'similar to mortals neither in body nor in thought', and is identical with the universe.[18]

Similarly Herakleitos, along with his pioneering focus on the ψυχή as the organ of comprehensive consciousness, also envisaged the cosmos as a single entity. Both ψυχή and cosmos are composed of fire, which embodies the λόγος (*logos*), an abstract formula. But how is this embodiment to be envisaged?

> You would not discover boundaries of ψυχή, even by travelling along every path: so deep a *logos* does it have.

> (B45)

About this astonishing statement, I will make two points. Firstly, Herakleitos is not denying that there are boundaries in the depth of the ψυχή. Nor is he affirming it: he writes 'boundaries' when he could have written 'the boundaries'. He means no more than that that we cannot be conscious of boundaries: the ψυχή is, *so far as we are concerned*, bottomless. Suddenly, for the first time (at least in a Greek text), we are presented with the *bottomlessness* of consciousness.

Secondly, 'so deep a *logos* does it have' implies the conception of a lower layer of consciousness that we may travel into, exploring along every path, with the possibility of finding there – within the same organ of consciousness (the ψυχή) – new thoughts or feelings. In Homer by contrast new thoughts or feelings arrived either from one of the various separate organs of consciousness (*thumos, noos, phrenes*, etc.),[19] or by the intervention of a deity.[20] The Herakleitean single organ of consciousness, the comprehensive inner self, is emerging at the price of being not simultaneously present to itself, even to the point of seeming bottomless.

Kingsley notes that 'Jung's two favourite terms for describing his descents, *katabasis* and *nekyia*, both derive straight from ancient Greece'.[21] The first of these terms means simply *descent*, the second refers to the *dead*. Another term that has often been used in this connection, and has had a strong hold on the Western imagination, is *abyss*, from the Greek ἄβυσσος, which means *bottomless*. It is generally used of the sea and of the underworld, which I call its cosmic use. It does not occur in Homer or Hesiod, for both of whom Tartaros is a long way down but not bottomless. Its first three occurrences are all in Aeschylus (525-456 BCE), a younger contemporary of Xenophanes and Herakleitos.

Two of the three occurrences are from the same tragedy (*Suppliant Women*), and they both refer – remarkably – simultaneously to the *cosmos* and to the *mind*. Pelasgos, the king of Argos, faced with a difficult decision, says that safety requires 'deep thought that goes into the depth like a diver' (407), and that 'I have entered this ἄβυσσος sea of ἄτη that is not easy to cross' (470): ἄτη has both an objective and a subjective aspect, as the disaster caused by delusion or the delusion that causes disaster. And so ἄβυσσος here *combines the cosmic with the psychic*, as does its occurrence later in the same tragedy when the chorus asks: 'how am I to see down into the mind (φρήν) of Zeus, an ἄβυσσος sight?' (1057-8). In Aeschylus both φρήν and ψυχή can refer to something like the inner self. Earlier in the same tragedy, Zeus is described as implementing his thought without moving from his throne (101-103), and elsewhere in Aeschylus he is identified with the universe (fragment 70): the Aeschylean Zeus resembles the one god of Xenophanes.

## 3 Parmenides

Parmenides is a younger contemporary of Herakleitos. One of the surviving fragments of his work consists of the so-called proem (B1), in which he describes being led in a chariot by maidens, the daughters of the Sun, who have left the house of Night. They lead him to the 'gates of the paths of Night and Day', which are enclosed (literally, held 'around' or 'on both sides': ἀμφίς) by a lintel and a stone threshold, and blocked by great doors of which Justice holds the keys. The maidens persuade Justice to unbolt the doors, they drive the chariot through the resulting gap, and Parmenides is welcomed and instructed by an anonymous goddess.

Among the influences that have been detected on this passage, two deserve our attention. One is the journey of the mystic initiate, which is suggested by – *inter alia* – the description of Parmenides as a knowing (εἰδότα) man, the divine revelation at the destination, and the anonymity of the goddess.[22]

The other is the Hesiodic description of the region of Tartaros, where there is the dark house of Night, in front of which Prometheus holds up the sky, and

> Night and Day coming near (ἆσσον ἰοῦσαι) greeted each other as they cross the great threshold (οὐδός) of bronze. One enters and the other comes out, and the house never holds them both inside, but always one of them is outside the house ranging over the earth while the other waits inside the house until there comes the time for her to depart.
>
> (744–754)

There is here a textual problem. For ἆσσον ἰοῦσαι there is a manuscript variant ἀμφὶς ἐοῦσαι, which produces the phrase ἀμφὶς ἐοῦσαι ἀλλήλας, 'being around each other'. And so according to West in his Commentary 'it could mean that Night and Day are constantly apart from each other (as described in 750ff.), but in spite of that they meet in this unusual place'. The unusual place is a threshold (οὐδός). This is surely the text that inspired Parmenides' description of the threshold (οὐδός) that holds on both sides (ἀμφὶς) the gates of the paths of Night and Day. But Parmenides has entirely omitted the elaborate description of the constant alternating apartness of Night and Day, even while keeping the same word (ἀμφὶς) that in Hesiod expressed their *togetherness* at the threshold.

The mystic gold leaves and Hesiod are, like Parmenides' proem, composed in hexameter verse. Both influences, the mystic journey and Hesiod, suggest that the journey of Parmenides was to the underworld, as does a hint of death in words spoken to Parmenides by the goddess ('it was not a bad fate that brought you here'). And it was surely taken in this way by the earliest hearers of the proem. But Parmenides does not say it, nor even that the journey was downwards: on the contrary, the gates are described as aetherial (αἰθέριαι), that is, in the sky. But this does not mean that those interpreters are right who regard the journey as upwards. Burkert observes that the gate is rooted in the earth but reaches up to the sky, and so 'combines the regions of sky and earth, just as it encloses the paths of night and day' (12). Kingsley notes that the journey belongs to a type of other-world journey in which it is important to arrive 'at a place which simultaneously gives access to the lowest depths of the cosmos and to the greatest highs of heaven'.[23] Both these remarks are much to the point. For my part, I will develop the theme in a way that will help to relate it to our theme of the abyss.

In Aristophanes' *Frogs* the torchlight in the Eleusinian nocturnal festival is imagined as the sunlight which shines on mystic initiates in underworld.[24] Pindar, in a passage full of mystic allusions, claims that after death the 'good' have sun by night as much as by day.[25] Aeschylus' lost tragedy *Bassarai* was, I have argued, based on the idea – derived from the near-death experience and enacted in mystic initiation – of the sun seen in the underworld.[26] In an inscription, an Eleusinian initiate states that she will never forget the 'nights shining with the beauty of the sun'.[27] For Cleanthes (331–232 BCE) the cosmos is a μυστήριον (mystery) in which the sun is a torchbearer.[28] A Latin text of the second century CE describes initiation into the mysteries of Isis as a journey through all the elements, entry into the underworld and seeing the sun at midnight.[29] The point to emphasise here is that, with the sun in the underworld, the initiands – like Parmenides on his journey – experience the integration of cosmic opposites: of sky with earth and of night with day. For the initiands this is associated with salvation.

The togetherness of Night and Day in Parmenides' proem has to be seen in relation to two of his 'philosophical' passages. The first is as follows:

> They made up their minds to name two forms, of which it is not necessary to name one (τὼν μίαν οὐ χρεών ἐστιν) – it is in this that they have gone astray. And they separated them as opposite in appearance and assigned them signs separately from each other: to one the aetherial flame of fire, gentle and very light, and in every direction identical with itself but not identical with the other. That other is in itself the opposite, dark night [...].
> (B8.53-59)

The first sentence means that they named two forms (light and night) but regarded it as unnecessary to name *one* (i.e., a unity of the two), and this was a mistake: that is, Parmenides means (a) that they should have named their unity,[30] and so (b) that aetherial fire (light) and night *are* a unity, insofar as that is possible: not only have 'all things been named light and night', also 'everything is full simultaneously of light and obscure night, both equal, since neither has any share of nothing' (B9). They both belong to Being. Similarly Herakleitos, even with his very different view of the cosmos, reifies the unity of day and night: 'god is day night, winter summer, etc' (B67).

This has to be taken in conjunction with our second 'philosophical' passage (B4):

> But look at things that being absent are firmly present to the mind (νοῦς). For you will not cut off for yourself what is from holding on to what is, neither scattering in order everywhere in every way, nor drawing together.

This fragment was probably an argument (from introspection) for the continuity and indivisibility of Being that Parmenides insists on elsewhere (B8.22-5). The words 'neither scattering in order everywhere in every way, nor drawing together' imply a *cosmic* cycle. And indeed they are generally regarded as negating the cosmic doctrine of Herakleitos that there is a universal process of constant change resembling a river that 'scatters and again draws together, approaches and goes away' (B91). What this implies is that the continuity and indivisibility of what the mind sees, which Parmenides contrasts with Herakleitos' universal cyclical change, is itself universal. For Parmenides what is universal is – in contrast to the Herakleitean cosmos – unchanging abstract Being that is continuous and, he emphasises, *limited* (B8.22-33), its existence assessed not by the senses but by *logos*.[31] Things absent are not perceived by the senses but 'seen' by the mind as 'present' and continuous. *In contrast to Herakleitos and Aeschylus, the contents of the Parmenidean mind are simultaneously 'present' to itself.* That contents is Being, which is within the mind but also – despite being limited – universal, all that exists. The contrast with Herakleitos is also with Herakleitos' conception of the inner self as having a lower layer that is in effect bottomless.

Parmenides' journey may easily seem at once cosmic and mental, both an outer and an inner journey. But in contrast to the journey of Herakleitos into the depth of his ψυχή (travelling along every path and not finding boundaries), it is not bottomless, nor even downwards (or upwards): it is through a gate that brings together cosmic opposites (sky and earth, night and day). In the Hesiodic account of Tartarus quoted above as influencing Parmenides, there is a gap or chasm (χάσμα) in which someone would, 'once inside the gates', take a year to reach the floor (740–741). In Parmenides too there is a χάσμα, but not downwards. It is created by the opening of the doors and leads only to the goddess welcoming and instructing Parmenides. The journey is to a gate that brings together cosmic opposites and gives access to the revelation of Being. It lacks the basic features that would be expected of a journey to the house of Night: a descent, a deep downward chasm, the alternation of cosmic opposites.

The gold leaves reveal a mystic doctrine of two paths down to the underworld for souls (ψυχαί).[32] One, recommended to the mystic initiand, leads to the waters of memory; the other, to be avoided, leads to the waters of forgetfulness. So too Parmenides' goddess distinguishes between a right path and a wrong path, but these are paths *of thought* (B2.2-6). The spatial journey of mystic initiates down to the underworld is in Parmenides *internalised*, and no longer downwards. Parmenides' poem survives only in fragments, but even from these it seems that the self-contained, perspicuous inner self implied by Parmenides was antithetical – in effect if not in intention – to the sense of a bottomless inner self that found expression in Herakleitos and Aeschylus.

An aspect of this distinction is the opposition between the individualism of Parmenides and the communality propounded by Herakleitos. The *internalisation* of mystic initiation is generally also its *individualisation*, and so it is with Parmenides: he represents the wisdom of the goddess as revealed to himself alone, setting him apart from the ignorance of mortals. He is carried, as 'the man who knows', along a path that is 'far from the treading of humankind' (B1.2-3, 27), to the goddess, who warns him off the path followed by 'mortals knowing nothing' (B6.3-7). Contrast the transition to communal joy at Eleusis described by Plutarch, and the initiate on the Hipponion gold leaf who is told that, after following the recommended path and drinking from the waters of memory, she 'will go along the sacred path on which other glorious initiates and *bacchoi* travel'. Herakleitos insists that people should listen 'not to me but to the *logos*' (B50), which is 'communal' (B2): the communal *logos* here is both an abstract formula and the sacred *logos* revealed in mystic initiation.[33]

Despite mystic initiation being generally an experience of the *group*, the experience of mystic descent into the underworld was in myth projected onto superhuman *individuals*: apart from Persephone notable examples are Orpheus and Herakles. Herakles claimed to have defeated Kerberos on his visit to the underworld because he had been initiated (Euripides, *Herakles* 614); but on a fragmentary papyrus of the late second century CE he claims that his descent was an 'initiation into truer mysteries' (than the Eleusinian): the fragments of the papyrus then allow us to discern '[...] I [...] through the night [...] the fire whence [...] I saw Kore'.[34] The idea of wisdom truer than what is obtained in mystic *ritual* is implicit also in philosophy: in Parmenides, in Plato, and in Herakleitos, who condemn the mysteries as actually practised (B14).

On the mystic gold leaves the recommended path, and drinking the waters of memory, leads to permanent well-being in the beyond, whereas the wrong path, and drinking the waters of forgetfulness, leads to reincarnation.[35] For Parmenides the goddess distinguishes between two 'paths of enquiry', one accompanied by Truth, the other completely indiscernible (B2). She also mentions a second mistaken path, followed by ignorant mortals who trust their senses and believe that Being and not-Being are 'the same and not the same, and the path of all is backward-turning (*palintropos*)' (B6.9). *Palintropos* here is generally taken to mean 'contradictory', which it does, but I suggest that it also evokes the path to reincarnation (*turning back* to this world, rather than going to the blessed place):[36] the believer in variety and change is disqualified from permanent well-being. The traditionally concrete paths in the underworld leading respectively to eternal well-being and reincarnation have been transformed by Parmenides into paths of *thought* leading to new abstractions (eternal Being and contradiction).

## 4 Plato

Plato infers from mystery cult that the path to the underworld has many forks and windings, with different destinations for the good and the bad ψυχή (*Phaedo*, 108a-c). The (philosophical) ψυχή that avoids the body and 'is gathered itself into itself [...] goes away into what is like itself [...] and, as the initiated say, lives truly in all remaining time with the gods', whereas the ψυχή dominated by bodily pleasures and pains is subjected to the cycle of reincarnation (*Phaedo*, 80d-81e), and ψυχαί in the underworld who drink excessively of the waters of forgetfulness are sent upward for rebirth (*Rep.* 621a-b). Plato adapts to his philosophy the mystic doctrine of two paths, as had before him Parmenides. But from the copious surviving writings of Plato, we learn much more than we do from the few surviving fragments of Parmenides about what happens in this process to the *soul* (ψυχή).[37]

In Plato's *Meno* (81) Socrates maintains that 'the ψυχή is immortal and has been born many times', a doctrine he attributes to a *logos* told by priests and priestesses (i.e., almost certainly in mystery cult). From this doctrine he infers that

> the ψυχή has seen the things here and the things in Hades and has acquired knowledge of everything; so that it is no wonder that it can recollect what it previously knew about virtue and other things.

It follows that the completeness of the ψυχή, knowledge of everything, can be achieved by the exercise of *recollection*. As he says in *Phaedrus* (249c),

> he who uses such recollections rightly, always being initiated into complete/perfect mysteries (τελέους ἀεὶ τελετὰς τελούμενος), becomes alone truly τελέος (perfect/complete).

'Such recollections' are used rightly by understanding a general conception going from many sense perceptions into a unity (εἰς ἓν) collected by reasoning.[38] This is a recollection of those things which our ψυχή once saw when it journeyed with god (249bc). Recollection or memory, identified here with *unification* of the inner self, derives from a pre-natal mystic vision seen by souls (ψυχαί) not yet entombed in the body:[39]

> Mysteries which it is right to call most blessed, which we celebrated ourselves whole (ὁλόκληροι) [...] with the gaze of our final initiation on whole (ὁλόκληρα) and simple and untrembling *(ἀτρεμῆ)* and blessed apparitions.

> (250b8-c4)

All this, together with certain other texts, implies that the inner self of the mystic initiands is united (made whole), as well as assimilated to what they see in initiation. It is also similar to what Parmenides says of the One (Being): 'it is whole-limbed and untrembling (ἀτρεμὲς) and not uncompleted' (B8.5).[40] The rare word ἀτρεμής implies a subject but is in both Plato and Parmenides applied to the object. Just as in Plato both subject and object are 'whole', so in Parmenides B4 – we noted above – both the One and what the mind sees within itself are continuous and undivided, that is, whole. What Plato adds to Parmenides' conception is that it is by recollection (of pre-natal knowledge) and reasoning (beyond sense perceptions) that the ψυχή achieves wholeness, and that this enlightenment is connected with mystic initiation.

For Plato the chaos in the depths of what we call the unconscious can be collected into an ordered, self-contained whole by methodical recollection and by reason. The result is the inception of the Western individual mind. Even our mystic understanding comes to us, as it did to Parmenides and Plato, as *individuals*, without the shared action of mystic initiation.

The mental-cosmic abyss briefly glimpsed in Herakleitos and Aeschylus was by Parmenides and Plato excluded from philosophical thought. But it was not thereby abolished. It has remained, beneath the surface, ready to open up with the suddenness with which the ground gave way beneath Jung's feet, or Hades' chariot emerged to abduct Persephone to the depths.

## Notes

1 C. Jung, *Memories, Dreams, Reflections*, tr. R. and C. Winston, London: Flamingo, 1983, p. 203. For further such descents, see pp. 205–206.
2 P. Kingsley, *Catafalque: Carl Jung and the End of Humanity*, 2 vols, London: Catafalque Press, 2018, vol. 2, pp. 497–498.
3 Notably the purification, fasting, abstention from wine, *aischrologia*, and drinking of the *kukeōn* (192–211); see N. Richardson, *The Homeric Hymn to Demeter*, Oxford University Press, 1974, pp. 211–217.
4 Clement of Alexandria, *Protrepticus*, 2.12.2; Lactantius, *Div. Inst. Epit.*, 18.7. See further R. Parker, *Polytheism and Society at Athens*, Oxford: Oxford University Press, 2005, p. 355; K. Clinton, (1992), *Myth and Cult: the Iconography of the Eleusinian Mysteries*, Stockholm: Svenska Instituet i Athen, 1992, pp. 85–90; C. Sourvinou-Inwood, 'Aspects of the Eleusinian Cult', in M. Cosmopoulos (ed.), *Greek Mysteries*, London: Routledge, 2003, pp. 25–39; and R. Seaford, *Cosmology and the Polis*, Cambridge: Cambridge University Press, 2012, pp. 24–9.
5 Fragment 178; this almost certainly means (or at least includes) the Eleusinian: Sourvinou-Inwood, 'Aspects of the Eleusinian Cult', p. 33.
6 W. Burkert, *Homo Necans*, Berkely, Los Angeles, London: University of California Press, 1983, p. 280. In Lucian, *Cataplous* (22) a dead man, just after disembarkation from Charon's boat, describes the effect of the darkness, then says to another dead man, 'you were initiated into the Eleusinian mysteries. Are not things here similar to them?', and receives a positive answer.
7 Sourvinou-Inwood, 'Aspects', pp. 29–34; Parker, *Polytheism and Society at Athens*, pp. 355–356.
8 Burkert, *Homo Necans*, pp. 154–161.
9 Livy, 39.13.13.
10 R. Seaford, 'The Tragic Wedding', *Journal of Hellenic Studies*, 1987, vol. 107, pp. 106–130.
11 R. Sinos, 'Wedding Connections in Greek and Roman Art', in J. Benekeer and G. Tsouvala (eds), *The Discourse of Marriage in the Greco-Roman World*, Madison: University of Wisconsin Press, 2020, pp. 20–67.
12 F. Graf and S. Johnston, *Ritual Texts for the Afterlife*, Routledge, 2007, no. 1 (p. 4) and no. 3 (p. 8).
13 Olbian bone plates: M. West, *The Orphic Poems*, Oxford University Press, 1983, pp. 17–19. See Pindar, *Olympian* 2.68-73, in West, p. 100, n. 82; Aristophanes, *Clouds* 319; Euripides, *Bacchae* 72–5; and R. Seaford, *The Origins of Philosophy in Ancient Greece and Ancient India: A Historical Comparison*, Cambridge: Cambridge University Press, 2020, pp. 221–222.
14 For a defence of this view, see Seaford, *Origins*, pp. 54–57 and 304.
15 I have argued in detail for the factor of *monetisation*: for example, in Seaford, *Origins*, pp. 253–70.
16 D. Claus (in *Toward the Soul*, Newhaven: Yale University Press, 1981, p. 125) claims that there are only six occurrences of ψυχή as a 'psychological agent' before the fifth century; compare Herakleitos B12, 36, 45, 67a, 77, 85, 98, 107, 115, 117, 118; also B26, 88, 136, A16.

17  Seaford, *Origins*, pp. 223–225 and 230–234.
18  A4, A29-31, A34-6; B23-6.
19  For example, in the frequent phrase θυμὸς ἀνώγει.
20  For example, Athena 'put' it into the *phrenes* of Penelope to appear to the suitors, and 'gave' strength and courage to Diomedes; see *Odyssey* 18.158; *Iliad* 5.2.
21  Kingsley, *Catafalque*, vol. 2, pp. 493 and 528–529.
22  W. Burkert, 'Das Proömium des Parmenides und die Katabasis des Pythagoras', *Phronesis*, 1969, vol. 14(1), 1–30 (pp. 5 and 13); see most recently S. Tor, *Mortal and Divine in Early Greek Epistemology*, Cambridge: Cambridge University Press, 2017, pp. 267–273; and Seaford, *Origins*, 225–226.
23  P. Kingsley, *Ancient Philosophy, Mystery, and Magic: Empedocles and the Pythagorean Tradition*, Oxford: Oxford University Press, 1995, p. 252. In his *In the Dark Places of Wisdom* (Inverness, CA: The Golden Sufi Center, 1999), he argues for the importance of the practice of incubation for understanding Parmenides.
24  454–6; cf. 155, 446–7, 312–4, 340, 351.
25  *Ol.* 2.61-3, with F. Solmsen, 'Two Pindaric Passages on the Hereafter', *Hermes*, 1968, vol. 96, 503–506 (esp. p. 504); cf. *fr.129* Snell; Virgil, *Aeneid* 6.641.
26  R. Seaford, 'Mystic Light in Aeschylus' Bassara', *Classical Quarterly*, 2005, vol. 55, 2005, 602–606.
27  *IG* II² 4058.
28  *Stoicorum Veterum Fragmenta* I 538 von Arnim.
29  In the cult of Isis: see Apuleius, *Metamorphoses* 11.6, 21, 23.
30  Reference to proponents of this interpretation are in A. Mourelatos, *The Route of Parmenides*, 2nd edn, Las Vegas, Zurich, Athens: Parmenides Publishing, 2008, pp. 81–82. He and some others prefer the translation 'one of which it is not right to name', which in my view would certainly require ἑτέρην for μίαν, as well as giving inferior sense.
31  B7; I agree with Kingsley (*Reality*, Point Reyes, CA: The Golden Sufi Center, 2003, pp. 566–569) that *logos* here can not yet mean 'reason'. It must at the least *connote* discourse, as well as connoting a faculty employing abstraction: similar (what we call) ambivalence occurs in the use of *logos* by Herakleitos: see note 33 below.
32  Graf and Johnston, *Ritual Texts*, no. 1 (p. 4) and no. 3 (p. 8).
33  R. Seaford, *Money and the Early Greek Mind*, Cambridge: Cambridge University Press, 2004, pp. 233–234.
34  *Pap. Univ. Milan* I 20.18-32; in R. Seaford, *Cosmology and the Polis*, Cambridge University Press, 2012, p. 27.
35  Seaford, *Origins*, p. 226.
36  Parmenides and reincarnation: B12.4; in Tor, *Mortal and Divine*, pp. 237–239.
37  For the detail on which what follows is based, see Seaford, *Origins*, 225–34.
38  Cf. *Phaedo* 67c, 80e, 83a; Plotinus, *Enneads* 1.6.5; and Augustine, *Confessions*, 10.11.18. See C. Riedweg, *Mysterienterminologie bei Platon, Philon und Klemens von Alexandrien*, Berlin and New York: de Gruyter, 1987, pp. 11, 19, 27, and 53.
39  For the importance of mystic initiation throughout this passage of *Phaedrus* see Riedweg, *Mysterienterminologie*, pp. 30–69.
40  For more detail, see Seaford, *Origins*, 228, 231–2.

# Chapter 2

# *Katabasis* in Reverse

## Heraclitus, the Archaic, and the Abyss

*Paul Bishop*

In Psalm 42 (or in the Vulgate, Psalm 41) we find the evocative line, 'deep calls unto deep' (42: 8). This line is quoted by the medieval German mystic Johannes Tauler (c. 1300–1361), in his sermon for the Thirteenth Sunday after Trinity. In this sermon, Tauler exhorts his listeners: *entsink, entsink in den grunt*, i.e., 'sink into thy inmost soul, into thy nothingness'.[1] Tauler goes on to interpret the line from Psalm 42 as follows: 'The created abyss, with its boundless knowledge of its own nothingness, calleth into itself the uncreated abyss that is the infinite God', and Tauler draws a link between this exhortation and what Pseudo-Dionysius the Areopagite says about the soul's knowledge of God.[2]

Tauler is, as I have explored elsewhere, pre-eminently a thinker of the abyss.[3] In a sermon on Pentecost, for instance, he contrasts the response to the outpouring of the Holy Spirit of the foolish and the wise man. Whereas the former enjoys the comfort of the Paraclete but, by falling in love with this enjoyment, loses the 'true ground' (*dem woren grunde*), the wise man, by contrast, gives himself up utterly to the 'origin' (*ursprung*), achieves 'enlightened purification' (*verklerte lúterunge*), and sees only God.[4] Yet, for Tauler, God Himself is a form of abandonment, being the 'divine desolation' of which Tauler speaks in highly mystic terms in a sermon on the hidden nature of God:

> Then Man can see the quality of divine isolation in silent emptiness, in which no word in the essence is ever spoken in an essential way, nor is any work ever done. For there everything is so silent, so secret, and so empty [*denne do ist es so stille, so heimelich und so wuest*].[5]

And a contemporary of Tauler, Heinrich Seuse (c. 1293–1366), depicted God in *The Little Book of Eternal Wisdom* as telling his servant that 'the highest path of all beings away from their first origin is taken (in accordance with the natural order) through the noblest beings to the lowest; but the return to the origin is taken from the lowest to the highest', and that 'no one should seek the groundless ground of my secrecy and my hiddenness, in which I arrange all things according to my eternal providence, for no one can understand it'.[6]

DOI: 10.4324/9781003054139-4

The rich tradition of meditation on the abyss found in German mysticism (to which, of course, Meister Eckhart (c. 1260–1327) should also be reckoned)[7] extends from the medieval period, over two centuries later, to the mature mysticism of Jakob Böhme (1575–1624), known as the *theosophus teutonicus* ('Teutonic theosopher') or (in deference to his trade) the Shoemaker of Görlitz. It is in Böhme's work that the notion of the 'groundless ground', the *Ungrund*, is explored in its fullest theological implications.[8] In *De incarnatione verbi, or Of the Incarnation of Jesus Christ* (1620), Böhme writes:

> In eternity, as in the *Ungrund* outwith nature, there is nothing other than a silence without being; there is nothing to give rise to anything, it is an eternal silence, and there is nothing like it, an *Ungrund* without beginning or end: there is no goal nor resting-place, nor any searching or finding, or anything that could be possibly be.[9]

And Böhme has a striking image for this *Ungrund* (which may, in turn, have had an influence on Schopenhauer)[10]:

> This *Ungrund* is like an eye, for it is its own mirror, it has no being, neither light nor darkness, and it is above all a *magia*, and has a will after which we should neither strive nor enquire, for it disturbs us. With the same will we understand the ground of the divinity, which has no origin, for it contains itself in itself, about which we ought properly remain silent; for it is outwith nature.[11]

Böhme's subtle, even paradoxical thought regards the ground of divinity as having no origin, as being nothing, yet being full of desire, or so he explains in *Mysterium pansophicum, Or Complete Account of the Earthly and Heavenly Mysteries* (1620):

> The *Ungrund* is an eternal nothing, but it creates an eternal beginning as a desire. For the nothing is a desire for something: and since there is nothing that could give rise to something, the desire is itself what gives rise to something that is nothing other than a longing desire.[12]

For all its apparent abstraction, Böhme's thinking had its source (or so it is said) in Böhme's sensory experience of sunlight and observing its reflection on a metal dish:

> Sitting one day in his room, his eye fell upon a burnished pewter dish, which reflected the sunshine with such marvellous splendour that he fell into an inward ecstasy, and it seemed to him as if he could now look into the principles and deepest foundations of things;

believing it to be 'only a fancy, and in order to banish it from his mind, he went out upon the green', but 'he remarked that he gazed into the very heart of things, the very herbs and grass, and that actual nature harmonized with what he had inwardly seen'.[13]

## Hermann Fränkel on Tauler, Heraclitus, and the abyss

In a footnote to an article published in 1938, the German American classical scholar Hermann Fränkel (1888–1977) noted the similarities between these passages in Tauler and some of the fragments of the Presocratic thinker, Heraclitus.[14] (Professor of Classics at Stanford, Fränkel had been born in Berlin in 1888; studied in Bonn and Göttingen; and after the First World War had returned to Göttingen as *Privatdozent*, then Professor Extraordinarius. When Hitler came to power, Fränkel was invited to join the faculty at Stanford and moved to the USA. His scholarly work focused on Homeric similes (1921), intellectual and artistic history from Homer to Pindar (1948), as well as Ovid (1945); in his later years, he worked on a new theory of grammar.) Fränkel's work is central to the problem of this volume, that is to say, central to the problem of *katabasis*: namely, how do we get out of the abyss? In a way, this is, too, Jung's central problem, as reflected in his earliest major work, *Transformations and Symbols of the Libido* (1911–1912), and its discussion of the figure of Peirithoos.

According to mythological tradition, Theseus descends to Hades to carry off Persephone from the underworld, and the centaur Peirithoos joins him. But the mission turns into a disaster; after their failure and imprisonment, Theseus is subsequently rescued by Heracles, but Peirithoos remains behind – for Jung, a powerful symbol. For 'if, like Peirithoos, [the individual] tarries too long in this place of rest and peace', Jung writes, 'he is overcome by torpor, and the poison of the serpent paralyzes him for all time'; and 'if he is to live he must fight and *sacrifice his longing for the past*, in order to rise to his own heights'.[15] In terms of the life of the individual, this means that, 'having reached the noonday heights, he must also *sacrifice the love for his own achievement*, for he may not loiter', and in this respect a cosmic pattern may be discerned:

> The sun also sacrifices its greatest strength in order to hasten onwards to the fruits of autumn, which are the seeds of immortality; fulfilled in children, in work, in posthumous fame, in a new order of things, all of which in their turn begin and complete the sun's course over again.[16]

In his article, Fränkel suggested that of these similarities (i.e., these various parallels in image and expression) between Tauler and Heraclitus, some turn around self-knowledge and some around the concept of the abyss. As far as the former is concerned, one example is as follows. 'Children, what do you think can be the reason that so many men cannot enter in and examine the inner life of their own souls?', Tauler asks, and he answers:

> It is because a veil is drawn over their interior eyes [...]. Men shut their souls up so close that they keep both God and themselves entirely

outside – they shut up their spirits with thick, coarse, black hides [...].
And what do I mean by these hides? Everything to which thou devotest
thy will; [...] in a word, pleasure in anything whatsoever without God.[17]

And as far as the latter is concerned, one example is the following passage.
'Men will come to thee with overbearing manners and hard words, telling thee
high-sounding and subtle things of the intellect, as if they were Christ's apos-
tles', says Tauler, adding: 'Dear child, get away from them and sink into thy
inmost soul, into thy nothingness [...] it will all help thee wonderfully, if thou
wilt but turn inward to the study of thy nothingness: that is "the best part"'.[18]
Indeed, 'the soul sunken into the deepest depths of humility attracts the best
gifts of the divine abyss of love', Tauler concludes, exhorting his listeners to

> the union [...] in which the soul knows God, and yet, as St Dionysius says,
> knows Him as like nothing that it ever knew before; for God is nothing
> like the things that man knows or can ever express. Herein the spirit of
> a man is truly humbled and self-abandoned. So that it if pleased God to
> annihilate him [...], he would gladly be annihilated – for he knows noth-
> ing, loves nothing, enjoys nothing, but the One.[19]

Fränkel constellates these passages with the following fragments of Heraclitus
(referred to using the conventional Diels-Kranz referencing system). First,
DK 22 B 101: 'I inquired into myself';[20] second, DK 22 B 45: 'If you travel
every path you will not find the limits of the soul, so deep is its account
[*logos*]',[21] translated by Fränkel as 'the boundaries of soul you will not find,
wandering in whatever direction, so deep is the logos it possesses';[22] and third,
DK 22 B 18: 'If you do not expect the unexpected you will not discover it; for
it cannot be tracked down and offers no passage',[23] translated by Fränkel as
'unless one hopes against hope, he will not find out that which is indiscover-
able and inaccessible'.[24]

   In Heraclitus, the notion of the abyss is associated with filth – indeed, with
'revelling in filth', to cite a phrase attributed to Heraclitus by Clement of
Alexandria in his *Stromates*, I. 2 (DK 22 B 13).[25] This idea is found in several
other fragments of Heraclitus, including a critique of (an Orphic?) purification rite in fragment 5:

> They vainly purify themselves with blood when they are defiled: as
> though one were to step in the mud and try to wash it off with mud. Any
> man who saw him doing that would think he was mad. And they pray
> to these statues as though one were to gossip to the houses, not knowing
> who the gods and who the heroes are
>
> (DK 22 B 5)[26]

The significance of this passage is aptly characterized by Fränkel as
follows:

Not even in his religious acts does man succeed in establishing a contact with the beyond. Instead, he clings to "these" images […], which may or may not be the dwelling places of divinity but certainly are not themselves divine. He cannot escape the mire of this superficial reality; and, when he tries to do so, he only covers himself with more of the same substance. How, then, should he be able to visualize that which is beyond the ken of trivial experience? The vicious circle of ignorance and faulty behavior closes and imprisons its victim in a grave of "filth". In this sense Heraclitus had exposed ordinary man as "burying himself in filth"'.[27]

The fixation on filth can even be found, or so Fränkel suggests, in the late legend on the life and death of Heraclitus recorded by Diogenes Laertius (*Lives and Opinions*, book 9, chapter 3), according to which the philosopher 'fell into misanthropy' and had, in fact, buried *himself* in filth:

Finally, he became a hater of his kind and wandered on the mountains, and there he continued to live, making his diet of grass and herbs. However, when this gave him dropsy, he made his way back to the city and put this riddle to the physicians, whether they were competent to create a drought after heavy rain. They could make nothing of this, whereupon he buried himself in a cowshed, expecting that the noxious damp humour would be drawn out of him by the warmth of the manure. But, as even this was of no avail, he died at the age of sixty.[28]

A resonance of this tradition can be found in Jung's *Red Book* in the astonishing episode at the end of the chapter titled 'Death': 'I perish on a dung heap, while peaceful chickens cackle around me, amazedly and mindlessly laying their eggs', the narrator figure records, then 'a dog passes, lifts his leg over me, then trots off calmly' – 'I curse the hour of my birth seven times, and if I do not choose to kill myself on the spot, I prepare to recognize the hour of my second birth'.[29]

That Heraclitus uses the image of 'revelling in filth' to denounce the pleasures of the unenlightened is confirmed by other thinkers. For instance, in his *Protrepticus* (otherwise known as 'Exhortation to the Heathen' or 'Hortatory Discourse to the Greeks') (chapter 10; 92, 4), Clement of Alexandria writes, attributing this image to Democritus:

Some there are, who, like worms wallowing in marshes and mud in the streams of pleasure, feed on foolish and useless delights – swinish men. For swine, it is said, like mud better than pure water; and, according to Democritus, "doat upon dirt".

(DK 68 B 147[30]; cf. Plutarch, On Preserving Health,<br>chapter 14, 129A).[31]

And in his *Enneads* (I. 6. 6) Plotinus declares:

> For, as was said in old times, self-control, and courage and every virtue, is a purification, and so is even wisdom itself. This is why the mysteries are right when they say riddlingly that the man who has not been puri- fied will lie in mud when he goes to Hades, because the impure is fond of mud by reason of its badness; just as pigs, with their unclean bodies, like that sort of thing.[32]

In fact, Fränkel even suggests that Heraclitus might be a source, not just for the passage in the *Republic* where Socrates describes 'the dialectical way of inquiry' and observes that 'when the eye of the soul is really buried in a barbaric bog [*borborōi barbarikōi*], dialectic gently draws it forth and leads it up above' (533c-d),[33] or the passage where Adeimantus, drawing on Orphic theology, reminds Socrates that 'they bury the unholy and unjust in mud in Hades' (363d),[34] but for the entire allegory of the cave Socrates develops in book 7. For his part, Heraclitus had contended that 'man is buried in filth and that thereby his spiritual view is obstructed', while Plato 'sets forth how man is, as it were, buried in a subterranean cave, unable to see the daylight of spiritual truth'; as a consequence, the allusion to Heraclitus (DK 22 B 107) later on in book 7 of the *Republic* (533d) was a way of 'paying homage to the archaic author who, by his blunt and crude verdict on the human state, had given him the inspiration for his consummate parable of the cave'.[35]

Here Fränkel describes Heraclitus as an *archaic* author, and what consti- tutes the archaic nature of Heraclitus's though resides in the fact that, unlike modern or postmodern thinkers who wish to keep us in the abyss and in its filth, he wishes to raise us *up out of* the filth of the abyss. How does he pro- pose to do this? The answer lies in precisely what another American classicist, the independent scholar Raymond A. Prier, Jr. (b. 1939), has described as 'the archaic configuration of mind' found in Heraclitus.[36]

## Prier on archaic logic

By 'archaic', Prier means an early, non-Aristotelian configuration of mind, and he insists that pre-Aristotelian does *not* mean 'antiquated', 'underde- veloped', or even 'embyronic'.[37] Rather, he argues, archaic thought is 'a self-contained and self-supporting point of view, possessed of its own struc- ture and symbols and totally independent of the so-called rational patterns of Descartes or numerous logical patterns traceable from Aristotle to the present', and he defines it as 'comprehensive and all-inclusive in nature, based on one or more *a priori* structures, established not only as the base or "begin- ning" of thought but also as the ruling pattern of the thought itself'.[38]

This 'archaic configuration' of mind expresses itself through its 'graphic' or 'pictorial' nature, thus establishing an important relationship to the *sym- bol*; not surprisingly, Prier pays tribute to the work in this area of three thinkers – C.G. Jung (1875–1961), Claude Lévi-Strauss (1908–2009), and Ernst Cassirer (1874–1945).[39] Prier describes this 'graphic' or 'pictorial' nature as 'the basic constituent of the thought's deceptive simplicity or seeming one-dimensional nature', for 'the oppositional and symbolic character is a given, a phenomenon that can generally be drawn or sketched', and yet 'beyond mere opposition there exists a third term that works between or behind given sets of oppositions'.[40]

In so arguing, Prier acknowledges his intellectual debt to Ernst Cassirer, noting that one observation by Cassirer in particular had 'opened' his own thinking greatly in terms of 'the archaic configuration of mind in early Greek literature'.[41] According to Cassirer, it is 'a fundamental trait in mythical thinking' that 'wherever it posits a definite relation between two members it transforms this relation into an identity'.[42] In the case of Heraclitus, Prier argues, this mythical 'identity' disrupts 'an inbred linguistic opposition to prefigure structural oppositions', and Prier recognises the contribution to understanding the archaic not just of Cassirer but also of Jung and Lévi-Strauss, each of whom tried, in his own way, to reveal 'the widespread oppositional structure of archaic thought'.[43] This structure is, as Prier argues, a *symbolic* logic, defined as follows:

> Both symbol and structure are primarily logical phenomena as I shall use them. Logic is a cognitive method by which two or more phenomena are related. What properties this relationship assumes depends entirely on the type of logic under consideration. It should be clear by now that these properties I describe do not fit into modern logical frameworks. An archaic symbol in its logical sense is an uniquely used picture represented more and more consciously in terms of a noetic area of experience. This symbolic word forms an immediate representation of logical structure itself and/or is, in a less comprehensive sense, used within a structure as a logical term.[44]

This kind of symbol can be discerned, Prier argues, in such archaic Greek literature as the *Homeric Hymns* and the works of Hesiod, for example, in the 'Hymn to Aphrodite' or in the figure of Eros in the *Theogony*, as well as in the thought of Heraclitus, Parmenides, and Empedocles. How does this work in practice? Or to put it another way, how can Heraclitus – thus read – help us to climb out of the abyss?

To begin with, Prier distinguishes between two schools of Heraclitean scholarship.[45] One school is associated with the edition of Heraclitus by the English classical scholar (1840–1914) and with the work of such commentators as the Scottish classicist John Burnet (1863–1928) or the Scottish classical scholar W.K.C. Guthrie (1906–1981). This school approaches the question of how to study the specific meanings of terms in materialistic or scientific terms. For instance, in fragment DK 22 B 31 – 'Turnings of fire: first, sea; of sea, half is earth, half lightning-flash [*prēstēr*]. [...] Sea is dissolved and measured into the same proportion that existed at first' (DK 22 B 31 a and b)[46] – Heraclitus refers to *pyr* and to *prēstēr*, two sorts of primordial elements translatable as 'fire' or as 'a hurricane accompanied by a fiery water spout'.[47] For such critics, Heraclitus's cosmology propounds a physical theory, one that could be transcribed (as it has been by Charles H. Kahn) as follows:

> The reversals of sea (or the reverals of fire starting from sea) means that part of the sea moves in the dry (and cold) direction, further away from its starting point in fire, and becomes earth; part moves back towards fire and warmth and becomes atmospheric vapor, clouds, and wind, thus filling the region between earth and celestial fire, and proving nourishment for the fires aloft.[48]

Yet instead of offering a systematic account of the atmosphere, Heraclitus introduces the notion of *prēstēr*, interpreted by critics variously as a tornado or a waterspout or a lightning storm.[49] Aristotle, for instance, associates the *prēstēr* with a whirlwind or tornado, explaining that it is a hot or rarified wind that is drawn down from the clouds and 'sets the air on fire (*synekprimprēsi*) and colors it by its conflagration'.[50]

By contrast, a second school, exemplified by such German Idealists as Friedrich Schleiermacher (1768–1834), G.W.F. Hegel (1770–1831), or Ferdinand Lassalle (1825–1864), takes a more general – but ultimately more fruitful – approach. In his *Lectures on the History of Philosophy*, Hegel writes:

> This universal principle is better characterized as Becoming, the truth of Being; since everything is and us not, Heraclitus hereby expressed that everything is Becoming. Not merely does origination belong to it, but passing away as well; both are not independent, but identical. It is a great advance in thought to pass from Being to Becoming, even if, as the first unity of opposite determinations, it is still abstract.[51]

Or in Prier's terms, Hegel shares with Heraclitus 'a similar hierarchical and heuristic movement' that is 'structured upon a dialectic of opposites', inasmuch as Hegel identifies in Heraclitus 'a speculative method of thought' that can deal validly with 'becoming' as well as with 'the One'.[52] On Prier's account of how Hegel reads Heraclitus, the German Idealist has succeeded in uncovering 'the most pertinent characteristic of Heraclitean thought' – i.e., the structure of an 'oppositional logic' that both regulates and is separate from 'the objective world of naïve sense perception'.[53]

Following Hegel, Lassalle took up the examination of 'the symbolic qualities of the logic of opposition', arguing that a number of terms found in Heraclitus – such a fire, time, necessity, the way up and the way down, flux, justice, and peace – were in fact *symbols for the same principle or idea*. On this account, such Heraclitean topoi as fire, time, flowing represent *in themselves* 'a unity made up of a type of oppositional process between Being and Non-Being'.[54] Although Lassalle considers these symbols ultimately to be religious in nature, what interests Prier is Heraclitus's argumentational *logic*, i.e., its structure and its symbol. Rather than conceiving opposites as static, i.e., as x versus −x, they are seen as correlates that are united on a higher plane.[55] Correspondingly, an examination of the symbolic content of Heraclitean thought is interested in 'the possible significance of those words which act as key concepts or points of meaning', such as the term *logos*, but also *physis*, *nomos*, the circle, strife (or *eris*), and the sun.[56]

In particular, Prier focuses on the symbol of fire (*pyr*), which he reads as yet another 'predominant' or 'primary' symbol for *logos*.[57] Outside the specifically Heraclitean context, fire is used in a non-material sense. For instance, in the *Iliad* (book 13, l. 688), Homer compares the god-like Hector to a flame:

> There the Boiotians, and Ionians with their trailing tunics, / the Lokrians and the Phthians, with the shining Epeians / tried to hold him as he swept hard for the ships, but they could not / avail to beat brilliant flame-like Hektor back from them.[58]

In the *Odyssey* (book 4, l. 662), the anger in the eyes of Antinous is said to burn like fire when he speaks to his fellow Greeks: 'Antinoos, son of Eupeithes, spoke out to them, / Troubled. For his heart, black all round, was greatly filled / With rage. And his eyes resembled a shining fire'.[59] In one of the *Homeric Hymns* dedicated to Pythian Apollo, the god is described with emphasis on his flame (*phlox*):

> Then, like a star at noonday, the lord, far-working Apollo, leaped from the ship: flashes of fire flew from him thick and their brighness reached to heaven. He entered into his shrine between priceless tripods, and there made a flame to flare up bright, showing forth the splendour of his shafts, so that their radiance filled all Crisa, and the eives and well-girded daughters of the Crisaeans raised a cry at that outburst of Phoebus; for he cast great fear upon them all.[60]

In the *Theogony* (ll. 689–699), fire is used as a symbol of the destructive fury of Zeus:

> Now Zeus held in his strength no longer. Straightway his lungs were filled with fury, and he began to display his full might. From heaven and from Olympus together he came, with continuous lightning flashes, and the bolts flew thick and fast from his stalwart hand amid thunder and lightning, trailing supernatural flames. All around, the life-bearing earth rumbled as it burned, and the vast woodlands crackled loudly on every side. The whole land was seething, and the streams of Oceanus, and the undraining sea. The hot blast enveloped the chthonic Titans; the indescribable flames reached the divine sky, and the sparkling flare of the thunderbolt and the lightning dazzled the strongest eyes.[61]

Yet another example of many of the 'non-materialistic' uses of fire can be found in the 'startling' use made of it by Pindar in the opening to the first of his *Olympian Odes*: 'Even as water is most excellent, while gold, like fire flaming at night, gleameth more brightly than all other lordly wealth; even so, fond heart, [...] let us think to praise a place of festival more glorious than Olympia'.[62] But how does it help us understand Heraclitus to say that fire (and its 'cognates' such as lightning or flames) is a 'symbol' for the *logos*? How does the symbolic logic of Heraclitus's thought actually work? There are two ways in which the symbol functions in Heraclitus's philosophy.

## Oppositional structure

One of them is exemplified by the image of the bow and the lyre (as found in fragment DK 22 B 51) which, for reasons of space, I will discuss on another occasion. Another of them is the way in which his concept of 'the measured oppositional and structural nature' of *logos* led Heraclitus to express *not only* 'an oppositional structure involving a third connecting or underlying term' *but also* 'a structure and its dynamics in which this third term unifies and identifies phenomena that are by nature qualitatively superior or inferior to one another'.[63] In the case of *prēstēr* and *pyr*, this means reading the two parts of one fragment cited by Clement of Alexandria in his *Miscellanies*: 'Turnings of fire: first, sea; of sea, half is earth, half lightning-flash [*prēstēr*]. [...] Sea is dissolved and measured into the same proportion that existed at first' (DK 22 B 31 a and b) in terms of the structure found in another, cited elsewhere by Clement in his *Miscellanies*: 'A man in the night kindles a light for himself, his sight being quenched: living, he kindles the dead; awake, he kindles the sleeping' (DK 22 B 26).

On this account, both fragments exhibit a similar structure:

> sea: fire- *prēstēr*:: fire- *prēstēr*: earth
> and
> death: sleep-waking:: sleep-waking: life

In other words, the structure of this thought defines and at the same time overrides its hierarchical nature,[64] in this case when 'oppositions entailing a third term are used to imply a three-termed opposition of one order higher'.[65] As Prier acknowledges, this structure of thought is the one that had been discovered in the Thirties by Fränkel.[66]

Fränkel summarizes the role of fire in Heraclitus's thought as follows: 'the soul of man consists of divine and living fire', but in most individuals 'the flame is soiled and deteriorated by a considerable admixture of water, preventing the mind from shining brightly and understanding clearly'.[67] This reading is not controversial; after all, Jung wrote in a paper given at Eranos in the early 1930s that 'when our natural inheritance has been dissipated, then the spirit too, as Heraclitus says, has descended from its fiery heights'.[68]

'For Heraclitus the soul at its highest level is fiery and dry, because *psychē* as such is closely akin to "cool breath" – *psychē* means "to breathe", "to blow"; *psychōs* and *psychos* mean "cold, "chill", "damp"'.[69] Yet Jung, too, sees this fire in a metaphorical sense, associating 'the Heraclitean *pūr aei zōon* (ever-living fire)' with 'the primitive notion of an all-pervading vital force, a power of growth and magic healing that is generally called *mana*'.[70]

In a way that might well have appealed to Jung, the originality of Fränkel's approach lies not in simply describing the Heraclitean symbol of fire in terms of other concepts, whether material (e.g., fiery dryness) or metaphysical (e.g., *mana*), but in analysing its function in 'the logical apparatus of the Heraclitean dialectic' (as Prier calls it),[71] and, in particular, in terms of 'a device to express the inexpressible and to explain the unexplainable' – i.e., the use of the *geometrical mean*.[72] Given there are three planes, his thought reveals 'a movement embracing lowest and highest by means of the middle term', i.e., the geometrical mean.[73] Some examples should suffice to show how this works in practice.

For instance, in a fragment recorded by Origen in his treatise *Against Celsus*, Heraclitus says: 'A man is called foolish by a god as a child is by a man' (DK 22 B 79).[74] This saying can be analysed as exemplifying the geometrical mean and transcribed as follows, viz.:

God / Man = Man / boy
or
A / B = B / C
or
divinity : human being :: human being: child

Or as Fränkel explains this formula: 'Man, being the geometrical mean, may be called wise when compared to a boy, and childish when compared to God', or in other words 'B (man) is tantamount to C (child) when compared to A (God)'.[75]

Or to go back to the example discussed earlier by Prier: in DK 22 B 31, consisting of two fragments found in the *Miscellanies* of Clement of Alexandria, Heraclitus is recorded as saying: 'Turnings of fire: first, sea; of sea, half is earth, half lightning-flash. [...] Sea is dissolved and measured into the same proportion [*logos*] that existed at first'.[76] Just as it was difficult to say what *pyr* or *prēstēr* might be, so it is even harder for us to say what the *logos* actually is, but its function as a 'proportion' or 'correspondence' emerges when the statement is analysed as follows:

fire/sea = sea/earth
fire: sea :: sea: earth

Whatever the ratio may be, Fränkel argues, the proportion or *logos* prevails in both directions, upwards and downwards, so that it is the sea from which 'both ways are open, the way upward through the rising fiery whirlwind to fire, and downward to earth'.[77] The function of the middle term (in this case, 'sea') is to combine opposite qualities, and it can do this because 'its relations to the things above are the opposite of those to the things below it'.[78]

Then again, take fragment 61, 'The sea is most pure and most polluted water: for fish, drinkable and life-preserving; for men, undrinkable and death-dealing' (DK 22 B 61).[79] Here the middle term is again the sea, something at once pure and polluted:

pollution: sea :: sea: purity

How can the sea be both? Because, on the one hand, pollution collects in the sea, while on the other its water is used in purification rituals; because, on the one hand, compared to dirt, water is pure, while on the other, compared to purity itself, water is polluted; and because, for 'base animals' with an 'earthy' constitution (cf. *Timaeus*, 92a-b), the sea is life, while for higher life endowed with a fiery soul, it is death.[80]

Yet it is not the sea itself as an aquatic phenomenon in which Heraclitus is interested, as the first school of Heraclitus scholarship identified by Prier believes but rather the sea as an element in a symbolic economy, in which life in general and the soul of man in particular is viewed as 'a process sustained by continuous conversion of "water" into its opposite, "fire", i.e., through evaporation', which (on the accounts of Heraclitus offered by Aristotle, Aetius, and Sextus Empiricus) supplies air for respiration, enables the assimilation of food, and supports consciousness and reasoning (DK 22 A 15, 16). By the same token, its opposite, i.e., precipitation, implies death for souls, or as Heraclitus puts it, 'For souls it is death to become water, for water death to become earth; but from earth water comes into being, from water soul' (DK 22 B 36).[81] Analysing this fragment as follows,

soul → water, water → earth:: earth → water, water → soul
death: water :: water : birth

Fränkel notes the equivalence between the two downward conversions (soul → water, water → earth) and the two upward conversions (earth → water, water → soul), arguing that they amount to a 'twofold death' and a 'double birth' in which 'water' (rather than 'sea') occupies the 'central position' at the point where 'the ways of birth and death meet'.[82]

What this pattern implies is that 'the middle element B, when considered from a higher standpoint, is no better than its apparent opposite C', or in this case, with reference to fragments DK 22 B 82 and DK 22 B 83, that 'the most beautiful ape is ugly when compared with another species' and 'the wisest of men, when compared to a god, will seem an ape in wisdom and beauty and everything else'.[83] But what it also means is that the equation can be reduced by Heraclitus to a shorter form, or in other words to the assertion that 'B virtually amounts to its opposite C'.[84] In this sense, the opposites can be said to be equivalent.

(In fact, the notion of the identity of opposites is central to the thought of Heraclitus, as the Open University scholar C.J. Emlyn-Jones has discussed,[85] and it is a distinctive feature of Heraclitean philosophy.[86] While Parmenides emphasized the separateness of opposites, Anaxagoras based his assertion of the inseparability (and hence identity) of opposites on his belief in the infinite divisibility of matter, and Plato (in *Theaetetus*, 152c-e) linked the doctrine that objects simultaneously possess opposite attributes to the doctrine of flux, Aristotle (in *Metaphysics*, Γ 1005 b 17-20) argued that the very doctrine of the identity of opposites was a violation of the law of contradiction, one of the basic laws of logic. Of more recent critics, W.K.C. Guthrie paid Heraclitus something of a backhanded compliment, arguing that 'by boldly stating the absurd consequences of neglecting [logical distinctions]', the philosopher of Ephesus 'unintentionally paved the way for their recognition'.[87] Then again, the Serbian American philologist Miroslav Marcovich (1919–2001) suggested that the opposites were not literal or logical opposites but rather *extremes* – and hence not really opposites at all.[88] And the Cambridge classicist G.S. Kirk (1921–2003) defended Heraclitus against the Aristotelian criticism of violating the law of contradiction by conceding that this criticism applied to the expression, but not the intention, of Heraclitus's assertions.[89] For his part, Chris Emlyn-Jones proposes that Heraclitus may 'most plausibly be associated' with Anaximenes, suggesting a parallel between Anaximenes's explanation of physical opposites as modifications of one primary substance and Heraclitus's statement that the opposites are unified or identical by virtue of the fact they are all modifications of fire.[90] Of course, in the twentieth century, Jung picked up the doctrine of the unity of opposites and, while acknowledging Heraclitus as its source, interpreted it in essentially psychological terms.[91]

While agreeing with G.S. Kirk that, 'instead of seeing [the unity of the world] in its origin from a single substance [...]', Heraclitus 'conceived of a single arrangement or formula in all separate things which connected them into a determinate whole',[92] Emlyn-Jones wants to go further and insists that 'the opposites were not merely extremes of a continumm or examples of the variety of πάντα, but concrete entities whose mutual dynamic relationship was one of Heraclitus' main preoccupations'.[93] Moreover, when Emlyn-Jones notes that the element of paradox in Heraclitean thought is not attributable to 'stylistic or rhetorical idiosyncracy' but is rather associated with 'a mode of thought whose linguistic origins' constitute for Heraclitus 'the ultimate origin' of his belief in the identity of opposites, it is precisely this *mode of thought* that Prier and, before him, Fränkel are seeking to uncover.)

Now in all these statements by Heraclitus that are cited by Fränkel, we find the following pattern:

- term C varies and, with it, the predicate of the statement: in the case of DK 22 B 79, it is the 'child'; in DK 22 B 82 and 83, an 'ape'; in DK 22 B 1, the 'sleeping'; in DK 22 B 6, the 'deaf';
- term B is a constant, referring to ordinary humankind;
- term A refers in some sense to God or the Absolute.[94]

As Fränkel points out, this scheme also implies that term C is something well-known, but defective; term B denotes something supposedly well-known, but in fact misrecognised and erroneously valued; while term A represents something unknown and possibly unknowable. Hence, the scheme of the geometrical mean is not merely 'a method of denouncing and humiliating humanity' while 'praising and extolling the divine', it is also 'a device to express the inexpressible and to explain the inexplicable'.[95] And so the equation A/ B = B / C (or A : B :: B : C) can be rewritten as A : x / B = B/C (or A: x/B :: B: C).

Let's work this schema through when applied to fragment DK 22 B 117, 'A man when he is drunk is led by a boy, stumbling, not knowing where he goes, his soul moist'.[96] When interpreted in accordance with this scheme, DK 22 B 117 gives this result,[97] i.e.,

> Man : drunk/child = child/man: sober
> or
> Man : drunk / child :: child / man : sober

Fränkel relates this fragment to another, to DK 22 B 1,

> Of this account [logos] which holds forever men prove uncomprehending, both before hearing it and when they first have heard it. For although all things come about in accordance with this account, they are like tiros as they try the words and the deeds which I expound as I divide up each thing according to its nature and say how it is. Other men fail to notice what they do when they are awake, just as they forget what they do when asleep.[98]

In the case of fragment DK 22 B 1, Fränkel interprets it as exemplifying 'the scheme of double proportion', viz., 'ordinary people are equally uninformed before and after they have been told the truth', they 'do not experience their own experiences', and 'even while awake they are like sleepers, unaware of what they had ever known before',[99] while he reads DK 22 B 117 as representing only one half of a 'double proportion'.[100]

The common element in both fragments is the term, 'not knowing where he goes' or 'do not know what they do when awake', or as Fränkel paraphrases the essential meaning of these two fragments when read in a combined form with a third fragment, i.e., DK 22 B 118, 'A dry soul is wisest and best':[101]

> What is divine clarity of mind and the insight of an illuminated soul, burning in a clear, unadulterated fiery glow? It is a state in comparison to which ordinary consciousness is like sleep, and sober reasoning like the numbness of a drunken man, not knowing whither he goes, his soul being moist.[102]

Fränkel's method allows for the meaningful combination of other fragments: for example, fragment 99 ('if the sun did not exist it would be night'; DK 22 B 99),[103] fragment 3 ('the sun as to its size has the breadth of a human foot'; DK 22 B 3),[104] and fragment 45 ('if you travel every path you will not find the limits of the soul, so deep is its account [*logos*]'; DK 22 B 45)[105] could originally have been connected in terms of the following equation

$$\text{fires / sun} = \text{sun / soul}$$
$$\text{fires : sun :: sun : soul}$$

to argue that 'the sun by far surpasses all other fires, but the sun itself is equally surpassed by the soul'.[106] After all, in the opening to the fragmentary remains of his paean to the Thebans, Pindar exclaims, 'Beam of the sun! O thou that seest afar, what wilt thou be devising? O mother of mine eyes!' (*Paean*, 9, 2),[107] but what are our bodily eyes compared to the soul that contains the living, perceiving *logos*?

## Conclusion

By offering an interpretation of the fragmentary Heraclitean corpus that not only uncovers their logical structure but allows for their meaningful combination, Fränkel's structural approach reveals a way to reconstruct the thought of Heraclitus as a whole; restoring it (insofar as this is possible) to something that begins to approach its original integrity; and by the same token it allows us to appreciate its applicability as a tool for understanding the archaic. In the terms on which we are addressing his fragments in this paper, Heraclitus show us both what it is to be in the abyss and how an archaic mode of thought can help us out of it – by pointing us towards the inexpressible and the inexplicable, about which we can know next to nothing, and not even that it exists, were it not for the argumentational method of using the geometrical mean. As Fränkel puts it, the thought pattern of the continued proportion was primarily used, if not invented, by Heraclitus in order to clarify the contrast between the mundane' – the excrement-filled abyss of the day-to-day – 'and divine'.[108]

The approach taken by Raymond A. Prier to 'archaic thought' in general and by Hermann Fränkel to the fragments of Heraclitus in particular helps us make sense of this ancient work by conforming to the task of interpretation as defined by the British secularist philosopher, Richard Robinson (1902–1996); namely, that 'the purpose of an interpreter [...] is to make himself and others rethink the very thoughts that were thought by someone long ago'.[109] Like Apollo, whose oracle at Delphi 'neither speaks nor conceals but indicates' (DK 22 B 93),[110] Heraclitus asks his readers – through 'the device of the double proportion'– to 'find the transcendental by the indirect means of extrapolation'.[111] Or, in terms of *katabasis*, to find their way out of the abyss.

On this account, 'the greatness of the metaphysical organization' and 'the perfection of the hidden harmony' – a harmony which is far finer than the apparent one of a 'nature' that, according to Heraclitus, 'likes to hide itself' (DK 22 B 123) – are expressed by Heraclitus as follows: 'The most beautiful world is like a heap of rubbish aimlessly piled up' (DK 22 B 124).[112] Unlike Theophrastus who, in his *Metaphysics* where he gives this quotation (7a10- 15), interprets this to mean that 'while the whole heaven and each of its parts all have order and reason in their shapes and powers and periods, there is no such thing in the first principles',[113] Fränkel would have us read this fragment as meaning that 'the most beautiful world is like a heap of rubbish aimlessly piled up' – compared, i.e., to *the less obvious organization behind and beyond the manifest regularity of sun, stars and life.*[114] To cast this idea as a paraphrase of a famous remark by Oscar Wilde: *we are all in the abyss, but some of us are looking at the stars.*

## Notes

1  J. Tauler, *The Sermons and Conferences*, tr. W. Elliott, Washington, CD: Apostolic Mission House, 1910, p. 501.
2  Tauler, *The Sermons and Conferences*, p. 503.
3  For further discussion, see 'Introduction: A Brief History of the Archaic', in P. Bishop (ed.), *The Archaic: The Past in the Present*, London and New York: Routledge, 2012, pp. 3–54 (pp. 9–11).
4  J. Tauler, Sermon 26 ('Repleti sunt omnes Spiritu Sancto'), in *Die Predigten Taulers: Aus der Engelberger und der Freiburger Handschrift sowie aus Schmidts Abschriften der ehemaligen Straßburger Handschriften*, ed. F. Vetter, Berlin: Weidmann, 1910, p. 107; see H. Holzhey and D. Schoeller Reisch, 'Ursprung', in *Historisches Wörterbuch der Philosophie*, vol. 11, ed. J. Ritter, K. Gründer, and G. Gabriel, Basel: Schwabe, 2001, cols 417–24 (col. 418).
5  Tauler, Sermon 83 ('Audi, Israel'), in *Die Predigten Taulers*, p. 277.
6  H. Suso, *Das Büchlein von der ewigen Weisheit*, Neu-Ruppin: Alfred Oehmigke, 1861, part 1, §1 and §2, pp. 4 and 8.
7  For further discussion, see P. Bishop, 'Can analytical psychology provide a framework for a comparative approach to mysticism? C.G. Jung and Meister Eckhart as a case study', forthcoming.
8  For an overview of Böhme and his teaching, see R.M. Jones, *Spiritual Reformers in the 16th and 17th Centuries*, London: Macmillan, 1914, chapters 9, 10 and 11, pp. 151–234; and J. Boehme, *Essential Readings*, ed. R. Waterfield, Wellingborough: Crucible, 1989.

9  J. Böhme, 'De incarnatione verbi, oder Von der Menschwerdung Jesu Christi', in *Sämtliche Schriften*, ed. W.-E. Peuckert, vol. 4, Stuttgart: Frommanns-Holzboog, 1957, part 2, chapter 1, §8, pp. 120–21.

10  See A. Schopenhauer, *The World as Will and Representation*, tr. E.F.J. Payne, 2 vols, New York: Dover, 1969, vol. 1, §36, where he describes genius as 'the ability to leave entirely out of sight our own interest, our willing, and our aims, and consequently to discard entirely our own personality for a time, in order to remain *pure knowing subject*, the clear eye of the world [*klares Weltauge*]' (p. 186); cf. §38 (p. 198), §54 (p. 282) and vol. 2, chapter 30, p. 371. In *The World as Will and Representation* Schopenhauer describes the self-knowledge of the will as 'the objectivity, the revelation, the mirror of the will' (§29, p. 165), the subject purified of will as 'the clear mirror of the inner nature of the world' (§36, p. 186).

11  Böhme, 'De incarnatione verbi', p. 121. Here, 'magia' means the transition from a possible to a real existence in a material sense (see 'Glossar', in J. Böhme, *Von der Gnadenwahl*, ed. R. Pietsch, Stuttgart: Reclam, 1988, p. 244). See also *The Signature of All Things* (*De Signatura Rerum*), chapter 3, §2: 'Without nature God is a mystery, understand in the nothing, for without nature is the nothing, which is an eye of eternity, an abyssal eye, that stands or sees in the nothing, for it is the abyss; and this same eye is a will, understand a longing after manifestation, to find the nothing; but now there is nothing before the will, where it might find something, where it might have a place to rest, therefore it enters into itself, and finds itself through nature' (J. Boehme, *"The Signature of All Things" with Other Writings*, tr. C. Bax, London and Toronto: Dent; New York: Dutton, 1912, p. 22).

12  J. Böhme, 'Mysterium Pansophicum, Oder Gründlicher Bericht von dem Irdischen und Himmlischen Mysterio' [1620], in *Sämtliche Schriften*, vol. 4, Text 1, p. 97.

13  H.L. Martensen, *Jacob Boehme: His Life and Teaching, or Studies in Theosophy*, tr. T. Rhys Evans, London: Hodder and Stoughton, 1885, p. 7; cf. C. Wilson, *Religion and the Rebel*, Bath: Ashgrove Press, 1984, pp. 153–54, who sees in Böhme's experience a confirmation of Paracelsus' principle that 'we may look into Nature in the same way that the sun shines through a glass'.

14  H. Fränkel, 'A Thought Pattern in Heraclitus', *American Journal of Philology*, 1938, vol. 59, no. 3, 309–337 (p. 325, n. 35).

15  C.G. Jung, *Psychology of the Unconscious: A Study of the Transformations and Symbolisms of the Libido: A Contribution to the History of the Evolution of Thought*, tr. B.M. Hinkle, London: Routledge, 1991, §566.

16  Jung, *Psychology of the Unconscious*, §566.

17  Tauler, *The Sermons and Conferences*, p. 499.

18  Tauler, *The Sermons and Conferences*, p. 501.

19  Tauler, *The Sermons and Conferences*, p. 503.

20  J. Barnes, *Early Greek Philosophy*, Harmondsworth: Penguin, 1987, p. 113.

21  Barnes, *Early Greek Philosophy*, p. 106.

22  Fränkel, 'A Thought Pattern in Heraclitus', p. 327.

23  Barnes, *Early Greek Philosophy*, p. 113.

24  Fränkel, 'A Thought Pattern in Heraclitus', p. 319.

25  Cf. J.-P. Dumont, *Les Présocratiques*, Paris: Gallimard, 1988, p. 149.

26  Barnes, *Early Greek Philosophy*, p. 118.

27  Fränkel, 'A Thought Pattern in Heraclitus', p. 324.

28  Diogenes Laërtius, *Lives of the Eminent Philosophers*, tr. R.D. Hicks [Loeb Classical Library], 2 vols, Cambridge, MA: Harvard University Press, 1925, vol. 2, p. 411; cited in Fränkel, 'A Thought Pattern in Heraclitus', p. 309.

29  Jung, *The Red Book: Liber Novus*, ed. S. Shamdasani, tr. M. Kyburz, J. Peck, & S. Shamdasani, New York and London: Norton, 2009, p. 275.

30  Clement of Alexandria, 'Exhortation to the Heathen', tr. W. Wilson, in *The Ante-Nicene Fathers*, vol. 2, *Fathers of the Second Century: Hermas, Tatian, Theophilus, Athenagoras, and Clement of Alexandria*, Edinburgh: T. & T Clark, 1885, pp. 163–205 (p. 198).
31  Barnes, *Early Greek Philosophy*, p. 262.
32  Plotinus, *Porphyry on Plotinus; Ennead I*, tr. A.H. Armstrong, Cambridge, MA: Harvard University Press, 1966, pp. 249–251. (Armstrong notes that two critics, Diels and following him Henry-Schwyzer, see in this passage an allusion to the fragment by Heraclitus discussed above (DK 22 B 13), but wonders whether Plotinus could have thought of this point by himself.)
33  Plato, *The Republic*, ed. and tr. Allan Bloom, New York: Basic Books, 1968, p. 212.
34  Plato, *Republic*, tr. Bloom, p. 41.
35  Fränkel, 'A Thought Pattern in Heraclitus', p. 312.
36  R.A. Prier, *Archaic Logic: Symbol and Structure in Heraclitus, Parmenides, and Empedocles*, The Hague and Paris: Mouton, 1976.
37  Prier, *Archaic Logic*, p. 1.
38  Prier, *Archaic Logic*, p. 1.
39  Prier, *Archaic Logic*, p. 2.
40  Prier, *Archaic Logic*, p. 1.
41  Prier, *Archaic Logic*, p. 4.
42  E. Cassirer, *The Philosophy of Symbolic Forms*, vol. 2, *Mythical Thought*, tr. R. Manhim, New Haven and London: Yale University Press, 1955, p. 250; cited in Prier, *Archaic Logic*, p. 4.
43  Prier, *Archaic Logic*, p. 4.
44  Prier, *Archaic Logic*, p. 5.
45  Prier, *Archaic Logic*, pp. 57–62; cf. R.A. Prier, 'Symbol and Structure in Heraclitus', *Apeiron*, 1973, vol. 7, no. 2, 23–37.
46  Barnes, *Early Greek Philosophy*, p. 122.
47  Prier, 'Symbol and Structure', p. 23.
48  C.H. Kahn, *The Art and Thought of Heraclitus: A New Arrangement and Translation of the Frgaments with Literary and Philosophical Commentary*, Cambridge: Cambridge University Press, 1979, p. 141.
49  Kahn, *The Art and Thought of Heraclitus*, p. 141.
50  Aristotle, *Meteor.* III.1, 371a 15-17; in Kahn, *The Art and Thought of Heraclitus*, p. 142.
51  G.W.F. Hegel, *Lectures on the History of Philosophy*, vol. 1, *Greek Philosophy to Plato*, tr. E.S. Haldane [1892], Lincoln and London: University of Nebraska Press, 1995, p. 283.
52  Prier, *Archaic Logic*, p. 60.
53  Prier, 'Symbol and Structure', p. 24.
54  Prier, 'Symbol and Structure', p. 25.
55  Prier, 'Symbol and Structure', p. 25.
56  Prier, 'Symbol and Structure', pp. 25–27.
57  Prier, 'Symbol and Structure', p. 30.
58  Homer, *The Iliad*, tr. R. Lattimore, Chicago and London: University of Chicago Press, 1951, p. 289.
59  Homer, *The Odyssey*, tr. and ed. Albert Cook, 2nb edition, New York and London: Norton, 1993, p. 48.
60  *Hesiod, The Homeric Hymns and Homerica*, tr. H.G. Evelyn-White, Cambridge, MA; London: Harvard University Press; Heinemann, 1982, pp. 355–357.
61  Hesiod, *Theogony and Works and Says*, tr. M.L. West, Oxford and New York: Oxford University Press, 1988, pp. 23–24.
62  Pindar, *Odes*, tr. J. Sandys, London; New York: Heinemann; Putnam, 1927, p. 5.

63  Prier, 'Symbol and Structure', p. 31.
64  Prier, 'Symbol and Structure', p. 32. Compare with the **diagramming** of the first fragment offerered by Marcovich:

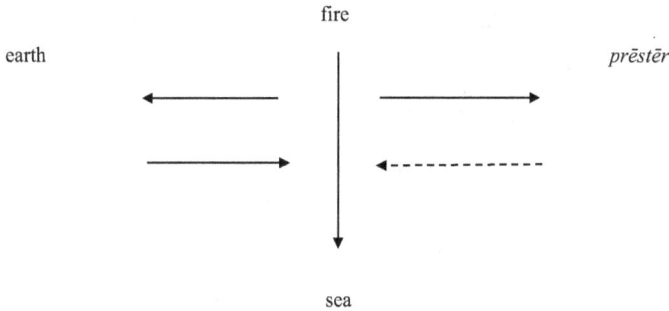

fire

earth                                                                                    *prēstēr*

sea

(M. Marcovich, *Heraclitus Editio Maior* [Greek Text with a Short Commentary], Merida: Los Andes University Press, 1967, p. 287), whose three-termed opposition Prier suggests replacing with a more advanced three-termed opposition as captured in the following diagram:

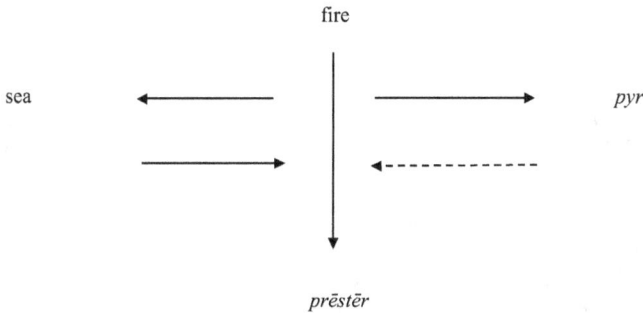

fire

sea                                                                                      *pyr*

*prēstēr*

(Prier, 'Symbol and Structure in Heraclitus', p. 37, n. 39).
65  Prier, 'Symbol and Structure in Heraclitus', p. 32.
66  For Prier, Fränkel's work constitutes, as opposed to the Burnet and Guthrie school *and* the Schleiermacher, Hegel, and Lassalle school, the key to 'a third point of view' that solves 'the dilemma of a certain overly scientific philology on the one hand that cannot see the forest for the trees and of a certain overly idealistic philosophy on the other that sees the forest but neglects the trees' because it is based on 'symbolic and structural principles' (*Archaic Logic*, pp. 61–62). In other words, Fränkel's thought is itself a third term of the kind that he discerned in the thought of Heraclitus.
67  Fränkel, 'A Thought Pattern in Heraclitus', p. 310.
68  C.G. Jung, 'Archetypes of the Collective Unconscious' (1934; 1954), in *The Archetypes of the Collective Unconscious* [*Collected Works*, vol. 9/i], tr. R.F.C. Hull, Princeton, NJ: Princeton University Press, 1968, §1–§86 (§32).
69  Jung, 'Archetypes of the Collective Unconscious', §55.
70  Jung, 'Archetypes of the Collective Unconscious', §68.
71  Prier, 'Symbol and Structure in Heraclitus', p. 31.

72  Fränkel, 'A Thought Pattern in Heraclitus', p. 318.
73  Fränkel, 'A Thought Pattern in Heraclitus', p. 31.
74  Barnes, *Early Greek Philosophy*, p. 112.
75  Fränkel, 'A Thought Pattern in Heraclitus', pp. 314–315.
76  Barnes, *Early Greek Philosophy*, p. 122.
77  Fränkel, 'A Thought Pattern in Heraclitus', p. 333.
78  Fränkel, 'A Thought Pattern in Heraclitus', p. 333.
79  Barnes, *Early Greek Philosophy*, p. 104.
80  Fränkel, A Thought Pattern in Heraclitus', p. 334.
81  Barnes, *Early Greek Philosophy*, p. 121.
82  Fränkel, 'A Thought Pattern in Heraclitus', p. 335.
83  Barnes, *Early Greek Philosophy*, pp. 115–116.
84  Fränkel, 'A Thought Pattern in Heraclitus', pp. 315–316.
85  C.J. Emlyn-Jones, 'Heraclitus and the Identity of Opposites', *Phronesis*, vol. 21, no. 2 (1976), 89–114.
86  See the remark by G.S. Kirk: 'An idea which Heraclitus particularly stretched' was 'his discovery of the unity that subsist in apparent opposites' ('Natural Change in Heraclitus', *Mind*, 1951, vol. 60, 35–43 [p. 35]).
87  W.K.C. Guthrie, *History of Greek Philosophy*, vol. 1, *The Earlier Presocratics and the Pythagoreans*, Cambridge: Cambridge University Press, 1962, p. 443.
88  Marcovich, 'Herakleitos', RE = *Realencyclopädie der classischen Altertumswissenschaf*, or *Pauly-Wissowa*, supplement 10 (1965), 246–320 (286–297); and *Heraclitus Editio Maior*, pp. 158–159.
89  G.S. Kirk, *Heraclitus: The Cosmic Fragments*, Cambridge: Cambridge University Press, 1954, p. 94.
90  Emlyn-Jones, 'Heraclitus and the Identity of Opposites', pp. 91–92.
91  For Jung, the union of opposites is indexed to the concept, attributed to Heraclitus, of *enantiodromia* (see C.G. Jung, *Psychological Types* [1921] [*Collected Works*, vol. 6], tr. R.F.C. Hull and H.G. Baynes, Princeton, NJ; Princeton University Press, 1971, §708–§709).
92  Kirk, *Heraclitus: The Cosmic Fragments*, p. 402.
93  Emlyn-Jones, 'Heraclitus and the Identity of Opposites', p. 111.
94  Fränkel, 'A Thought Pattern in Heraclitus', pp. 317–318.
95  Fränkel, 'A Thought Pattern in Heraclitus', p. 318.
96  Barnes, *Early Greek Philosophy*, p. 109.
97  Cf. Fränkel, 'A Thought Pattern in Heraclitus', p. 318, n. 18.
98  Barnes, *Early Greek Philosophy*, p. 101. For further discussion, see C. Brown, 'Seeing Sleep: Heraclitus fr. 49 Marcovich (DK 22 B 21)', *American Journal of Philology*, 1986, vol. 107, no. 2 (Summer), 243–245.
99  Fränkel, 'A Thought Pattern in Heraclitus', p. 316.
100 Fränkel, 'A Thought Pattern in Heraclitus', p. 319, n. 18.
101 Barnes, *Early Greek Philosophy*, p. 109.
102 Fränkel, 'A Thought Pattern in Heraclitus', p. 318.
103 Barnes, *Early Greek Philosophy*, p. 123.
104 Barnes, *Early Greek Philosophy*, p. 123.
105 Barnes, *Early Greek Philosophy*, p. 106.
106 Fränkel, 'A Thought Pattern in Heraclitus', p. 328, n. 40.
107 Pindar, *Odes*, tr. Sandys, p. 547.
108 Fränkel, 'A Thought Pattern in Heraclitus', p. 328.
109 R. Robinson, *Plato's Earlier Dialectic*, Ithaca, NY: Cornell University Press, 1941, p. 4. As if anticipating the relativistic trends in deconstructive and post-structuralist approaches, Robinson argues that 'interpretation is not just any sort of commentary, including the revelation of the historical causes and consequences of a given thought', but rather 'it is the recreation of that thought' (p. 4).

110 Barnes, *Early Greek Philosophy*, p. 118. For further discussion, see B. Snell, 'Die Sprache Heraklits', *Hermes*, 1926, vol. 61, no. 4 (October), 353–381 (p. 371).

111 Fränkel, 'A Thought Pattern in Heraclitus', p. 319.

112 Barnes, *Early Greek Philosophy*, p. 123.

113 Barnes, *Early Greek Philosophy*, p. 123.

114 Fränkel, 'A Thought Pattern in Heraclitus', p. 319.

# Chapter 3

# Virgil, Epicureanism, and Unseemly Behaviour

## The Epyllion in *Georgics* 4 and Its Three *Katábases*

*Terence Dawson*

David Slavitt describes the *Georgics* as 'probably the most literary work of all classical poetry'.[1] Ostensibly 'about agriculture', it consists of four books, or sections, each of about 550 lines. The first looks at how to till the soil and care for crops; the second, how to look after one's trees and vines; the third, how to care for one's farm animals; the last and fourth is devoted to bee-keeping. A whole book is given to beekeeping because, in the ancient world, honey was the usual way to sweeten food. Almost everyone who had any land sought to attract and to keep at least one colony of bees. In the spring, a part of each colony would swarm, that is, fly away to start a new colony, usually quite close by. A beekeeper would want to know where the new colony was; if this was inconvenient, and still on land to which he had access, he would move the new colony closer to where he could manage it.[2]

Halfway through book four, Virgil discusses what a beekeeper should do if all his bees swarm and cannot be recovered. He should engage in a practice called *bugonia*. He must wait until the early spring, then take a two-year-old bullock and beat it to death in such a way that, although its flesh is pounded to a pulp, the skin remains unbroken. Then he must leave the carcass in an enclosed space, covered with thyme and cassia. Nine days later, a new swarm of bees will have grown from within the fermenting flesh. Various possible explanations have been offered for this apparently widely held belief, none of them very persuasive. It is unlikely that Virgil gave them *any* credence. He was merely preparing his big question: 'Which of the gods devised this custom?'.

It is an *unexpected* question – for he had a strong interest in the teachings of the Greek philosopher Epicurus (341–270 BCE). Epicurus believed in the gods as images of perfection that *might* come to human beings from distant space. But he strongly rejected the view that they took any kind of interest in human affairs. He was a materialist and an empiricist. He thought everything in the world was composed of indestructible atoms, and he prioritised the experience of our senses. He distinguished between 'passing pleasures' (all forms of self-indulgence, unnecessary ambitions) and 'fixed pleasures' (friendship, the pursuit of philosophy). He argued that the *best* life was one lived in obscurity, and which sought *ataraxia* (freedom from all worries, unshakable peace of mind, equanimity).[3]

DOI: 10.4324/9781003054139-5

Throughout the Roman world of the first century BCE, possibly stimulated by the political turmoil, there was considerable interest in his ideas. This was strengthened by the publication of Lucretius' *On the Nature of Things* (*De Rerum Natura*, *c*. 60 BCE), a philosophical and speculative poem written in dactylic hexameters. It quickly became recognised as the key work of Epicureanism. In 2011, Stephen Greenblatt identified its *re*-discovery in the early fifteenth century as the beginning of modernity.[4] He argued that its theory of atoms helped Renaissance scholars to gradually move away from understanding our place in the world through religion towards one in which they learned to think scientifically.

Lucretius, however, was not only interested in atoms. Several of his other views may also be pertinent to the beginnings of modernity. *On the Nature of Things* pours scorn on the convoluted scenarios of mythology. It suggests that, albeit unintentionally, belief in the gods can lead to unpardonable violence, such as that inflicted on Iphigenia (book one). It argues that the gods have no interest in human beings and that they are not moved either by their entreaties or by their prayers (book 2). It maintains that the sufferings of characters condemned to eternal torture in Hades (for example, Tantalus and Sisyphus) are merely symbolic representations of the consequences of man's obsessive desires, such as greed or ambition (book 3). That is, it advances views about the nature of *myth* and the *imagination* which might be described as 'modern'.

Virgil was a teenager when the work began to circulate widely, and it impressed him deeply. Following Epicurus and Lucretius, he came to regard not only the gods but all mythological figures as embodiments of *human* tendencies.

The second half of book four of the *Georgics* is often referred to as an *epyllion* (little epic). It consists of two stories, both ostensibly taken from mythology – and, almost certainly, Virgil was the first to connect them. The 'frame story' is about Aristaeus, who has lost his bees (137 lines). To help him find his bees, he is told the myth of Orpheus and Eurydice (74 lines). Although fragmentary references to earlier Greek versions of this myth survive, Virgil's account of it in Latin verse happens to be the earliest extant version of the myth – and it is an 'embedded story': a story *within* a story. Improbable as this might seem, Virgil's *apparent* purpose in recounting this myth is to indicate how Aristaeus can find his bees. As we shall see, however, he has little interest in the story *per se*. His focus is on the implications of the *behaviour* he ascribes to Aristaeus, and its relation to the first three and a half books of the *Georgics*.

This chapter explores Virgil's 'little epic'. It examines the relation between the stories of Aristaeus and of Orpheus, the implications of the metaphor of a 'downward journey' (*katábasis*), and the connection between the poet's wit and the serious implications of his poem.

It has four objectives. Firstly, to show how each of the three 'downward journeys' at the heart of his epyllion represents a journey 'inward': that is, to suggest that the metaphor invites interpretation of what, today, we might refer to as its psychological implications. Secondly, through an analysis of the insistent two-part narrative structures, to present an unexpected reading of his seminal account of the myth of Orpheus and Eurydice. And thirdly, to argue that his version of the myth is not about its celebrated 'story', ostensibly about love. It is a carefully crafted *jeu d'esprit* – a cleverly sustained exhibition of literary wit – devised to illustrate an aspect of Virgil's interest in Epicurean philosophy.

The *Georgics* is widely regarded as being about the rhythms of nature and the seasons, and about the labour of man.[5] Whilst not disputing this view, this chapter argues that the poem is less about man and nature than it is about the cultivation of a proper *attitude* towards life, especially in the face of the unexpected vicissitudes and challenges that life can present.

## Unbearable Loss (1): Aristaeus and Cyrene

Popular anthologies of the Greek myths often include the story of Aristaeus losing his bees as if it were part of an ancient Greek myth about Orpheus and Eurydice. Virgil probably concocted the story himself. It is not a myth (an *oral* genre pertinent to a community). It is a deliberately ridiculous story carefully constructed to both resemble and *parody* a myth: that is, it consists of a sequence of intense episodes that harbour resonant metaphors. The reader is intended to smile at its absurdity while simultaneously noting its serious implications. For Virgil would have agreed with Horace: the purpose of poetry is not only to please but also *to be useful*.[6]

Aristaeus is one of the more curious figures of Greek mythology. Although stories may have been told about him in the eighth century BCE, our earliest extant reference to him is in the *Theogony* (*c*.680 BCE), where we learn that he had long hair and married Autonoê, one of the daughters of Cadmus and Harmonia.[7] The earliest substantial reference to him is in Pindar's ninth *Pythian Ode* (*c*.474 BCE), which tells the story of Apollo's love for Kyrene and the birth of their son. Aristaios is fed on ambrosia and nectar, the food and drink of the gods. He is to be both a hunter and a shepherd: hence his other names, Agreus (hunter) and Nomios (shepherd). More strikingly, he is to be both another Zeus and another Apollo. Aristaios will be 'the best god' (*aristos* = best).[8] About two hundred and thirty years later, the Alexandrian Greek poet Apollonius of Rhodes further describes him as a healer and prophet.[9] Such attributes signal unusual expectations.

And yet no one seems to have known what more they could say about him. Interest in him gradually evaporated, and his early attributes were forgotten until he became a figure from folklore rather than myth. Apollodorus (second century BCE) mentions him only in passing and, a century later, following Apollonius of Rhodes, Diodorus of Sicily repeats the claim that he 'learned from the Nymphs' how to make cheese and beehives, and how to cultivate olive-trees, and he was 'the first to instruct men in these matters'.[10] This is a long way from the achievements predicted for him by Pindar – and yet it does explain why Virgil chose him for his hero. He would have expected his readers to remember the fortunes forecast for Aristaios by Pindar – and to smile at the wit with which he recasts the new 'Zeus and holy Apollo' as an over-anxious adolescent beekeeper.

It has long been recognised that Virgil creates his myth about Aristaeus almost entirely from episodes borrowed from other myths.[11] In this section, we reflect on the implications of this.

Aristaeus has lost his bees, and like Little Bo-Peep, he 'doesn't know where to find them'. He looks everywhere. He quickly reaches the end of his tether. Not knowing what to do, he begins wandering idly up the Peneus (*Peneios*), a small river which flows through the spectacular six-mile gorge of Tempe (modern *Témpi*) between Mount Olympos and Mount Ossa. According to Herodotus, its residents attributed their rough countryside to the conse-quences of the *Gigantomakhia*, the war between the Gods and the Giants.[12] The magnificently jagged landscape thus echoes the emotional upheaval affecting Aristaeus.

The gorge of Tempe is where Apollo killed the Python, after which he puri-fied himself in the river Peneios. Then, from its banks, he cut a branch of laurel (*daphne*), which he took back to his shrine at Delphi and planted it. From this shrub were made the wreaths with which the winners were crowned at the various events of the Pythian Games, which were held every four years above and behind the famous sanctuary. The reference to Tempe thus con-trasts heroism and athletic prowess with the comically *un*-heroic quest of Aristaeus.

Ignoring a famous temple to his father Apollo, he wanders aimlessly *upstream* until he comes to the river's source, where he starts whining to his mother. This, of course, is a witty parody of one of the most comical and yet poignant episodes from the greatest work of Greek literature. Shortly before the opening scene of Homer's *Iliad*, the Greeks had captured a small town near Troy. Chryseïs is taken prisoner and awarded to Agamemnon as his 'prize'. Her father, Chryses, a priest of Apollo, goes to the Greek camp to offer a hugely generous ransom in exchange for her. The Greeks loudly applaud his request, but their commander is stubborn: Agamemnon will not surrender his prize. His offer refused, Chryses asks Apollo to punish the Greeks, and the god obliges.

The Greek army immediately finds itself ravaged by plague. On the tenth day of the plague, Achilles calls an assembly, at which Calchas, a Greek seer, tells Agamemnon why Apollo is punishing the Greeks. He *must* return Chryseïs. Agamemnon agrees – but only on condition that Achilles surren-ders to him the prize that he was awarded: his 'rosy-cheeked Briseïs'.

Outraged by the suggestion, Achilles is about to draw his sword and kill his commander-in-chief when Athene, visible only to him, descends from heaven to tell him that if he restrains himself, he will receive three times the value of the prize awarded him. Whereupon Achilles glowers at the assembled Greeks and prophecies that Hektor will wreak havoc amongst them, and they will tear their hearts out for not having shown more respect to 'the best of the Achaians'. Everyone is shaken by the prophecy, even Agamemnon. He orders sacrifices to be offered to Apollo and asks Odysseus to oversee the return of Chryseïs, together with handsome gifts. This done, he promptly sends two heralds to fetch Briseïs from the tent of Achilles, who greets them politely and hands her over.

Achilles, however, is in despair. He wanders along the seashore until he comes to a place where he sits down and weeps. Looking out over the sea, he raises his arms in prayer. 'Mother!' he moans. 'Since it was destined that I should have only a short life, you and Zeus might at least have ensured it was glorious! How could you stand by while Agamemnon dishonoured me?' His mother, Thetis, who had been sitting on the seabed beside her father Nereus, the old man of the sea, rises like a mist from the water, sits down in front of her son, and asks him why he is crying. 'You know why', Achilles whines, 'because you know everything'. He begs her to persuade Zeus to help the Trojans push the Greeks back onto the beaches. He wants them to learn what kind of general they follow, and Agamemnon to repent the way he has treated 'the best of the Achaians'. His mother, of course, agrees – indeed, her name, *Thetis*, suggests 'one who pledges' (θέτης).

So begins the *Iliad*. It is an extraordinary scene. We expect the gods to deal honestly with those whom they address. We discover that the world of the *Iliad* is *a*-moral and self-centred. When it suits them to do so, even the gods deceive. Athene forgets to tell Achilles that, because of her advice, he too (like Orpheus) will *lose* the person he loves most. In a similar fashion, we expect heroes to behave like heroes. The 'greatest' of the Achaians betrays his countrymen and behaves like a spoiled brat. He prays that the Trojans will make a bloodbath of his own companions. Because Agamemnon is a brute and a cad, hundreds of his men will be killed unnecessarily. Because Achilles behaves like a petulant teenager, his friend Patroklos will borrow his armour and be killed. Only when he has suffered this *unbearable loss* will Achilles snap out of his sulk and do what only he can do: become the killing machine he is, kill Hektor, and reverse the tide of war. His action is not dictated by heroism but by a horrific, and all-too-human desire for brutal and *excessive* revenge.

We laugh at Aristaeus for his childish whining, until we realise that the loss of his bees is being equated with the double loss of Briseïs and Patroklos suffered by Achilles. Like Achilles, Aristaeus is an adolescent who, when upset by something, instinctively whines about it to his mother. Like Thetis, Cyrene is a minor goddess who lives in an 'other' world below the surface of a pool. And with his tongue firmly in his cheek, Virgil models the behaviour of Aristaeus ('the best god') on Achilles, 'the best of the Achaians' (*Aristos Achaiōn*).

Virgil's epyllion not only parodies this episode from Homer's *Iliad*; it parodies the entire Trojan War. Just as Menelaos wakes one morning to find that his wife Helen has slipped away with Paris and sailed for Troy, so Aristaeus wakes one morning to learn he has lost his bees, and Orpheus will learn that Eurydice has died of a snake bite. Just as the Trojan War was fought to recover Helen from Troy, so Aristaeus desperately wants to recover his bees, and Orpheus will descend even into the underworld in his endeavour to recover Eurydice. Just as the Trojan leaders, smitten by Helen's beauty, are reluctant to return her, so Proteus will be reluctant to tell Aristaeus what he wants to know, and Aidoneus will be reluctant to let Eurydice go. Virgil would have expected his readers to enjoy the wit and audacity of his carefully calculated allusions.

Now comes the first 'downward journey' (katábasis) of the epyllion. No sooner has Cyrene learned that her son is on the banks of her pool, than she invites him inside. Aristaeus *plunges* into the pool.

This motif is borrowed from a later episode in the *Iliad*. The death of Patroklos finally rouses Achilles from his sulk and he does what only he can do: he kills the great Trojan hero. Then, to avenge his wild and monstrous grief, he attaches the corpse of Hektor to his chariot and, for twelve days, he drags it around the city. As he does this, Homer quietly reflects on the fate that now awaits him, for it has been foretold that Achilles will not long survive his great rival. The gods send Iris to warn Thetis of her son's impending death. Iris *dives* into the sea and finds Thetis in a hollow cave, distraught because her son will soon be killed.[13]

Virgil knows that a beekeeper's difficulties are not resolved inside a pool of water. He is using the motif of a 'downward journey' to contrast two *kinds* of reality. The river and the surface of the pool represent Aristaeus' habitual (or social) world. By plunging into the pool, he finds himself in an 'other' or *mythic* world. Crossing the threshold between these two worlds symbolises a shift from a more-or-less credible 'social' reality to an entirely 'imaginal' reality: a reality of the imagination. Virgil is exploring how these might be connected.

He is also exploring one of the most shattering of all human experiences: the loss of something so highly valued that the individual cannot imagine life without it. In his 'social' world, Aristaeus has looked everywhere for his lost bees. He cannot think where else to look for them. He has come to the end of his conscious resources. Without knowing why, he follows a river to its source *not* because bees usually build their colony close to water (which they do), but because the source of a river is a *metaphor* for the 'source' of the kind of information he requires.

Virgil is *playing* with mythic and literary motifs. But he is also exploring a serious question: How might Aristaeus overcome an apparently insoluble difficulty? The answer is unexpected: by finding the solution to his difficulty in the realm of myth: that is, from an Epicurean perspective, in the human imagination. The 'source' of the information Aristaeus seeks lies *within* himself. In other words, Aristaeus is presented with an implicit challenge – and this challenge would *seem* to be: Will he find his bees? Or will he, like Achilles, and like Orpheus after rejecting the advances of the Maenads, soon be killed? As we shall see, he misconstrues the challenge facing him.

Having plunged into the pool, Aristaeus finds himself inside a huge underground cavern through which flow *all* the rivers of the world. The cavern represents the boundless nature of the imagination – of inner experience – a container space whose rivers suggest that it is endlessly fecund. Aristaeus must walk through this almost unimaginable cavern, which suggests that the help he will receive comes from the 'imagination'.

Cyrene's name is suggestive of 'something that will happen', or 'one who grants'. Virgil probably derived the motif of a hero being *granted* something by a water-goddess from a contemporary of Pindar. Bacchylides tells how Minos once challenged Theseus to prove he is the son of Poseidon by throwing a ring into the sea from a speeding ship and asking Theseus to retrieve it.[14] Without a second thought, Theseus plunges into the sea and dolphins lead him down to the home of his mother, Amphitrite. She hands him a purple cloak and the garlanded headband that Aphrodite gave her on her wedding day. He then rises to the surface, thereby proving his parentage. The story thus anticipates a motif not only pertinent to Aristaeus but also central to the embedded story of Orpheus: the *descent* into an 'underworld' with the *hope* of returning with something sought.

Cyrene tells her son that his first task is to propitiate Ocean. In literal terms, this makes no sense at all, for a vast expanse of seawater can neither know nor care where anyone's bees have fled. But Virgil is playing with a metaphor. The Ocean represents the unfathomable nature of Aristaeus' own resources. It is not enough for him to *admit* that he does not know where else to look for his bees. He must *confirm* that he has come to the end of his conscious resources. For only then will he be ready to heed intuitions or suggestions that come to him from … 'Aye, there's the rub'. Where *do* they come from?

C.G. Jung argued that such intuitions come from the unconscious. Others challenge the very existence of an unconscious: they insist that the imagination pieces together creative products (whether dreams or literary works) by adapting memories.[15] Virgil's epyllion provides clear evidence for the latter view: his epyllion is composed of scenes adapted from works with which he was almost certainly familiar. This, however, does not explain *why* he should have remembered scenes from the *Iliad* when thinking about lost bees. These scenes appear to have suggested themselves to him *autonomously*: that is, he remembered them not because of their narrative incidents *per se*, but because of the resonance of the motifs and the metaphors they harbour – metaphors of *loss*, *descent* and its corollary, *otherness*.

Once Aristaeus has paid his dues to Ocean, we assume that his mother will be able to help him. To the reader's surprise, Cyrene tells him: 'sorry, I *can't* help, but I know someone who can'. Aristaeus must seek the help of Proteus, the Old Man of the Sea, who happens to be at Pallene.

## Intuition and Determination: Aristaeus and Proteus

Novelist and classicist Robert Graves asserts that 'Virgil's account of Aristaeus' visit to the river Peneus illustrates the irresponsible use of myth'. He considers everything about Virgil's epyllion to be 'mythologically absurd'. He pours scorn on the idea of having Aristaeus wander up the Peneus when there is 'a famous Oracle of Apollo at Tempe', which, as Apollo's son, 'he would naturally have consulted' before looking for his mother. He waxes indignant at the image of an underground cavern that can house entire rivers as far apart as the Phasis, the Tiber, and the Hypanis. And he objects to the story of Proteus being dragged in 'by the heels'.[16] Graves knows that Proteus does *not* live at Pallene. He lives on the low-lying island of Pharos, just off the Nile delta: Homer says so.[17]

It is not easy to understand why an eminent classicist with a keen sense of humour of his own should take such exception to Virgil's wit. For all his mystical tendencies, Graves understood myth in a surprisingly literal fashion – and myth is *not* a realist mode. The creations of mythology can be introduced *wherever* a poet chooses: the only question is whether the location is appropriate for the purpose in question. Opposite the estuary of the Peneus is the perfect site for Virgil's purpose.

It allows him to introduce his *second* 'downward journey'. Cyrene wraps Aristaeus in a perfumed mist and takes him *down* the river Peneus to its estuary, opposite which lies the peninsula of Pallene (modern-day Kassandra). That is, in the language of metaphor, she takes him 'deeper' into his own imaginal reality. As soon as they arrive at Pallene, she places him in the corner of a huge cave where Proteus likes to rest from the noonday sun.

The encounter with Proteus is composed of two motifs: an ambush and determination. Virgil borrowed the episode from book four of the *Odyssey* in which Telémakhos visits Menelaos, in the hope of learning something about his father. Instead, Menelaos tells him how he was delayed on his journey home from Troy.

Stranded near Pharos by adverse winds, Menelaos had lost hope that he would ever be able to return to Greece, when Eidothea (divine form or image), a sea-nymph, rises from the sea and offers to help him. She tells him that he must capture her father Proteus who, being a seer, will be able to answer his question. And she warns him of her father's tricks. Menelaos must *compel* Proteus to speak. Menelaos does as instructed, and he learns what he wants to know.[18] In Virgil's poem, the part of the delightfully helpful, even if somewhat un-filial Eidothea is taken by Cyrene, and yet the description of Aristaeus' struggle with Proteus is surprisingly faithful to Homer.

We associate Proteus with his ability to change form: hence our adjective, *protean* (= prone or able to change form). That is, we think of the episode in relation to the *object* of experience: this is highly misleading. In both the *Iliad* and in the *Georgics*, the significance of Proteus stems not from *his* ability to change form but from the determination of the *subject* to prevent him from doing so. Indeed, this is implicit in his name (Proteus), which is probably an archaic form of *Protogonos* (first-born).[19] That is, in ancient Greece, Proteus was associated with *origin*. In the story of Proteus, what is at stake is not *his* ability to transform himself, but the determination of the human *subject* (Menelaos and Aristaeus) to hold onto him through whatever forms he assumes until he reverts to the one in which they *first* saw him emerge from the sea. For only if they can do this, will he help them with their immediate problem.[20]

Menelaos and Aristaeus are in despair. Proteus represents the possibility of finding a solution to their impasse. He has the form of a seal on a beach, surrounded by other seals. This is because, as soon as disturbed, a basking seal will slip back into the sea with surprising agility. In other words, Proteus is a metaphor for a potentially useful intuition but which all-too-easily slips back into the unconscious. Other images/notions come to him – but they have no bearing on his immediate predicament; they cannot help him. It is only by forcing Proteus to revert to the form in which he *first* appears, that he will reveal what both Menelaos and Aristaeus seek to know.

In short, the frazzled teenager is confronted by an implicit challenge. He cannot resolve the difficulty in which he finds himself unless he actively *engages* with his imaginal experience. He must struggle with 'Proteus' until the seer tells him what he wants and *needs* to know. The struggle with Proteus is a vivid metaphor for the way in which a useful intuition can slip away from us before we can fully grasp it – unless we are determined to explore in what way it might be useful to us.

Virgil, however, makes one significant amendment to his source. In Homer, Proteus gives Menelaos *direct* answers. That is, in the *Odyssey*, Proteus is an all-seeing and helpful minor deity: he serves a narrative purpose. As an Epicurean, Virgil did not believe in all-seeing and helpful deities. His Proteus does *not* tell Aristaeus where to find either his lost bees or another colony to replace them. He provides an *indirect* answer in the form of an account of the myth of Orpheus and Eurydice. That is, he invites Aristaeus (and by extension also the *reader*) to interpret the connection between the challenge facing Aristaeus and the metaphors harboured in the myth.

The encounter with Proteus illustrates a 'theory' about a specific kind of psychological difficulty. It suggests that when an individual is faced by an insoluble dilemma (whether a practical challenge or an intellectual problem), their 'unconscious' imagination *might* provide a solution. But if it does, it will be in the form of a vague and fleeting intuition; and unless held fast, this will metamorphose into fresh but irrelevant notions. Even if held fast, however, the imagination will not provide a *direct* answer. It will provide an *indirect* answer, very probably composed from *memories*: that is, it will compose a 'myth' from fragments of other remembered stories (or experiences) and adapt these to its purpose.

## Unbearable Loss (2): Orpheus and Eurydice

Proteus begins by telling Aristaeus that Orpheus is angry with him – and for good reason. It was while fleeing from Aristaeus' unwelcome attentions that Eurydice was bitten by a snake and died. Virgil may have been the first to give this explanation of her death.

We tend to think of this myth as a *story* – and for good reason. Virgil's account of the myth *is* a well-told story. The popular imagination, however, assumes that because this story describes a kind of love, the myth must be *about* love. Virgil, however, makes no mention of either Orpheus or Eurydice having enjoyed any kind of ordinary, earthly happiness *before* the latter's death. Virgil is not exploring love: he is exploring how Orpheus responds to a tragic accident.

The story of Aristaeus is about unbearable loss and his yearning to recover his bees. For his embedded myth, therefore, Virgil needed a 'myth' about unbearable loss. He remembered the myth of Orpheus and Eurydice. He also knew that the best known of the Greek heroes to descend into the under-world are Odysseus and Herakles. In the story told in ancient Greece, Orpheus may also have been invested with heroic qualities. In contrast, throughout his epyllion, Virgil *parodies* heroic qualities. He wants the hero of his version of the myth to reflect the character he has ascribed to Aristaeus: that of a con-fused and petulant teenager. So, he casts Orpheus as an equally self-engrossed adolescent, equally shattered by *his* unbearable loss. That is, he adapts the existent myth to his purpose.

We learn nothing about Eurydice, except her name, which suggests some-thing like 'wide-ranging law'. Orpheus has lost the 'law' which guided him – and he finds life without this 'law' unbearable. He has lost his sovereign good, his highest value, which is so important to him that he cannot imagine his life without it. The myth is not about love for an individual; it is about an ardent longing to recover something without which his life feels meaningless. A myth is always about something *other* than its story.

Virgil was an Augustan, and most Augustan poets were *ludic*. They liked to poke fun at their subject and to do so with apparent effortlessness. The links between the myth of Aristaeus and Orpheus are particularly clever. They rest on an intriguing series of associations and allusions which the reader today might miss, but which Virgil's intended reader would have recognised and relished.

Aristaeus learned how to keep bees from dryads, that is, from wood-nymphs who were the companions of Artemis, one of whose primary sym-bols was the bee.[21] Virgil tells us that, before her marriage to Orpheus, Eurydice was a dryad. In the Graeco-Roman world, bees were not only iden-tified with dryads; they were also associated with *purity*. The priestesses of Apollo at Delphi were called *melissae* (= bees or honey), so too were the priestesses of Demeter, presumably because young women dedicated to either a god or goddess were considered as sweet and pure as honey: they were 'pleasing to the soul'. The verb *melítzo* means to strum or to play an instrument, or else to sing a song. That is, Orpheus' double musical talent – he both sings and plays the lyre – is also related, metaphorically, to the sweetness of honey. In Orphic teaching, the bee was a symbol of the soul and a late neo-Pythagorean tradition – a tradition possibly known to Virgil and his Epicurean friends – identified Eurydice as Orpheus' *soul*.

The entire epyllion is thus built on an unexpected series of playful associations:

| bees = | sweetness = | (a) the dryads | = Eurydice | = the soul |
|--------|-------------|----------------|------------|------------|
|        |             | (b) music      | = Orpheus  |            |

By carefully choosing his words, Virgil fuses a story about the loss of a colony of *bees* with a myth about the loss of Orpheus' *soul*. He would have wanted his readers to recognise every allusion and to enjoy (and admire!) both the skill and the wit with which he brings such different issues together. His epyllion invites the reader to smile, sometimes even to laugh out loud, and yet never to forget that it harbours a serious concern.

Orpheus feels that he must recover Eurydice. Following her death, he sings of her from morning until night for as long as he can bear. Then, as if this were a perfectly natural thing to do, he determines to brave the 'jaws of Taenarus'.

That is, he sets off on the third *downward journey* of Virgil's epyllion, which 'echoes' the imaginary descents of Aristaeus: a descent into the gloom of the underworld, the realm of the dead.

Today, it is difficult to get to Cape Tainaron (modern-day Matapan, the southernmost tip of the Peloponnesos) and, apart from the magnificent views from the steep cliffs, there is little reason to do so. Virtually nothing is left to indicate its former importance. The fifth-century BCE Temple of Poseidon, a major centre of worship for the surrounding area until well into Roman times, is almost entirely concealed by the much later chapel of Asómatos. It is not obvious why Hellenistic and Latin writers regarded Taenarus as a principal entrance to the underworld: perhaps because there was said to be a large cavern there from which black smoke would billow. Virgil may also have intended his readers to remember a story about Herakles, who guarded the entrance of the underworld. Whatever the case, Virgil describes the episode not with reverential awe but with gently mocking irony.

He parodies the heroism implicit in the determination to outface Death by conjuring a deliberately *un-heroic* metaphor. He likens the approach of Orpheus through the gloom of the underworld to that occasioned by someone rambling past shrubbery at the approach of evening, unwittingly disturbing the small birds that had settled there for the night. With deadpan humour, he imagines the effect that the sound of Orpheus' lyre and voice have on some of the best-known residents of the underworld. As he advances, not only the Furies, but even the snakes writhing in their hair fall silent. The wheel of

Ixion stops turning so it can listen. And all three of Cerberus' mouths fall open 'in wonder'. Virgil was clearly enjoying himself.

In Greek, *orphne* means 'darkness' or 'night'. Orpheus may be the son of Apollo, but his name is suggestive of the 'darkness' in which Dionysian rites were performed, and of the 'gloom' of the underworld. Just as the initiate seeks to recover a belief that their life has a lasting meaning, so Aristaeus wants to recover the bees which gave his life meaning, and Orpheus seeks to recover Eurydice, who gave his life meaning.

In myth (and myth-like narratives), the *downward journey* (*katábasis*) is rarely problematic. Aristaeus sinks all-too-easily into a self-pitying slough of despond. He follows his mother on their journey down the Peneus. The motif of a downward journey tells us only that the *subject* has accessed an *imaginal* reality. Orpheus descends into the underworld without difficulty. The challenge facing him will come at the nadir.

Orpheus is now in the deepest part of the underworld. He has come to persuade Aidoneus to release Eurydice to him and to be allowed to return to his *social* world with her. But just as Aristaeus misconstrues the challenge facing him, so too does Orpheus.

## The *Anábasis*: Orpheus Alone

Every *downward* journey supposes two corollaries: an *implicit challenge* and an *upward journey* (*anábasis*): in other words, a challenge to recover (or learn) something from the underworld (= imaginal experience) and an attempt to *return* to one's habitual or *social* world with this something. Every *downward journey* implies the question: Will the *upward journey* be successful?

Intriguingly, Virgil does not describe the scene of Orpheus pleading with the lord of the underworld. But he does tell us the condition the latter imposes.

No mention of the critical condition imposed on Orpheus by Hades has survived from either Greek or Hellenistic times. Such conditions are not at all common in Greek mythology. They appear, for example in the *Odyssey*, in the condition which Aíolos attaches to the wind bag which he gives to Odysseus (book 10), or in Kirke's various warnings about the Sirens, Skylla and Charybdis, and the sheep and cattle of Helios (book 12). But such episodes resemble folk motifs rather than myth. The condition *may* have belonged to Greek versions of the story, but because it would have been unusual, one would have expected some mention of it to have survived. Today, although it is still popularly assumed that the condition was part of the Greek myth, most scholars believe that Virgil was the first to introduce it.

Orpheus has no sooner entered the underworld than he is on his way out. And, as everyone knows, just as Orpheus is about to re-emerge into the light of day, for no clear reason, he looks back at Eurydice. She immediately cries out 'What madness caused you to destroy us both?' But even as she speaks, she is drawn back into the underworld forever. She has died a second death.

The ancient Greeks told a few stories about 'successful' descents into the underworld: notably those of Odysseus and Herakles. But Virgil was not an ancient Greek, and he did not believe in the gods of the Greeks. He was writing in different times. He remembered the story about Orpheus, and he adapted it to his own purpose.

He included the famous condition because it teases the reader into believing that the *impossible* (to come back from the dead) is nonetheless *possible*. Virgil tempts us to believe that Orpheus was at fault: that had he not turned to ascertain whether Eurydice was still following him, he would have succeeded in recovering her from the underworld. But no one returns from the realm of the dead to a social reality, and Virgil would have expected his readers – especially his Epicurean friends – to realise this.

Orpheus has achieved nothing by his descent. His failure to recover Eurydice leaves him so distraught that he *loses* his grip on reality – that is, on life. Aristaeus began his quest by seeking the *source* of the river Peneus, where he found his mother. Virgil now repeats this motif in a grim and tragic mode. Orpheus sets off on a further *anábasis* – a journey *up* the river Strymon (towards or into modern-day Bulgaria): that is, away from Greece – his *social* reality – and into lands imagined as bleak and backward: that is, suggestive of depression and despair.

In Greek culture, one of the oldest and most resonant images of Orpheus is that of a semi-divine musician who can charm wild animals with his playing and singing. He can make all nature stop to listen to him.[22] He represents not only the power of music to remind human beings of the natural harmony of the world but also, by extension, the relation between music, transformation, and regeneration.

Virgil *parodies* this image. Orpheus is traumatised by the unbearable loss of his 'sovereign good'. So plaintive is his song that it draws tigers and oak trees to gather round him. But there is nothing either transformative or regenerative about the description of him singing to them. In its *context*, this is an image of hopeless and self-indulgent despair. Orpheus is likened to a nightingale endlessly lamenting the theft of her chicks by an uncouth ploughman. Virgil is poking fun at the traditional image of Orpheus charming animals. But he is also trying to shake the reader into recognising the psychological implications of his account of the myth.

Orpheus refuses any suggestion that he might love again, let alone consider re-marriage. This paralysis of his emotional life is reflected in the aimlessness of his wanderings: first, north-east, away from the Mediterranean, around the north coast of the Black Sea to the estuary of the Don – and then back again to Thrace. And yet, wherever he is, he does nothing but lament the loss of his Eurydice. He is consumed by his unbearable loss.

Prior to Virgil, the story of the death of Orpheus belonged to a separate tradition from that of his journey to the underworld. An Attic red figure *stamnos* by Hermonax from Nola, dating from about 460 BCE, shows female figures attacking Orpheus with a roasting spit, a pestle, and a rock.[23] This is *not* an illustration of the last scene in the story of Orpheus and Eurydice. It represents the same moment as Aeschylus explores in the *Bassarai*, a play we know of only from later references to it. In the *Bassarai*, Orpheus rejects Dionysos in favour of the sun, which he identifies as Apollo; that is, Orpheus turns his back on the darkness in which Dionysian rites were performed in order to pay homage to Apollonian clarity. Whereupon Dionysus takes his revenge: he sends his followers, the Bassarids, to dismember him. Their fury symbolises how a man who turns his back on Dionysian intoxication and affect will be consumed by those Dionysian elements in his own personality which he has repressed. In Greek art, Orpheus is punished for shunning the possibility of personal salvation advocated by the Dionysian mystery rites in favour of the communal worship of Apollo.

Virgil was probably the first to connect the *death* of Orpheus to the story of his attempt to recover Eurydice from the underworld. His primary debt, however, is not to the play by Aeschylus but to the later play by Euripides. In the *Bacchae*, Maenads attack and kill Pentheus for refusing to join them in their Dionysian rites. In Virgil's epyllion, Maenads attack Orpheus and kill him. They then dismember him and throw his head into the Hebrus, a river whose source is in modern Bulgaria. As the Maritsa, it first flows eastward; then, as the Hebrus (it is now the border between Greece and Turkey), it flows south into the Aegean. There are few more poignant images in litera-ture than that depicted in the final lines: the head of Orpheus floating down the Hebrus, still singing plaintively, 'Eurydice! Eurydice!'

As soon as he has finished his story – and *without* offering any explanation why he told it – Proteus slips back into the sea.

Aristaeus is left thoroughly nonplussed. He is no further advanced than he was before consulting his mother. He has no idea what the myth of Orpheus and Eurydice has to do with his bees. He does not even appear to consider himself responsible for Eurydice's death. He personifies someone who cannot see beyond the end of his nose. The myth means nothing to him. He cannot interpret the metaphors of which it is composed. He is unable to make con-nections. He has had the experience but missed its meaning.[24]

## Narratives with a Two-Part Structure

A myth is determined by its context: in ancient Greece, either the *social* con-text which triggered it, or the needs of a *narrative*. An example of the latter is provided by the *Odyssey*. The purpose of the embedded stories that compose Odysseus' account of his adventures to the Phaeacians is to encourage his hosts to let him go home.[25]

In contrast, when Virgil uses embedded stories (those of Aristaeus in rela-tion to the *Georgics*, and of Orpheus in relation to Aristaeus), he is not devel-oping a 'narrative'. He is signalling a shift to a different *kind* of narrative space. The first three and a half books of the Georgics are about 'agricul-ture'. In the middle of book 4, Virgil 'plunges' the reader into the world of myth. Aristaeus *plunges into* the underwater home of his mother, then he *travels down* the river Peneus to its estuary, opposite which he forces Proteus to explain how to find his bees. To his surprise, the seagod tells him a myth, in which Orpheus *descends* into the underworld. In all three cases, the downward journey (or *katábasis*) is a metaphor representing a shift from a quasi-*social* reality (that of a smallholder, or a beekeeper, or of Orpheus's hypothetical 'habitual' reality) to an *imaginal* reality (that of myth) in which the protagonist hopes to find a solution to his difficulty.

The key to both the epyllion and to the *Georgics* lies in the repeated division into two parts. The *Georgics* is divided into two parts (the first three and a half books and the epyllion). The epyllion is in two parts (the frame story about Aristaeus and the embedded myth about Orpheus and Eurydice) – and both these stories have a two-part structure. In a myth, or other work with a two-part structure, one often finds that the *first* part describes an implicit challenge, and (in a tragic narrative) the *second* part illustrates the consequences of failing to meet this challenge.

Myths and myth-based narratives that divide into two parts existed long before Virgil. For example, in the first half of *Antigone*, each episode represents an aspect of a challenge implicitly facing Kreon (to listen to others, most obviously to Antigone and Teiresias); in the second half, the episodes represent the inevitable consequences of his failure to meet this challenge, a failure which Kreon only *partly* deciphers at the end. It is left to the spectator/reader to decipher the broader implications of his failure.[26] Although these reflect the attitude and behaviour of the protagonist, Sophocles is not exploring the 'psychology' of an *individual*. Kreon is a figure from myth: that is, he is a *carrier* of attitudes and tendencies pertinent to a *community* (the *pólis* of Athens).

Virgil's epyllion, however, does not reflect the concerns of any community, even those of an Epicurean community. It explores his own views – through metaphor.

The first part of the story of Aristaeus presents the beekeeper with a challenge. Readers might *assume* that this challenge has to do with recovering his lost bees. But this is a tease, for a myth is never about its story: it is about the metaphors harboured in the story. The issue that Virgil emphasises is how, when faced by a relatively minor difficulty, Aristaeus falls apart and sinks into helpless despair. But he misconstrues the challenge facing him: it is not to find his bees: it is to stop behaving in such an excessive or *unseemly* fashion.

As an embedded story, the first part of the myth of Orpheus reflects this issue. He too is presented with an implicit challenge – and, once again, most readers will assume that this challenge has to do with him recovering Eurydice from the underworld. This too is a tease. As an Epicurean, Virgil did not believe in the literal truth of myth. He did not believe that any god, whether of the upper world or of the underworld, would help a human – least of all to return from the dead. Orpheus also misconstrues the challenge facing him. It is *not* to recover Eurydice from the realm of the dead; it is to neither ask nor hope for the impossible. In other words, it is to *come to terms* with both his mistaken sense of entitlement and with Eurydice's death, that is, to behave in a less inappropriate and unseemly fashion.

The second part of the myth illustrates the consequences of his inability to understand this challenge. On returning to his social world alone, Orpheus becomes ever more fixated on his loss. He slips into a paralysing depression. Whereas in the first part of the myth, his sense of entitlement was reflected in his belief that he could recover Eurydice from the underworld, in the second part, it is reflected in the image of his music – his grief – being so beautiful that even tigers and trees come to listen to him. This illustrates not the harmony but a *reversal* of nature. He rejects the advances of women, which is a *refusal* of nature. And in a further rejection of nature, his body becomes no more than a head, singing of his longing. The second part of the myth represents the failure of Orpheus to come to terms with Eurydice's death.

As part of an embedded story, the tragic ending of the myth reflects the failure of Aristaeus to understand what is required of him. And thus, the *second* part of the story of Aristaeus' story is deliberately *ambiguous*.

This ambiguity is evident in three ways. Firstly, although Cyrene overheard Proteus tell Aristaeus that *Orpheus* is angry with him, she now tells him it was the *dryads* who caused his bees to swarm. They are angry with him, she insists, for having caused the death of their friend, Eurydice. This teases the unwary reader into trying to explain this difference. Was Proteus mistaken? Is Cyrene correct? These questions are *irrelevant*. Virgil is teasing his reader. As an Epicurean, he does not believe that deities take the slightest interest in either the entreaties or the prayers of human beings.

Secondly, Cyrene tells Aristaeus that if he wants to recover his colony of bees, he must sacrifice a bull and a heifer on each of four separate altars to the dryads. In addition to which, he must offer a black ewe to Orpheus, at whose shrine he must also leave funeral dues. And even though she will already have been appeased, he must make a further offering of a calf to Eurydice. In Greek religion, sacrifices were communal rites performed on behalf of a community. A priest, a leader, or other representative of this community would offer a sacrifice to one or more of the Olympian gods in exchange for a hope of divine favour. Homer sometimes tells us that the ancient Greeks offered sacrifices to dryads: for example, in the *Odyssey*, book 13.[27] But this is poetic license. It is highly unlikely that the Greeks offered sacrifices to dryads – especially on such an extravagant scale as Cyrene dictates, or to atone for a *personal* shortcoming. If they wanted to foster the goodwill of the dryads, they left them 'gifts' in front of a small wayside altar.[28] Offering dryads such an excessive sacrifice as Virgil describes, and for such a reason, is *burlesque*. He is poking fun at the idea that the gods can be persuaded, by means of sacrifices and offerings, to take an interest in human beings – that is, at the very practice he so vividly describes.

Thirdly, Aristaeus discovers bees rising from the rotting cattle to form 'grape-like clusters' in the trees. The reader is teased into believing that he has appeased not only the dryads but also Orpheus and Eurydice. Aristaeus has a new stock of bees. The unwary reader assumes this is a happy ending – and Virgil clearly wanted to oblige this expectation. He encourages the reader to think his epyllion has a happy ending. And yet, there is no indication that his beekeeper has learned anything from his experience. He has not understood why Proteus told him the myth of Orpheus and Eurydice.

All of these suggest that the second part of the story of Aristaeus is *ironic*. The ending is ingeniously ambiguous. The reader is invited to contrast the *ostensibly* happy ending with the implications of the *tragic* ending to the myth of Orpheus and Eurydice. And the fate of Orpheus suggests that Aristaeus remains as he always was – a comic representation of a human *type*: that of a person who becomes flustered and helpless at the first difficulty in his life. There is no indication that he has changed. His response to his situation will remain as excessive and inappropriate as it was at the outset. And that Orpheus wastes away until calamity overtakes him suggests that the same *might* happen to any person who cannot face the vicissitudes of life is a more appropriate and responsible fashion.

This is further suggested by the brief coda, in which Virgil tells his readers that he wrote the *Georgics* while Octavian was engaged in the events leading up to the Battle of Actium. He might have hoped that Octavian would restore a measure of peace and political stability to Rome and the 'empire', but he could not have known that – as Emperor Augustus – he would subsequently achieve this. The final envoi to the *Georgics* suggests that he was keenly aware that the political situation was still highly precarious. His poem represents a personal response to this uncertainty – a response rooted in his Epicurean convictions.

Thus, as one would expect, the key to the epyllion rests in its relation to the first three and a half books of the *Georgics* – and the relation between them shows a similar two-part structure.

The first three and a half books of the *Georgics* are about the proper management of a small farm. They are about *husbandry*, a word which, in our consumer-driven age, seems quaint and old-fashioned. But for Virgil, it held a deeper meaning. Husbandry refers to the skill of managing one's smallholding: it describes the art of taking good care of one's fields and livestock.[29] But by extension, it also applies to the proper care of *all* one's responsibilities, including one's family, one's home, and one's finances. It implies careful management of *everything* for which an individual is responsible. The poem suggests that good husbandry represents a *proper* attitude towards life. A person who practices good husbandry – a person deeply in touch with the seasonal challenges that confront a smallholder – will not be shaken by the vicissitudes of life, whether political calamity or natural disaster. He will enjoy an unshakeable peace of mind.

The story of Aristaeus offers a witty illustration of the consequences, not of poor husbandry *per se* (bees swarm regularly, usually in the spring) but of the beekeeper's overblown, and thus *unseemly* response to the setback he suffers. He loses only his bees, and yet in the mythic imagination – and in comically exaggerated form – this is represented as the loss of a beloved spouse. That is, the inability of Aristaeus to find his bees is represented by an *excessive* feeling of unbearable loss. Faced by a difficulty which he should have been able to anticipate and resolve, Aristaeus becomes flustered; his life falls apart; and he loses his peace of mind. The same holds for Orpheus when he loses Eurydice.

Virgil is suggesting that good husbandry is measured *not* by competence in 'normal' circumstances but by the ability to manage an unforeseen mishap. His epyllion illustrates the consequences of not having the kind of firm moral attitude (Epicurean philosophy) which would allow the individual to calmly meet every challenge with which they are presented.

## Conclusions

Because the *Georgics* includes the earliest extant rendering of the myth of Orpheus and Eurydice, we tend to think of it as *the* myth. It is not. It is only one poet's clever and witty adaptation of the myth as he knew it. It is an ingenious *parody* not only of the myth he inherited but also of the notion that human beings can hope for help from the 'gods'.

We also tend to think of a myth as a self-contained story. But in his epyllion, Virgil is not really interested in either *story*. The story of Aristaeus hinges on his unbearable loss and longing, but its purpose is to illustrate un-heroic and *unseemly behaviour*. Virgil is drawn to the myth of Orpheus and Eurydice because of its metaphors of *loss* and *yearning*, which he translates into *unbearable* loss and *impossible* yearning (and thus also unseemly behaviour). That is, he adapts the myth to serve as a comically exaggerated, but also inexpressibly poignant analogy to the challenge facing Aristaeus.

The key to both Virgil's account of the myth of Orpheus and Eurydice and to the *Georgics* is his clever use of two-part structures. For the first half of his epyllion, Virgil devises the story of Aristaeus to illustrate *how not to behave* when confronted by a mishap: the challenge facing Aristaeus is to realise that he needs to recover his *peace of mind*. In the second half of the epyllion, Virgil adapts the myth of Orpheus and Eurydice not only to amplify the helplessness he attributes to Aristaeus but also to illustrate (in the language of metaphor and myth) the consequences for a man who crumbles in the face of a tragic event. The first three and a half books of the *Georgics* gently exhort farmers to adapt to the changing seasons and to take proper care of their soil and of their livestock: that is, to manifest good husbandry. The epyllion is a sophisticated and endlessly amusing illustration of what might happen to an individual who loses his equanimity. The sense of unbearable loss which characterises both Aristaeus and Orpheus represents the sense of unbearable loss which might be experienced by anyone whose peace of mind has been shattered by personal misfortune.

Virgil lived through unusually turbulent times. The first forty years of his short life were dominated by almost incessant, brutal, and destabilising civil wars. The allusions to episodes from the Trojan War reflect his horror at the damage that human ambition, lawlessness, and misfortune can inflict on private individuals. The *Georgics* is a reminder that Virgil's family lost their lands during the wars, and he had to fight long and hard to recover them (or to have them replaced). His poem illustrates the importance he gave to his Epicurean desire for a peace of mind that can withstand 'the slings and arrows of outrageous fortune'; in other words, his desire to cultivate his *ataraxia*.

In ancient Greece, myths reflected the concerns of the communities in which they arise. The *Georgics* may be the first work in which the challenge facing the protagonist of a *myth* reflects a concern primarily related to an *individual*. Virgil is thinking of myth in a new way: *not* as a story 'out there', about a hero belonging to a mythic reality, but as a *representation* of the attitudes and behaviour of an individual rooted in a quasi-*social* reality. Virgil very probably thought of his two protagonists (Aristaeus, Orpheus) in *behavioural* terms – and so should we. Nonetheless, the relation between the two parts of the epyllion invites consideration in *psychological* terms. It illustrates a response to, and interpretation of, a myth which might be described as 'modern': it anticipates, for example, the importance that C.G. Jung would ascribe to myth almost nineteen hundred years later.

Stephen Greenblatt argues that modernity begins in 1417, with the rediscovery of Lucretius' *On the Nature of Things*. Virgil, however, saw no reason to wait for this work to be lost, and then found again. Within a generation of its original publication, he was responding not to its theory of atoms but to its theory of myth based on *human* nature. The *Georgics* taught subsequent generations of writers how to turn to myth to explore their own concerns; and, by doing so, little by little, gradually to better understand the issues that interest them. Modernity is not just about applying empirical methods to our exploration of the 'outer' world. Just as importantly, it is about exploring and thus better understanding the nature and function of our concerns, our interests, and the way these manifest themselves in our 'inner' experience. Virgil's *Georgics* represents an early milestone on the long and winding road to modernity.

## Notes

1  David Slavitt, *Virgil*, New Haven: Yale University Press, 1991, p. 50.
2  In Roman times, beehives were simple containers, some natural (hollowed out logs), others man-made (pottery) and collecting the honey usually meant destroying the entire colony. The movable comb hive, which made this unnecessary, did not come into use until the eighteenth century.
3  See George K. Strodach, 'Introduction', Epicurus, *The Art of Happiness*, tr. George K Strodach (1963), London: Penguin, 2012, pp. 26–27.
4  Stephen Greenblatt, *The Swerve: How the World Became Modern*, New York: Norton, 2011.

5  Charles Segal is representative: 'The fundamental theme of Virgil's Georgics is the relation between man and nature'. See *Orpheus: The Myth of the Poet*. Baltimore: Johns Hopkins University Press, 1989, p. 36; also, Kimberly Johnson, 'Introduction' to her translation: *Virgil's Georgics: A Poem of the Land*. London: Penguin, 2009. For recent appraisals, see Nicholas Freer and Bobby Xinyue (eds.), *Reflections and New Perspectives on Virgil's 'Georgics'*, London: Bloomsbury, 2019, esp. chapters by Tom Mackenzie ('*Georgica* and *Orphica*: The *Georgics* in the Context of Orphic Poetry and Religion') and Nicholas Freer ('Virgil's *Georgics* and the Epicurean Sirens of Poetry').

6  Horace, 'Ars Poetica' (*ll.* 343, cf. 333), in *Satires, Epistles, and 'Ars Poetica'*, tr. H. Rushton Fairclough (1926), Cambridge, MA: Harvard University Press, 1929, pp. 478–479. The *Ars Poetica* was written some twelve or fifteen years after the *Georgics*.

7  Hesiod, *Theogony* (*ll.* 975–978), Hesiod, *Theogony, Works and Days, Testimonia*, tr. Glenn W. Most, Cambridge, MA: Harvard University Press, 2018, pp. 80–81.

8  'For Telesicrates of Cyrene, winner, race in armor, 474 BCE', in Pindar, *Olympian Odes, Pythian Odes*, tr. William H. Race (1997), Cambridge, MA: Harvard University Press, 2012, pp. 356–359.

9  Apollonius of Rhodes, *Argonautica* (bk. 2: 500ff.), in Apollonius Rhodius, *Argonautica*, ed. and tr. W.H. Race, Cambridge, MA: Harvard University Press, 2008, pp. 152–155.

10  See Apollonius of Rhodes, *Argonautica* (bk. 4: 1128–1133), pp. 418–421; and Diodorus of Sicily, *Library* (bk. 4: 81), in *Library of History*, vol. 3, tr. C.H. Oldfather, Cambridge, MA: Harvard University Press, 1939, pp. 73–75.

11  See C. Segal, *Orpheus*, esp. pp. 36–53 and 73–94; also M. Owen Lee, 'The Epyllion', in *Virgil As Orpheus: A Study of the Georgics*, New York: State University of New York Press, 1996, pp. 101–126.

12  Herodotus, *Histories* (7: 129), in *The Landmark Herodotus: The Histories*, ed. Robert B. Strassler, New York: Pantheon Books, 2007, p. 546.

13  *Iliad* (24: 77–99), Homer, *The Iliad*, tr. Richard Lattimore, Chicago: University of Chicago Press, 2011, pp. 499–500.

14  Bacchylides, Dithyramb 17 ('The Young Athenians or Theseus for the Ceans to Perform in Delos'), in *Greek Lyric: Vol 4: Bacchylides, Corinna, and Others*, tr. David Campbell, Cambridge MA: Harvard University Press, 1992, pp. 216–227.

15  For example, Nick Chater, *The Mind is Flat: The Illusion of Mental Depth and the Improvised Mind*. London: Allen Lane, 2018.

16  Robert Graves, 'Aristaeus', section 5, *Greek Myths*, 2nd ed., London: Cassell, 1958, pp. 280.

17  Homer, *Odyssey* (4: 351ff.), in *Odyssey*, tr. A.T. Murray, rev. G. Dimock (1919), Cambridge, MA: Harvard University Press, 1998, p. 144ff.

18  See Homer, *Odyssey* 4: 351–425, in Homer, *Odyssey*, tr. A.T. Murray (1919), rev. George E. Dimock, 2 vols. Cambridge, MA: Harvard University Press, 1998, pp. 144–149.

19  Protogonos is also another name for *Phanes*, the 'Radiant Light' which emerged from the primal Orphic egg, and which Zeus swallows in order to become one with the primal energy it contains: See Radcliffe G. Edmonds III, *Redefining Ancient Orphism: A Study in Greek Religion*, Cambridge: Cambridge University Press, 2013, esp. part II, ch. 6, pp. 160–191.

20  One notes the same insistence in Ovid's far more disturbing account of Peleus' rape of Thetis: see Ovid, *Met.* (11: 221–265), in *Metamorphoses*, tr. Frank Justus Miller, 2 vols. (1916), Cambridge, MA: Harvard University Press, 1984, pp. 136–139.

21  See Marcel Detienne, 'The Myth of 'Honeyed Orpheus'', in *Myth, Religion, and Society: Structuralist Essays by M. Detienne, L. Gernet, J-P. Vernant, and P. Vidal-Naquet*, ed. R.L. Gordon (1981), Cambridge: Cambridge University Press, 2009, pp. 95–110.

22  See for example, Antipater of Sidon, in *The Greek Anthology: Books VII and VIII*, tr. W.R. Paton, Cambridge MA: Harvard University Press, 1917, pp. 6–7; also Diodorus of Sicily, *The Library of History: Vol. 2, Books 2:35-4:58*, tr. C.H. Oldfather, Cambridge MA: Harvard University Press, 1935, pp. 424–425.

23  In the Louvre, Département des Antiquités grecques, étrusques et romaines, Gallerie Campana (G. 416).

24  See T.S. Eliot, 'Dry Salvages', ii, from *Four Quartets*, in *The Complete Poems and Plays of T.S. Eliot*, London: Faber and Faber, 1969, p. 186.

25  See Glenn W. Most, 'The Structure and Function of Odysseus' Apologoi'. *Transactions of the American Philological Association* (1974–2014), Vol. 119 (1989), pp. 15–30.

26  See T. Dawson, 'Gender and the Political in *Antigone*: The Need to Listen to *Others*', *Exploring Depth Psychology and the Female Self*, London: Routledge, 2021, pp. 94–112.

27  For example, Homer, *Odyssey* (13: 349–355), see vol. 2, p. 26–27.

28  Homer, *Odyssey* (13: 356–360), vol. 2, pp. 28–29.

29  See Kimberly Johnson's translation: *Virgil's Georgics: A Poem of the Land*, London: Penguin, 2009; or a recent translation into French: Frédéric Boyer, *Le Souci de la terre: Nouvelle traduction des Géorgiques*, Paris: Gallimard, 2019.

Chapter 4

# The Neoplatonic *Katabasis* of the Soul to the World of the Senses

## Language as a Tool for Regaining Self-Consciousness

*Maria Chriti*

The subject of this paper is the Neoplatonic treatment of the *katabasis* of the soul from the upper world of the One to the world of senses in texts between the fifth and sixth centuries CE, from the perspective of what Carl Jung would call 'an attempt of the soul to regain self-consciousness'.[1] The influence of ancient Greek reflection on Carl Jung and, more specifically, his debt to Neoplatonism has been acknowledged by scholarship. However, there are writings of Neoplatonic commentators on Aristotle from the School of Alexandria which have not been taken into account by Jungian scholars, it is this gap which the present study aims to fill.

Neoplatonic philosophers who comment on Aristotle in the metropolis of Egypt are active as teachers and authors during a transitional historical period in an area witnessing the coexistence of pagans and Christians, with a complicated network of contacts. In addition, given that the Neoplatonic School of Alexandria has Christian teachers after a certain period, the doctrines regarding the soul have to be carefully contextualized, in the frame of both the reception of Platonic metaphysics and the possible theological influences from the new religion. A few general remarks about the tradition of these commentaries are worth formulating by way of introduction.

Neoplatonic commentaries as a deposit of valuable material for the discussion of Plato's and Aristotle's philosophy, as well as their reception in Late Antiquity and in the Middle Ages, have been increasingly studied[2] during the past decades. Special attention has been given by scholarship to those philosophers who explain Plato and Aristotle through the lenses of Neoplatonism and – in their majority – adapted them to the curricula of the Schools of Athens and Alexandria.[3] Studying Neoplatonic commentators is still a work in progress, but it is this specific aspect that renders an approach to their views with a contemporary apparatus so exciting. More specifically, taking into consideration that: (a) Platonic views on the soul are strongly evoked by the fifth- to sixth-century Neoplatonic commentators and (b) in contemporary psychology, Neoplatonic elements are considered to survive in several formulations of Carl Jung, it would be of high interest for the history of depth psychology to apply a Jungian perspective to such Neoplatonic texts of Late Antiquity.

DOI: 10.4324/9781003054139-6

According to the above preliminary remarks, the first section of this article deals with Jung's relation to Neoplatonic principles. The next part takes as its subject terms and issues of the residual content in the embodied soul, as they occur in Neoplatonic commentaries of the fifth and sixth centuries, themes which have not been related to Jung's Neoplatonism. Emphasis is put on these philosophers' theories regarding the effort of the soul to regain its lost self-consciousness, by means of the discussed residual remnants that are activated by language, a treatment which has not been investigated in the frame of depth psychology. It is hoped that in the conclusions the fruitful results that can enrich the history of depth psychology are underlined, in terms of approaching the effort of the soul to recollect its own identity.

## Carl Jung and Neoplatonism

Although Carl Jung himself does not discuss it explicitly,[4] Neoplatonism is considered to have played a significant role in the formation of his views. His formulations regarding the 'universal unconscious', his so-called 'archetypes' and 'archaic patterns' of the soul are treated as having counterparts in Plotinus's discussion of the Universal Soul and also the Platonic transcendent Forms.[5] Neoplatonic All-Soul has been paralleled with Jung's collective unconscious despite the differences and regardless of the less metaphysical character of Jung's theory.[6] Jung believed in an always-present religious/moral instinct; according to his position, there is a 'universal unconscious' which consists of non-personal experiential data, existing independently from individual souls and these data are evoked by individuals when they react in varied circumstances. His archetypes are primary universal principles which are indigenous in human souls as a potential.

Neoplatonists also believed in the need to locate ourselves in relation to a larger but also superior context to which we are linked by means of our souls: Souls originate from the divine Neoplatonic One and they used to be united with it, but they 'fell' onto the earth, i.e., the world of matter and senses, resulting in bodies. This position echoes Plato's formulations on the soul's liberation from the body after death.[7] According to Plotinus, this fall was inevitable, but the souls boasted of their detachment and forgot their own origins with arrogance.[8] What is interesting for the present discussion is that, when souls were united with the *intelligibles*, they were in direct contact with the Platonic Forms, a connection which is now broken.[9]

An aspect of Neoplatonic philosophy that hasn't been underlined from the perspective of depth psychology is the conviction that the souls kept a souvenir from their past identity, something that remains inside them as a residual content, during their habitation in the bodies; it is a kind of 'psychic concept' with a formative potential, since they can produce the forms of beings. The first technical term by which the innate soul content is expressed is *logoi* (λόγοι)[10] and it is used by Plotinus,[11] Porphyry,[12] Syrianus,[13] and Proclus.[14] Proclus clarifies that these specific *logoi* are in every human soul and the same for all human beings, as well as the same with the *logoi* of the World Soul, from which the natural objects originate. Proclus thus justifies the fact that the *logoi* are connected with sensible things; however, Proclus's student Ammonius of Hermeias, as well as Ammonius's students in the School of Alexandria,[15] deal with the way that *logoi* are actually activated in mankind, embarking on issues of semantics. Furthermore, 'λόγοι' are interchangeable with 'νοήματα' and 'ἔννοιαι' in their writings, as a result of treating Aristotle's semantics.

## Neoplatonic Soul and Self-consciousness

Let us start with Ammonius[16] and his commentary on Aristotle's *Categories*[17]: Ammonius expresses the irreversible situation of the soul's captivity in the body, by emphasizing that when it was 'up', it was 'at home' (*In Cat.*, 15.4-9):

Εἰ μὲν αἱ ψυχαὶ ἄνω ἦσαν χωρὶς τοῦ σώματος τούτου, πάντα ἂν ἐγίγνωσκον ἑκάστη οἴκοθεν μηδενὸς ἑτέρου προσδεόμεναι, ἀλλ᾽ ἐπειδὴ κατεληλύθασι πρὸς τὴν γένεσιν καὶ συνδέδενται τῷ σώματι καὶ τῆς ἐξ αὐτοῦ ἀχλύος ἀναπιμπλάμεναιἀμβλυώττουσι καὶ οὐχ οἷαί τέ εἰσι τὰ πράγματα γινώσκειν ὡς ἔχει φύσεως, διὰ τοῦτο τῆς ἀλλήλων ἐδεήθησαν κοινωνίας διακονούσης τῆς φωνῆς εἰς τὸ διαπορθμεύειν ἀλλήλαις τὰ νοήματα.

If souls were on high, separate from the body, each of them would on its own know all things, without need of anything else. But they descend at birth and are bound up with the body, and, filled up with its fog, their sight becomes dim and they are not able to know things it is in their nature to know. This is why they need to communicate with one another, the voice serving their needs in conveying their thoughts to one another.
(tr. S. M. Cohen and B. Matthews)

Ammonius' conditional clause that expresses the impossible is accompanied by an adverb which is intriguing – 'οἴκοθεν'. It might be said that the English translation does not render it properly, since 'on its own' does not shed light on the meaning of 'home', which is prior to and more important than 'being on someone's own'.[18] Eventually, the soul's home is the upper realm and the translation 'from home' would be more compatible with the importance of the origins of the soul in Neoplatonism.

In Ammonius's text, knowledge of the soul would only come from its homeland, meaning that the souls were supplied with what they needed to know when they were 'up', where they should be, and where they belong. Now that they are expatriated, there is distance between them and their homeland and this is why their identity is forgotten. The soul's genuine self is linked to the divine according to Ammonius, but as long as it became attached to birth and corruption by means of its embodiment, oblivion covered the knowledge that it had like a mist. As we read in this text, the souls can no longer recognize beings as they should and could do according to their nature: it was an inherent capacity for them to know all things but now they have to find a way to remember what they knew.

So far we have to place emphasis on the following: (a) the souls' identity and nature are situated in a past era, in a 'lost paradise', and (b) knowledge that is forgotten is related to communication by the Neoplatonic philosopher: something known has to be shared and communicated, as expressed by the verb 'διαπορθμεύειν'. Voice is the bodily organ for the transmission of the soul's content,[19] and it seems that conveying a content is as much important as possessing it for the philosopher, the term used to designate the soul's content being 'νοήματα' and not 'λόγοι'. This specific term appears in the commentators' discussion on the purpose of Aristotle's *Categories*. Ammonius adopts Porphyry's theory regarding the subject matter of the *Categories* as 'words that signify things via νοήματα', a 'formulaic purpose',[20] influenced by Aristotle's 'semantic triangle' in *On Interpretation*: things – concepts (= νοήματα) – words.[21]

Moving to Ammonius's student Simplicius, it must be pointed out that he uses three terms to refer to the soul's content: 'λόγοι', 'νοήματα', and 'ἔννοιαι'. In his commentary on Aristotle's *Categories*,[22] Simplicius refers to the *logoi* that the soul brings when it distances itself from the νοῦς,[23] by separating these 'λόγοι' from beings, with which they used to be united.[24] Therefore, Ammonius's 'οἴκοθεν' is illustrated by Simplicius who emphasizes the origins of the soul by insisting on Neoplatonic metaphysics: he refers to the unification between νοῦς and πράγματα at the level where νοῦς, πράγματα, and their νοήματα, i.e., the mental entities which correspond to things/beings, constituted a whole. In Simplicius's text too, communication is significant, as he explains that when souls were united with things, communication was held without voice. The souls were not in need of an intermediate instrument to share their contents, because they were identified with those contents and so voice was useless. Simplicius refers to 'there' (ἐκεῖ), designating the forgotten place and era of non-vocal communication. Ever since a distance was put between the soul and the intelligible beings, something is required to bring forward the remnants of the latter, so that the contact of the soul with beings is possible again.

Immediately after this point, Simplicius argues that the concepts in the soul are in a state of frigidity now, i.e., in the world of senses, where and when the souls are obliged to remain captivated in the bodies. Their mental entities are now like fossils, waiting to be revived. This residual content is no longer active, as if it urges for the appropriate stimulus (Simplicius, *In Cat.*, 12.26-30):

πεσοῦσα δὲ εἰς γένεσιν κα ιλήθης ἀναπλησθεῖσα ἐδεήθη μὲν ὄψεως, ἐδεήθη δὲ ἀκοῆς πρὸς ἀνάμνησιν· δεῖται γὰρ τοῦ ἤδη τεθεαμένου τὴν ἀλήθειαν διὰ φωνῆς ἀπὸ τῆς ἐννοίας προφερομένης κινοῦντος καὶ τὴν ἐν αὐτῇ τέως ἀπεψυγμένην ἔννοιαν· καὶ οὕτως ἡ τῆς φωνῆς ἐγένετο χρεία προσεχῶς μὲν τοῖς νοήμασι ἐξομοιοῦσθαι σπευδούσης, δι' ἐκείνων δὲ καὶ τοῖς πράγμασιν ἐφαρμοττούσης...

When, however, the soul has fallen into the realm of becoming, it is filled with forgetfulness, and requires sight and hearing in order to be able to recollect. For the soul needs someone who has already beheld the truth, who, by means of language (phônê), uttered forth from the concept (ennoia), also moves the concept within [the soul of the student] which had until then grown cold. This, then, is how the need for language (phônê) came about: on the one hand, it strives immediately to assimilate itself to notions (noêmata), while, on the other, by means of them it adjusts to realities and becomes of one nature with them...

(tr. M. Chase)

In Simplicius's 'palaeontology' it is explained how corporeality fatally affected the soul's conditions of living: alienation from νοῦς means that νοήματα can no longer be projected without a bodily organ. The *katabasis* of the soul in the sensible world and its consequent 'forgetfulness' rendered bodily functions (ὄψεως, ἀκοῆς) indispensable for the stimulation of 'remembrance'. Simplicius utilizes the term 'ἔννοιαι' for the frigid content in the soul and 'νοήματα' for what the voice tries to assimilate itself with (in order to be adjusted to 'πράγματα'). However, as Paraskevi Kotzia has rightly argued,[25] Simplicius applies these two terms interchangeably in his commentary on the *Categories* to denote mental states that correspond to things, being stirred up by linguistic utterances[26]: the voice can intrigue a mental entity in the soul and thus vocal sounds can assimilate themselves with such entities and regain their past contact with them.[27]

Neoplatonic metaphysics of the soul are depicted in a particular way by another of Ammonius's students, namely John Philoponus in his discussion of the same issue (Philoponus's commentary on the *Categories* generally reflects Ammonius's teaching).[28] His treatment is extremely interesting, given that he became a Christian. The term 'νοήματα' is also chosen by Philoponus in his commentary on the *Categories* to designate the souls' contents that have to be communicated after the fall (Philoponus, *In Cat.*, 9.31-34),[29] but his formulations can give us even more striking material:

εἰ μὲν γὰρ γυμναὶ σωμάτων ἦσαν αἱ ψυχαί, γυμνοῖς ἂν προσέβαλλον τοῖς νοήμασι· νῦν δὲ τοῖς σώμασιν ἐγκαθειργμέναι οὐκ ἄλλως ἢ διὰ τῶν φωνῶν δύνανται σημαίνειν ἀλλήλαις τὰ ἴδια νοήματα.

If the souls were bare and disposed of bodies, they would attend to bare notions; but now that they are shut in the bodies, there is no other way but via vocal sounds for them to denote their proper notions.

(my translation)

Philoponus uses a term that does not occur in the texts of the pagan commentators: he refers to the concept of 'bareness' (γυμναὶ, γυμνοῖς) in order to express (a) the soul's state before its embodiment and (b) the mental states' (νοήματα) condition before the fall, since the souls were in the position of communicating them directly to one another. 'Bareness' is related to the past but lost ideal era of the soul's existence. The commentator emphasizes that souls are no longer bare, but 'dressed' with bodies and restricted, and he also uses a conditional expressing the impossible: if it had been possible to de-corporealize souls so that they could be 'bare', they would have been able to share concepts also as *bare* contents, and not 'dressed' with vocal sounds. The motive of communication is also indispensable here: concepts are there to be designated and shared. 'Bareness' used to render communication easy but, ever since it had to be replaced by 'dressing' for the soul, its concepts had to be 'dressed', too, in order to be expressed.

A little further on in his commentary, Philoponus again uses the almost formulaic expression of the 'bare soul', by stating that the voice serves to signify νοήματα, by means of which the souls can communicate πράγματα, adopting the tripartite of the purpose of the *Categories*, as Ammonius and Simplicius agree (Philoponus, *In Cat.*, 14.1-5):

Αἱ ψυχαὶ αἱ ἡμέτεραι γυμναὶ μὲν οὖσαι τῶν σωμάτων ἠδύναντο διὰ τῶν νοημάτων σημαίνειν ἀλλήλαις τὰ πράγματα· ἐπειδὴ δὲ σώμασι συνδέδενται δίκην νέφους περικαλύπτουσιν αὐτῶν τὸ νοερόν, ἐδεήθησαν τῶν ὀνομάτων, δι' ὧν σημαίνουσιν ἀλλήλαις τὰ πράγματα

When our souls were bare, i.e. without bodies, they were able to designate things to one another via notions; since they were tied with bodies, due to a cloud their intelligible part is covered and so they needed words, via which they signify things to each other.

(my translation)

It is indeed intriguing that, in the writings of a Christian Neoplatonist, 'bareness' is identified with archetypal origins and homeland. According to Philoponus, body and language do not belong to the soul's home, the realm of the original intelligible entities. Both material organs are considered as 'garments' of the souls and the 'νοήματα', respectively, existing not for reasons of protection but as a burden: the souls' genuine identity and divine character are identified with bareness. The nostalgic character of the once-upon-a-time bare state of the soul can hardly be questioned here, as well as the similarities with the Old Testament: the 'protoplast' soul used to be 'bare', but it fell down and now it is obliged to be dressed with the body. Just like Adam and Eve – who used to be close to God and at home, bare and innocent, but afterwards they had to be dressed: the soul's homeland is far away now and the age of innocence has irreversibly gone.

## Concluding Remarks

Neoplatonic philosophers from the School of Alexandria are preoccupied with the soul's content in the past and present, emphasizing psychic/mental entities which are universal and not individual, immanent in the embodied souls, as well as able to help it regain its lost identity. More specifically, Ammonius, Simplicius, and Philoponus (a) describe the pre-existing content of the souls, a remnant which connects them with the universal One; (b) identify this content with the soul's genuine self; and (c) treat the way of activating and communicating this content by means of language as a procedure of recollection.

The transition from 'λόγοι' to 'νοήματα' and 'ἔννοιαι' can easily be observed in the terminology used, a development which is in part due to the treatment of Aristotle's semantics by the commentators. Be that as it may, the new designations of the soul's content can be smoothly contextualized in their approaches to the soul's recollection. According to the texts of Ammonius, Simplicius, and Philoponus, the psychic remnants do not consist of subjective mental constructions which cannot be perceived when communicated, but of conceptions with an archetypal and objective character that can be recognized and comprehended if (or when) shared and notified. The psychic remnants evoke a past era: the belonging to an ideal past, a universal frame, is undisputed, as formulated in the reckoning of the primitive divine situation, where and when everything was known and explicit and nothing was hidden or implicit.

The nostalgic reminiscence is totally compatible with both the formulations of the irreversible fall and the urge of the soul to be in contact again with what used to be its true nature. It was only then and there that the soul was happily identified with itself and its genuine character. The conditionals which express the impossible and are used by the commentators reveal the extent to which the 'fall' is considered as absolutely finalized. The *katabasis* of the soul has ended up in a dreadful situation, as a result of which the contribution of voice is necessary, in order to achieve communication. The Neoplatonic formulations are distinctive of the drastic distance between the 'upper' and the 'lower' worlds, as well as of the soul's chains:

- before, in 'heaven': ἄνω, ἐκεῖ, ἀλήθεια, τεθεαμένου, τέως;
- now on the earth: κατεληλύθασι, πεσοῦσα, συνδέδενται, ἐγκαθειργμέναι, συνδέδενται, λήθης, ἀνάμνησιν, ἀπεψυγμένην, ἀχλύος, νέφους, διακονούσης τῆς φωνῆς, διαπορθμεύειν.

According to the Neoplatonic commentators discussed so far, knowing the self on behalf of the soul should be treated in the frame of the soul's *katabasis* from the One to the earth and the following struggle to ascend. From the perspective of depth psychology, it is case of us having to stare up at a height, because the soul is already in the depth, in deep oblivion of who it formerly was. The formation of self in this case is not a look into the abyss, but a look 'into the sky'. The soul has to be healed from oblivion and, in its bodily condition, language helps to take a step towards the timeless, archetypal self.

Thus, linguistic utterance is, for the first time, related to the soul's *katabasis* in ancient Greek thought. Language emerged to help the soul recollect its fossils, so to speak. The soul's genuine self has to do with communicating these fossils: it is in its inability to express and share its contents that its for-getfulness is obvious, since these contents need to be stirred up as they are no longer projected. It is of great interest for depth psychology that the loss of identity means communicative incompetence in ancient philosophical texts. Knowing the self implies being able to communicate it, and vice versa: not being in a position to communicate who it is means that the soul does not know who it is. Consequently, knowing the self (or self-consciousness) is the means for the soul recollecting and recognizing the archetypal mental entities that it once possessed and could project in an unprohibited way. Thus, the soul's identity is defined and located in a common, broad, and originally framed context.

The purpose of this paper is not to suggest that Carl Jung must have read some of the above ancient texts, but to show that some commonly treated *topoi* may be found in various periods of philosophical reflection on the soul. When we talk about Neoplatonic elements in scholars like Jung, we might conclude that there is maybe more to be studied and discovered – and that interdisciplinary perspectives are essential for a better evaluation of ancient philosophical texts.

## Notes

1 I would like to express my warm thanks to Leslie Gardner, Terence Dawson, and Paul Bishop for organizing a wonderful conference and inviting us to submit our papers.

2 See P. Hadot, 'Philosophie, exégèse et contresens', in P. Hadot (ed.), *Études de phi-losophie ancienne*, Paris: Les Belles Lettres, 1998, pp. 3–10; apart from P. Hadot and I. Hadot (in 'The Life and Work of Simplicius in Greek and Arabic Sources', in R. Sorabji (ed.), *Aristotle Transformed*, London: Duckworth, 1990, pp. 275–304), K. Praechter's studies emphasized the philosophical value of the commen-taries of this era ('Richtungen und Schulen im Neoplatonismus', in H. Dörie (ed.), *K. Praechter: Kleine Schriften*, Hildesheim and New York: Olms, 1973, 165–216); and see P. Moraux, *Der Aristotelismus bei den Griechen*, vol. 2, *Der Aristotelismus im I und II Jh. N. Chr.* [*Peripatoi*, vol. 6], Berlin: de Gruyter, 1984. On the way that the philosophy of the commentators between 200 and 600 CE connects ancient with medieval philosophy, with Latin-speaking Christianity, and with medieval Islam, see R. Sorabji, *The Philosophy of the Commenta-tors, 200–600 AD: A Sourcebook*, Ithaca, NY: Cornell University Press, 2004.

3 Thanks to the enormous enterprise of the series *Ancient Commentators on Aristotle* directed by Richard Sorabji and his collaborators, the study of Aristotle's commentators in particular has been shedding light on crucial issues of the Neoplatonic literature. The published volumes with English translations of many of these texts facilitates in general the accessibility to this specific tradi-tion and, at the same time, reveals the stabilization of their study by contempo-rary scholarship. In his introductions to *Aristotle Transformed* (pp. 3–17) and *The Philosophy of the Commentators* (pp. 1–28), R. Sorabji addresses the kind of thorny issues that a scholar has to cope with before and during the treatment of Aristotle's Neoplatonic commentators.

4 See H. E. Barnes, 'Neoplatonism and Analytical Psychology', *The Philosophical Review* 1945, vol 54.6, 558–577 (p. 558).

5  For a general account of the influence of Eastern religions and culture on Carl Jung, see C. Douglas, 'The Historical Context of Analytical Psychology', in T. Dawson and P. Young-Eisendrath (eds.), *The Cambridge Companion to Jung*, Cambridge: Cambridge University Press, 1997; ²2008, pp. 19–38 (pp. 20–22). Jung's conviction that unconscious images can have teleological influence brought him in opposition to Freud. Jung used the term *archetype* in 1919 and later he was probably influenced by his travels to such places with indigenous populations as Mexico. Jung's archetypes have provoked much debate; however, his way of uniting philosophy with religion is widely recognized. For further discussiom, see H.-R. Schwyzer, 'Archetyp und absoluter Geist: C.G. Jung und Plotin', *Neue Zürcher Zeitung*, 1975; H.-R. Schwyzer, 'The Intellect in Plotinus and the Archetypes of C. G. Jung', in J. Mansfeld and L. M. de Rijk (eds.), *Kephalaion: Studies in Greek Philosophy and its Continuation offered to Professor C. J. de Vogel*, Assen: Van Gorcum, 1975, pp. 214–222; and R. Robertson, 'Stairway to Heaven: Jung and Neoplatonism', *Psychological Perspectives: A Quarterly Journal of Jungian Thought*, 2002, vol. 44 (1), pp. 80–95.

6  See Barnes, 'Neoplatonism and Analytical Psychology', p. 562.

7  Plotinus, *Enneads*, III.4.2-3. See J. Dillon and L. P. Gerson, *Neoplatonic Philosophy: Introductory Readings*, Indianapolis and Cambridge: Hackett, 2004, pp. 35–37; K. Corrigan, *Reading Plotinus. A Practical Introduction to Neoplatonism*, West Lafayette, ID: Purdue University Press, 2005, pp. 16–17. On the dichotomy between body and soul with the consequent superiority of the soul, see Plato, *Phaedo*, 79e-80a and 247c; and on the immortality of the soul as one of the essential principles of Neoplatonism, see P. Remes, *Neoplatonism*, Berkeley and Los Angeles, CA: University of California Press, 2008.

8  Plotinus, *Enneads*, IV.9.3.

9  On the relation between concepts and Form, see L.P. Gerson, *Plotinus [The Arguments of the Philosophers]*, London: Routledge 1999; and on the role of *concepts* in thought from Plato to the Neoplatonists, see the profound study of C. Helmig, *Forms and Concepts: Concept Formation in the Platonic Tradition* [Commentaria in Aristotelem Graeca et Byzantina, vol. 5], Berlin and Boston: de Gruyter, 2012.

10  The term *logoi* probably originates from the Stoic term 'σπερματικοὶ λόγοι' (or 'seminal *logoi*'), designating the 'seeds of things'. Michael Chase explains that '*logoi* are soul-portions as a spark buried in ashes, the stimulating of which brings the wished 'recollection' and constitutes the process of learning', in M. Chase, *Simplicius On Aristotle, Categories 1-4 [Ancient Commentators on Aristotle]*, London: Duckworth, 2003, p. 108. Also useful is Kevin Corrigan's argument about the Stoics who considered God as an immanent rational principle organizing everything, a principle to which we belong as 'individual intelligences', in the sense of being fragments of it (Corrigan, *Reading Plotinus*, p. 114).

11  Plotinus talks about the soul's *logoi* after its separation from the One as the forming principles of the sensible entities: see *Enneads*, IV.7.2 and IV.8.6, as commented on by Dillon and Gerson (in *Neoplatonic Philosophy*, pp. 35–49 and 56–58).

12  In his writings from Plotinus's *Enneads* known as *Aids to the Study of the Intelligibles* 16.1-5 (Αφορμαὶ πρὸς τὰ νοητά; see Dillon and Gerson, *Neoplatonic Philosophy*, pp. 178–179), Porphyry discusses the *reasonable soul*, which bears the *logoi* of things since it was free from the body. By using the term *logoi*, Porphyry mainly means the projection of Platonic ideas; see Dillon and Gerson, *Neoplatonic Philosophy*, p. 178, n. 3.

13  Syrianus, *In Metaph.*, 12.35-36, 24.21-24. See Helmig, *Forms and Concepts*, pp. 184–186.

14  Proclus explicates the role of *logoi* in his commentary on the *Parmenides* (981.11-13; 1081.1-11), explaining that they are a kind of psychic concepts which immanently exist in us, being representations of things; see also his commentary on *Timaeus* (1.248.7-252.10; 3.338.6-13), where he points out that the *logoi* are stifled by oblivion.

15  For an earlier discussion of the ancient texts that follow from the perspective of the negative character attributed to the origins of language, see M. Chriti, 'The Neoplatonic commentators of Aristotle on the origins of language: a new Tower of Babel?', in P. Golitsis and K. Ierodiakonou (eds.), *Aristotle and His Commentators: Studies in Memory of Paraskevi Kotzia* [*Commentaria in Aristotelem Graeca et Byzantina*], Berlin: de Gruyter, 2019, pp. 95–106.

16  Ammonius was the student of Proclus in the Athenian School and the teacher of Philoponus, Asclepius, Simplicius and probably Olympiodorus in Alexandria. Many of the commentaries were written 'according to the sayings of Ammonius' (ἀπὸ φωνῆς Ἀμμωνίου); for the specific type of texts, see the classic article by M. Richard, 'Apo Phônes', *Byzantion*, 1950, vol. 20, 191–222. On the School of Ammonius, son of Hermeias, see L.G. Westering, J. Trouillard, and A.P. Segonds, *Prolégomènes à la philosophie de Platon*, Paris: Les Belles Lettres, 1990; ²2003, pp. x–xlii; and H.J. Blumenthal, 'Alexandria as a Center of Greek Philosophy in Later Classical Antiquity', *Illinois Classical Studies*, 1993, vol. 18, pp. 307–325. On Ammonius, see K. Verrycken, 'The Metaphysics of Ammonius son of Hermeias', in R. Sorabji (ed.), *Aristotle Transformed*, 1990, pp. 199–231; and D.L. Blank, *Ammonius on Aristotle's "On Interpretation" 1-8*, London: Duckworth, 1996, pp. 1–2.

17  As it is known, this commentary is considered to be 'ἀπὸ φωνῆς Ἀμμωνίου', i.e., based on the oral teaching of Ammonius; see P. Kotzia, *Ο σκοπός των Κατηγοριῶν του Ἀριστοτέλη. Συμβολή στην ιστορία των αριστοτελικών σπουδῶν ως τον 6ο αιών* [i.e., *The Purpose of the Aristotelian Categories: A Contribution to the History of Aristotelianism until the 6th Century*], Thessaloniki: Aristotle University of Thessaloniki, 1992, p. 137.

18  On a similar issue of a questionable English translation of the same stem in Aristotle, see M. Chriti, '*Oikeiôs* as designating 'familiarity' and not 'appropriateness' in Aristotle's creation of words', *Labyrinth*, 2019, vol. 21(2), 88–105.

19  For the use of bodily organs by the soul as being superior to the body, see also Proclus, *On Plato's "Republic"*, 1.171.20-172.6.

20  Ammonius, *On Int.*, 10.4 ff.

21  Ammonius, *On Int.*, 17.24-28. Ammonius repeats his position in his commentaries on *On Interpretation* (24.8; 24.30; 89.23) and on the *Analytics* (1.9 and 1.18). He insists on the view that words, concepts and things are inextricably connected with one another, an approach which is also supported by Philoponus (*On Cat.*, 9.28-31), Simplicius (*On Cat.*, 12.1-3 and 13.16), and Olympiodorus (*On Cat.*, 41.1-34).

22  Philoponus, *In Cat.*, 12.20-21.

23  According to the Neoplatonic theory of the three hypostases, which are the One, the Mind and the Soul (see Plotinus, *Enneads* V.1.10), Simplicius refers to the unification between νοῦς and πράγματα at the level where νοῦς, ὄντα/πράγματα, and their νοήματα constitute a whole (*In Cat.*, 12.17-19): 'ὁ μὲν γὰρ νοῦς αὐτὰ τὰ πράγματα ὢν καὶ αὐτὴ ἡ νόησις ταὐτὸν ἔχει τά τε ὄντα καὶ τὰ τῶν ὄντων νοήματα διὰ τὴν ἀδιάκριτον ἕνωσιν...' ('For Intellect, being identical with realities and with intellection, possesses as one both beings and the notions of them, by virtue of its undifferentiated unity [...]', tr. M. Chase). For a more detailed discussion of the specific text, Kotzia, *Ο σκοπός των Κατηγοριῶν του Ἀριστοτέλη*, pp. 118–119.

24  Simplicius, *In Cat.*, 12.19-25.

25  See Kotzia, *Ο σκοπός των Κατηγοριῶν του Αριστοτέλη*, p. 133.
26  See also Simplicius, *In Cat.*, 24. 6 ff.
27  See Kotzia, *Ο σκοπός των Κατηγοριῶν του Αριστοτέλη*, pp. 119–121.
28  See the analysis in Kotzia, *Ο σκοπός των Κατηγοριῶν του Αριστοτέλη*, pp. 139–140.
29  Philoponus's commentary on the *Categories* is also considered to be 'ἀπὸ φωνῆς Ἀμμωνίου'; see *Commentaria in Aristotelem Graeca*, IV.4, v–vii and *Commentaria in Aristotelem Graeca*, XIII.1.

Chapter 5

# Acting Out, Science Fiction and Lucian's *True History*

*Leslie Gardner*

My paper is exploratory and light-hearted about a great satiric piece of writing which appeared in second empire Rome – by a foreigner, a native of what is now Syria, Lucian of Samosata, 'The True History'.[1] An extraordinarily popular itinerant performer/orator and writer in his time, he produced numerous dialogues as well as narratives, often using the voices of mythic figures, invented or common folk, to compose his commentaries. This was a time of wonder tales, a burgeoning genre of history-chronicle writing genre and travel narratives that crossed over.

It is an easy leap to talk about the performance of writing science fiction (and Lucian's 'True History' is touted as one of the first pieces of science fiction ever[2]) as a form of 'acting out': it is a compensation (or escape?) from contemporary and uncomfortable life, and also as the manifestation of a common psychological state in human beings. Lucian was sending up history and travel writing of his time which claimed to be describing true event and place with no grounding anywhere on earth. Fiction and history have long shared a common origin, and science fiction is perhaps incongruously a ruder and grander claimant to 'reality'.

Darko Suvin's (b. 1930, Yugoslav-born academic) famous 20th-century characterisation of sci-fi's rhetorical mechanism as 'cognitive estrangement'[3] shares traits with Freud's discussion 'uncanny'[4] in his commentary on E.T.A. Hoffman's 'The Sandman' and its creating an eerie shimmer to the ordinary traumatising a boy fearful for his eyes. Similar to developments in psychological theory outside depth psychology's remit, for example in CBT therapy's coordinates – cognitive behavioural therapy. Lucian pushed those buttons in the salty and explosive talk of world-weary courtesans knowingly assessing their marks and each other. While I won't explore CBT, which is outside my focus here, I want to demonstrate that Lucian engaged with technique we'd recognise is shared by both the great science fiction writers and the depth psychology theoreticians of the 19th and 20th centuries, alluding to 'real' event/science in their narratives: Ursula Le Guin, Jack Vance, even Jules Verne as well as obvious writings of psychic challenges in Freud, Jung and others.

DOI: 10.4324/9781003054139-7

Vance contemplates in one volume 'new' unearthly dark energy that warps the speed of earth out of danger – Jung's ideas of accommodating transformative energies as archetypal drive fit in here ('active imagination' – conscious dreaming) – which idea is mocked by Lucian in his imagery of propping open the mouth of a giant whale to escape its innards. Le Guin's perennial theme of the fictive composition of reality leads her often to include demurrals about the 'truth' of what she was doing as a novelist. Verne's *Twenty Thousand Leagues under the Sea*' includes sea creatures described in great detail – imaginary or 'real' – and the effects of deep sea diving on human psyche.

It is no mystery why Suvin turned to what was almost-faddish psychological language in his theoretical discussion of the genre in writing about science fiction as cognitive event in Freudian language which were invading literary commentary (along with applied Marxism especially in Suvin's case) at the time. In his time, Lucian was not only nudging competitive travel writers who he was fairly certain (as were readers) were made up places and events (and thereby sending up writers of history – including Herodotus) with fake vehicles, alien beings and places, but he was also teasing his readers who thought they knew the literature and satire of the times, by mocking them and mentioning great names as if his readers should know them: often they did not exist. In effect, he created meta-dissonance not only typically as a satirist but created uncanny compositions of dissonance of place and time, believable but not true.[5]

A descent into the abyss of the unknown whether it be metaphorically 'up' to the moon or into the bowels of an alien planet is tracked by Lucian as the familiar/unusual in the travel and satiric genres of the time. In its very recounting, compensatory psychic revolt erupts in the form of lashing out against the troubling psychological disturbance with anomalous or telling portrayals of other worlds and alien creatures or impulses that he proposes to be faithfully narrating.

There is a serious problematic involved in such an examination of a psychological dimension to Lucian's work. How can I comment on a writer/orator in those ancient times, focusing on the theme of depth psychology? The psyche's interior was an unknown or at least unarticulated 'place'. Many commentators however have pointed to ancient Greek notions of 'phrene' (location of thought or contemplation, not only pertaining to humans but throughout the universe) or 'thumos' (passion) as also bodily linked elements of what we would call the psyche (see the discussion in *Aeschylus' Use of Psychological Terminology: Traditional and New* by Shirley D Sullivan [McGill-Queen's University Press, 1993].) These words designate and locate a formulaic bodily reaction rather than a personal psychological event. Ruth Padel in her volume *In and Out of the Mind: Greek Images of the Tragic Self* (Princeton UP, 2016) points out how images of consciousness connect with language in a range of gender-specific and cultural points. She discusses that we may use these words to point to what we might today call feeling and thinking. When we read Lucian's works in later Roman times, these formulations of psychology seem to hold: as below, events with the vine women and the ass-legged women reveal a 21st-century knowledge of male desire: even to Padel's point that females were associated to Hades and animal depredation.

In Lucian's work, he implies a psychic interior whether he fully defines it as we might in the 20th and 21st centuries or not. Karen ni Mheallaigh in *Reading Fiction with Lucian: Fakes, Freaks and Hypereality* (Cambridge UP, 2014) claims that his psychic manoeuvres of thought and feeling assume a register abstracted from the conventions of bodily reaction. In other words, 'real' psychology drives his dialogues – his 'Dialogue with Courtesans' mentioned above is only one example.

Indeed, we note self-reflexive commentary by the narrator and among the crew who experience the adventures on the moon – aware of their personal failings and desires. In his dialogue among courtesans, for example, meaningful exchanges of envy and smug knowingness are carefully parsed out in the conversational exchanges, as here the crew warn each other of the attractions of females and fear of competition with alien warriors.

Suvin's discussion of science fiction, like Freud's 'uncanny', refers to homely strangeness. Science fiction affords an experience of fiction in which the familiar is disrupted by unlikely or alien shadings of agency or predication in the aesthetic product. In fact, inevitably, because it is anomalous and without apparent source, these odd turnings must derive from our perceptions of them or so we believe – and so in that way erupt from an interior which we sense, thereby, has shaped and driven what becomes the cultural product although we don't know how. That's where defensive action comes into the picture.

There are features and motifs in Lucian's long piece that I will show relate to a compensatory impulse as well as revealing an awareness about the interior register of human life. My endeavour is to show common themes that issues of depth psychology have with science fiction as a vehicle, deployed in one of its earliest performances. Due to space, I can allude only to some themes. But first follows a summary of the story.

## The story

After opening caveats in which Lucian insists that unlike others who make such claims, the history he is about to set out is all a lie, and 'that's the truth'. Having laid down the terms of narrative engagement, we are immediately told he and his crew travelled past the Pillars of Hercules and were blown off course, arriving at a wine island, where Heracles and Dionysus clearly have been – the trees are female, and several men in the crew engage with them, drinking wine from their lips. The ensuing sexual congress leads to permanent bodily entanglement/attachment – of necessity those men are left behind when the others leave the island.

But now, the ship is caught up in a whirlwind that takes them to the Moon where they are drawn into a battle with the Sun; the battle is led by the Moon's leader Endymion and the crew support them; to their surprise, they note that their fellow Moon warriors are hybrid, alien creatures who Lucian describes in great detail. The Sun's forces vanquish the Moon's army by blocking out the Moon's essential light (the science of the time suggesting that it is the Sun who radiates the Moon) and so they prevail; they arrange a harmonious peace. It is here on the Moon Lucian and his crew observe the Earth through a mirror-like disc – reflecting themselves on the Moon even as they look back.

They transport back to earth but are blown off course again by a tumultuous sea which plunges them inside a large whale through his huge open jaw. There they find familiar earth people who speak with them, and hybrid amphibious beings imprisoned too. They've built homes and villages and developed agriculture for sustenance. Lucian and crew hole up with an elderly earth man and his son who have both despaired and settled in, anticipating a long stay, they fear – battles are constantly brewing with other inhabitants, many of them brutish alien figures, but finally Lucian and his crew assist them all in escaping when the whale is killed and they can prop open its mouth.

Encounters then follow in a sea of milk where you can elect oblivion, and an island of cheese before they arrive at the bliss of the Island of the Blessed – encountering there Trojan heroes and other mythical figures, as well as a chatty Homer and Pythagoras. They stay in this salubrious place as long as they can, but since they are not dead, they must finally leave after giving invaluable advice to the inhabitants. Odysseus gives Lucian a letter to deliver to Calypso who resides on the next island in their journey – it's an apology for having left her abruptly behind (as per the myth). They sail around a great chasm in the sea, and Lucian ends, promising more (which never came).

## Themes

I will develop briefly in this paper that not only is Lucian's satire a form of defensive 'acting out' – as all fiction is such 'acting out' or compensatory activity, and science fiction in a particular way – but it is acting out just as such defensive activity is performed in the 21st century in ways we certainly recognise.

There is much to 'act out' about in Lucian's considerations of society. Padel and ni Mheallaigh both point out that images of male consciousness are contrasted to the darkness of Hades and to females. Padel particularly analyses biological metaphors for what is within. Patriarchal organisation of society sets females offstage, for example – fearful magnets for erotic loss of male senses and rationality. Hypocrisies of behaviour from intimate one-on-one contact to community ethos are drawn into his poetic world. Exploring hypocrisy in his dialogues and in his travel works seems his primary satiric purpose.

Additionally, in 'True History' Lucian comments on what we call 'fake news' and explores the all-too-familiar motivations for human's firmly believing what they know is not true (that's the 'cognitive dissonance' Suvin and Freud allude to).

But there is another psychological element of the commentary he engages in alluded to above. He observes his audience inflating themselves: he game-plays as Tim Whitmarsh points out with reception of his satire.[6] He snares his unaware audience in one-upmanship, tweaking their self-esteem and engaging them in hypocrisy. Reading or listening to orators, such as Lucian, delivered a pleasure for the audience in acknowledging erudition, their knowingness – for one thing recognising allusions to other writers. Tim Whitmarsh and ni Mheallaigh have pointed out that Lucian frequently invented those references. This is a meta-game with the formula of travel writing in this case – alluding as he does, for example, to a famous battleship Herodotus wrote about. (In fact, centuries later such a ship was discovered – so Lucian was wrong about the ancient historian's error – it was 'real'.) This de-stabilising form sends up the narrative and sends up the writers he alludes to who he accuses of fakery. It also upends the reader's expectations and tweaks the willing suspension of disbelief a reader engages in reading such material.

The deadly females recur and is perhaps Lucian's mocking patrician attitudes in Roman society – their reproductive purpose is taken away on the moon too – the males 'give birth' from their calves.

To explore the psychological and rhetorical devices he deploys, I want to refer to two classics in the literature of psychological delusion or hallucination as backdrops to the psychological angle I am pursuing: Victor Tausk's and Carl Jung's essays.

## Tausk

A brilliant disciple of Freud, Victor Tausk wrote an 'On the Origin of the "Influencing Machine"' in 1918.[7] In it he sets out his ideas about the pathology of schizophrenia (among other things). He focuses on a schizophrenic who insists he is being controlled by a long cylindrical object in the sky – he comments that he is one among others with the same complaint. This object has a mystical nature for them, Tausk reports, and patients are mostly vague about its construction: but it is notable that whatever is currently popular technologically and attributable to non-human origin seems relevant. This object makes the patient see pictures; it produces (and removes) thoughts and feelings by means of rays or other forces; it produces motor effects in the human body (erections, seminal emissions) and at times, depriving the patient of his specifically male potency; it creates indescribable sensations; it also causes physical effects in forming abscesses, or other pathological processes (Tausk, p. 186).

Tausk points out this has only occurred in males – they are persecuted in this way by their enemies. (Oddly despite this claim, two of his examples are female in this essay!) Since there is no obvious means their enemies might do this, they attribute it to an alien machine under that enemy's influence. The idea of the influencing machine 'originates in the need for causality that is inherent in man [sic]' (p. 187). Causality is linked to truth claims.

Tausk points out this is analogous to ideas of the persecutions invented by paranoids. Patients may originally not attribute the 'visions' they see to anything else, except that they 'see' them. They sense an 'inner estrangement' that can develop into a feeling that it originates from the outside. Often he points out observers (therapists/analysts?) confuse the stages of this development for depression or hysteria and do not note the development of a schizophrenic delusional pathology.

He explores one patient's pathology more closely – she identifies closely with the one who she perceives as her enemy, which Tausk points out is an attempt to 'project the feelings of the inner change [the inner estrangement] onto the outer world': it is a 'kind of intermediary position between the feeling of self-estrangement and the delusion of reference […] the discovery or invention of a hostile object' (p. 189). This process is a progression that may look like lesser or different disorders in the patient. This is a kind of 'projective identification' as it is known. It leads to a compensatory activity which is 'acting out'.

Tausk has concluded that this progression is common, and he now turns to the plausibility of the 'influencing machine' – setting aside its not being real. It is an elaborately constructed machine – that's for sure, and the patient gets more and more familiar with it as he examines it. He concludes without question they are symbols of genitalia, and the visions are masturbatory escape episodes. The issue is impotency – and its causes are displaced to an alien machine.

He continues in describing alternatively the female patient's illusion: she'd been rejected by a suitor, which Tausk finds important. She increasingly felt the deleterious effects of the invented (or discovered) machine that was slowly robbing her of sexual response altogether, and then robbing her of sensation in all her body parts – it is the ex-suitor's manipulation of the machine that is the source.

It was clear to her doctor that this lack of response presented and was symbolised not only in her genitalia but in her entire person. She became increasingly inaccessible and antagonistic to family and friends and to her doctor. He claims that it is her repugnance to the sexual attributes of her body that caused her to defuse and alienate – in fact, dismember – her own body relocating it into the machine so that she could refute it. 'It is a defence mechanism which has as its aim the protection of the conscious ego against the appearance or reappearance of undisguised fantasies' – in this case (but in many cases according to Freudian tradition) to sexual arousal.

He then explores a related disorder: the distortion of feeling that all inner thoughts/secrets are known to others. He associates to this mechanical distortion the pathological lying that adolescents engage with – again, as a defensive measure, acting out to protect the secret uses and arousals of the body – especially the penis. He outlines how it is an attribute of ego development that the child has a sudden guilty realisation that he can control his own thoughts and pleasures.

This discussion goes towards pointing out normative developmental progress and the involvement of delusions of references as a tool, almost a feature of this sequence. By the time of his conclusion, Tausk quotes Freud (and observes something that we will also find in Jung): 'It may be said that, in a certain theoretical sense, symptoms are formed only in order to forestall an otherwise inevitable development of anxiety'. Delusional tools and inventions are necessary to psychic development. Repression and guilt of the individual go into these byways as defensive acts of supporting guilt or shame. Lucian's choice of a flying ship and the distortion in the crew's and Lucian's (as leader) choices and fears and their encounter with alien vehicles fulfil these problematic observations neatly for me.

## Flying saucers

Jung extends these ideas to the collective psyche, discussing the phenomenon of the prevalent sighting of flying saucers especially in the 1950s USA to cultural anxieties of a similar order (a good defence and 'reason' for fiction altogether too).

In Jung's essay 'Flying Saucers' of 1958,[8] he talks about ubiquitous 'rumours' of disc-shaped objects in our skies at the time, beaming down control and/or sucking up human energies. He points out that scientists are implicated – they see a blip in their readings that 'confirms' observers' reports of UFOs. He'd been approached by American commentators including the CIA wondering what he made of this widely noted observation in US life. (See the article about recently declassified CIA documents at https://wpas.worldpeacefull.com, claiming evidence for what Jung experienced hearing from the US government, and there is much discussion of Jung's involvement in President Truman's inquiries in the 1950s in *The Man from Mars: Ray Palmer's Amazing Pulp Journey* by Fred Nadis [Tarcher Perigee, 2013].)

Discussion of what Jung refers to as 'visionary' occurrence brings up themes of causality for him as with Tausk: not as nearest-to-hand explanation but as possibly 'synchronistic' occurrence. Simply put: synchronic events form meaningful alignments, bringing historical 'fact' together in timely and significant ways. In his preface to the essay, he points out that the alacrity with which the press took up the story that he, a prominent psychologist, was a 'saucer-believer' meant to him that 'skepticism [on this topic] seems to be undesirable':

> To believe that UFOs are real suits the general opinion, whereas disbelief is discouraged. This creates the impression that there is a tendency all over the world to believe in saucers and to want them to be real,

unconsciously helped along by a press that otherwise has no sympathy with the phenomenon. This fact in itself merits the psychologist's interest. Why should it be more desirable for saucers to exist than not?.[9]

Again such a defensive tool was operative and 'normal.

Projections in Jung's analysis operate in a different but related way:

> It boils down to nothing less than this: that either psychic projections throw back a radar echo, or else the appearance of real objects affords an opportunity for mythological projections [...] even if UFOs are physically real, the corresponding psychic projections are not actually caused, but are only occasioned, by them. [...] These statements depend in the first place on the peculiar nature of the psychic background, the collective unconscious, and for this reason have always been projected in some form.
>
> (p. 122)

He explains that in our time the Christ figure – a god/man mediator – no longer does the trick, so alien mediation instead is thrown up to fill the gap by this collective psychic necessity. The psychic energies require a form to absorb them since Christianity does not fulfil the role any longer.

Both Tausk and Jung come close to proposing that these 'hallucinations' are normative. They underpin psychologically the production of Suvin's 'cognitive estrangement' of what we can safely, I believe, also call Lucian's 'True History' – satire: that is, science fiction.

And while Tausk as a committed Freudian attributes this configuration of the individual psyche due to a repressed death wish and guilt, Jung attributes these to projections of the collective unconscious, agreed on even by scientists, after the trauma of war – and eventually determining that individual reports are tantamount to being 'visions' just as Tausk does.

Other ancient evidence in our traditional literature even from the Old Testament (if we would like to stay with Western tradition) in the book of Ezekiel. Famously at the opening of the book, the Prophet sees something like a glinting metallic shimmer in his vision of the prophets and they pivot as if on wheels that move without any mechanical underpinnings. This occurrence in the Old Testament expands on Jung's theme of 'collective psychic symbol – a machine in the sky.

## Forms of 'acting out' and Lucian's truth

What I am proposing here, about surreal fiction, is that it is a form of 'acting out', and there is plenty of evidence for me that Lucian particularly and many sci-fi writers in general, imagining a world different to what it is and playing it out, are assuming the defensive posture of such 'acting out'. And in Lucian's case, asserting that the 'as if' they report is real – in fact, insisting that it is more truly real that some historical accounts of other geographies, and events – chiming with contemporary tradition of the wonder tales at the time of the second empire in Rome. This is the defensive posture undertaken in the projection onto the world of particular anxieties, including personal fears.

Of course, Lucian's is a well-formulated kind of 'acting out' in this recounting of a voyage off the earth: he keeps contact throughout with his audience who are the 'ground' – constantly describing events and creatures and places in detail to persuade his audience of their reality (what ni Mheallaigh calls 'pseudo documentation' used conventionally in science fiction), but I'd suggest that his choices of themes and sequence suggest a 'projection' from the psyche that both Jung and Tausk would call 'visionary' – and, like Jung, I prefer this designation to 'hallucination' with its pathogenic flavour. Lucian is all the time telling us that this is the truth – the form of metaphysical truth that is fiction.

To absorb or legitimise the fictional underpinnings of truth, Jung claimed in the epilogue to the *Flying Saucer* essay that he engaged with 'real' scientists – like J.B. Rhine (1895–1980) whose controversial parapsychological scientific work he had time for (so did Duke University who housed him at the time, and see letter by William Sloane recounting the meeting between Jung and J.B. Rhine)[10] and citing a 'prominent expert', a disreputable scientist named Donald Keyhoe (1897–1988) who was also, incidentally, given to writing for Ray Palmer's 'Astounding Tales', the popular previously mentioned rag of science fiction tales. Jung does not mention Keyhoe's sideline when he cites Keyhoe as a credible source, but he undoubtedly knew it. At this point, before his discrediting, however, Keyhoe was widely regarded as leader in the field of ufology.

In his essay, Jung uses the example of a vision taken straight from the pages of 'Astounding Tales' (and in fact it was a ghosted and doctored-up report from a man who claimed he had been taken up into a spaceship, but whose story was much embellished by the famous hack journalist/publisher as mentioned above, Ray Palmer, just after WW2).[11] The story was sensationalised to garner more magazine sales. Certainly Jung must have known the vision's provenance, although there is no evidence he did except in his faux wide-eyed tone.

Further in line with the theme of *katabasis*, I'd suggest that the entire structural edifice of the 'True History' is a depth, an abyss. No matter in the sky or on the sea, the depths are where all the events of Lucian's history take place – a grand metaphor for the underground that is the psyche, projected into contrived events that yet are true – after all where else would we find such fiendish temptresses as the vine women? It's about leaving and burrowing under the empirical ground/reality. In fact, related to this repression and state of covert space, there are themes about women in the 'True History' that would have Freudians particularly alerted.

The first instance is the 'vine women'. Several of Lucian's crew in the ship are physically entangled in perpetuity as they are drawn into sexual encounter with the alien female bodies, drinking wine from their branches. This enforced entanglement is the dark side of sexual engagement with women – and Lucian is dredging up such familiar and ubiquitous male fears of women in his fiction.

Later when the crew and Lucian get to the moon, they discover there are no women: the reproductive means and relationships on the Moon require no female presence – babies spring from men's calves, and erotic relations are conducted among men – older and younger men who raise the children. Larmour in *Rethinking Sexuality: Foucault and Classical Antiquity* (Princeton UP, 1997) and ni Mhaileagh (2014) point to this being targeted and satiric commentary on Greek patrician life which excluded women in all ways, except for biological necessity. Here, Lucian obviates even that necessity as a sarcastic comment on systemic misogyny. Freud might call this wish fulfilment. Lucian reflects on a collective and deep cultural desire.

After encountering the lethal devouring vine women, Lucian and his crew encounter the beautiful and fatally alluring ass-women with their hidden donkey's legs. They invite the crew into their homes with sexual congress apparently in mind. But Lucian is distracted by all the bones lying around their homes, and catching sight of non-human ass legs under their skirts, he shouts for his crew to leave them! The women immediately dissolve when they are found out – but Lucian stabs the puddle with his sword, drawing blood – and they flee. Different forms of misogyny and fear of females!

Similarly or not – it is a psychic truth that males fear women, sexually and fear being swallowed up, and Lucian knows full well that he can play on that effectively. It is a truth. As in all fictional tales, the agreement with the audience is that they suspend one kind of epistemological reception for another.

## Imagination and truth

The human imagination and psyche concoct such 'visions' – and the impulse of the acting out of these constructions traverses time – and, indeed, this impulse is ubiquitous. These 'delusional', 'estranged' visions also connect repeatedly to the notion of lying not only for Tausk and Jung but in commentators on the divide between hallucination or vision and lying: which is purportedly a conscious decision to mislead, and to a tone and mode that accommodates but at the same time undermines the prose of empirical and so-called fact-based assertion.

Science fiction writer Ursula Le Guin, like Lucian, proclaims the dilemma at the opening of her important novel *The Left Hand of Darkness* in sentiment very close to Lucian's opening statement in *True History*:

> Science fiction is not predictive [of reality] [...[ A novelist's business is lying. [....] All they can tell you is what they have seen and heard, in their time in this world, a third of it spent in sleep and dreaming,

another third of it spent telling lies. [...] They may use all kinds of facts to support their tissue of lies. [...] [the] weight of verifiable place-event-phenomenon-behaviour makes the reader forget that he [sic] is reading a pure invention [...] in fact while we read a novel we are insane [...] we have to know perfectly well that the whole thing is nonsense and, then, while reading, believe every word of it [...].[12]

Lucian and Le Guin establish a contract with their audiences. To engage his audience more closely, when Lucian read these out to his audience, gestures and tone were means of adherence! Le Guin's narrative drive on the page provides that adherence (we want to find out what happens next), what is the contract? It is the demand that we all know we are in a different register, so let's agree to suspend an empirical notion of 'reality' – a prejudice, anyway – 'reality' is a kind of religion as Jung's dining companion Einstein put to him. This epistemic shadiness is itself 'acting out': a way of problematising, cocking a snook at historians, in Lucian's case, and psychologists who were inclined to be positivists in Jung's case.

## Lucian and psychology

To reiterate: approaching a second empire Roman writer/orator's work directly in a psychological way is probably anachronistic. The sense of an interior and of psyche itself was clearly in a different register for him than it is for us. Despite that worry, I am encouraged to risk it after reading Karen ni Mheallaigh's persuasive *Reading Fiction with Lucian*, which suggests that we can *claim* that Lucian explored at least fiction in a psychological way – Lucian engages in speculating why people liked to read what they know is not true, and theorised about it in his works.

We see this in his other satires – when Lady Clothos and Charon bargain with Hermes about the disposition of a tyrant who refuses to accept death – the psychological punishment of disallowing him to drink from the river Lethe so that he may NOT forget his sins committed in his past life is seen as far greater than what a cobbler who lead a hard life may 'suffer' for his sins. The laugh is on the tyrant. (See 'Dialogue of Courtesans' in Delhi editions).

Lucian's psychological insights could easily sit in dialogue with Freud's ideas or else they might sound like parodic appendices in dialogue with Victor Trausk's centuries later.

There are similar impulses at play in Jung's work on synchronicity and in his exploration of the psychological ramifications of flying saucers to Lucian's impulses. Jung's suggestions about synchronicity are more than simply coincidence; it's meaningful emergence of the converging events or impulses exploding into a new truth. How can 'truth' in its basic definition be contingent ... isn't for all time and places? In this way truth is problematic for Jung as well who was inclined to eschew positivist science (although he dutifully tried to engage with it).

Other typical elements of science fiction appear in Lucian's work. As mentioned above, hyper-detailed descriptions and/or 'pseudo documentation' seeming to authorise a reality play a role. When Lucian and his crew find and engage with 'aliens', they are minutely described. But, also, at times he says, 'I won't describe them because you won't believe me'. Among the many aliens: the vine women, and the ass-legged women who they manage to escape with help of the locals, their allies and enemies in the battle with the Sun's warriors. Indeed, in those adventures inside the whale, encounters with seemingly rational but physically monstrous aliens and the appearance of fully vivacious dead people – the fictional character Ulysees, and Homer – fully described who could easily inhabit John Wyndham's worlds of densely conceived beings, or Olivia Butler's (with her biologically altered women) or Brian Aldiss's plant-eating-humans world, science fiction writers of the 20th century. He certainly joins in their endeavours to upend ways of knowing: how we ascertain that what we see is true or not – and indeed how we can recognise alien 'others' for example. These issues are interrogated by Lucian.

Mythological figures are vivacious and psychologically valid human beings: such as Endymion, now awake from his mythic slumbers and the leader on the Moon, guiding the earthly crew after they help him in his battle with the Sun. And then, finally, at Endymion's suggestion, they inspect a giant mirror/disc which the inhabitants of the Moon use to witness events on the Earth (which similarly functioning disc we find again in Jung's essay). The disc sits in a well, and you can hear what's said on Earth as you watch, and the 'mirror' shows you what's happening – but mirrors also reflect you back to yourself and Lucian engages in a self-reflexive scrutiny. This is perplexing for him and for us, reminding of the contemporary encounter with the self we've been examining: perhaps the phenomenon of counter-transference is applicable here. In the encounter between patient and doctor in the analytic situation, the analyst imputes her own reactions and dreams to the analysand, influencing communication. You are not sure who you are witnessing – the listener is confused with its object.

The reciprocity epitomised here involves a self-reflexion – or is it mutual self-delusion? – inherent in our regard of the depths of Hades or of interiority – or, again, as political scientist and science fiction writer China Mieville calls it, a 'defamiliarisation' perpetrated by the writer in collusion with an audience and reflecting back on them.[13]

Looking at the moon, and 'going' there is to go into yourself – mirroring back at you ... a self-defensive mechanism in lieu of facing the abyss directly? Is that it? Is it a hidden and shameful desire to elude the abyss.

This idea of reciprocal projection is a recurring theme in Jung's work, and it is explored in the 'Flying Saucers' essay, too – lying is a way of knowing, and a way of reporting knowledge – Gorgias' dialogue on knowing nothing (his reference is to Parmenides): just as it is difficult to recount 'nothing' it is hard to report anything about that 'nothing' and if you could there is no way to say it.

Paradox and metafictional manoeuvres were deployed by Lucian, as they are by science fiction writers to engage in a contractual relationship between writer and reader (orator and listener) who agree among them that the lies they are about to hear are licensed and provisional reality for the duration. Implied is that how we know alters what we know, and I propose this is a modernist position which, Jung, as a certain kind of psychologist particularly, can accommodate. It is a form of 'acting out' with its shadow side of escapism and shame. Paul Bishop explores this theme in his book *On the Blissful Islands with Nietzsche and Jung: In the Shadow of the Superman* (Routledge, 2016) – without mentioning shame – but the shadow aspect of an art performance or product is explored. Wasn't Jung acting out in his essay in *Mysterium coniunctionis* (Collected Works of C.G. Jung, vol. 14; Princeton UP, 1977) when he engaged in scholarly commentary on a faux inscription on a gravestone in Bologna, knowing it was a hoax? He called the essay 'The Enigma of Bologna'. In it he responded to medieval interpretations by serious scholars like Nicholas de Cusa, who were not aware it was a fake – as if he were commenting on a real object. As Whitmarsh comments in an essay on the pragmatics of reception, it is 'the *provisional* nature of fact' that is under scrutiny – [14] and that makes up both the entertainment value and the deeper engagement with the fiction for the reader.

Lucian famously opens his *True History* with the caveat that he is the only one of the many historians telling the truth: and the truth is that these are all lies. As Whitmarsh continues, '[this] 'provisionality' is a complex phenomenon: for not only do we not 'know' the past, we also do not 'know' what we are doing with it in the present' (p. 107). Exploration of other worlds and the facts of those worlds is an exploration of *contingency*, and present fact.

Jung was also exploring the credibility of sentiments expressed in the riddle of the faux gravestone inscription which he wrote about in *Mysterium coniunctionis*, where he includes a chapter where he talks of 'the enigma of Bologna'. In a cemetery there is a gravestone referring to the death of a young woman. According to the inscription she was much loved. The language focuses on the young woman buried beneath it and frames their speculations as if by close friends or family, pondering the irony of early death. In his own commentary on the inscription, miraculously, in fact, Jung finds specifically Jungian significance: discovering and therefore confirming his own theoretical precepts in his discussion of this gravestone which he knowingly takes *as if* real – with our compliance – and his psychological precepts are rediscovered even in those ancient times. For him, this is a *projection* of archetypal meaning. Rumour run amock in plausible ways.

An anachronistic frisson of transgression is explored – and this again is about the viability of psyche's reaction to unpalatable or alien 'truths' – admittedly the frisson is different for second empire people, hearing Lucian humanise mythic figures or giving body and language to Homer, or Odysseus outside his usual dialogue and intentions (it is a meta-meta narrative moment when Odysseus asks for help to communicating with Calypso – outside the story where he only has presence!) and hilarious. Here, too, we see the figure of the usually sleeping mythic persona, Endymion, loved for his beauty by the moon – here speaking and organising battles, etc., seemingly out of character for him – but relegating the figure at the same time to a psychological human level: mythic figures have a stated, rigid purpose in the panoply, and don't deviate – that's not the point. Our accommodation of a speaking and acting mythic figure lacks some of that pleasurable frisson Lucian afforded his listeners, but we get some of it ... and it is reliant on psychological *nous*.

I'll finish with another quote from Le Guin, this time from her *Earthsea Trilogy*:

> I'll make my report as if I told a story, for I was taught as a child on my home world that Truth is a matter of imagination. The soundest fact may fail or prevail in the style of its telling. [...] Facts are no more solid, coherent, round and real...and if at moments the facts seem to alter with an altered voice why then you can choose the fact you like best; yet none of them is false, and it is all one story.[15]

This for me is the greatest argument for the designation of fiction as an 'acting out' in a specific register, and I suggest Lucian fully and even knowingly engaged with it.

## Notes

1   There are many versions/translations. I used the Delphi Classics volume, *Delphi Complete Works of Lucian* (2016), with translations by H.G. and F.G. Fowler (from OUP text); and A.M. Harmon (in the Loeb Classical Library), particularly 'True History' (or 'A True Story') and 'Dialogues of the Gods' and 'Dialogues of the Courtesans'.

2   See A. Roberts, *The History of Science Fiction*, London: Palgrave, 2016; and R. Luckhurst, *Science Fiction*, Cambridge: Polity, 2005.

3   See D. Suvin, *Metamorphoses of Science Fiction: on the poetics of a Literary Genre*, Oxford: Lang, 2016.

4   Freud's essay 'The Uncanny' was first published in *Imago*, 1919, vol. 5, translated by A. Strachey.

5   I draw this from discussions by Tim Whitmarsh, *Beyond the Second Sophistic*, Berkeley, CA: University of California Press, 2013; and various articles by James I. Porter, particularly 'Foucault's Ascetic Ancients', *Phoenix*, Spring-Summer 2005, vol. 59, no. 2, 121–132; and 'Making and Unmaking: Limits of fictionality in Homeric criticism', *Transactions of the American Philological Association*, Spring 2011, vol. 141. no. 1, 1–36; as well as Karen ni Mheallaigh's *Reading Fiction with Lucian: Fakes, Freaks and Hyperreality*, Cambridge: Cambridge University Press, 2014.

6   Whitmarsh, *Beyond the Second Sophistic*, chapter 11.

7   V. Tausk, 'On the Origin of the "Influencing Machine" in Schizophrenia', first published in 1919 in *Internationale Zeitschrift fur Psychoanalyse* and translated by D. Feigenbaum in *The Psychoanalytic Quarterly*, 1933, vol. 2, 519–556; reprinted in *Journal of Psychotherapy Practice and Research*, Spring 1992, vol. 1, no. 2, 185–206.

8  C.G. Jung, *Flying Saucers: A Modern Myth of Things Seen in the Sky*, tr. R.F.C. Hull, London: Ark 1977 [Routledge, 1959].

9  Jung, *Flying Saucers*, p. 9.

10  See 'Jung and Rhine', *The Free Library* [2006 Parapsychology Press, 26 March 2021] Available online HTTP: https://www.thefreelibrary.com/ Jung+and+Rhine.-a0168586754. This letter appeared originally in *Quadrant: The Journal of the C G Jung Foundation for Analytical Psychology*, Winter 1975, vol. 8, no. 2, 73–75.

11  See Nadis, *The Man from Mars*, chapter 5

12  U. Le Guin, *The Left Hand of Darkness*, London: Gollancz, 2017.

13  See Chia Mieville in a blog on the Verso publishers' site, promoting his book *October* (May, 2018).

14  T. Whitmarsh, 'True Histories: Lucian, Bakhtin, and the Pragmatics of Reception', *Classics and the Uses of Reception*, ed. by C. Martindale and R.F. Thomas, Oxford: Blackwell, 2006, pp. 100–132.

15  U. Le Guin, *Earthsea Trilogy*, Harmondsworth: Puffin, 1987, p. 6.

# Part II

# Katábasis, Goddesses, and Saints

Chapter 6

# Inanna's Descent to the Netherworld and Analytical Psychology

## What Has the Mistress of All the Lands Done?[1]

*Catriona Miller*

In *The Dream and the Underworld*, the analytical psychologist James Hillman made a startling claim. 'A fundamental tenet of archetypal psychology', he said, is 'the interchangeability of mythology and psychology. Mythology is a psychology of antiquity. Psychology is a mythology of modernity'.[2] This seems to work both ways, with those studying mythology sometimes looking to psychology to better understand their source material. Mythological stories continue to exert fascination because we intuit, as Hillman went on to say, that they 'are not simply part of the past [...] Myth lives vividly in our symptoms and fantasies and in our conceptual systems'.[3] Jung himself saw myth even more specifically as an elucidation of the psyche, saying, 'myths are original revelations of the preconscious psyche, involuntary statements about unconscious psychic happenings'.[4] Thus from a classical Jungian perspective, myth both comes *from* the psyche and is fundamentally *about* the psyche. As I have discussed elsewhere,[5] in considering Sumerian myth from a specifically Jungian perspective, my focus here is less on the myth's historical or cultural context and more upon the potential psychological insights that these stories might offer us today as an expression of an inner psychic world.

Mythological stories are the creation of human beings for whom they express an essential truth of some kind. Sometimes this 'truth' has been explained as a kind of proto-science accounting for elements of the natural world (such as the rising and setting of the sun), and sometimes as a (mis) remembering of actual historical events (such as the story of Troy perhaps). Over and above such explanations, however, the 'truth' being expressed is also likely to contain some kind of 'psychological savour' that resonated sufficiently with others to ensure the stories were taken up, reimagined, and retold over and over again. Myths are stories worked upon time and again until they are eventually codified sufficiently to be written down. Thus, I would argue that myths cannot be taken as 'pure' statements about unconscious psychic happenings, as individual dreams might, because the form that survives is one that has always been worked on collectively. In this scenario, an inner psychological reality that meets with external social reality then bounces back towards the psyche once more and so on.

DOI: 10.4324/9781003054139-9

In this chapter, I make the assumption that the 'essential truth' and 'psychological savour' being set out in the Sumerian myth *The Descent of Inanna to the Netherworld* is a codified description of the psychological ecosystem itself. In doing so I make a connection, as Jung, Campbell, Hillman, and others have done before, between stories of journeys to the underworld and stories about journeys into the psyche. I do not seek to explore what the myth may have meant to the Sumerians themselves, though I have tried to make use of Sumeriologists' best contemporary understanding of the text and its context.

## The Descent of Inanna to the Netherworld

Sumerian culture is perhaps the oldest human civilisation, or, at least, it is the first literate society that we know about.[6] Its literature means we may encounter Sumerian culture and thought in their own words and not just through archaeological remains. Archaeological finds in the region date back to at least 5,000 BCE though the height of Sumerian civilisation dates to between 3,500 and 2,350 BCE, where Sumerian was spoken, the cuneiform writing system developed along with urban civilisation in cities such as Eridu and Uruk. A complicating factor is that Sumerian remained the written language of the educated long after the civilisation itself had faded, and scribal schools which lasted into the Babylonian period (1,750 BCE till about the sixth century BCE) continued to use and circulate Sumerian texts. This long period of Sumerian use by subsequent cultures along with a relative lack of historical contextualisation does make the meaning and significance of some texts difficult to fully fathom.

*The Descent of Inanna to the Netherworld* is a long text in two parts, and as is the case with all Sumerian literature, its rediscovery and translation was the result of many years of painstaking work from both archaeologists and Sumerian scholars. The task of drawing together the fragments of the clay tablets began in 1914 with the publication of the first elements but it was another two years before it was recognised that they belonged to the same text. Work continued, though it was not until 1937 that about two-thirds of the text was assembled by Samuel Noah Kramer, with the final third finally emerging in the early 1960s[7] but other missing lines continued to be found into the 1970s. Katz, writing in 2003, noted that there are about thirty copies of the piece, which is why there is now a near-complete text.[8]

For this chapter, I have made use of several translations of the text beginning with Sladek's unpublished doctoral thesis from 1974. Kramer, working with folklorist Wolkstein, produced a less technical edition in 1983, with Jacobsen's version following in 1987. In this chapter, I also make use of de Shong Meador's 1992 rendering of the text, along with the Electronic Text Corpus of Sumerian Literature (ETCSL), a project by the University of Oxford running between 1997 and 2006, which aimed to provide a comprehensive collection of transliterations and translations of all available Sumerian literature.

For those not familiar with the story, I will begin with a fairly straightforward recounting of the main points before circling around it once more, in what Jungian therapist Berry called a 'restatement'. 'If we are stumped by a dream [or an image]', she says, 'there might be nothing better to do than replay it, listening until it breaks through in a new key'.[9]

At the start of the narrative, the Goddess Inanna decides to visit the underworld. Precisely why she decides to do this is not clear and demonstrates some of the difficulties of translation. Sladek (1974) offers a seemingly straightforward rendering of the opening line: 'From the "great heaven" she has set her mind on the "great below"'.[10] However, the literal meaning of the opening line appears to be 'had her ear stand',[11] and Wolkstein and Kramer choose to keep more of the original sense by rendering it 'opened her ear to the Great Below',[12] while de Shong Meador uses the phrase 'turned her ear'.[13] It is certain that she turns her attention to the Great Below, but the motivation is less obvious. Sladek is happy to assume that this is with an acquisitive eye 'because she is not satisfied with what she has in heaven and wants to extend her control to the netherworld'.[14] Although it is true that many of the stories about Inanna relate to her desire to acquire more power in the form of the *mē*,[15] it is also true that Inanna perhaps already has *mē* that relate to the underworld, those of 'descent into the underworld' and 'ascent from the underworld',[16] which Inanna gains in the narrative *Inanna and Enki*. That being the case, perhaps the goddess is just ready to try out these skills.

Whatever the reason for her decision, Inanna then dresses in her best finery, including makeup and jewellery and 'come hither' perfume. These are not the warlike accoutrements of her battle with the mountain Ebih,[17] but instead the more seductive outfit she puts on to ask An for help in the same poem. She then picks up her symbols of power and sets out, taking leave of a series of temple sites along the way. Inanna does seem to have some idea that her visit to the underworld is going to be problematic because as she travels, she gives detailed instructions to her right-hand woman Ninshubur on what to do while she is away. Ninshubur is to mourn Inanna (loudly and publicly), then she is to go to three senior gods in turn: Enlil, Nanna, and then Enki and ask for help.

Inanna, arriving at the gates to the underworld palace, then knocks loudly, perhaps even rudely, and demands to be let in. In the later Akkadian *Descent of Ishtar*, she is more aggressive, threatening to smash the gate and shatter the bolt,[18] and to raise up the dead to eat the living if they do not let her in, but in the Sumerian version she has come in her seductive guise, rather than her warrior one. The gatekeeper confers with Ereshkigal the Queen of the Underworld (Inanna's sister) about what to do. Ereshkigal agrees to let her in but stipulates that at each of the seven gateways, Inanna must remove one of her garments. Inanna reluctantly agrees to do so in order gain entry, and by the time she arrives in front of Ereshkigal she is naked and without her symbols of power.

In a frustratingly brief but explosive moment in the narrative, the sisters come face to face, whereupon Inanna, in some way, attempts to replace

Ereshkigal on the throne. The gathered underworld gods are utterly appalled and Inanna is killed and her corpse is hung on a hook.

After three days, Ninshubur carries out her instructions and Enki (as predicted) is the one who agrees to help. He sends two little creatures made from the dirt under his fingernails into the underworld, where they find Ereshkigal in a sorry state, perhaps giving or having given birth (Sladek, de Shong Meador, and ETCSL follow this reading), or perhaps she is crying out like a woman *about* to give birth (Wolkstein and Kramer's preferred reading), but certainly no one is looking after her. She has no cover or shawl upon her and her hair stands out like leeks. As directed, the two little creatures empathise with the goddess and, when offered a reward, ask for the corpse of Inanna. They sprinkle the corpse with the water of life and the food of life, and Inanna is revived.

The second part of the narrative concerns a deal that is suddenly thrust upon Inanna just at the moment she is leaving. The Anunna (the assembled gods of the underworld) abruptly decide that someone else has to take Inanna's place, and the next part of the story follows Inanna as she decides who that will be. She returns home, accompanied by minor underworld deities, eventually to discover that her husband Dumuzi has not been mourning her as he should and instead is sitting on her throne. Inanna makes her decision that he is the one to take her place. His sister tries to help him, and eventually Inanna decrees that he will spend half the year in the underworld, and his sister the other half.

There is evidence to suggest that 'while its first part was originally an Inanna myth that ended with her release from the Netherworld through Enki's trick, the intervention of the Anunna gods in Inanna's release was added later for the purpose of integrating the Inanna myth with a Dumuzi myth'.[19] For the sake of brevity, my focus here will remain on the first part of the narrative. I will explore what we know about the location of Inanna's descent, and then introduce the main characters of the story in a little more detail, before finally reconsidering the story from a more psychological point of view.

## Inanna's Destination: The Great Below

Alongside regular developments in the finer points of translation, concerted scholarly effort also continues to be devoted to understanding how the Sumerians conceptualised the world in which they lived, including its cosmic geography, as one scholar terms it.[20] The exact nature of the Sumerian 'land of the dead', or 'land of no return', is still under active discussion by academics and linguists.

The land of the dead has many names: *ki-gal*, that is, literally 'great earth', or 'the great place', or 'great below' (since *ki* meaning 'earth' is usually contrasted with *an* meaning 'sky'); *edin*, that is, the steppe; *kur nu gi*, that is, 'land of no return' or 'earth of no return'.[21] However, a large part of the difficulty lies in the semantic field of the word which is most often used for the land of the dead – or *kur*, where the original meaning of the word is thought to be 'mountain' or 'mountainous region'.[22] Since the mountains of the Iranian highlands are in stark geographical contrast to the plain of Sumer and were home to peoples hostile to the 'black headed ones', as the Sumerians called themselves, the chain of association includes the idea of foreignness, even hostility. Hence, the extension of *kur* to mean the most hostile of place of all, 'death' itself. Katz (2003) also discusses a linguistic binary that sees the meanings of *kur* ('mountain'; 'foreign land', 'hostile land') pitted against the concept of *kalam*, which means the 'heart of the land' of Sumer, which lends further weight to this point of view. After an expansion of Sumer in the middle of the third millennium, this concrete distinction became more conceptual, with *kur* increasingly coming to designate the land of the dead.[23] In other places the land of the dead is referred to as the 'Great City hidden from the sight of the living'[24] and in a hymn to the underworld goddess Nungal, her temple is described as 'House, with a great name, nether world, mountain where Utu [sun god] rises; no one can learn its interior!'[25] At least, this is how one line of argument goes.

Artemov (2012) is less sure of this chain of association, particularly as dating the origins of texts is difficult, but he also points out that it still tells us little about the cosmic geography of the land of the dead itself and whether the distinct regions of heaven, earth, the land of the dead, and another Sumerian cosmological region of the *abzu*, is accurate. Nor does it say much about their relative positions – up, down, beside, within, and so on. Should the 'land of no return' even be considered an *under*world *per se*? Some translations favour 'netherworld' though, of course, this comes from an Indo-European root also meaning 'down'. Was it originally a specific mountain, or more generally 'in the mountains' (whether in the east or the west, that is, the place of the rising sun, or the place of the setting sun), or possibly underground but with an entrance in the mountains, or reached by river? All these options occur at various points in the literature, and while Katz assumes a chronological development, with the later texts (insofar as it is possible to tell) moving more decisively towards the land of the dead being 'below', Artemov argues that the idea of the land of the dead existing in the mountains is in fact concurrent with the idea of it being 'below'.

The nature of land of the dead itself is, perhaps surprisingly, not described directly in *The Descent of Inanna*, although the later Akkadian version is more evocative, describing the place that Ishtar is travelling to as:

> [...] the house where those who enter are deprived of light
> Where dust is their food, clay their bread.
> They see no light, they dwell in darkness.[26]

In fact, Sladek sums it up rather well when he says 'it is the realm of death and the antithesis of life and all of its pleasures',[27] though this seems to rely upon the later Akkadian concept more than the Sumerian one.

However, trying to reconcile written evidence with archaeological evidence about the land of the dead raises further questions. As discussed, the written evidence suggests the netherworld was conceptualised as a dry, dusty place of perpetual thirst,[28] and yet the archaeological evidence of grave goods suggests an expectation of a more comfortable place that might have use for musical instruments and even board games[29], but, in any case, Katz makes clear that the idea of the dead as either paradise or hell 'is non-existent in the Sumerian texts'[30] and that essentially the land of the dead is simply where the dead are.

This inability to clearly describe this deep region, the Great Below, where 'no one can learn its interior', makes some evocative associations when considered through the lens of analytical psychology. Although Jung accepted the idea of a personal unconscious, he also posited a further deep region of the psyche, which he termed the collective unconscious, which had its roots in biological systems, and was home to patterning forces Jung called archetypes. The archetype is, he said, 'a condensation of the living process',[31] whereas the archetype *an sich* is irrepresentable.[32] The collective unconscious cannot be directly apprehended by the conscious part of the psyche and so also cannot be described, though it remains an active participant in the overall psychic ecosystem. It too is neither good, nor bad, but simply is and has its role to play in psychic health.

It was to this unknown and perhaps unknowable region that the goddess Inanna turns her ear. Her name probably means 'Lady of Heaven', but she 'wears the robes of the old, old gods',[33] and her power seems to reach back into a pre-patriarchal period.

## Inanna's *Katabasis*: A Tale of Three Deities

For Jung, mythological stories of descent are stories about an encounter with the unconscious, both personal and collective. In one passage, Jung uses the word *nekyia*, alluding to one part of *The Odyssey* where the hero must undertake a journey to Hades, stating that this is 'no aimless and purely destructive fall into the abyss', as he said, 'but a meaningful *katabasis eis antron*, a descent into the cave of initiation and secret knowledge'.[34] He draws on the term *katabasis* for the sense of 'going down' or descent, though this term is interesting because according to one writer, etymologically it 'could refer to a place from which descents are made, such as a cave mouth, or to a military manoeuvre involving a descent'.[35] It was the term 'used by the Greeks more particularly to refer to a story about a living person who visits the land of the dead and returns more or less unscathed'.[36] However, for Jung, a successful descent (or encounter with the unconscious) is one which results not just in return but in renewal. For example, in *Symbols of Transformation* he makes clear that 'in the act of sacrifice the consciousness gives up its power and possessions in the interests of the unconscious', and 'this makes possible a union of opposites resulting in a release of energy'.[37] And in *The Spirit in Man, Art and Literature*, he more directly associated the term with a journey within that activates the transcendent function, saying:

> With my patients [...] the *katabasis* and *katalysis* [literally 'loosen down', but 'dissolution' seems a fair translation] are followed by a recognition of the bipolarity of human nature and the necessity of conflicting pairs of opposites. After the symbols of madness experienced during the period of disintegration there follow images which represent the coming together of the opposites: light/dark, above/below, white/black, male/female, etc.[38]

*The Descent of Inanna to the Netherworld* is one of the oldest myths following the pattern of both *katabasis* and *katalysis* but unlike subsequent iterations of similar narratives, the central character is not male but female, a fact not lost on Brinton Perera (1981) and de Shong Meador (1992), who have both read the myth from a Jungian perspective. They have found plenty of 'psychological savour' in engaging with the *Descent of Inanna*, with invigorating images of reorientation and renewal in this oldest of descent narratives. Brinton Perera explored the myth as route for modern women to reconnect with their 'dark sister', the deep primal feminine of Ereshkigal, ignored, suffering, and alone, buried by the everyday world of patriarchy. De Shong Meador also used the narrative to explore 'the drama of individuation as the innate self strives for full realisation against the demands of cultural adaptation'.[39] In her reading, 'the descent' is that which strips a person of adaptation to patriarchal culture, leaving a more fundamental feminine self. De Shong Meador saw this as a necessary task for women trying to uncover authentic selves from the accretions of patriarchal expectations.

However, although Inanna is certainly a central character in the tale, I do not choose to characterise her as the lone heroic protagonist, because there are in fact *three* major deities invoked in the first part of the *Descent:* Ereshkigal, Enki, and Inanna. Although they do not exactly come face to face, they are intimately connected with one another, forming the ecosystem of the story, and it is their *collective* actions and decisions that form the core drama.

Ereshkigal, whose name can be translated 'Queen of the Great Below' is a much less prominent member of the Sumerian pantheon than either Enki or Inanna. The earliest reference to Ereshkigal is a dedication inscription of the ruler of Umma in Old Akkadian Period where she is called 'the lady of the place of sunset',[40] but, as already discussed, very little is known about the geography or interior of the underworld itself, which like the collective unconscious cannot be known, but it is to her palace that Inanna seeks entry. In approaching the myth from a psychological perspective where a descent to the underworld is understood as a movement within the psyche, Ereshkigal must be seen as the personification of the indescribable collective unconscious.

By way of contrast, I have suggested elsewhere that Enki can be seen as a god of consciousness and directed thinking.[41] He is manifestly not a warrior god and only rarely resorts to violence; instead, he persuades and holds debates. His realm is the *abzu*, where he is often to be found at the start of tales, in a lowered state of awareness, sometimes sleeping, sometimes drunk. He is sleeping in the *abzu* when Nammu rouses him to deal with the complaints of the labouring gods. He gets drunk there with Ninmah, and on another occasion with Inanna, leading on the one hand to a lengthy drunken debate with Ninmah and on the other foolhardy gifts of *mē* to Inanna. The *abzu* can perhaps be associated with a personal unconscious, because it is a private interior space, which Enki and the other gods can enter and leave at will. It is a place where directed thinking is not always to the fore but where creativity germinates, and when travelling away from the *abzu*, Enki has a more focussed persona.

He is often called *Lord Nudimmud*, which may mean something like 'image fashioner'[42] or 'shaper-creator'.[43] In *Enki and Ninmah*, he is also called *geštú dagal* which has been rendered as 'wise one',[44] 'the one with the cunning grasp',[45] 'he of the vast intelligence',[46] 'the one of great wisdom',[47] but which others suggest is better rendered simply as 'understanding/knowledge personified'.[48] He is also the keeper of the *mē* and is often to be found spreading the *mē*, the knowledge and crafts of urban civilisation. So when Enki is roused from an unfocussed state of mind in the *abzu*, he becomes the god of technical skills, organised planning, abundance and knowledge, and the multitude of *abzu*-shrines in Early Dynastic Sumer points to a prominent role.[49] He also has a close association with Inanna and they are linked in no fewer than three major mythological narratives: *The Descent of Inanna*, *Enki and the World Order*, and *Inanna and Enki*.

Inanna herself is also one of the major gods of the Sumerian pantheon, which had somewhere around five thousand minor deities but about a dozen major ones.[50] However, as one writer points out, 'her relationship to the rest of the pantheon is far from clear'.[51] The pantheon did not have a fixed hierarchy, but rather one which tended to fluctuate over time depending on the relative political fortunes of the city-state associated with the temple devoted to each god. Inanna had important temples in Nippur, Lagash, Shuruppak, Zabalam, and Ur, but she was especially associated with Uruk.[52]

She is proud, sure of herself, and capable of great violence. In one narrative, for example, she single-handedly destroys the mountain Ebih that had refused to offer her proper respect. She was well known for her delight in violence, with battle being referred to as the 'dance of Inanna'. One hymn describes her so eager to get to battle that she has not even finished putting on her shoes:

> fighting is her play
> she never tires of it
> she goes out running
> strapping on her sandals.[53]

She is a 'great fierce storm' who makes 'a lion's body and lion's muscles rise up'.[54] She is the 'battle planner' and 'foe smasher'.[55]

However, Inanna is also addressed as a young woman who delights in eroticism, desire, and sex, not marriage or motherhood for whom other goddesses existed. There are many instances of Inanna's pleasure in sex, both for herself and for others. Her temple at Uruk is described as 'perfectly shaped fresh fruit, dazzling in [its] irresistible ripeness', and there are a great many hymns celebrating the sexual prowess of Inanna and her husband Dumuzi in the 'sacred marriage'.

At times her power is described as coming through An or Enlil (who is sometimes her father), the two gods most often at the head of the pantheon, or sometimes through Nanna (who is also sometimes) her father. Power, for the Sumerian deities, is usually expressed in terms of how many of the *mē* they possess and, as noted earlier, Inanna gathers rather a lot of them. In *Inanna and Enki*, while Inanna is visiting, Enki drinks a lot of beer and in a moment of drunken largesse, gives Inanna many of the *mē* in his keeping. In the morning he wants them back, but Inanna has already left and declines to hand them over. *Hymn to Inanna B* or the *Exultation of Inanna* calls her the 'Lady of all the divine powers', which de Shong Meador renders as the 'lady of blazing dominion',[56] but is perhaps more literally 'Queen of all the *mē*',[57] and sometimes her power is so great it seems to rival the other gods and she frightens them. One hymn describes how

> the magnificent lady who gathers up the divine powers of heaven and earth and rivals great An, is mightiest among the great gods – she makes their verdicts final. The Anunna gods crawl before her august word whose course she does not let An know; he dares not proceed against her command.[58]

In *Enki and the World Order*, Inanna protests that Enki (who has been travelling the cosmos, distributing *mē* to various deities) has not assigned *her* any special responsibilities. Enki reacts with surprise, taking some time to praise her and enumerate her powers and abilities before asking, 'What more could we add to you?'.[59] But Inanna is always open to enlarging her holdings, so to speak, and does not always seem to know when to stop. 'Inanna', says Enki later,

> you heap up human heads like piles of dust, you sow heads like seed. Inanna, you destroy what should not be destroyed; you create what should not be created. [...] You never grow weary with admirers looking at you. Maiden Inanna, you know nothing of tying the ropes on deep wells'.[60] However, Inanna is correct in her complaint to Enki – she does not have an obvious purpose or dominion. In contrast to the other major deities, Inanna has control of a lot of the *mē*, but it does not seem to add up to anything very focused. Jacobsen points out that perhaps her special

feature is that 'she is a goddess of infinite variety',[61] while Vanstiphout describes her 'unique complexity.[62]

Inanna is loud, sometimes hair-raisingly violent, also actively desiring, insistent on her due respect, and always open to receiving more power if the opportunity presents itself. Her powers encompass heaven, earth, and perhaps the even underworld. She is always being accused of wanting it all. In fact, whilst keeping a due eye on any unconscious bias towards misogyny, Inanna in the round, *is* perhaps just a bit too much! Another writer points out that the Mesopotamian pantheon is remarkably peaceable, at least with each other, and that suggests Inanna's 'gift' is controversy and strife.[63] Inanna is always moving things around, mixing things up but she also brings the gods and their cosmological realms *together* in interesting ways.

## Inanna as Transcendent Function

As suggested earlier, for Jung the psyche was a kind of ecosystem (though this is not an analogy he used himself), where the ego was only the most conscious part of a much larger system, and where the unconscious remained an important and active participant, and to stretch the ecosystem metaphor a little further, consciousness grows out of deep pre-conscious structures that ultimately have their roots in biology. Campbell's model of the hero's journey involves the heroic ego figure, descending to the unconscious underworld before returning renewed. However, given the importance of the *three* deities involved in the Descent of Inanna, I prefer a different reading of the goddess, because in this case, the potential to illuminate a path towards greater psychic balance arises through activation of what Jung called the transcendent function which brings together the conscious and the unconscious.

The transcendent function is a psychic activity that weaves together symbols that contain both conscious and unconscious material in order to foster a transition from one psychological attitude to another. As Jung put it in *The Structure and Dynamics of the Psyche*: 'The tendencies of the conscious and the unconscious are the two factors that together make up the transcendent function. It is called "transcendent" because it makes the transition from one attitude to another organically possible, without loss of the unconscious'.[64] So Jung called it 'transcendent', not in a religious sense but in the sense of transcending two opposites: in this case, conscious and unconscious, through symbolic images which contain both.

With this in mind, I suggest that Inanna is a not personification of the 'ego', but of the transcendent function itself. Inanna spans paradox and contradiction but not in the more negative way that a Trickster figure might exacerbate paradox and conflict. Tricksters, for Jung, were associated with the Shadow archetype and as such tended towards destruction rather than synthesis, whereas Inanna, according to Harris, 'embodied within herself polarities and contraries, and thereby she transcended them',[65] which is echoed by

Selz who pointed out that 'she encompassed contradictions and recognised opposites'.[66] Inanna's sigil was the reed post (or ring post), the gatepost that stood on either side of the doorway to the storehouse, an emblem that marked the point between outside and inside, but with a symbolism doubled when the material of its construction is also taken into account. Made of reeds, the ring post was thus 'made of the common building material that fills the marshlands, that liminal space separating the river waters and the dry land'.[67] We can see here that Inanna does not just represent paradox but also audaciously contains it, bridges it, perhaps even reconciles it.

With this in mind, *The Descent of Inanna* is a story about an approach to the unconscious, where Enki can be viewed as representing socially adapted consciousness, and Ereshkigal, the neglected unconscious, but where Inanna becomes a personification of the transcendent function who connects Enki and Ereshkigal. These two gods cannot directly interact with one another. There is a mutuality between the three gods in the story that has been overlooked and is also interesting that in order for the story to unfold, Inanna, Ereshkigal, and Enki are *all* doing things that are outwith their usual behaviour and spheres of influence.

Inanna, 'impetuous lady' as she is called in *Hymn to Inanna C*,[68] sets off to the underworld, arrayed like a Queen and rudely demands to be let in to Ereshkigal's domain. When asked directly to account for this behaviour, she says that she is there for the funeral of Ereshkigal's husband, although she says nothing of an invitation. She is making demands that should not be satisfied, by insisting on entrance to a place she is not supposed to be. As a furious Nanna says later: 'Who, having got to that place, could then expect to come up again?'.[69] Impetuous she may be, but Inanna is not completely heedless because she has also planned ahead in sending her right-hand woman to ensure that Enki will come looking for her. Just as Inanna 'turned her ear to the Great Below', she has also made sure that Enki's attention will be drawn to the situation.

Meanwhile, Ereshkigal is also doing something that she should not. Ereshkigal should just tell Inanna to go away, but curious about Inanna's approach, she cautiously agrees to let her in, although she takes the precaution of craftily arranging for Inanna to have all her finery and symbols of power removed step by step as she approaches. A rebuff does not seem to be contemplated and direct attack would be unlikely to work on the warrior maiden Inanna, but this 'one by one' approach seems to confuse her and she complies. The radiant Inanna is gradually dimmed as she passes gate by gate further into Ereshkigal's domain, till at last, she arrives in front of Ereshkigal naked and divested of her usual gifts of seduction and violence.

What happens next is unclear. It seems as if despite her powerless state, Inanna cannot help one final provocation: she tries to replace Ereshkigal on the throne. It is an awful, terrible moment. So terrible in fact, it is almost like the Great Below itself, as if it cannot be even spoken about let alone described. This moment, which should be the crux of the whole narrative, is very brief, but the complexity of the grammar makes the action difficult to parse. As Katz explains, 'because of the indeterminate syntactic structure, the obscure subject and object of the verbs, and the suffix/-ta/in line 166, these lines are still in dispute'.[70] So there is confusion over subject and object, and 'the two motion verbs are in opposite directions'.[71] Consequently, the translations of this pivotal moment offer different options, depending on whether the translator accepts Ereshkigal or Inanna as the subject of the sentences.[72] Does Ereshkigal rise voluntarily from her throne, which then opens up an opportunity for Inanna to take her place? This is the preferred option for Sladek, Wolkstein and Kramer, and de Shong Meador, while Jacobsen, the ETCL and Katz (via Falkenstein's German 1965 version) prefer a translation where Inanna *causes* Ereshkigal to stand up. All, except Wolkstein and Kramer think that Inanna then actually takes a seat on the throne.

From a Jungian perspective, however, the difficulty of conveying this key moment is in fact to be expected, because the land of the dead/collective unconscious cannot be described. The conscious cannot directly apprehend the unconscious. It is as if matter and antimatter collide causing each other's destruction; it is over in a flash; it is a calamity, a total disaster. The Anunna (the assembled underworld gods) are utterly furious. 'They looked at her – it was the look of death. They spoke to her – it was the speech of anger. They shouted at her – it was the shout of heavy guilt'.[73] Their anger causes Inanna to become a piece of spoiled meat (not just dead, but rotting) and hung on a hook. What a catastrophe!

In many ways, although Inanna chose to come to the gates of Ereshkigal's palace, Ereshkigal then tricked Inanna into entering a place where she should not be, with no powers to deploy in her defence.[74] However, *at the same time*, Inanna has tricked Ereshkigal, because Inanna has opened a path to the underworld goddess and her presence there forces Enki, the god of consciousness, to pay close attention to Ereshkigal. The senior gods, Enlil and Nanna, are furious and will not help Inanna, but Enki seems more exasperated than in a rage, asking: 'What has the mistress of all the lands done? She has me worried'.[75]

Enki cannot go himself, but after more exasperated remonstrations he sends little creatures made from dirt under his fingernails into the land of the dead. He already knows that Ereshkigal is sorely neglected. He tells them: 'Her nails are like a pickaxe [...] The hair on her head is bunched up as if it were leeks'.[76] As discussed earlier, she is in a bad way, perhaps mourning a husband and perhaps giving birth, but regardless no one is looking after her. The little creatures, as directed by Enki, empathise with her pains, and Ereshkigal is so grateful that she eventually gives them Inanna's corpse. They sprinkle her with water and food, and she comes back to life, and then prepares to leave the land of the dead.

The transcendent function, then, 'mediates opposites' and, 'expressing itself by way of the symbol, it facilitates a transition from one psychological attitude or condition to another'.[77] This function is the 'bridge between'.

Which 'involves a dialogue between consciousness and the unconscious through the instrumentalities of fantasy and symbol'.[78] Ereshkigal cannot (and should not) be overcome, but she should be respected. Instead, she is sorely neglected. Perhaps Enki is too busy doling out the *mē*, the accomplishments and activities of civilisation, to pay much attention to the Great Below, until Inanna forces his hand by going somewhere she should not. Inanna is the one who piques Ereshkigal's curiosity and manages to get herself invited in, even though Ereshkigal should not be making that invitation. Inanna is the one who calls Enki's attention to Ereshkigal and ensures that he empathises with her, to ensure her own release.

Jung regarded the unconscious as an active participant in the psychic eco-system, but felt that the demands of conscious, logical, directed thinking resulted in a neglect of the unconscious. A focus solely on the ego, the most conscious part of the psyche, could only lead to an unbalanced psychic system. A meaningful *katabasis* is therefore one where attention is drawn to the unconscious, resulting in a better psychic balance, and if so, following this reading of the *Descent of Inanna*, we might expect the narrative reward to be demonstrated in terms of a release of energy, a coming together of opposites and renewal of some kind. However, the blending together of the Dumuzi myth with the *Descent* does make the ending seem rather unsatisfactory in this regard. Just at the moment of her return, the Anunna tack on a fresh stipulation that someone else must take her place, and the narrative pivots towards Dumuzi. But what if we consider an ending where Inanna, revived by Enki's clever empathy with Ereshkigal, simply leaves?

The Queen of Heaven goes into the most indescribable place because she is an audacious goddess, but even Inanna cannot rule this land. In so many of her hymns and stories she is energetic, fierce, restless, always on the move, mixing things up, but in the *Descent of Inanna*, she is brought to a complete halt, hung as a corpse on a hook, in order to force Enki, god of consciousness and civilisation, to turn his attention to the neglected, tormented Ereshkigal in the realm of the unconscious. Inanna is the one who stands between, a personification of the transcendent function, able to contain paradox and contradiction, and so somehow she gets away with it. She is restored to life and eventually, paradoxically, allowed to leave the land of no return. Inanna, always the dashing *agent provocateur*, undertakes a dangerous task of forcing confrontation and dialogue between conscious and unconscious, becoming the transcendent function in action bridging (for a split second) conscious and unconscious in the symbol of the alive/dead/alive goddess. She actively seeks out both Ereshkigal and Enki to become the link between them.

'In the act of sacrifice', Jung says, 'the consciousness gives up its power and possessions in the interests of the unconscious', and 'this makes possible a union of opposites resulting in a release of energy'.[79] Inanna at last finds the limits of her power and is renewed; Enki is drawn from his tower in Eridu to become more grounded, and Ereshkigal is ministered to and consoled. The result is not a dramatically overturned psychic ecosystem, but rather one that is deepened and strengthened with bonds of mutual respect. In the end, Ereshkigal is soothed, because Inanna forced Enki to listen to her pain, and the final line of the narrative reasserts her importance. 'Holy Ereshkigal, Sweet is your praise'.

## Notes

1 Enki speaking in *Descent of Inanna*, see online HTTP http://etcsl.orinst.ox.ac. uk/section1/tr141.htm; accessed 02.02.2021.
2 J. Hillman, *The Dream and the Underworld*, New York: HarperCollins Publishers, 1979, p. 23.
3 Hillman, *The Dream and the Underworld*, p. 23.
4 C.G. Jung, 'The Psychology of the Child Archetype', in *The Archetypes and the Collective Unconscious* [*Collected Works of C.G. Jung*, vol. 9/i], London: Routledge & Kegan Paul, 1968, pp. 151-181 (= §259-§305) (p. 154 [= §261]).
5 See C. Miller, 'Becoming Queen: Inanna and Claire Underwood', in L. Gardner and C. Miller (eds), *Exploring Depth Psychology and the Female Self: Feminist Views from Somewhere,* Abingdon and New York: Routledge, 2021, pp. 79–93.
6 M. Chahin, *Before the Greeks*, Cambridge: Luterworth Press, 1996, p. 6.
7 See W.R. Sladek, *Inanna's Descent to the Netherworld*, Baltimore, MD: Johns Hopkins University Press, 1974.
8 See D. Katz, *The Image of the Netherworld in the Sumerian Sources*, Bethesda, MD: CDL Press, 2003, p. 251.
9 P. Berry, 'An Approach to the Dream', *Spring: A Journal of Archetype and Culture*, 1974, 58–79 (p. 73).
10 Sladek, *Inanna's Descent to the Netherworld*, p. 154.
11 T. Jacobsen, *The Harps that Once...: Sumerian Poetry in Translation*, New Haven: Yale University Press, 1987, p. 206.
12 D. Wolkstein, and S.N. Kramer, *Inanna: Queen of Heaven and Earth: Her Stories and Hymns from Sumer*, New York: Harper & Row, 1983, p. 52.
13 B. de Shong Meador, *Uncursing the Dark: Treasures from the Underworld*, Illinois: Chiron, 1994, p. 19.
14 Sladek, *Inanna's Descent to the Netherworld*, p. 17.
15 The *mē* are a specifically Sumerian concept that relate to skills, abilities, or knowledge relating to the various accoutrements of civilisation from baking bread to lovemaking.
16 From the opening of *Inanna and Enki*, in Wolkstein and Kramer, *Inanna: Queen of Heaven and Earth*, p. 15.
17 See *Inanna and Ebih*; available online HTTP https://etcsl.orinst.ox.ac.uk/cgi-bin/ etcsl.cgi?text=t.1.3.2&charenc=j#; accessed 02.02.2021
18 S. Dalley, *Myths from Mesopotamia Creation, The Flood, Gilgamesh, and Others*, Oxford: Oxford University Press, 1998, p. 155.
19 D. Katz, 'How Dumuzi Became Inanna's Victim: On the Formation of "Inanna's Descent"', *Acta Sumerologica*, 1996, vol. 18, 93–102 (p. 93).
20 W. Horowitz, *Mesopotamian Cosmic Geography*, Winona Lake, IN: Eisenbrauns, 1998.
21 See G. Leick, *A Dictionary of Ancient Near Eastern Mythology*, London: Routledge, 1991, p. 159.
22 See N. Artemov, 'The elusive beyond: Some notes on the netherworld geography in Sumerian tradition', in C. Mittermayer and S. Ecklin (eds), *Altorientalische Studien zu Ehren von Pascal Attinger*, Göttingen and Fribourg: Academic Press, 2021, pp. 1–30 (p. 3).

23  See Katz, *The Image of the Netherworld in the Sumerian Sources*, pp. 105–106.
24  Artemov, 'The elusive beyond', in Mittermayer and Ecklin (eds), *Altorientalische Studien zu Ehren von Pascal Attinger*, p. 16.
25  *Hymn to Nungal A*; available online HTTP: https://etcsl.orinst.ox.ac.uk/cgi-bin/etcsl.cgi?text=t.4.28.1&display=Crit&charenc=gcirc&lineid=t4281.p1#t4281; accessed 02.02.2021.
26  Dalley, *Myths from Mesopotamia Creation, The Flood, Gilgamesh, and Others*, p. 155.
27  See Sladek, *Inanna's Descent to the Netherworld*, p. 66.
28  J. Black and A. Green, *Gods, Demons and Symbols of Ancient Mesopotamia: An Illustrated Dictionary*, London: British Museum Press, 1992, p. 180.
29  See C.E. Barrett, 'Was Dust Their Food and Clay Their Bread? Grave Goods, The Mesopotamian Afterlife and the Liminal Role of Inana/Ishtar', *Journal of Ancient and Near Eastern Religion*, 2007, vol. 7(1), 7–65.
30  Katz, *The Image of the Netherworld in the Sumerian Sources*, p. xvi.
31  C.G. Jung, *Psychological Types* [*Collected Works*, vol. 6], London: Routledge and Kegan Paul, 1971, p. 445 (= §749).
32  C.G. Jung, *The Structure and Dynamics of the Psyche* [*Collected Works*, vol. 8], London: Routledge and Kegan Paul, 1960, p. 214 (= §417).
33  B. de Shong Meador, *Inanna, Lady of Largest Heart*, Austin: University of Texas Press, 2000, p. 92.
34  C.G. Jung, *The Spirit in Man, Art, And Literature* [*Collected* Works, vol. 15], London: Routledge and Kegan Paul, 1966, pp. 139–140 (= §213).
35  R. Falconer, *Hell in Contemporary Literature: Western Descent Narratives since 1945*, Edinburgh: Edinburgh University Press, 2005, p. 2.
36  Falconer, *Hell in Contemporary Literature*, p. 2.
37  C.G. Jung, *Symbols of Transformation* [*Collected Works*, vol. 5], London: Routledge and Kegan Paul, 1956, p. 432 (= §671).
38  Jung, *The Spirit in Man, Art, And Literature*, p. 140 (= §213).
39  De Shong Meador, *Uncursing the Dark*, p. xi.
40  Katz, *The Image of the Netherworld in the Sumerian Sources*, p. 171.
41  C. Miller, 'Enki at Eridu: God of Directed Thinking', in L. Gardner and P. Bishop (eds), *The Ecstatic and the Archaic: An Analytical Psychological Inquiry*, London and New York: Routledge, 2018, pp. 147–60.
42  P. Espak, *Ancient Near Eastern Gods Enki and Ea: Diachronical Analysis of Texts and Images from the Earliest Sources to the Neo-Sumerian Period*, unpublished MA thesis, Tartu 2006, pp. 111 and 26.
43  H.D. Galter, 'The Mesopotamian God Enki/Ea', *Religion Compass*, 2015, vol. 9/3, 66–76 (p. 69).
44  H. Sauren, 'Nammu and Enki' in M. Cohen, D. Snell, and D. Weisberg (eds), *The Tablet and the Scroll: Near Eastern Studies in Honor of William W. Hallo*, Bethesda, MD: CDL Press, 1993, pp. 198–208 (p. 200).
45  S. Kramer and J. Maier, *Myths of Enki, the Crafty God*, Oxford: Oxford University Press, 1989, p. 32.
46  T. Jacobsen, *The Harps that Once...*, p. 154.
47  *Enki and Ninmah*; available online HTTP http://etcsl.orinst.ox.ac.uk/section1/tr112.htm; accessed 02.02.2021.
48  C. A. Benito, *"Enki and Ninmah" and "Enki and the World Order"*, unpublished Ph.D dissertation, Philadelphia 1969, p. 22, line 12, and commentary on p. 49; cited in Espak, *Ancient Near Eastern Gods Enki and Ea*, p. 117.
49  See Galter, 'The Mesopotamian God Enki/Ea', 66–76.
50  W. Hallo, 'Enki and the Theology of Eridu', *Journal of the American Oriental Society*, April-June 1996, vol. 116, no. 2, 231–234 (p. 233).

51  H.L.J. Vanstiphout, 'Inanna/Ishtar as a Figure of Controversy', in H.G. Kippenberg and I. Finkel (eds), *Struggles of Gods: Papers of the Groningen Work Group for the Study of the History of Religions (Religion and Reason)*, Berlin: de Gruyter, 1984, pp. 225–238 (p. 225).
52  Leick, *A Dictionary of Ancient Near Eastern Mythology*, p. 87.
53  De Shong Meador, *Inanna, Lady of Largest Heart*, p.118.
54  *Hymn to Inanna A*; available online HTTP https://etcsl.orinst.ox.ac.uk/cgi-bin/etcsl.cgi?text=t.4.07.1&charenc=j#; accessed 02.02.2021.
55  De Shong Meador, *Inanna, Lady of Largest Heart*, p. 91.
56  De Shong Meador, *Inanna, Lady of Largest Heart*, p. 91.
57  Leick, *A Dictionary of Ancient Near Eastern Mythology*, p. 87.
58  http://etcsl.orinst.ox.ac.uk/section4/tr4073.htm *Hymn to Inanna C.*
59  Kramer and Maier, *Myths of Enki, the Crafty God*, p. 55.
60  *Enki and the World Order*; available online HTTP http://etcsl.orinst.ox.ac.uk/section1/tr113.htm; accessed 02.02.2021.
61  T. Jacobsen, *The Treasures of Darkness: A History of Mesopotamian Religion*, New Haven and London: Yale University Press, 1976, p. 135.
62  Vanstiphout, 'Inanna/Ishtar as a Figure of Controversy', in Kippenberg and Finkel (eds), *Struggles of Gods*, p. 228.
63  Vanstiphout, 'Inanna/Ishtar as a Figure of Controversy', in Kippenberg and Finkel (eds), *Struggles of Gods*, p. 232.
64  Jung, *Structure and Dynamics of the Psyche*, p. 73 (= §145).
65  R. Harris, *Gender and Aging in Mesopotamia*, Norman: University of Oklahoma Press, 2000, p. 159.
66  G. Selz, 'Five Divine Ladies: Thoughts on Inana(k), Ištar, In(n)in(a), Annunītum, and Anat, and the Origin of the Title "Queen of Heaven"', *NIN, Journal of Gender Studies in Antiquity*, 2000, vol. 1, 29–62 (p. 39).
67  De Shong Meador, *Inanna, Lady of Largest Heart*, p. 15.
68  *Hymn to Inanna C*, available HTTP https://etcsl.orinst.ox.ac.uk/cgi-bin/etcsl.cgi?text=t.4.07.3&charenc=j#; accessed 02.02.2021.
69  *Descent of Inanna*; available HTTP http://etcsl.orinst.ox.ac.uk/section1/tr141.htm; accessed 02.02.2021.
70  Katz, *The Image of the Netherworld in the Sumerian Sources*, p. 261.
71  Katz, *The Image of the Netherworld in the Sumerian Sources*, p. 261.
72  Katz, *The Image of the Netherworld in the Sumerian Sources*, p. 261.
73  *Descent of Inanna*; available HTTP https://etcsl.orinst.ox.ac.uk/cgi-bin/etcsl.cgi?text=t.1.4.1&charenc=j#; accessed 02.02.2021.
74  Katz, *The Image of the Netherworld in the Sumerian Sources*, p. 265.
75  *Descent of Inanna*; available online HTTP https://etcsl.orinst.ox.ac.uk/cgi-bin/etcsl.cgi?text=t.1.4.1&charenc=j#; accessed 02.02.2021.
76  *Descent of Inanna*; available online HTTP http://etcsl.orinst.ox.ac.uk/section1/tr141.htm; accessed 02.02.2021.
77  A. Samuels, B. Shorter, and F. Plaut, *A Critical Dictionary of Jungian Analysis*, London: Routledge, 1991, p. 150.
78  J.C. Miller, *The Transcendent Function*, Albany, NY: State University of New York, 2004, pp. 54–55.
79  Jung, *Symbols of Transformation*, p. 432.

# Chapter 7

# *Katabasis* in an Ancient Indian Myth

## Savitri Encounters Yama

*Sulagna Sengupta*

## The Cultural Sphere of the East

In October 1933, the Swiss psychoanalyst Carl Jung returned to lecture at the ETH after a gap of twenty years. By Jung's own admission, he had left university teaching in 1913 'consciously, deliberately' in order to 'understand something about psychology in the first place'.[1] Underlying this decision of moving away from public lecturing amidst his breakup with Freud was Jung's desire to explore cultures and traditions outside modern West.[2] In the decades of twenties and thirties, Jung traveled to America, Africa, and India, encountering indigenous people and archaic traditions in places where scientific psychology had not taken root. 'I then withdrew, and traveled the world, since our cultural sphere simply fails to supply us with an Archimedean point'.[3] The Archimedean point is a point outside, from which a different, perhaps objective or true picture of something is obtainable.[4] In Jung's case, this was a standpoint outside Western science and a monotheistic Judeo-Christian tradition where scientific psychology had originated. Jung's links with India can be traced to these early thoughts and a series of synchronistic events that led to his journey to India bringing eastern culture in contact with Western psychology for the first time. What is evoked in this paper from that transcultural history is a depth psychological exploration of an Indian myth, the psyche as seen envisaged in a culture distinct from Jung's own.[5]

Jung's lecture at the ETH contained references to religions where the phenomenon of the soul could be found contained.[6] Cultures living within such effective religious forms where doubts about the soul had not yet surfaced could function without a scientific psychology. 'In Buddhism, Islam, Confucianism, and so forth, too, the life of the soul is expressed in symbols. [...] But once doubt sneaks in, the life in the symbol gutters out, and actual psychology begins'.[7] While the origins of Western psychology can be traced to the first seeds of doubt and the rupture of relations with the Church,[8] it is pertinent to remember that such a radical rift with religion had not transpired in India, although religious disputes had surfaced often and fueled important social reformation since the Middle Ages.[9] Hence, even as

DOI: 10.4324/9781003054139-10

scientific reason was steering the birth of psychology in modern West, a pluralistic and polytheistic culture was aiding the development of knowledge in India, in literature, art, religion, philosophy, and the sciences.[10] This point is reiterated here to show that the east Jung pursued in his inquiries, essentially religious-oriented, contrasted diametrically with his own Western inheritance. The myth of Savitri draws from that eastern world and reveals the notion of the psyche that can perhaps be compared with Jung's notions of the unconscious or its scientific equivalent.

## Savitri's Descent

In chapter 18 of *Vana Parva: Book of Forests* in Vyasa's *Mahabharatha*, the story of Savitri and Satyavan is recounted.[11] In mainstream Indian culture, the myth is used to illustrate feminine devotion and sacrifice. We make a departure from the conventional metaphor of idealized womanhood and read the myth from a depth perspective of the unconscious.

In the land of Madra in ancient India, a childless king Asvapati, desirous of sons, offered many oblations to the sun god Surya and the goddess Savitri who inhered in him. After eighteen years, the goddess emerged from the sacrificial fire and offered the king not a hundred sons as he had wished, but a spirited daughter. She asked him to accept this boon ungrudgingly. The girl born to Asvapati was named Savitri in honor of the sun god from whose boon she was born. Savitri grew up to be beautiful, with radiant eyes, exuding a golden sheen, but when time came for her to marry, no man dared approach her daunted by her brilliance. Concerned, Asvapati asked her to find a husband on her own by which he would be able to fulfill his duties as a father. Savitri could travel anywhere to accomplish this and so the princess followed by a retinue, visited many kingdoms, towns hermitages, and forests, seeing the world by herself. When it was time for her to return, she came back to find her father in the company of sage Narada, who as a traveling bard knew about the happenings of all the three worlds. Savitri revealed to her father the man she had chosen as her husband. He was the Salva prince Satyavan, son of Dyumatsena, the blind and exiled king who had been driven away from his kingdom by his enemies and who now lived with his wife and son on the edge of the forests in poverty. On hearing of Savitri's decision, Narada informed them that although Satyavan was upright, handsome, artistic, and fond of horses, he was destined to die in a year. When Asvapati asked Savitri to reconsider her decision following Narada's counsel, she insisted that it was her mind she would follow whatever be her destiny and her mind had chosen Satyavan as her husband. On hearing this, Asvapati began preparations for visiting the forests with the intent of having Savitri and Satyavan married. On an auspicious day the wedding was solemnized, even though Dyumatsena expressed his concern about the princess' ability to give up her royal comforts and take up life in the forests. But Savitri settled in her new surroundings without difficulty and soon made everyone happy. Despite the couple's happiness, not a day passed without Savitri recalling Narada's ominous words about Satyavan.

Four days before the portended event, Savitri took on severe austerities upon herself, praying, fasting, and withdrawing into solitude. On the fateful day, she informed her parents-in-law, that she would not accept food until sunset, till her prayers were completed. When she saw Satyavan heading off to the forests with his axe, she asked if she could accompany him. He resisted, knowing that she was too weak to undertake a forest trail and unaccustomed to do one. But Savitri insisted, and finally when Dyumatsena gave his nod, the couple set off for the forests. The glorious sight of trees, rivers, and animals delighted Satyavan, but all along Savitri wondered about Narada's prophecy. At the destined hour, Satyavan picked up his axe and began to fell a tree, while Savitri sat watching nearby. Within moments, he felt weak and breathless and lowered himself on Savitri's lap. Bewildered, Savitri waited wondering what would follow, when a terrifying figure emerged before her and staked claim on Satyavan's life. Astonished, Savitri asked who he was and what his purpose was in coming there. It was then that Yama, who presided over hell and arbitered the fate of the dead, met the radiant and beautiful Savitri standing before him, having escorted her ill-fated husband Satyavan into the forests on the day of his death.

Readers may acquaint themselves with the myth of the sun god Surya at this point to see how these two seemingly unrelated characters, Yama and Savitri, met and sparked off a friendship that was unexpected and heart-warming. Reference to the sun god Surya can be found in the *Rig Veda* and the *Upanishads*. Known as Mitraya (friend), Ravaye (shining), Bhanave (illuminator), Khagaya (swift mover), Pushne (one who gives strength), Hiranayagarbha (golden womb), Aditya (son of the cosmic mother), Bhaskarya (enlightened), the sun is a symbol of consciousness and the highest atman (self) in the mythology of Vedic India.[12] Myth has it that Sanjana, daughter of the cosmic architect Vishwakarma, desired Surya and married him but unable to bear his intensity left him soon after. Yama was Surya's son born from his marriage to Sanjana. When the latter chose to go away to the forests leaving Surya, she created out of herself her look-alike, the dusky Chhaaya (Sanskrit for shadow), to replace her. Being dark, Chhaaya was able to absorb the sun's rays and went on to live with Surya, undetected. It was only when she was cruel to Sanjana's children that Chhaaya was confronted by Yama and her identity was revealed. Yama told his father that Chhaaya was not their mother. Surya then went to look for Sanjana and asked her to return but she refused asking him to reduce his brightness instead. Sanjana returned only when this was done, and Chhaaya, Sanjana's shadow lived with them in that marriage.[13] Depth and darkness was an essential foil to the sun god's unrestrained and blinding brilliance.

This story reveals Yama's solar antecedents and his unusual perspicacity, since even the sun god did not notice his wife's absence from the household till Yama informed him. Born to luminous parents, the dark and terrifying

Yama was a complete opposite of the dazzling Surya – a *coincidentia opposi-torum*.[14] Assigned the task of mediating dead souls, Yama presided over the darkest realm in the universe away from the dazzling skies where his father reigned. Although brilliant, the sun's intensity blinded all including Surya himself, who was ignorant of his wife's departure from their marriage. The sun's brightness lacked the dark and penetrating depth of Yama. This gap is bridged mystically through Surya's union with Chhaaya, where the latter absorbed some of the sun's brilliance. Light and dark and opposites of all manner surrounded Surya and hinged on all whom he created or beget. Yama's encounter with Savitri seen against this backdrop is a meeting of not two unrelated figures as one would think, but two kindred souls born from the sun's luminosity and darkness, its dual nature and twofold movement across the skies.

When Yama tied the noose around Satyavan's lifeless body and pulled him towards hell, Savitri followed. Asked by Yama to return as she had nothing more to do, Savitri said that she could not leave Satyavan having vowed in marriage to be with him forever. Yama was surprised that as the most feared of gods whom no one dared approach Savitri seemed unafraid of him. The distant cries of animals, the eerie presence of ghouls, and spectral beings did not seem to deter Savitri. Yama looked back to see her trudging along, ready for a conversation. She looked up at him and said that she had heard of his virtues and timeless wisdom and knew of all that he had to oversee in hell. When asked why she was not afraid of him, Savitri said that she had walked more than seven steps with him and she thought that this signified friendship. She said that while his outer demeanor was terrifying, his company was far from loathsome. Indeed, Yama's deathly appearance belied the fact that he was of glorious lineage and impeccable conduct. Savitri's candor and spirit-edness baffled Yama. When they had walked thus for long, Yama urged her again to leave. He offered her a boon hoping that this would turn her away. She could ask for anything he said, except the life of her husband. Savitri paused, thinking for a moment, and then asked if her father-in-law Dymutsena could have his vision restored and his kingdom returned, as after losing Satyavan he would have nothing left to live for. Yama was ready to fulfill this, pleased all along with her spiritedness, seeing that her life was indeed ill-fated at so young an age. Yet, when many more furlongs had been crossed, Yama saw that Savitri had not turned back nor left the trail. Aggravated, Yama told her that they were now close to the gates of hell from where he would have to take away Satyavan forever. Savitri recounted to Yama the story of her mar-riage to Satyavan and how she had chosen him after a long search, from among many others. She was destined to be with him. She asked Yama that as one who upheld truth and integrity in all his actions, if he would advise her to forsake her vows in marriage and abandon Satyavan. Yama repeated that he could not take her to hell as it was not time for her to die. Every mortal had to fulfill his or her task in life and Savitri had to do hers before she could be allowed to die. As for Satyavan, his life was destined to be brief. Yama asked that she take another boon instead as there was nothing more that he could do for her. Savitri enquired if her father-in-law could be blessed with a hundred sons as Satyavan would no more be there for him to rule his newly regained kingdom. Yama agreed and proceeded to complete the final leg of the journey. Seeing his companion, the bull near the gates of hell, Yama asked Savitri to bid a final goodbye as he prepared to go across. But Savitri prepared to cross over too, explaining that she would go till the end wherever this journey would take her. Yama insisted that she leave, as the gates of hell were open to only those who had shed their mortal life. She would have to return, he said; she could take a final boon if she wished but that was all. Savitri then asked if she could be blessed with a hundred sons with Satyavan in this life. What could she look forward to otherwise if she had to return? She had desired Satyavan and knew that life would not be the same without him. Yama was confounded. As a man of word, he could not retract his offer now. She had not asked for Satyavan's life but had insisted that she could not abandon him in this life. If he acceded to her request, he would have to release Satyavan from death, for only if he did so could Savitri have her boon fulfilled. It was a conundrum.

Yama stood pondering. He thought that Savitri had not bemoaned her fate or reproached him for taking Satyavan away but had accompanied him willingly, telling him all along that she understood the gravity of his tasks. He had felt cheerful and animated in her company. He could see that she was determined to be with Satyavan and he wondered if he should accede to her wish. A dead soul had never been returned before, but Yama thought that this was an unusual encounter. Savitri had changed something in this dark and desolate world, and in him. She had asked Yama, the god of death, who was forever ferrying dead bodies to restore the dead and birth new ones. A radiance emerged from their trail now, surrounding them both. Indeed, Satyavan had regained his life and Savitri was preparing to return with him. Myth has it that they lived a long and purposeful life together and when time came for them to die they surrendered themselves willingly to Yama.

## *Katabasis* in Myths

The psychological essence of *katabasis* found in myths is rich and varied. *Katabasis*, from Greek κατάβασις, from κατὰ 'down' and βαίνω 'go' (also called *nekyia*), evokes many ways of imagining the netherworld (also called *naraka*).[15] The notion of soul's descent can be found in a hero's encounter with dead spirits or in visions of tormented souls in hell. The Sumerian goddess Inana's journey into hell after she decides to take over her sister Ereshkigal's domain suggests power, envy, and hubris in psyche's depths. Inana's catastrophic journey in which she is stripped by Ereshkigal and Anunnaki and eventually killed depicts the ordeal of soul descents.[16] Indeed, journeys into hell often entail painful stripping of one's self and its dissolution. Soul descents are found symbolized through *nigredo* or blackness where a lightening of darkness may be seen sometimes, but the latter comes only after a long and difficult battle with the depths and the painful encounter of one's shadow.[17]

Myths of *katabasis* include themes of feminine initiation as the story of Persephone in the Eleusinian Mysteries reveals. Persephone's abduction and rape destroy her youthful innocence and disrupt her existence, nurtured all along on a one-sided relation with her mother Demeter. Her descent initiates her development and experience of the other but is brought about through violence, and unleashes interminable chaos, pain, and wrath around. The depths become an intrinsic part of her when she tastes the forbidden fruit of hell because having accepted it, she can no longer return to Demeter permanently. The rich and luscious pomegranate is symbolic of the abundance and delights of the underworld, a life that Persephone has partaken in. Her passage between the two worlds is therefore recurrent, cyclical, and eternal, calling for a relentless movement between opposites and bridging of the conscious and unconscious. It reflects an individuation motif and in experiences that are similarly constellated, we find that the psyche matures through such encounters and their accompanying pain, loss, and suffering.

Reference to myths of *katabasis* is incomplete without mention of Orpheus and the nymph Eurydice, whom Orpheus loved, lost, and followed into the underworld. Orpheus' story reflects the tragic fate of earthly unions, the impossibility of conquering death or of uniting the Apollonian and Dionysian worlds, as myths of descent often reveal. It raises other persuasive ideas as well.[18] Orpheus' descent is a contrast to the Vedic myth of Savitri, where the feminine is not relegated to a subterranean world of darkness and unknowing or even the unknowable feminine mystery but denoted instead as consciousness and agency. Like Orpheus, Savitri too descends into hell following her beloved, but unlike him, she is able to restore Satyavan's life. It is not this that makes the myth noteworthy, but the encounter between Savitri and Yama[19] that transforms a grim and ominous tale into one of hope and light. It suggests a view of descent that contrasts vividly with myths of *katabasis* elsewhere.

## The Essence of Solar Descents

'Myths are stories of archetypal encounters', writes Jungian analyst and writer Andrew Samuels.[20] Jung's experience of mythic images in his patients' dreams gave him his first inkling of the collective unconscious or the layer of the psyche that is common to all. The archetypal layer from where dreams, fantasies, and myths emerge denotes something universal about the psyche in Jungian parlance. Samuels writes that when mythic imagery crops up during analysis they express something vital about the psyche that needs to be brought into conscious realization. It is through conscious engagement with these images that their compulsive hold over the psyche is released. He draws parallels between myths and analysis and between mythology and pathology.

Any behavior that searches for mythologems in order to reconstruct reality is a sign of regression he says, that attempts to imitate archetypal behavior, avoid reality and reinforce psychic inflation.

Samuels speaks from a psychoanalytic tradition that has a specific history in the West, in particular Britain.[21] Myths have been used to construct psychoanalytic theory in that tradition in a way that is distinct from the way myths have been treated in the east. While Samuels is right that myths evoke something vital about the unconscious psyche that is necessary to bring into conscious realization, is it only the pathological aspect of the unconscious that is reflected in myths and unconscious fantasies? Jung's critical difference with Freud was that the psyche had a prospective aspect outside its reductive analytic dimension. The psychoanalytic and the psycho-synthetic are therefore distinctive approaches that distinguish Freudian and Jungian traditions of psychoanalysis. Paul Bishop explains this when he differentiates between the causal-reductive aspect of dream analysis and the emergent or prospective aspects of the psyche that dreams and images signify.[22] Jung's differences with Freud can be seen in his introductory essay in *Symbols of Transformation* titled 'Two Kinds of Thinking', where he writes of directed and fantasy thinking. Jung emphasized that fantasy thinking and mythological imagination, while arising from instinct are not necessarily pathological:

> To characterize them, we ought therefore not to use expressions borrowed from pathology. So also the myth, which is likewise based on unconscious fantasy process, is, in meaning, substance and form, far from being infantile, or the expression of an autoerotic and autistic attitude [...].[23]

If myth and mythical imagination are seen as originating in instinct but not entirely pathological, what could myths be signifying that is prospective or potential about the psyche? In *The Mythological Unconscious*, Michael Vannoy Adams says that Jung developed a specific technique by which he applied mythology to clinical practice.[24] Amplification of myths and their association to clinical material gave a foreground and context to a patient's irrational unconscious. While over-identification with myths and inflation could be the pitfalls of such an exercise, Vannoy Adams thinks that mythic images disturb, confront, and question defective psychic attitudes and are useful in analysis. I use the amplificatory approach that Adams refers to not for examining clinical material but to expand the myth in understanding its prospective, emergent character and in seeing how images of the psyche in this myth contrast and correlate with Jung's notions about the unconscious.

Among other things, Surya's myth denotes his union with Sanjana, an anima figure, who is both light and dark.[25] Sanjana's self-division, where she gives form and life to her own shadow suggests a step towards discernment and consciousness. The alchemical play of light and dark between Surya and Sanjana, a moderation of the sun's intensity or its absorption by Chhaaya in the marriage, makes consciousness inseparable from unconscious and integral for the sun's sustenance, lest he expels all around him through his sheer intensity. The sun is cosmologically tied to its shadow. This is mythically expressed through Surya's children who represent darkness in one form or another and remain related to him, cosmically and mythically.[26] Jung described the relation between light and dark when he said that consciousness necessitates the presence of the dark to fulfill itself: 'Just as the day-star rises out of the nocturnal sea, so, ontogenetically and phylogenetically, consciousness is born of unconsciousness and sinks back every night to this primal condition'.[27] Consciousness is inclined to align itself with darkness in many mythical motifs in India[28] and contrasts significantly with myths elsewhere where evil and darkness are often split off from the main body. Solar descents underscore sun's relation to darkness, and while the myth does not equate light with dark, treat them similar, or take away their essential polarity, it suggests a necessitous relation with the other in the basic structure of the myth. This hermeneutically differs from Jung's emphasis that consciousness births from the unconscious and needs the other for its fulfillment.

Primordial imagination on which myths are based are pre-psychological in tone, archaic conceptions about the mysteries of life and death that have been part of most cultures and civilizations. According to Paul Bishop, the archaic 'derives from the Greek arkhaios (ρχαῖος), which in turn is related to the word ρχή (or *archē*), meaning "principle", "origin", or "cause"'.[29] Early knowledge in India was an articulation of such an archaic worldview. The notion of archaic is therefore grounded in an actual body of texts in India where myths and imagination are encapsulated. But Bishop reminds us that the notion of archaic is not just chronological, rooted in history but timeless, contemporary, and qualitative.[30] I take the qualitative to mean a psychological essence, or the quality of the myth that is ahistorical, subjective, dialectical, and reflexive.

The qualitative essence of Persephone's descent is in its individuation motif. Any transformative effect that it has on her young, undifferentiated psyche is prospective in essence, unfolding and emergent as individuation journeys typically are. Persephone's descent results in a liminal and indeterminate passage between two worlds as she struggles to bridge her relation between Hades and Demeter. The intermediary ground which Persephone finds, a *tertium non datur*, or a supraordinate' third (as Jung says), is a realm that unites opposites.[31] The myth offers a view of the psyche that is prospective in essence, suggesting birth of a new attitude perhaps, that could offset Persephone's current predicament of her one-sided relation with her mother and regression into the maternal.

The qualitative and prospective aspects of the psyche in Savitri's myth are denoted in an entirely different manner. Savitri's descent, even when triggered by a stasis in her life does not originate in violence. Unlike Persephone, who is a symbol of feminine innocence, Savitri personifies wisdom and knowing, invested as she is with self-agency and consciousness from young age.

However, her luminous persona is imperfect and flawed and this surfaces in her youthful prime. Born spirited, as powerful as a hundred sons, Savitri displays her brilliance from birth. But her radiance intimidates prospective suitors, as the sun god's brilliance once drove away his own wife, and therein begins Savitri's difficulties. She has a dim forethought that her future lies not in her inherited glory but in a life that is somewhere else. She is drawn towards a poor, displaced, and ill-fated Satyavan, an unlikely choice for so extraordinary a princess. But Savitri notes that everything around her present life is exaggerated and unreal and fails to fulfill her desires of love and companionship. Satyavan's abject and miserable life appeals to her, much like the sun that is pulled towards darkness and begins to descend at noon to enter the realm of dusk. Savitri embraces this downward climb instinctively and unfeignedly. It marks the beginning of her descent, which unfolds not in hell but on earth, in a marriage of her choice, a willing retreat into the forest, and in a life of hardship and denial. It is a lowering of her worldly station and a relinquishing of a life that no more gives her meaning. Savitri initiates her descent and as all initiates in mystery cults of times foregone know, the task of coming in contact with the unknown necessitates a rudimentary stripping to the bone, a surrendering of the superfluous, and an acceptance of a mystery.

According to the classical scholar Yulia Ustinova, 'all initiates had to make efforts to become "fit for the purpose", an act that comprises austerities like fasting, exhaustion, fear, pain, sensory deprivation. It involves "the anthropologically attested archaic 'shaking the foundations of the personality'.[32] Savitri's willing surrender of her comforts, stripping away of royal pleasures in favor of a life of poverty is illustrative of a psychic attitude that has embraced descent consciously, determinedly. Following this downward movement, Savitri begins to prepare herself for the imminent. Tapas or tapasya, the ancient meditative practice of introversion, is quite simply an act of concentration and gathering of energy which Savitri believes will help her in facing the final ordeal.[33] Yet, she does not know what the ordeal would look like. When it does appear in the form of Yama, she is astounded but lets out no heart-wrenching cries or abject pleas. In sync with wherever Yama takes Satyavan's lifeless body, Savitri conveys to him about her intent of accompanying Satyavan. Her stark and bare life of the year past has sharpened her mind. She now perceives Yama not as a harbinger of death, terrifying or alien who has come to take away her husband, but a man of word, noble and perspicuous, committed to fair play. The seven steps she takes with him affirms her change of disposition. She realizes soon though that she is poised precariously between her beloved whom she will not forsake and Yama, who is bound by his own obligations. It becomes essential for her not to lose her composure as she witnesses a frightening terrain around her. It is Yama who begins to offer her boons to dissuade her from her journey, surprised by her courage and candor. Savitri tells him that while he would have to remain truthful to his role and fulfill what he has been assigned to do, she would have to remain committed to hers. How could these two opposing poles of life and death be reconciled? How could their promises be honored together?

The ensuing tension agitates Yama but Savitri sees no reason to veil her desires before his stern directives. Satyavan's bare and ordinary life shrouds his love for beauty, animals, and nature, and alludes to instincts and passions that could spring back to life under favorable conditions. Knowing that she can no more go back to the world she has left behind, Savitri seeks nothing for herself at first. She remembers instead her blind and helpless father-in-law and wonders how disconsolate he would be knowing about Satyavan's death. She thinks of how he would need to safeguard his kingdom once he has regained it, since there was no dearth of enemies around. How would he manage to do it without Satyavan? Her request for a hundred sons is symbolic of the strength and courage that she thinks Dyumatsena would need to retain his kingdom. When she is compelled by Yama to seek a boon for herself, Savitri can think of nothing other than a creative seed within her as a gift from the depths. The feminine potential for fertility and generativity, whether bodily or in spirit, can rise from ashes, or birth from darkness, as we see in all instances of rebirth and resurrection. It encapsulates a desire for the other, an embodied animus, and we note that Savitri cites Satyavan's name. What could she have envisioned from this plea knowing fully well that Satyavan was lost to her forever? Hovering near the gates of hell with the body of Satyavan beside her, Savitri makes an inconceivable request taking her conversation with Yama close to a breakdown. Their conversation is about to end but instead of a rupture, the air around lightens. Yama feels inclined to fulfill Savitri's request. Lives are born, kingdoms are regained, gifts of creation are received, and finally Satyavan is revived. The realm of hell changes momentarily from a vast expanse of doom and despair to one of hope and fertility. Yama goes beyond his ordinary call of duty but he tells himself that what he grants Savitri is perhaps as precious as what he has received from her.

The illumined air in hell is sign of a new birth, what Jung called a transcendent function,[34] a *tertium non datur*, where a reconciling third has emerged, reflecting the birth of a new experience and a new level of consciousness.[35] Both Yama and Savitri are transformed through their encounter, albeit differently. Savitri, no more *the beau ideal* whose unearthly brilliance daunted all, imperfect and incomplete in her perfection, but deepened and darkened now through love, loss, longing, and privation. Yama too is pervaded with a new lightness as he awakens to his creative powers, touched by a feminine luminescence from another world, witnessing as he does for the first time the sacred temenos of hell lit up. It is pertinent to note, that the emergent, reconciling transcendent third, symbolized through the illumination of hell, arises spontaneously, for neither Yama nor Savitri premeditated on or anticipated its appearance beforehand, even though they both deliberated consciously and purposefully into the conflicting nature of their goals in hell. Its spontaneous emergence renders the transcendent symbol with a numinosity that myths often carry in their final resolutions.

## Conclusion: Myths in a Post-Colonial Environment

According to the Jungian analyst Donald Kalsched, 'mythology is the most archaic and profound record we have of mankind's essential spirit and nature', for 'instead of concepts and facts that make logical sense, we find patterns of irrational imagery whose meaning must be discerned or experienced by the participant-observer'.[36]

In introducing Western psychology in India in early 1900s, a psychoanalytic approach was offered by Freud, Ernest Jones, and their cohorts Owen-Berkeley-Hill, C.D. Dally (among others),[37] where the study of patient cases, training of analysts, setting-up of mental institutions, and induction of psychology into Indian academia became the basis on which psychological knowledge was disseminated. Within that approach, psychoanalysis was used to critique religious and cultural attitudes in India which the colonizers felt could be replaced by scientific understanding of human behavior.[38] In this colonialist perspective, religion was a defensive compromise against instincts resulting in its discontents; the idealization of primitives was a blunder by early explorers. That they were inferior to the European psyche, developmentally, phylogenetically, and ontologically was taken to be a fact.[39] Thus, myths, literary narratives, religious symbols, and cultural constructs innate to Indian society, fragments of its early civilizational history, were excluded from psychology in favor of a scientific theory about the unconscious, developed in an intellectual climate quite distinct from the east. How universal could these theories be, evolving as they did in historical and intellectual climates far removed from India?[40] When pioneering Indian psychologist Girindrashekhar Bose encountered the notion of repression in his patients in Calcutta and corresponded with Freud about the differences he perceived in his own cases, these differences were not examined by Freud. Bose attempted to integrate knowledge of the Upanishads in affirming psychic unity of the self under his theory of opposite wishes.[41] Freud's lack of enthusiasm about Bose's suggestions due to his inadequate understanding of Indian culture and his need to create a 'Psychoanalytic International' or a universal psychoanalytic movement resulted in an eventual thawing of relations between the two and a dilution of the impact of scientific psychology in India.[42]

The colonization of psychology in early 1900s reduced the possibility of bringing eastern knowledge in dialogue with Western theory. Post-colonial psychoanalytical discourse in India, while attempting to analyze culture and psyche through the lens of repression, instincts, sexuality, body, and object relations has kept a vast body of symbols, myths, literary narratives, religious, and other cultural constructs outside the ambit of psychological discourse.[43] Michael Vannoy Adams has argued that the Freudian approach of defining 'primitive' as more identified with id and not the ego, automatically puts the colonized as inferior to the colonizer.[44] Although these binary divisions do not actually reveal the complexities of colonial history and the many layers of oppression and subaltern histories it contains, denoting the archaic as regressed, primitive and backward has been characteristic of psychoanalytic theory. The myth of Savitri brings to fore entirely other ideas. Savitri's descent underscores the dual nature of consciousness, the significance of shadow in the individual's developmental trajectory, the essence of solar descents, and the prospective and individuating quality of the psyche that exists alongside its one-sided, regressed, and morbid tendencies. The imagery of opposites in Surya's myth is indicative of psychic duality, the emergence of a mediating symbol, the luminous feminine that engenders a reconciling third are clearly discernible, but remain poorly harnessed themes in Post-Jungian and post-colonial psychology – a fact that analytical psychology needs urgently to address.

## Notes

1  C.G. Jung, *History of Modern Psychology: Lectures Delivered at ETH Zurich*, vol. 1, *1933-1944*, ed. S. Shamdasani, Princeton, NJ: Princeton University Press, 2018, p. 1. Jung lectured at the University of Zurich as a Privatdozent from 1905 to 1913.
2  C.G. Jung, *Memories, Dreams, Reflections*, ed. A. Jaffé, New York: Vintage Books, 1989, p. 238. Jung wrote that the period following 1913 after his break with Freud was a time of inner uncertainty, when he grappled with a new attitude towards his patients, searching for the myth in which the Western man lived. In 1920 he travelled to Tunis and said that he had longed to be in a country where no European language was spoken, no Christian conceptions prevailed, and where a different race and historical tradition could be found from where he could view the European.
3  Jung, *History of Modern Psychology*, ed. Shamdasani, p. 1.
4  See the definition available online at https://www.oxfordreference.com/view/10.1093/oi/authority.20110803095422175. Jung said in several places that analytical psychology lacks the possibility of objective verification of psychic facts. The observer is bound by his/her own subjective standpoint and observations and empirical verification of psychic phenomena are never exact but relative (see, for example, C.G. Jung, *The Development of Personality* [*Collected Works*, vol. 17], London: Routledge & Kegan Paul, 1977, §163 [pp. 88–89]). Jung's foray into other cultures was an attempt at having the European image reflected back, as a way of understanding the psyche from outside his own standpoint.
5  Jung's transcultural history with India can be found in S. Sengupta, *Jung in India*, New Orleans: Spring Journal Books, 2013. For Jung's experience of India as his cultural other, see S. Sengupta, 'Indeterminate States in Transcultural Histories: Cultural Other in Jung's India', *International Journal of Jungian Studies*, 2020, vol. 12, no. 1, 88–108.
6  In his first lecture at ETH Jung talked about the soul and its expression in religion. He said that everything outside the inner world that was concrete was explored by science but matters of the soul was left to the Church.
7  Jung, *History of Modern Psychology*, ed. Shamdasani, p. 3.
8  According to Jung, 'the Renaissance arose out of what, through doubt, had freed itself from Christianity. This was actually the first time that a psychological problem manifested itself' (Jung, *History of Modern Psychology*, ed. Shamdasani, p. 4).
9  See R. Thapar, *History of India*, Harmondsworth: Penguin, 1990. Here the Indian historian Romila Thapar outlines the advent of the Aryans in ancient India, followed by Islamic and British invasions. Buddhist, Jain, and other religious groups were also part of that history. Religion remained an important factor in India's evolution as a nation and played a definitive role in the development of knowledge, society, institutions, culture and philosophy.

10  See A. Sen, *The Argumentative Indian: Writings on Indian History, Culture and Identity*, Harmondsworth: Penguin. 2006. Here the noted writer and economist Amartya Sen says that the tradition of intellectual and religious pluralism has been part of India since ancient times. Buddhist, Jain, and Islamic intellectuals have critiqued dominant Hindu scriptures in a climate of intellectual heterodoxy. A culture of argumentation and public debating has helped religious, political and ideological differences thrive, which Sen believes is essential for sustaining a pluralistic society. The other side of this history which Sen does not dwell on, is the violence and hostility that religious and social differences have triggered in the subcontinent, threatening the cultural and political unity of India often.

11  See B. Sharma, *Vyasa's Mahabharatam in Eighteen Parvas*, Kolkata: Academic Publishers, 2008. The retelling of the myth here and its amplification is my version developed for this paper and aligns with popular narratives in Indian literature.

12  Surya, a major divinity in the Vedas, is known by various names such as Aditya, Arka, Savitri and is a symbol of supreme realization and spiritual enlightenment. Savitri is the goddess inhering in Surya, procreator, and a source of illumination and knowledge. For further discussion, see the entry available online at https://www.britannica.com/topic/Surya.

13  This myth, originally from the Puranas, is narrated orally in India in various languages and in children's literature. I have narrated the popular version of the myth here.

14  See J. Valk, 'The Concept of the Coincidentia Oppositorum in the Thought of Mircea Eliade', *Religious Studies*, 1992, vol. 28, no. 1, 31–34. The notion of paradoxical opposites or *coincidentia oppositorum* was proposed by Mircea Eliade in his concepts of sacred and profane. Eliade thought these opposites were logically contradictory but mutually complementary. The sacred needs the profane to express itself and each contradicts the other to affirm its own validity. The sun god's creative powers contradict death, but both life and death, Surya and Yama, need each other to express themselves. Without dark there would be no light, and without life there would be no death. The symbols are paradoxical, complementary, and simultaneously occurring. They are of dual nature: in the sun's dazzling brilliance is hidden its blindness, and behind Yama's dark demeanor lies his acuity and wisdom.

15  See S. Schuhmacher and G. Woerner (eds), *The Encyclopaedia of Eastern Philosophy and Religion*, Boston: Shambala, 1994, p. 241, where *naraka* is defined as a 'place of torture and torment, where the souls of the wicked go. Manu enumerates twenty-one hells, each with its own name'. In addition, 'the hells are places of torment and retribution for bad deeds; but existence in them is finite, i.e., after negative karma has been exhausted, rebirth in another better form of existence is possible'.

16  See S.N. Kramer, 'Inana's Descent to the Netherworld', *Proceedings of the American Philosophical Society*, 1950, vol. 94, no. 4, 361–363.

17  In 'A Black Blessing', Alexandra Fidyk discusses the pedagogy of suffering that begins with black. The abyss is experienced when conscious ego has exhausted itself in a given life attitude, when the call of the dark will have to be attended to give space for a new psychic movement to emerge. Jung called this meaningful *katabasis* which is symbolized through the colour black, the alchemical nigredo, symbolizing decomposition and dissolution of the soul, putrefaction and stripping to the bone. See A. Fidyk, 'A Black Blessing', in D. Jardine, C. Gilham, and G. MacCaffrey (eds), *On the Pedagogy of Suffering: Hermeneutic and Buddhist Meditations*, New York: Peter Lang, 2015, 101–106.

18  Sarah Burgess Watson suggests that Orpheus' erotic mysteries and *katabasis* had an effect on his sexuality, his homoerotic tendencies and his misogyny. See S. Watson, 'Orpheus' Erotic Mysteries: Plato, Pederasty, and the Zagreus Myth', *Phanocles: Bulletin of the Institute of Classical Studies*, 2014, vol. 57, no. 2, 47–71. Elsewhere, Helen Sword has argued that 'if, for many readers, Eurydice's fate may seem frustrating unfair, for others it has provided the very secret of her appeal', and noting that 'Rainer Maria Rilke saw Eurydice as the embodiment of feminine mystery, possessing powers of self-fulfillment inaccessible even to her archetypal poet-husband'; see H. Sword, 'Orpheus and Eurydice in the Twentieth Century: Lawrence, H. D., and the Poetics of the Turn', in *Twentieth Century Literature*, 1989, vol. 35, no. 4, 407–428.
19  See S. Bhattacharjee, *The Study of Indian Theogony: A Comparative Study of Indian Mythology from the Vedas to Puranas*, Camnridge: Cambridge University Press, 2007. Indian mythologist Sukumari Bhattacharjee gives detailed description of Yama, the god of death describing him in various incarnations. Hell, Yama's abode, is located in multiple regions of the underworld in mythology, described as a place for suffering and tormented souls. Yama's description includes reference to the two dogs who accompany him, his messengers (Yamadutas) and various other birds and animals.
20  See A. Samuels, B. Shorter, and F. Plaut, *A Critical Dictionary of Jungian Analysis*, London: Routledge, 1986, pp. 95–96.
21  See S. Shamdasani, *Jung and the Making of Modern Psychology*, Cambridge: Cambridge University Press, 2003; and P. Kuhn, *Psychoanalysis in Britain, 1893–1913: Histories and Historiography*, Lanham, MD: Lexington Books, 2017. British psychoanalysis evolved through various schools of thinking about the unconscious, their differentiation in medical, clerical and spiritual fields, psychical, psychotherapeutic, and psychoanalytic research and dissemination of Freud's ideas. In addition to psychoanalytic schools led by Anna Freud, Melanie Klein, and Donald Winnicott, Jungian psychology led by Michael Fordham made its contribution, with Fordham adding his interpretation and clinical emphasis to Jung's concepts, establishing SAP, and rendering British Jungian work with a particular identity distinct from Jungian schools elsewhere. Myths and religious concepts are not considered sources of scientific knowledge in that psychoanalytic tradition except for their reductive analysis; their contribution in the development of knowledge in non-western cultures is not considered relevant in this field.
22  See P. Bishop, *Jung in Contexts: A Reader*, London: Routledge, 1999, pp. 5–6.
23  C.G. Jung, *Symbols of Transformation* [*Collected Works*, vol. 5], Princeton, NJ: Princeton University Press, 1967, §38 (p. 29).
24  M. Vannoy Adams, *The Mythological Unconscious*, Putnam, CT: Spring Publications, 2010, pp. 36–51.
25  The anima is the contra-sexual unconscious other in a man's psyche. If his dominant identity is masculine, his inner other is feminine. Jung conceived that the psyche is made up of both masculine and feminine, conscious and unconscious parts. The anima typically represents according to Jung, the characteristics that are opposite of the conscious masculine. If the masculine reveals qualities such as assertive, thinking, and rational, then a man's inner undeveloped feminine would be his feeling and relational side. The anima acts like a bridge between conscious and unconscious psyche and is integral for psychological development. For women, Jung conceived of a corresponding figure called the animus. Post-Jungian discourse has defined masculine and feminine in more fluid ways without attributing fixed stereotyped qualities to men and women.
26  For instance, Yama, the god of death, is born from Surya and Sanjana. Other children include Yamuna, river of sorrow, and Shani or Saturn, a son born with Chhaaya.

27 Jung, *Mysterium coniunctionis* [*Collected Works*, vol. 14], §117 (p. 97).
28 Myth of Samudra Manthana in which Vishnu, the cosmic creator is seen performing ambiguous acts to retrieve the nectar in the fight between gods and demons. Vishnu is not a symbol of purity and perfection here. See S. Sengupta, 'Samudra Manthan: Reflections on an Ancient Indian Myth', in *Jung and India* [*Spring Journal*, Fall 2013].
29 P. Bishop, *The Archaic: The Past in the Present*, Hove: Routledge, 2012, p. 3.
30 See Bishop, *The Archaic: The Past in the Present*, p. 228.
31 C.G. Jung, *Aion* [*Collected Works*, vol. 9/ii], Princeton, NJ: Princeton University Press, 1968, §280 (p. 180).
32 Y. Ustinova, 'To Live in Joy and to Die with Hope: Experiential Aspects of Ancient Greek Mystery Rites', *Bulletin of the Institute of Classical Studies*, 2013, vol. 56, no.2 [Ancient History Issue], 105–123 (p. 113).
33 Jung writes in *Psychological Types* about opposites as follows: 'Liberation follows the withdrawal of libido from all contents, resulting in a state of complete introversion. This psychological process, is very characteristically, known as *tapas*, a term which can best be rendered as "self-brooding"' (Jung, *Psychological Types* [*Collected Works*, vol. 6], Princeton, NJ: Princeton University Press, 1971, §189 [p. 118]).
34 The 'transcendent function' is 'a function that mediates opposites' (Samuels, Shorter, and Plaut, *A Critical Dictionary of Jungian Analysis*, p. 150). Samuels has also discussed the transcendent function in his *Jung and The Post-Jungians*, London: Routledge & Kegan Paul, 1985, p. 59, where he underscores the role of ego in mediating opposites and in reconciling conflicts through discrimination of opposites, allowing for a conscious attitude to emerge and facilitating the production of new psychic contents.
35 C.G. Jung, *The Structure and Dynamics of the Psyche* [*Collected Works*, vol. 8], Princeton, NJ: Princeton University Press, 1960, §189.
36 D. Kalsched, and A. Jones, 'Myth and Psyche: The Evolution of Consciousness', published in the website of the C.G. Jung Foundation for Analytical Psychology, 1986; available online HTTP https://www.cgjungny.org/myth-and-psyche-sample-article/
37 See the history of Indian psychoanalysis in S. Akhtar, and P. Tummala-Narra, 'Psychoanalysis in India', in *Freud Along the Ganges: Psychoanalytic Reflections on the People and Culture of India*, New Delhi: Stanza, 2008, pp. 3–25.
38 As Salim Akhtar writes, two of the original members of the Indian Psychoanalytic Society, Owen Berkeley-Hill and Claude Dangar Daly, were British army officers: 'Tragically, both men used psychoanalysis as a vehicle of cultural prejudice and oppression in their studies of the Hindu personality. They displayed an astonishing lack of curiosity in the experiential individuality of their Indian subjects and in the positive aspects of Indian culture' (Akhtar and Tummala-Narra, 'Psychoanalysis in India').
39 M. Vannoy Adams, *The Multicultural Imagination: "Race", Color and the Unconscious*, Abingdon and New York: Routledge, 1996, pp. 51–55.
40 See Shamdasani, *Jung and the Making of Modern Psychology*.
41 A detailed list of Bose's psychoanalytic papers can be found in Christiane Hartnack's essays listed below (see note 43).
42 For an entire history, see C. Hartnack, *Psychoanalysis in Colonial India*, New Delhi: Oxford University Press, 2001; as well as C. Hartnack, 'Colonial Dominions and the Psychoanalytic Couch: Synergies of Freudian Theory with Bengali Hindu Thought and Practices in British India', in W. Anderson, R.C. Keller, and D. Jenson (eds), *Unconscious Dominions: Psychoanalysis, Colonial Trauma and Global Sovereignties*, Durham, NC: Duke University Press, 2008, 97–111.

43  This trend has been reversed to some extent in the works of Indian authors Sudhir Kakar and Ashis Nandy, who have introduced psychoanalytic perspectives in their studies of Indian culture, history, and society. Yet the symbolic, emergent, and the transcendent function in Jung's concept of individuation, along with symbols, archetypes, Self, have still remained outside these discussions. See S. Kakar, *Culture and Psyche: Selected Essays*, New Delhi: Oxford University Press, 1997; and A. Nandy, *The "Savage Freud" and Other Essays on Possible and Retrievable Selves*, Princeton, NJ: Princeton University Press, 1995.

44  M. Vannoy, *The Multicultural Imagination*, p. 54.

# Chapter 8

# *Katabasis* in Middle Eastern Female Hagiography

## A Post-Jungian Perspective

*Roula-Maria Dib*

### Introduction: What Is New about This Study

In older literary works, both fiction and nonfiction, sacred and profane, there are many examples but little highlights on the emergence of heroines and female fighters; in other words, while '[t]he female warrior is a potent activated archetype in fiction and reality',[1] most studies have concentrated more on the journeys of male heroes, with patriarchy somehow overlooking an important literary and historical manifestation of the feminine archetypes – namely that of the female hero or female warrior. But if Jung believes that 'individuation is a philosophical, spiritual and mystical experience',[2] then looking at the stories of female mystics, particularly saints, may shed light on the journey of the heroine. In 'Fierce Young Women in Popular fiction and Unpopular War', Elizabeth Eowyn Nelson asserts that 'the precise simultaneous fluorescence of fierce young women in fiction and reality indicates the activation of an archetypal pattern, the female warrior, long unrecognized in patriarchy'.[3] These 'fierce young women' appear in a unique literary form that is worth mining: hagiography. The synaxarion, which is a Byzantine anthology of hagiographies, along with oral storytelling, contains hundreds of stories on the lives of saints, which can offer a wealth of archetypal truths manifested in rich symbolism and story elements, particularly when studying the 'heroine' from a post-Jungian perspective, with a special focus on *katabasis*.

The role of *katabasis*, or 'descent' in the development of the spiritual psyche, is a topic that has been relatively unexplored in hagiographic literature, particularly in the stories of the Orthodox matericon, or 'mothers of the church' in the Middle East. Stories of these saints have survived both through oral tradition and through the synaxarion, which has not quite been approached from a post-Jungian perspective. Many female saints in these texts have, in one way or another, escaped patriarchy, embarking on journeys of ascension toward spirituality, but by *descending* into various circumstances of self-destitution. A post-Jungian revisiting of this literature will show how, in addition to eliding a patriarchic social system, female saints

DOI: 10.4324/9781003054139-11

such as Barbara, Thecla, and Marina the Monk have achieved spiritual development, or individuation, by seeking refuge in maternal landscapes; they fled to camouflaging natural environments, katabic womb-like abysses such as dark settings, cavernous spaces, and forests, which were sites where an inner *coniunctio* takes place. Nature, and these natural landscapes specifically, plays a very important role in the psychic development of these saints during *katabasis*, as it is also a reflection of the nature inside – the archetypes[4]; it is also through descension into the dark that these saints reach the 'light' of their sainthood, or individuation, for as Jung notes, '[W]hen they [the mystics] descend into the depths of their own being they find '"in their heart" the image of the sun'.[5] Nevertheless, the saints' descent into such settings in these hagiographies re-unites their human nature with that of the natural world, an important factor in individuation. As Susan Rowland opines,

> [...] for Jung nature is both inside the human in archetypes and outside in the synchronous universe. Myth is equally a personal, individual and also cultural language that unites psyche and nature; it is a language knitting the human into the nonhuman. [...] Myth in literature re-makes us as part of nature.[6]

Under the umbrella of *katabasis* and post-Jungian studies, feminine hagiographic literature has been relatively unexplored and under-approached as literary text, for as Maureen Murdock points out, the more commonly studied 'Hero's Journey' focuses on, spiritually, 'the masculine journey of up and out into the God realm instead of down and in into the realm of the Goddess'.[7] However, *Katabasis* in female hagiography, as a matter of fact, is this descent into the sacred feminine realm of nature, where bonding with the greater feminine in womb-like natural settings, allows for a journey toward inner balance. The result is the emergence of a heroine, a spiritually advanced 'holy' female figure.

## What Is *Katabasis*?

According to Jung, the 'motif of the Nekyia is found everywhere in antiquity and practically all over the world'.[8] From a literary standpoint, one can make the analogy that saints in hagiography are like heroes in myths, in that both saints and mythological heroes need to overcome some evil force, or dragon, which creates the Hero and Dragon motif. A variation of this motif, though, is what Jung speaks about in his Tavistock Lectures as the *katabasis*, the Descent into the Cave – also called the *nekyia*. Although there are some literal examples of these descents into caves in all three hagiographic stories to be discussed (which are part of the settings' natural landscape), these events reflect the changing psychic structures of the heroes through their own personal katabatic experiences, which 'expresses the psychological mechanism of introversion of the conscious mind into the deeper layers of the unconscious psyche'.⁹ Amid their passions and trials, as they descend into natural caves, they simultaneously enter a new womb, where they are cocooned before being liberated into a new state of individuation:

> [...] the Nekyia is no aimless or destructive fall into the abyss, but a meaningful *katabasis eis antron*, a descent into the cave of initiation and secret knowledge. The journey through the psychic history of mankind has its object the restoration of the whole man, by awakening the memories in the blood.
>
> (pp. 139–140)

Jung tends, then, to see the fruitfulness of what may seem like a dark period, a descent into hell, or a time of trials and hardships in the lives of heroes. It is a rite of passage, a necessary stage before an initiation into a new psychic experience. The depth of the descent, therefore, corresponds to the new explorations of the deeper layers of unconscious after which the hero changes forever; to quote James Hillman, '[T]he nekyia takes the soul into a depth for its own sake so that there is no "return,"'[10] for 'to know the psyche at its basic depths [...] one must go to the underworld'.[11] Thus, the stories of these saints tend to reflect the journey to the nekyia, in context of the heroine instead of the hero.

## Stories of the Saints

### Saint Thecla

Thecla, a young noblewoman, sits by the window for three days without eating or drinking, listening to Paul's teachings. She immediately becomes convinced of the idea of celibacy and rejects marrying her fiancé, Thamyris. As a consequence, Thamyris puts Paul in prison. Thecla, nevertheless, runs off to see Paul in prison, where her family 'went and found her, so to say, chained to him by affection'.[12] Thecla's mother, Theoclia, demands that her daughter be burnt, 'burn the wicked one, burn her who will not marry in the midst of the theatre, that all the women who have been taught by this man may be afraid',[13] and for Paul to be cast out of the city. While at the stake, Thecla sees the Lord in the likeness of Paul, ascending to heaven. She then crosses herself, and rain and hail fall, putting out the flames, and allowing her to flee: 'A cloud full of water and hail overshadowed the theatre from above, and all its contents were poured out so that many were in danger of death. And the fire was put out and Thecla saved'.[14]

Paul, meanwhile, was fasting on a tomb with his friend Onesiphorus and his family (for six days), and the latter's son is hungry so Paul gives him a cloak to sell and buy food with the money. While at the market, the boy sees Thecla, tells her about Paul, and leads her to him at the tomb, where all rejoice at the reunion. There, Thecla informs Paul of her wish to cut her hair and follow him: 'I will cut my hair off and I shall follow you wherever you go'.[15] Paul objects, and when Thecla also asks him to baptize her, he also refuses and tells her to be patient.

After that, Paul and Thecla travel to Antioch, where a Syrian influential citizen, Alexander, harasses her in the street: 'But he, being of great power, embraced her in the street. But she would not endure it'.[16] Thecla, to the amusement of the crowds, tears his clothes and throws his crown; as a result, he takes her to the governor for attacking a nobleman. Consequently, Thecla is condemned to the wild beasts, but the women objected. While waiting for her execution, Thecla was under Queen Tryphaena's protection. The latter had recently lost her daughter and was grieving, so Thecla consoled her. While there, a lioness was tied to Thecla's leg, but instead of harming her, the lioness licks Thecla's feet. Tryphaena asks Thecla to pray for her deceased daughter, and she cries for Thecla, who is taken to the beasts, naked. The lioness protects her, then dies with the lion while fighting it. After that, Thecla throws herself in water to baptize herself; 'and there was round her a cloud of fire so that neither the beasts touch her nor could she be seen naked'.[17] Bulls were tied to her feet, but as they charged, the fire consumed the ropes; Tryphaena then faints and the governor thinks that she is dead, so he then orders to set Thecla free, lest Caesar destroy the city because (they think) his relative Tryphaena is dead. The governor then asks Thecla who she is, to whom she replies: 'I am the servant of the living God'.[18] He then orders garments for her to wear and releases her. Afterward, Thecla stays with Tryphaena for eight days and preaches to the whole house, whom she converts to Christianity.

After leaving Tryphaena's house, Thecla seeks Paul by dressing like a man and going to Myra; she finds him, tells him about her experiences, and then gives him some of the riches Tryphaena gave her so he can donate them to the poor. Thecla then sets off toward Iconium, where she finds her mother (but Thamyris dead) and speaks to her about Christianity. Unsuccessful in changing her mother's mind, or softening her heart, Thecla proceeds to Seleucia,[19] where she preaches for 72 years.[20] According to the synaxarion, Thecla lived a hermetic life there, inside a cave, and developed the gift of healing, performing miraculous cures until she caught the annoyance of a local physician, since people would seek her out instead of coming to him. The physician attributed Thecla's healing powers to her virginity, so he hired a group of men to rape her at her old age; while fleeing from their attack, these men surround her. Praying to God for help, a rock that miraculously opened and closed her in.[21]

### Saint Barbara

Barbara was the beautiful young daughter of Dioscorus, a rich merchant in the Heliopolis region (Baalbek, Lebanon today). After the death of her mother, Barbara's father was obsessed about protecting her, so he kept her in a tower, where she would receive her food by pulling a basket tied to a rope. The only people allowed to see her were her pagan teachers and her father. She would, nonetheless, gaze at the hills and sky outside the window every day and wonder about the creating force behind them. She soon came to realize that there was a real power behind creation, unlike the soulless man-made idols that her father worshipped.[22] Therefore, she made it a life mission to know the Creator, the true God, and despite the many suitors who sought her hand in marriage, Barbara refused to get married and insisted on retaining her virginity. This worried her father, who thought the seclusion was beginning to affect her mind, so he decided to allow her some freedom to explore the world beyond the tower. Consequently, Barbara met many young Christian maidens, who taught her about the new religion; Barbara then was baptized by a priest who arrived from Alexandria dressed as a merchant.

Dioscorus, before traveling for business, asked for a private bathhouse to be built at his house, and he asked to have two windows in it. Despite that, Barbara asked the laborers to build a third window, in honor of the holy trinity, and she traced a cross with her finger on one of the walls, and her footprints were embossed on the steps of the bathhouse. The water of the bathhouse then became known for its healing powers and allowed for many miracles to happen. Upon discovering this after his return, Dioscorus was enraged at his daughter's conversion, and in his fit of anger, he attempted to strike her with a sword. Even so, Barbara, dressed in a disguise, fled before her father could hit her. She ran through the wheat fields as her father ran after her; miraculously though, Dioscorus's path was blocked by a hill, which opened up and hid Barbara inside it until she was able to find the path from the crevice up the hill, where she took shelter in a cave. Local oral tradition also has it that Barbara was dressed up in a disguise and camouflaged with the wheat fields in order to escape Dioscorus. Meanwhile, Dioscorus was still desperately seeking Barbara, and he asked a couple of shepherds about her whereabouts. He managed to make the second shepherd lead him to Barbara's cave, where he beat her and dragged her to Martianus, the prefect of the city, who ordered more corporeal punishment for the young girl, striking her with rawhide and rubbing her wounds with haircloth. At night, Barbara would pray to Jesus, who appeared to her and healed her wounds. After seeing her healed in the mornings, the torturers would subject Barbara to more punishments, but whatever damage they caused would be healed again overnight.

Among the crowd witnessing the trials of Barbara was a young pious woman named Juliana, who felt sorry for the tortured youth and also wanted to suffer for Christ. Juliana began to shout and protest against the torturers until they took her with Barbara; both were raked, pierced with hooks, and paraded naked in the streets – but upon the prayers of Barbara, they were both made decent by a splendid robe from an angel. After that, both women were beheaded, Barbara at the hands of her own father. The beheaders, though, did not survive after their wrongdoings, as they were both instantly killed by lightning strikes.

### Saint Marina the Monk

Saint Marina was born around the 5th century in North Lebanon, to pious parents Ibrahim and Baddoura (also known as Eugene and Theodora in some texts). Marina's mother died a few years after, while her daughter was still very young. Marina had a devout Christian upbringing by her father, and as she approached adulthood, her father decided to retire in a monastery after his daughter was married, since she was a woman and he did know what else to do with her. However, Marina refused to get married and insisted on following her father, asking him why he wanted to save his own soul and destroy hers. After that, Ibrahim/Eugene accepted and donated all his property to the poor before embarking on his journey with Marina, who shaved her hair and wore men's clothing in order to live the monastic life under the name of 'Marinos the monk'.

Ten years later, Ibrahim/Eugene died and Marina continued her ascetic life as a man at the monastery. None of the monks noticed her feminine traits, except for her soft voice, which they attributed to her alternations between silence and long periods of prayer. One day though, she was sent with three other monks on a church mission, and they had to spend a night at an inn during their long journey. On that same night, there was a Roman soldier also staying at the inn, and he took fancy in the innkeeper's daughter, thereby seducing her and taking away her virginity. He warned her that if she were to become pregnant, she should never let anyone know of the father's identity; instead, she was to say that it was Marinos the monk who had raped her. A few months later, this is what actually happened, leading Marinos into the abyss of predicament, as he was told to confess his sins and leave the monastery; he did not deny fathering the child and was made to sit at the gates of the monastery like a beggar for a long time.

When the innkeeper's daughter gave birth to a child, a boy, the grandfather took him and gave him to Marinos to raise. Marina stayed with the child in a cave, and she fed him sheep's milk until one day a miracle happened and she was able to nurse the baby with her own milk. Ten years later, Marinos's fellow monks were able to convince the abbot to bring him back to the monastery under the conditions that he must do some laborious tasks, such as cooking and cleaning in addition to his other monastic duties.

One day, Marina became severely ill and died after three days. Upon preparing the body for funeral rites, the monks discovered that Marinos the monk was actually a woman and not a man, thereby realizing her innocence in the whole innkeeper's story. This caused the abbot some great distress, and he prayed and wept bitterly by Marina's side before informing the innkeeper of the truth. The innkeeper and his daughter were forever tormented, and they cried and begged forgiveness for all their wrongdoings.[23]

## Common Factors in These Hagiographies

After reading these stories of saints Thecla, Barbara, and Marina the Monk, we notice that all three young women went against the current, which led to their descent into the hell of castration and suffering. Withal, going against their parental religion *per se* was not really the only reason that caused their fates, but upon looking closely (as that was not the case for Marina, for example), we realize that the culprit was actually their absconding patriarchy and the imposed social system that comes along with it (imposed marriage and/or sexual and religious identity). As Coline Covington asserts, '[A] female hero is essentially the woman warrior whose battles take place within the male world'.[24] Moreover, Bradley TePaske, in *Sexuality and the Religious Imagination*, points out at how 'Whitmont explores the ways in which patriarchal hierarchies enforce a repression of the feminine and effect a sharp dissociation between the heroic ego and the instinctual shadow'. Their heroic egos struggle to ultimately conquer their shadows (family, community, government) through their spiritual development in the end. The female saints discussed in this paper seem to be going against this patriarchic hierarchy, where there is the 'heroic ego-consciousness that identifies itself with the aerial solar pole of masculine spirit'.[25] In the discussed stories, the saints seem to move away from the masculine heroic ego-consciousness and toward nature during *katabasis*, when they hid and dwelled in caves and wheat fields: '[...] a movement towards reconnection with body, nature, and all things nonhierarchical'.[26]

Another obvious connection between Thecla, Barbara, and Marina, of course, would be that they all descend into *katabasis* on the road to ascension; they go through self-abnegation, persona suppression, disguising, and seeking refuge in maternal landscapes of cavernous nature – ultimately making a new connection not only with nature and spirit but also with their bodies. Consequently, their *katabasis* is a fruitful developmental stage that takes place within the inner folds of nature and the psyche; it is a 'cocooning' before the emergence of the hero-saint, the manifestation of the warrior within.

## Going against the Current and Separating from the Feminine

Part of the saints' escapes from the imposed patriarchic system is a separation from their own gender identities and their roles as imposed by society. These are women seeking individuation in a world where men hold power – an animus-possessed society that identifies itself with the masculine; however, as Elizabeth Eowyn Nelson asserts, 'for Jungians, viewing power as masculine is antithetical to the theory of individuation because it effectively truncates the possibility of a woman's wholeness.[27] Thecla, Barbara, and Marina's identification with the masculine is seen on many levels. But seeking wholeness, they need to go against patriarchy and at the same time identify with the masculine. This is what Maureen Murdock would see as the heroine's separation from the feminine on the heroine's journey, which would later conclude with an identification with the masculine.[28] First, they all separate from the feminine in many ways, first being a separation from the mother: Thecla's mother is evil and seeks to persecute her own daughter who flees, and both Barbara's and Marina's mothers die while they are at a young age. In addition to separation from their mothers, the three girls also separate from their expected cultural and institutional gender roles as wives, since all of them reject marriage: Thecla leaves her fiancé Thymiris, Barbara refuses all her suitors, and Marina leads a monastic life. Finally, they all disconnect from their feminine physical appearance. Perhaps this way they separate from all the negative associations with the feminine, where 'the splitting off of badness, and the bad mother, is somatized in a splitting off of the body'.[29] This is shown through the physical transvestitism — Marina and Thecla both shave their heads and wear men's clothing, while Barbara disguises herself, eliding her father by hiding in the wheat fields. Despite this, the heroine remains clean, pure, innocent, 'unconnected to her anger, i.e. shadowless, and is consequently persecuted'.[30]

## The Identification with the Masculine

Thecla, Barbara, and Marina further go against the current by identifying with the masculine. By dressing as men, Thecla and Marina not only separate from the feminine in order to escape their expected gender roles, but perhaps each of them 'wishes to identify with the masculine or to be rescued by the masculine. When a woman decides to break with the established images of the feminine she inevitably begins the traditional hero's journey. She puts on her armor […]'.[31] Therefore, they look for male role models — Christ being the primary one, as well as Paul (for Thecla) and the father (for Marina). In the case of Thecla, she identifies with Paul, whereas Marina, by following her father to the monastery, she becomes one of the father's daughters, who 'organize their lives around the masculine principle, either remaining connected to an outer man or being driven from within by a masculine mode'.[32] By separating from their feminine social aspect and escaping marriage, they decide to follow into the footsteps of the men idols in their lives, and connecting with a savior masculine image by declaring themselves the brides of Christ. This is the driving force that leads them to descend into a series of trials, and ultimately, in Barbara's case, martyrdom. Therefore, their identification with the masculine is not necessarily the saints' own inner masculinity, along with connecting with their male role models, but the outer patriarchal masculine with power as its driving force (be it dressing up as 'men' in society, standing up for their beliefs, or identifying with their inner masculine voices, mainly those of God or Christ). During their descent, and within the turmoil of persecution and the protective roofs of feminine landscapes, 'masculine consciousness often tries to help the feminine to speak. In other words, it jumps in and takes over'.[33]

During the descent, 'there is a desire to spend more time in nature being nurtured by the earth.'[34] This stage in the heroine's journey 'may involve a seemingly endless period of wandering, grief, and rage, of dethroning kings [...]',[35] of further escape from society and its institutionalization of many natural inclinations like gender roles and spirituality — the three women sought after a spiritual message that was not yet institutionalized, but one they reached through personal experiences and offered them mystical paths in life. The original religions that Thecla and Barbara were brought up in, for example, were imposed on them; yet the rebelliousness involved in adopting the 'new' religion was a breaking free from the chains of society, and a new adventure within the secret folds of nature. According to Richard Naegle, institutional religion protects and excludes — absconding institution had actually excluded the saints, who found protection in nature. Their *katabasis* was a descent resulting from exclusion, which ended them up in a protective (womb-like) subterranean setting, both mentally and environmentally. It is the fleeing from codified dogma in favor of the experience: 'The dogma, the religion protects us, because many scriptures say it's a terrible thing to fall into the hands of the living God, it's an awesome light and dark cosmic event, and so the myths or the religions contain us.'[36] The structure of their local religion, or even the social system (patriarchy) had traditionally helped contain, but when the saints embark on their individual journeys and descend into the 'darkness' of the unconventional, their *katabasis* allows them to have powerful mystical experiences that can be overwhelming.

### *Katabasis*, Nature Landscapes, Reconnection: from Institution to Instinct

Disconnection is always the way to reconnection, for as Susan Rowland points out, 'we cannot connect without first being separated, and vice versa'; these women have separated themselves from society and from the feminine as seen by it, escaping the popular beliefs of the 'fathers' (reflected through patriarchy), but by finding unity of this consciousness with nature. To achieve this, they wandered into their own *katabasis*, to unite this consciousness with nature. Jung claims that 'the heroes are usually wanderers, and wandering is a symbol of longing, of the restless urge which never finds its object, of nostalgia for the lost mother'.[37] Moving into the next stage then, is a time of wandering and hardship, for 'the female hero is also characterized by sacrifice'.[38] During this descent, the task is to reclaim the discarded repressed parts of oneself that were split off in the original separation from the feminine. These are the parts of the self that were perhaps ignored or devalued — feelings, connection with the body, with creativity, and intuition:

> A woman moves down into the depth to reclaim the parts of herself
> that split off when she rejected the mother and shattered the mirror of
> the feminine. To make this journey a woman puts aside her fascination
> with the intellect and games of the cultural mind, and acquaints herself,

perhaps for the first time, with her body, her emotions, […] her intuition, her images, her values, and her mind. This is what she will find in the depths. When a woman makes her descent, she may feel stripped bare, dismembered or even devoured by rage. She experienced it as a loss of identity, a falling away of the perimeters of a known role and the fear that accompanies loss […] and she may spend a long time there in the dark waiting while life goes on up above.[39]

This stage is also reminiscent of Campbell's monomyth, the idea of the descent, 'the courage to seek the depths',[40] where he talks about the call of the soul: these female saints consciously respond to the calls of their souls, accepting the spiritual invitation to re-create themselves anew, and undertake the challenges that the descent provides, despite feeling frightened or inadequate. The katabatic experience, therefore, is an opportunity to heal the part they had cut off of themselves during the initial separation from the feminine, the mother. Descending into *katabasis*-like settings is like a 'withdrawal into a maternal nexus in reaction to the paternal nexus',[41] where womb-like settings reconnect 'the maiden to a good, nourishing mother […]'[42] during the descent into nature, preparing them for the next stage. In their *katabasis* there is a return to the values of the gynolatric period, a descent to a realm where the Great Goddess, manifesting the archetypal feminine, is 'mistress of the stars and heavens, the beauty of nature, generating womb, nurturing power of earth and fertility, fulfiller of all needs, but also the power of death and the horror of decay and annihilation. From her all proceeds and to her all returns'.[43] The descent into the 'womb' of nature enriches the sainthood experience with the divinity of the feminine. Nature becomes a channel for divine expression; it is not the heroic masculine, but through *katabasis*, it becomes the home – the nurturing womb – of the heroine. This is what happens during a fruitful *katabasis*:

> The Feminine is not concerned with achieving or ideating. It is not heroic, self-willed and bent upon battling against opposition. Rather, it exists in the here and now and the endless flow. It values the vegetal dimension of growth-decay, the continuity and conservation of natural orders. It expresses the will of nature and of instinctual forces rather the self-will of a particular person. The feminine form of consciousness is global, field, and process oriented. It is functional rather than abstract and conceptual. It is devoid as yet of the strict dichotomy of inner-outer or body-mind.[44]

There are clouds, mountains, sudden chasmic formations, caves, thunder, and milk flow as part of this 'vegetal dimension'. The divine is seen to manifest itself through nature, showing the feminine counterpart of the male god worshipped by the newly initiated saints: 'The divine forces, intrinsic to nature and the object world, are worshipped and seen as manifest in human and animal bodies, plants, stones, earth, sky, and stars'.[45] The enwombment within nature, then, can be seen as a return to the instinctive side of humanity (from institution to instinct via nature). Katabatic landscapes are anima projections or manifestations of the realm of the anima with all its danger and darkness: 'With the archetype of the anima we enter the realm of the gods, or rather, the realm that metaphysics has reserved for itself. Everything the anima touches becomes numinous – unconditional, dangerous, taboo, magical'.[46]

Notwithstanding, the saint-heroine is not entirely alone during her journey. The people she meets on her way 'perform the task of the transcendent function and enable [the saints] to experience connectedness to a primal mother and to resolve an inner split'.[47] In the case of Barbara, there is Juliana to come to her rescue, eventually joining her in martyrdom. Thecla, on the other hand, takes Paul as a guide and teacher, and Marina, after her father's death, gains strength from the motherhood she is suddenly endowed with when receiving the child.

## The Effect of *Katabasis*

The periods spent by saints in the caves, wheat fields, and mountain crevices are times of reflection and spiritual incubation, in which their individuation processes are at work. The wilderness itself, with its darkness and danger, reflects the unconscious and its unknown, mysterious contents; furthermore, 'it symbolizes the maternal source from which the individual emerges as the tree is born within the forest'.[48] Thecla, Barbara, and Marina do not embark on adventures filled with conquests, dragon-slaying, or physical combats; their adventures are journeys of disconnection and separation from society and institutionalization of values and ideals, followed by a fleeing into nature after or during periods of physical and psychological torture seeking oneness of the self through ascetic experience. These three saints, engulfed within the folds of nature, turn their katabatic experiences into fetus-like periods of growth and nurture – within the different cavernous womb-like shelters. While hiding in the caves and no action seems to take place, these women are actually experiencing the most pivotal points in their individuation journeys, while in the darkest depths of the wilderness. This is when Thecla and Barbara develop healing powers, and when Marina is able to breastfeed and mother a child given to her. According to Covington again, 'The heroine cannot truly act for herself until she is able to internalize her experience of matter (mater or mother). What marks her out is not simply her state of dependency, but how her dependency is transformed'.[49] Thus, the saints' abilities to 'form an inner connection with mother' show by the development of their special healing/nursing powers: 'Autonomy for the heroine is achieved not through doing, or making things happen, or going out into the world. It is during her period in the forest, when nothing appears to happen, that things change and her plight is resolved'.[50]

## Conclusion

At some point in their journeys, the hero-saints connect with the feminine: after Thecla returns to unsuccessfully confront her biological mother, she leaves once more and becomes a healer in another land; Marina reconnects with the feminine in her body through the miracle of breastfeeding, and Barbara develops an awareness of her body (and asks the angels to make her decent by covering her nudity). But most importantly, they all achieve ascension as the 'brides of Christ'; hence, their *katabasis* succeeds in 'shifting the center of gravity from the ego to the self, from man to God', wherein 'the ego disappears in the self, and man in God'.[51] At the end of their journeys, their *coniunctio*, or sacred marriage, takes place: they integrate the masculine and feminine parts of the self through what they had learned along their road of trials. As 'brides of Christ', they have finally achieved the synthesis after their separation from the feminine and rejection of the masculine: they have developed a masculine consciousness after reconnecting with the feminine during their *katabasis*. This echoes Jung in Richard Evans's *Conversations with Carl Jung and Reactions from Ernest Jones*, where he comments on the role of the animus in a woman's mystical journey:

> When a woman realizes her shadow the animus can be constellated. If the shadow remains in the unconscious the animus possesses her through the shadow. When she realizes her animus, mystical generation can occur.[52]

Separating from the feminine, simultaneously recognizing their shadow and identifying their masculine, then, leads them to the series of events ultimately ending in their 'mystical generation'. Their trials and periods of seclusion were actually times of a fruitful darkness, when, as TePaske posits, 'The abysmal maternal aspect of the feminine is activated [...] the personal anima working in harmony with Mother Earth', giving them 'ambivalent archetypal power'.[53] As women, they all seem to remember their true nature and accept themselves as they are; they have developed a new feminine consciousness and are now aware of an equally strong masculine consciousness, which has helped them to get their voices out into the world, even at the cost of martyrdom (as in the case of Barbara). The lifelong task they succeed in is the integration of all aspects of their nature along the path of experiencing the divine outside of the convention of institutions.

## Notes

1 E.E. Nelson, 'Fierce Young Women in Popular fiction and Unpopular War', in *Feminist Views from Somewhere*, London: Routledge, 2017, pp. 99–117 (p. 109).
2 C.G. Jung, *Psychology and Religion: West and East* [*Collected Works*, vol. 11], Princeton, NJ: Princeton University Press, 1975, p. 294.
3 Nelson, 'Fierce Young Women', p. 100.

4 The archetypes as 'nature' comes from the notion that they exist within the psyche, rooted in the human body, within our biological being. In *Remembering Dionysus*, Susan Rowland comments on Ross Woodman's observation that 'Jung's notion of the archetype inheres in humanity through the body's connection to the psyche'; see S. Rowland, *Remembering Dionysus: Revisioning Psychology and Literature in C. G. Jung and James Hillman*, London: Routledge, 2017, p. 93.

5 C.G. Jung, *Symbols of Transformation: An Analysis of the Prelude to a Case of Schizophrenia* [*Collected Works*, vol. 5], London and New York: Routledge, 2014, p. 122.

6 S. Rowland, *Jungian Literary Criticism*, London: Routledge, 2018, p. 157.

7 Maureen Murdock, interview by David Van Nuys, 15 April 2007, in Shrink Rap Radio #85; available online HTTP: https://shrinkrapradio. com/85-the-heroines-journey/

8 C.G. Jung, *The Spirit in Man, Art and Literature* [*Collected Works*, vol. 15], Princeton, NJ: Princeton University Press, 1978, p. 38.

9 Jung, *The Spirit in Man, Art and Literature*, p. 38.

10 J. Hillman, *The Dream and the Underworld*, New York: Harper Collins, 1979, p. 168.

11 Hillman, *The Dream and the Underworld*, p. 46.

12 'The Acts of Paul and Thecla', in *The Apocryphal New Testament*, ed. and tr. by J.K. Elliott, Oxford: Oxford University Press, 1993, p. 180.

13 'Acts of Paul and Thecla', in *Apocryphal New Testament*, p. 180.

14 'Acts of Paul and Thecla', in *Apocryphal New Testament*, p. 180.

15 'Acts of Paul and Thecla', in *Apocryphal New Testament*, p. 180.

16 'Acts of Paul and Thecla', in *Apocryphal New Testament*, p. 180.

17 'Acts of Paul and Thecla', in *Apocryphal New Testament*, p. 181.

18 'Acts of Paul and Thecla', in *Apocryphal New Testament*, p. 182.

19 According to the version in the synaxarion, Thecla went to 'the Syrian Silifkia', or what is known today as Maaloula, Syria.

20 One version of the story, in the *Acts of Paul and Thecla*, mentions that afterwards, Thecla rests in a glorious sleep.

21 توما بيطار, سير القديسين و سائر الاعياد في الكنيسة الأرثوكسية (السنكسار), الجزء الأول: أيلول-تشرين الأول-تشرين الثاني, دوما: عائلة الثالوث القدوس, 2007
[T. Bitar, *Lives of the Saints and their Feast Days in the Orthodox Church (Synaxarion)*, vol. 1, 2nd edn, Douma, Lebanon: Holy Trinity Family, 2007, p. 118.]

22 توما بيطار , سير القديسين و سائر الاعياد في الكنيسة الأرثوكسية (السنكسار), الجزء الثاني:كانون الأول-كانون الثاني, دوما: عائلة الثالوث القدوس, 2009
[T. Bitar, *Lives of the Saints and their Feast Days in the Orthodox Church (Synaxarion)*, vol. 2, 2nd edn, Douma, Lebanon: Holy Trinity Family, 2009, pp. 32–33]

23 توما بيطار, سير القديسين و سائر الاعياد في الكنيسة الأرثوكسية (السنكسار), الجزء الثالث:شباط-أذار, دوما: عائلة الثالوث القدوس, 2017
[T. Bitar, *Lives of the Saints and their Feast Days in the Orthodox Church (Synaxarion)*, vol. 2, 2nd edn, Douma, Lebanon: Holy Trinity Family, 2017, pp. 94–95]

24 C. Covington, 'In Search of the Heroine', in L. Gardner and F. Gray (eds), *Feminist Views from Somewhere*, London: Routledge, 2017, pp. 70–79 (p. 70).

25 B. TePaske, *Sexuality and the Religious Imagination*, New Orleans: Spring Journal Books, 2008, p. 29.

26 TePaske, *Sexuality and the Religious Imagination*, p. 30.

27 Nelson, 'Fierce Young Women', p. 99.

28   Murdock, interview on Shrink Rap Radio #85.
29   Covington, 'In Search of the Heroine', p. 75.
30   Covington, 'In Search of the Heroine', p. 75.
31   M. Murdock, *The Heroine's Journey: Woman's Quest for Wholeness*, Boston: Shambhala, 1990, p. 36.
32   Murdock, *The Heroine's Journey*, pp. 29–30.
33   Murdock, interview on Shrink Rap Radio #85.
34   Murdock, *The Heroine's Journey*, p. 8.
35   Murdock, *The Heroine's Journey*, p. 8.
36   Richard Naegle, interview by David Van Nuys, 15 April 2007, on Shrink Rap Radio #295, available online HTTP: https://shrinkrapradio.com/295-mythology-and-the-spiritual-journey-with-richard-naegle-phd/
37   Jung, *Symbols of Transformation*, p. 203.
38   Covington, 'In Search of the Heroine', p. 70.
39   Murdock, *The Heroine's Journey*, p. 90.
40   J. Campbell and P. Cousineau (eds), *The Hero's Journey: Joseph Campbell on his Life and Work*, Novato, CA: New World Library, 1990, p. xxiv.
41   Covington, 'In Search of the Heroine', p. 74.
42   Covinton, 'In Search of the Heroine', p. 70.
43   E.C. Whitmont, *The Return of the Goddess*, New York: Continuum, 2001, p. 42.
44   Whitmont, *The Return of the Goddess*, p. 43.
45   Whitmont, *The Return of the Goddess*, p. 43.
46   TePaske, *Sexuality and the Religious Imagination*, p. 26.
47   Covington, 'In Search of the Heroine', p. 74.
48   Covington, 'In Search of the Heroine', p. 74.
49   Covington, 'In Search of the Heroine', p. 77.
50   Covington, 'In Search of the Heroine', p. 79.
51   Jung, *Psychology and Religion* [*CW* 11], §958.
52   R. Evans, *Conversations with Carl Jung and Reactions from Ernest Jones*, New York: Insight Books, 1964, p. 30.
53   TePaske, *Sexuality and the Religious Imagination*, p. 23.

# Part III

# Katábasis in Theory

# Chapter 9

# Raising Hell

## Freud's Katabatic Metaphors in *The Interpretation of Dreams*

*Jonathan Shann*

*Flectere si nequeo Superos, Acheronta movebo*[1]

This epigraph from Vergil's *Aeneid* (VII.312) stands on the title page of *The Interpretation of Dreams* (1900) – at the threshold of a new century and Freud the conquistador's entry into the kingdom of the dynamic unconscious.[2] Freud circles back to it again only a few pages before the volume's close where (from the 1909 edition onward) it is immediately followed by the most famous sentence in the whole book: '*The interpretation of dreams is the royal road to a knowledge of the unconscious activities of the mind*'.[3] In this chapter, I will explore some aspects of Freud's metaphoric invocation of the infernal regions – Furies, Titans, Tartarus, shades, Odysseus's *nekyia*, psychoanalysis as 'labour in the depths', underworld rivers, royal roads – in the context of the *katabasis*, or descent into the underworld. My main focus is on a handful of core metaphors from Freud's dream book, but I will also explore metaphors in later works that derive from or augment those core metaphors, especially the Vergilian epigraph. I will argue that Freud's distinctive use of metaphor holds polarities in creative tension, notably that of conquistador versus outsider and is both constitutive and subversive of his theory-building.

This line of Vergil's Latin lay long on Freud's mind. In a letter dated 4 December 1896, he shared with Wilhelm Fliess various mottoes for his work-in-progress, ascribing this one to a chapter on symptom formation. Again writing to Fliess some two and a half years later, Freud called it 'a reference to repression'. 'In addition to my manuscript', he said, 'I am taking the Lasalle [sic] and a few works on the unconscious with me to Berchtesgaden'.[4] The significance of this choice of holiday reading is illuminated by Freud's admission in 1927 to Werner Achelis that he borrowed the Vergilian epigraph from the Prussian-German Jewish socialist Ferdinand Lassalle (1825–1864), 'in whose case it was probably meant personally and relating to social – not psychological – classifications'. In Freud's usage, he said, it was 'meant merely to emphasize the most important part in the dynamics of the dream. The wish rejected by the higher mental agencies (the repressed dream wish) stirs

DOI: 10.4324/9781003054139-13

up the mental underworld (the unconscious) in order to get a hearing'.[5] Carl
E. Schorske notes that Lassalle used the epigraph in '[o]ne of his most brilliant pamphlets' – *The Italian War and the Task of Prussia* (1859) – and concludes that Freud probably read that book (although it may not have been his
1899 vacation reading).[6]

Freud's engagement with Vergil went much further back – to his school-
days: in his final exams, aged seventeen, he graduated *summa cum laude* –
and one of the papers he excelled at was a Latin-German translation of a
passage from Vergil's *Aeneid* which he'd already 'read for his own pleasure'.[7] Justin Glenn argues that Freud's boyhood fantasies included a strong
admiration for (or even an identification with) Aeneas, which influenced his
mature thinking.[8] But there's something dismissive about Freud's references to this epigraph – to Fliess, Freud writes, 'A motto for the dream
[book] has not turned up since you killed Goethe's sentimental one.[9] A
reference to repression is all that will remain', while Freud brushes off
Achelis' description of the Vergilian motto as 'Promethean' and says it
'merely' lends emphasis to the function of repression in dream-work. He
also attributes a 'personal' meaning to the phrase for Lassalle but implicitly
not for himself.[10]

Despite Freud's protestations, Achelis was not alone in finding Freud's epigraph Promethean:

> The mood of the conquistador is reflected in the motto Freud put under
> the title of *The Interpretation of Dreams*, "Flectere si nequeo superos,
> Acheronta movebo"… One can hardly imagine a word more fitting for
> the conqueror's or revolutionary's pride in the power of his discoveries.
> It has a Promethean ring to it, writes Ernest Schachtel.[11]

Yet the capitalized placing of the motto on the title page of *The Interpretation of Dreams*, its recapitulation some six hundred pages later, and
the fact that it remained the sole epigraph to Freud's acknowledged masterpiece through every subsequent edition – all suggest that there's more
to its significance than Freud was willing to admit: to downplay the value
of something prized is itself revealing. In 1925, he felt the need to offer
the public a narrow interpretative reading of it, as if to exclude other,
more suggestive or personal possibilities: it 'is intended to picture the
efforts of the repressed instinctual impulses', he reiterated.[12] Likewise, on
neither occasion when Freud quotes the epigraph does he name either the
author or the speaker, as if to let the words stand for themselves, shorn of
context – Richard Sterba shows how Freud's use of classical quotations
and his expectation that cultivated readers would be familiar with (or at
the very least able to translate) them were hallmarks of his humanistic edu-
cation and spirit, a pervasive influence shaping his thought and values.[13]
I read that as implying both concealment and invitation in Freud's use of
resonant literary quotations.

Vergil's line does neatly suggest the operation of repression, but also the subversion of seemingly impervious higher powers by infernal forces. The link to Lassalle evokes associations with revolution and defiance of the establishment, the clash of old and new. As Henri Ellenberger says, there's 'an element of deliberate but well concealed provocation' here: a challenge to the higher echelons of the Viennese academic and medical community. Peter Heller also reads the epigraph as Freud's riposte to the unbending 'gods of academe'. Peter Gay notes that this 'enigmatic motto [...] subtly intimates that he was both nervous and prepared to be angry [...] the truculent tone of the verse [...] fits well into Freud's defiant mood'. And, we might add, Freud's discreet defiance of bourgeois values generally – Leonard Shengold refers to '[t]his motto of a conquistador with its sexual implications'. It also implies, as Shai Frogel observes, a rejection of some supposedly higher forms of thought (religion, metaphysics) and a tendency to offer reductive explanations of others (art, literature, ethics) by reference to lower mental states (the emotions, the unconscious).[14]

By contrast, James Naiman sees in the Vergilian motto a less aggressive, more depressive reflection of Freud's state of mind: a mixture of self-deprecation, fatalism, and anxiety in the face of the anticipated negative reaction to his work. Percival Bailey takes a more damning view: 'He had failed as a scientist; he had failed as a philosopher; he had never been a physician at heart. So, in the words of Virgil, he wrote: "*Flectere...*"'. Helen Walker Puner proposes a 'freer translation' of the epigraph, 'in the language of Freud's purpose in writing the book': 'If I cannot change my father's attitude towards me, I will let all hell loose'.[15] Perhaps Freud's downplaying of the epigraph and insistence on its narrow reference to the mechanics of repression cloaked more tangled feelings.

Or the focus implied by Freud's narrow construal of the epigraph may, as Jean Starobinski suggests, emphasize or establish 'an isomorphism, or at least an occasional equivalence, between myth and psychological theory', the epigraph offering 'an interpretive illustration, an imaged equivalent of the theory'[16] – not concealment but revelation through the metaphoric invocation of a canonical forbear. Starobinski stresses that the second appearance of the epigraph (which precedes the 'royal road' dictum) is itself immediately preceded by a crux statement which the epigraph itself then crystallizes, condenses, and renders *personal*:

In waking life the suppressed material in the mind [*Das seelisch Unterdrückte*] is prevented from finding expression [*Ausdruck*] and is cut off from internal perception owing to the fact that the contradictions present in it are eliminated – one side being disposed of in favour of the other; but during the night, under the sway of an impetus towards the construction of compromises, this suppressed material finds methods and means of forcing its way into consciousness.[17]

(*Interpretation of Dreams*, 608)

Starobinski presents a close reading of both this passage and the epigraph itself, which has not been bettered (402–405). He highlights the chiastic structure of the epigraph (i.e., a sequential pattern which is repeated in reverse): verb – mythic noun – mythic noun – verb. The first verb is a verbal phrase (*flectere si nequeo*), comprising an active infinitive (to bend) negated by a present tense of impotence (I am not able). The object of this verbal phrase is a mythic noun (*Superos*). The second mythic noun (*Acheronta*) is the object of the final verb (*movebo*). The chiasmus establishes two polarities, one spatial, one temporal: above and below (*Superos/Acheronta*); present (*nequeo*) and future (*movebo*). Each is aligned with states of impotence or action: the present inability to bend the higher powers, the willed future action of moving the lower regions. In Freud's theoretical passage, Starobinski notes the opposition between the neuter and passive *seelisch Unterdrückte* ('suppressed material in the mind'), which is denied *Ausdruck* ('expression'), and the doubled verbs of action *findet* [...] *aufzudrängen* ('finds methods and means of forcing its way into consciousness'). Jumping from the theoretical passage to the epigraph, Freud moves from a realm of non-localized impersonal forces to a personal conflict between supernatural powers. In each case, the forces from below are temporally prior to the forces from above which repress them.

In January 1897, Freud declared to Fliess that his chapter on sexuality would bear another infernal motto: '*vom Himmel durch die Welt zur Hölle*' – [18] a clear image of descent to the underworld, which he later quoted in the *Three Essays on the Theory of Sexuality* (1905).[19] Noting the possibilities for Freud's identification with the hero Aeneas, Didier Anzieu highlights themes from book 6 of the *Aeneid*, in which Aeneas descends into the underworld to consult his dead father, Anchises. Here Aeneas, a martial hero, fled from fallen Troy, encounters a riddling Sybil, an incestuous father (not his own), and terrifying monsters who turn out to be mere shades. The parallels with Freud are striking: outsider status, heroic ambitions, his childhood military fantasies, the work of mourning his father (Jacob Freud died on 23 October 1896),[20] the ambiguous nature of dreams, incestuous wishes, and imaginary terrors – all resonate with Freud's dream book.[21] Stanley Edgar Hyman sees the epigraph as a refutation of Freud's father's prophecy that the boy wouldn't amount to anything in life: 'Freud is a mythic hero who has made the dangerous journey into the underworld and come back with the treasure, and in this respect the book's form is that of a successful mythic quest'.[22]

Yet Freud's epigraph is not from book 6 of the *Aeneid* but the book which follows it. The *Aeneid* tells the epic tale of Aeneas's flight from Troy and the foundation of Rome: the first six books are his *Odyssey*, his wanderings from Troy to Latium to find his true home, the second six his *Iliad*, the war with Turnus. The *katabasis* of book 6 therefore closes the Odyssean section (love and home) and our epigraph comes from the beginning of the Iliadic part (hate and strife). The speaker of the motto is the goddess Juno. She is cursing Aeneas – to whom she is implacably opposed. It's a cry of defeat, albeit a defiant one: 'But I, great wife of Jove [...] am vanquished by Aeneas', she says, a couple of lines earlier.[23] As she cannot persuade her husband, Jupiter, to prevent Aeneas from escaping and going on to found Rome, the eternal city, she calls on the forces of the underworld – and sets a snake-haired Fury, Allecto, on Aeneas's trail. If she can't halt destiny, Juno will delay it – and make Aeneas suffer, if only for a while.

For Anzieu, Allecto personifies persecutory anxiety – and the episode tells us that the descent into the unconscious springs unknown powers into action. By contrast, Naiman thinks the quotation inapposite, because Juno's words are charged with aggressive, not sexual, wishes.[24] We might counter that Freud did not hold that all dreams were rooted in sexual wishes (aggressive wishes are apparent in the foundational dream of psychoanalysis, the dream of Irma's injection,[25] and elsewhere in Freud's dream book) – and that the primacy of aggression in Juno's words anticipates Freud's later focus on hatred, sadism, destructiveness, and his later postulation of the death drive.[26]

Jean-Bertrand Pontalis regards the themes of death and sexuality as equally constitutive of psychoanalysis, holding that sexuality is often given greater prominence to eclipse death's import, rooting his analysis in Freud's own fears of mortality. He argues that *The Interpretation of Dreams* marks a shift in Freud's attitude to death, a metaphoric move from death imaged as a figure in a painting to a psychic drama. Death, he contends, is no longer seen primarily as an external threat to psychosomatic integrity but as a wish framed by the Oedipal triangle and focused on the parental rival.[27] By its complex, implicit, and discreet foregrounding of Juno, I suggest, the Vergilian epigraph conveys Freud's official, literal message (the repression of prohibited, primarily sexual, wishes) while concealing an underlying theme of destructiveness, defeat, death, and loss. Hence, Freud's insistence that the epigraph be read simply as a technical description of the operation of repression. Both sexual and aggressive feelings are centred upon the mother, and both are suppressed, such that the image of the mother herself is veiled. Hyman identifies a succession of path and landscape metaphors in *The Interpretation of Dreams* and concludes that 'all of these dark woods, narrow defiles, high grounds and deep penetrations are unconscious sexual imagery, and we are exploring a woman's body, that of Freud's mother'.[28] We can add that the archaic, hating mother, Juno, is evoked still more elliptically than the erotic mother. Yet she, too, is here. For Frogel, the epigraph 'indicates that Freud's thinking was rooted in death from its very beginning'.[29]

While both the Faustian tag '*vom Himmel durch die Welt zur Hölle*' and Aeneas's descent to the underworld imply *katabasis*, Juno's words invoke the *raising* of an infernal power, Allecto, from the depths as a scourge to the living human world – an *anabasis*, a return of the repressed.[30] Allecto, whose name means 'the unstoppable, the unabating, the ceaseless one',[31] was one of the three *Erinyes* (or Furies) in Greco-Roman mythology, who were chthonic deities of vengeance for wrongs and blood-guilt (especially within the family).[32] As soon as Juno summons her, Allecto visits Queen Amata of Latium, the mother of the woman Aeneas is destined to marry, Lavinia. Allecto tears a snake from her gorgon hair and casts it at Amata. In imagery that is both erotic and menacing, the snake slides between the Queen's breasts and her dress, then twines around her head like a golden necklace, and slithers down her limbs, stirring up her anxiety and rage by its venomous bite (*Aeneid* VII.341-358[33]). War between Aeneas and Turnus, his rival for Lavinia's love, ensues – and ultimately Amata commits suicide by hanging. Aeneas marries Lavinia. Jupiter prevails.

Allecto's snake-hair resembles Medusa's head, which Freud later links to the castration complex; it is, he says, 'a representation of the female genitals', which 'isolates their horrifying effects from their pleasure-giving ones'.[34] The phrase '*Acheronta movebo*' is a metonymic evocation of Allecto (the name of the infernal river Acheron substituted for Allecto herself, a denizen of that region),[35] and the Vergilian epigraph conceals, beneath the divine mother who, in the shadow of the prohibitive father, speaks it, the unnamed figure of the gorgon-headed Fury. Hans Loewald contrasts 'the proud and rebellious motto of *The Interpretation of Dreams*, '*Flectere si nequeo superos, Acheronta movebo*', with the quotation which closes the first section of *Civilization and its Discontents*:

> But I am moved to exclaim in the words of Schiller's diver: —
> '... *Es freue sich,*
> *Wer da atmet im rosigten Licht.*'[36]

For Loewald, Freud was no longer willing (as he had been in 1900) to take the plunge into the depths; he was reluctant to explore primary narcissistic stages associated with the maternal, the 'oceanic feeling' of mysticism which Freud associates with regressive longing for the intra-uterine state. Perhaps we can read back into Freud's motto ambivalence towards a maternal figure who is 'proud and rebellious' yet also associated with a monstrous, castrating gorgon and who finally (fulfilling the son's wish) submits to the law of the father.

Neither Juno nor Allecto are named in the epigraph; they lie hidden behind a screen of literary allusion. The metonymic reference to Allecto suggests that she is unnameable, may only be referred to indirectly. (The Greeks (notably, Aeschylus) sometimes referred to the Furies as the *Eumenides*, or kindly ones, in an apotropaic euphemism.) On the surface, the motto evokes heroic masculine figures: Vergil, Dante's guide to the underworld, and Aeneas, founder of Rome, respectively author and hero of the poem, quoted – a netherworld guide-cum-interpreter-of-visions and a founder of empire, two aspects of Freud himself in the foundational text of psychoanalysis. We have already noted the link between the motto and Ferdinand Lassalle, the founder of the German Social Democratic movement – another inaugurator-hero. But veiled behind these potent males stand two angry, violent, and vengeful female figures, Juno and Allecto: the defeated mother – and the undefeated Fury. Lassalle himself died in a duel for love of a woman.[37]

David L. Pike reads Aeneas's *katabasis* in book 6 of the *Aeneid* as 'the destined, eschatological march of history' against which Juno in book 7 presents 'a counterblast of protest'. Drawing on Walter Benjamin, he associates Aeneas with what Benjamin called 'the tiger's leap into the past', the appropriation of the past to render present resonance in the service of the powerful. This contrasts with the truly revolutionary and dialectical 'leap in the open air of history' which Pike locates in Juno's summoning of Allecto. Thus, the metaphor of the underworld holds 'both the master narratives and their countercurrents, both the will to transcendence and the movement toward entropy'.[38]

## Tectonic Titans and Labours in the Depths

Jeff Rodman attributes an 'analeptic value' to the Vergilian epigraph, which 'will have received its relevance and sense once we, its readers, have completed the epic journey through the dream book and are at that vantage point where a glance backward reveals all'.[39] The repetition of the quotation near the end of the text facilitates such a backward glance. Rodman's observation implies that the reader experiences a kind of *après-coup*,[40] the second time we encounter the quotation we have been changed by what we've seen since we first read it, and we experience the fullness of its meaning for the first time, thereby retroactively transforming our initial encounter with it. Starobinski makes a similar point: Freud's 'royal road' dictum marks a culmination; looking back, our journey through Freud's text reveals only in retrospect a triumphal march to knowledge.[41]

Richard H. Armstrong contrasts the temporal perspective of the ancient authors with that of Freud: the *katabasis* of Aeneas in book 6 of the *Aeneid* (following the pattern of that of Odysseus in book 11 of the *Odyssey*) is a *nekyia*, in which the hero questions the dead about the future; by contrast, Freud denies divination and takes the descent into the unconscious to be a turn to the past.[42] Freud does later evoke the Odyssean *nekyia* when he writes, the 'wishes of the past which have been abandoned, overlaid and repressed [...] are not dead in our sense of the word but only like the shades in the Odyssey, which awoke to some sort of life as soon as they had tasted blood'.[43] Yet the oracular dimension of the *nekyia* is here occluded, and instead we have the living presence of archaic wishes: desire concerns what has happened, has been felt, has been repressed, and its propensity to awake to vampiric life in the present, not a revelation of what will happen. Starobinski likewise speaks of the 'double narrative' in Aeneas's *katabasis*: the encounter with dead comrades (Palinurus, etc.) is backward-looking (analeptic), Anchises' prophecy forward-looking (proleptic); Freud favours analepsis (psychoanalysis as katabatic recollection or anamnesis) while suppressing prophetic prolepsis (dreams as portents).[44] This is the temporality of *après-coup*, not of precognition or prognosis.

In his discussion of the epigraph, Armstrong speaks of Freud's 'appropriation of the [Greek and Roman] underworld as a trope for the unconscious', highlighting two further examples: Freud's reference to *repressed wishes as Titans*, confined in the underground prison of Tartarus as punishment for their rebellion against the gods, and Freud's later metaphor of *psychoanalysis as labour in the depths*.[45] Let us follow Freud deeper down into these two metaphors.

> These wishes in our unconscious, ever on the alert and, so to say, immortal, remind one of the legendary Titans, weighed down since primaeval ages by the massive bulk of the mountains which were once hurled upon them by the victorious gods and which are still shaken from time to time by the convulsion of their limbs. But these wishes, held under repression, are themselves of infantile origin, as we are taught by psychological research into the neuroses. I would propose, therefore, to set aside the assertion made just now [p. 551], that the place of origin of dream-wishes is a matter of indifference and replace it by another one to the following effect: *a wish which is represented in a dream must be an infantile one.*
>
> (*Interpretation of Dreams*, 553; original italics)

Tartarus, the place where the Titans are imprisoned, lies as far below the realm of Hades as earth lies beneath the sky.[46] It is where criminals are punished after death. The mountains burying the Titans represent the weight of repression holding down archaic wishes. At the risk of pushing the topographical metaphor too far, the underworld as a whole corresponds to the descriptive unconscious, Tartarus to the dynamic unconscious, and Hades to the preconscious. We descend with Freud to the depths of the underworld not to divine the future but to learn of the titanic, tectonic pressure of upward forces from the past: '*a wish which is represented in a dream must be an infantile one*'. As in the Vergilian epigraph, the threat is of vertical pressure from below, of forces breaking back out from the underworld, and the temporality is past-, not future-oriented. The metaphor bears the weight of (and introduces) one of Freud's central propositions – the infantile nature of dream-wishes. As with Juno and Allecto, the titanic upward force in the myth is primarily aggressive rather than sexual. The Tartarus metaphor refigures the Vergilian tag, rather than breaking with it. And feel how it, too, is heavy with furious defeat.

Freud here echoes Josef Breuer, who had previously invoked the Titans in *Studies on Hysteria* (which he and Freud co-authored). Breuer notes how in his and Freud's patients' cases 'the part of the mind which is split off is "thrust into darkness", as the Titans are imprisoned in the crater of Etna, and can shake the earth but can never emerge into the light of day'.[47] The quotation within a quotation (*in die Finsternis gebracht*) is from Goethe's *Faust*, where Mephistopheles is speaking of himself.[48] Breuer is distinguishing his and Freud's pre-psychoanalytic repression model (horizontal splitting of consciousness from the underlying dynamic unconscious) from Pierre Janet's model of dissociated personalities (vertical splitting with each separate part comprising both conscious and subconscious layers); the Titans and Mephistopheles both stand for the repressed dynamic unconscious. Freud's version thus elaborates Breuer's metaphor, in the context of infantile wishes and the formation of dreams.

Jason Dean suggests that Freud's Titan metaphor echoes Nietzsche's use of a similar image: 'the Titanic forces of nature, that *moira* [Fate] [...]'. And again: 'under the influence of the Apolline instinct (*Trieb*) for beauty, the Olympian divine order of joy developed out of the original Titanic divine order of terror in a series of slow transitions, in much the same way as roses burst forth from a thicket of thorns'.[49] Dean reads Nietzsche as equating the Titans with the Dionysiac, whereas I would follow Albert Henrichs in regarding the Dionysos of *The Birth of Tragedy* as 'sui generis', neither Titanic nor Olympian.[50] Starobinski likens the furious delirium of Queen Amata and her women in the *Aeneid* to Dionysian frenzy – which, he asserts, was interpreted in the late nineteenth century as hysteria. He also reminds us that the Olympian gods belong to a later generation than the Titans: 'The repressing force is an aftereffect'.[51] On that reading, I suggest, Nietzsche's Titanic forces could be likened to the Freudian drives, the return of the repressed resulting in hysterical symptoms, and the Olympian order of joy representing the emergence of sublimated cultural achievement.

In 1925, Freud employed yet another metaphor of libidinal forces coming from below:

> Human civilization rests upon two pillars, of which one is the control of natural forces and the other the restriction of our instincts. The ruler's throne rests upon fettered slaves.[52] Among the instinctual components which are thus brought into service, the sexual instincts, in the narrower sense of the word, are conspicuous for their strength and savagery. Woe, if they should be set loose! The throne would be overturned and the ruler trampled under foot. Society is aware of this – and will not allow the topic to be mentioned.[53]

Again, this refigures (without breaking with) the Vergilian epigraph. The metaphor draws on classical architecture; the 'instinctual components' (*Triebkomponenten*) are now caryatids; civilization rests on old (unstable) pillars which rely on mastery (*Beherrschung*) and constraint (*Beschränkung*). It is as if repression turns the vital drives to stone but is constantly threatened by the possibility of a magical reversal of that process, an explosion of animal energy. The new metaphor makes explicit what the epigraph and the Titanic metaphor implied: the collective (social, political, and cultural) dimensions of repression. In civilization, Freud says, there is slavery.

Moving on from the literary to the literal, we find another possible source for Freud's Titan metaphor in some caves near Trieste, which he and his brother Alexander visited over the Easter weekend of 1898. Freud reported back to Fliess on 14 April 1898:

> On the same evening [Easter Day, April 10] we got to Divaça on the Carso, where we spent the night so as to visit the caves on the next and last day, Monday. In the morning we went to Rudolf's Cave, a quarter of an hour from the station; it was full of all sorts of strange stalactite formations – giant horsetail, pyramid cakes, tusks growing upward, curtains, corncobs, richly folded tents, hams and poultry hanging from above. Strangest of all was our guide, in a deep alcoholic stupor, but completely surefooted, and full of humor. He was the discoverer of the cave, obviously a genius gone wrong [*ein verkommenes Genie offenbar*]; constantly spoke of his death, his conflicts with the priests, and his conquests in these subterranean realms. When he said that he had already been in thirty-six 'holes' in the Carso, I realized he was a neurotic and his conquistador exploits [*Konquistadorentum*] were an erotic equivalent. A few minutes later he confirmed this, because when Alex asked him how far one could penetrate into the cave, he answered, 'It's like with a virgin; the farther you get, the more beautiful it is.'
>
> The man's dream is one day to come to Vienna, so as to gather ideas in the museums for naming his stalactites. I overtipped the 'biggest blackguard in Divaça,' as he called himself, with a few guilders, so that he can drink his life away faster.
>
> The caves of Saint Cangian, which we saw in the afternoon, are a gruesome miracle of nature [*ein schauerliches Naturwunder*], a subterranean river running through magnificent vaults, waterfalls, stalactite formations, pitch darkness, and slippery paths secured with iron railings. It was Tartarus itself [*Der reine Tartarus*]. If Dante saw anything like this, he needed no great effort of imagination for his inferno. At the same time the master of Vienna [*Der Herr von Wien*], Herr Dr. Karl Lueger, was with us in the cave, which after three and a half hours spewed us all out into the light again.
>
> (Masson, 308–309)

'Rudolf's Cave' (now known as the Divača Cave or Divaška Jama) is a Karst cave some eight and a half miles east of Trieste in what was Habsburg Austria and is now Slovenia, discovered in 1884 by Gregor Žiberna (1855–1929), Freud's guide, a local butcher (smoked sausages a speciality) and amateur speleologist. The cave opened to the public in 1887 when it was visited by (and named in honour of) Crown Prince Rudolf von Habsburg.[54] The thirty-year-old Prince notoriously died in a suicide pact with his teenage mistress in his hunting lodge at Mayerling in January 1889. The 'caves of Saint Cangian' are now known as Škocjan Caves and became a UNESCO world heritage site in 1986. The written record of the Škocjan Caves begins with Poseidonius of Apamea (135-50 BCE). The archaeological record reaches much further back – to the late Bronze Age and includes burial sites and evidence of sacrificial rites.[55]

Dr. Karl Lueger, 'the master of Vienna', Freud's fellow tourist in the Škocjan Cave, had won the popular vote for the office of Mayor of Vienna in 1895, but the Emperor Franz Josef had refused to install him; Gay reports that Freud celebrated the emperor's veto 'by indulging in proscribed cigars'.[56] On 8 April 1897, Lueger again won the vote, the emperor reluctantly endorsing him on April 16, and he took office on April 20 – 'his fight against Liberalism and Jewry' resulting in 'final and glorious triumph', in the words of an Irish Jesuit who went on to quote Lincoln's Gettysburg address in support of Lueger's popular mandate.[57] Lueger remained in office as *Bürgermeister* until his death in March 1910. As Lueger celebrates his first anniversary as Mayor, Freud follows Dante in encountering a political enemy in hell.

Schorske quotes Hugo von Hofmannsthal's dictum: 'Politics is magic. He who knows how to summon the forces from the deep, him will they follow [*Politik ist Magie. Welcher die Mächte aufzurufen weiß, dem gehorchen sie*]', and he elaborates: Lueger 'the spellbinder' began as a liberal but skilfully 'traversed the road… from the politics of reason to the politics of fantasy'.[58] Lueger's populist, antisemitic rhetoric and agenda influenced Hitler. Slavoj Žižek, himself a Slovene, detects a pun in Freud's encounter with this black magician of reaction in the Škocjan cave – after all, Lueger implies *Lüge* (in German, a lie). For Žižek, what psychoanalysis finds in the depths of the psyche is not a true self to be liberated but a primordial, constitutive *lie*.[59]

Freud's lively account of his 1898 Easter journey was partly an attempt to cheer up Fliess, whose weekend had not been such fun. Yet it strikingly evokes many katabatic themes. In the Divača Cave, Freud's underworld guide, Gregor Žiberna, is a parodic psychopomp, a comic 'Vergil' – or perhaps a Charon,[60] whom he pays in coin – or even an uncanny, caricature double of Freud himself, a 'conquistador', 'obviously a genius' (albeit one 'gone wrong'), a critic of religion, master of the depths. The tenor (or target domain) of Freud's underworld metaphor is rendered explicit by sexual symbols, obscene, misogynistic jokes – and intimations of death. Rachel Falconer notes how in Greek myths the katabatic hero is gendered male, whereas 'the object of the quest as well as the medium through which the quest is realised is gendered female'.[61] Žiberna's neurotic fears of mortality echo Freud's own, as described by Max Schur, revealingly cloaked here in Mayerling's black veil.[62] Murderous aggression (turned against his own double) is implied by Freud's overgenerous tip to hasten Žiberna's death. In the Škocjan Caves, Freud witnesses an Acheron-like river, a scene that 'was Tartarus itself', he thinks of Dante, meets a politico-magician skilled in summoning up dark forces from underground (a reactionary *Doppelgänger* of Freud's hero Lassalle), experiences a Jonah-like anabatic return, 'spewed' from the belly of the beast – all in a site redolent of antiquity and the dead.

Let us now turn to Freud's metaphor of psychoanalysis as underworld work. He dismisses Adler and Jung in the final paragraph of *On the History of the Psychoanalytic Movement* (1914) with the following scathing words:

> Men are strong so long as they represent a strong idea [*eine starke Idee*]; they become powerless [*sie werden ohnmächtig*] when they oppose it. Psycho-analysis will survive this loss and gain new adherents in place of these. In conclusion, I can only express a wish that fortune may grant an agreeable upward journey [*eine bequeme Auffahrt*] to all those who have found their stay in the underworld of psycho-analysis [*der Aufenthalt in der Unterwelt der Psychoanalyse*] too uncomfortable [*unbehaglich*] for their taste. The rest of us, I hope, will be permitted without hindrance to carry through to their conclusion our labours in the depths [*ihre Arbeiten in der Tiefe*].[63]

The underworld is no longer simply a metaphor for the unconscious but '*der Unterwelt der Psychoanalyse*'. Those leaving it are not Furies or Titans but men such as Adler and Jung who have abandoned psychoanalysis ('*eine starke Idee*') and have therefore become '*ohnmächtig*', which means not only 'powerless' but also 'unconscious'. The true psychoanalysts continue their '*Arbeiten in der Tiefe*'. The trope of the underworld as the unconscious here redefines Freudian analysis as work of the depths – as *Tiefenpsychologie*.[64] Purporting to leave the underworld labours of psychoanalysis beneath them (Freud says), Adler and Jung paradoxically fall back into unconsciousness; their agreeable upward journey is in fact a swooning descent; and, finding the underworld uncomfortable, they are condemned to live unwittingly trapped within it, imagining they have escaped. The tone is comic, an absurd *katabasis*. As Peter Homans observes, it is a passage marked (and marred) beneath the surface wit by bitterness and hatred; Jung's religious sympathies are parodied in the echoes of Christ's katabatic descent into hell, resurrection, and ascension. For Homans, *On the History of the Psychoanalytic Movement* (especially its savagely sarcastic close) exhibits Freud's inability to mourn the loss of Jung.[65] I agree with Homans' reading, but I now want to tease out some other implications of Freud's self-identification as a labourer in the depths.

Edgar Michaelis, a Berlin neurologist, draws a parallel between this passage and the Vergilian epigraph itself: Freud's decision to pursue his labours in the depths (which seems so free and objective) is in fact involuntary, for it arose from his failure to move the heavenly powers, his having failed to attain the ideal.[66] Freud's modest plea for him and his loyal colleagues to 'be permitted without hindrance to carry through to their conclusion our labours in the depths' is, on this reading, born of necessity.

Gregory A. Staley also finds a Vergilian echo in Freud's notion of labour in the depths:

*facilis descensus Averno*:
*noctes atque dies patet atri ianua Ditis*;
*sed revocare gradum superasque evadere ad auras*,
*hoc opus, hic labor est*[67]

(*Aeneid*, VI.126-129)

Here the Sibyl of Cumae warns Aeneas of the dangers of the *katabasis* on which he is embarking:

[...] easy —
the way that leads into Avernus: day
and night the door of darkest Dis is open.
But to recall your steps, to rise again
into the upper air: that is the labor;
that is the task.

(Mandelbaum (trans.), 137)

Jung himself used this same Latin quotation as an epigraph to his 1935 paper 'Individual Dream Symbolism in Relation to Alchemy'.[68] Sonu Shamdasani observes that this citation by Jung 'can be read as a riposte to Freud's citation of the *Aeneid* at the beginning of *The Interpretation of Dreams*', and links Aeneas's *katabasis* to Jung's 'confrontation with the unconscious' and his turn to alchemy: 'The return to the upper air, by means of comparative historical scholarship, was to be his task and his toil'.[69] But perhaps, I suggest, it was also a riposte to Freud's 1914 sneer at Jung for abandoning psychoanalytic orthodoxy: Jung's rejection of Freud's labour in the depths, Jung implies, opened an upward path to the alchemical opus of analytical psychology.

Staley teases out the bidirectionality implicit in the metaphor used in both Vergilian epigraphs – the return of the repressed as *anabasis*, and the act of interpretation entailing a descent to the depths. Juno's *movebo* ('I shall move') evokes both the upward journey from the depths (raising hell) and the act of interpretation by the heroic analyst who descends to the depths. For Staley, the Acheronta epigraph anticipates Freud's later dictum, 'Where id was, there ego shall be',[70] which I take to imply that the analyst-hero descends to the depths to bring back the gold of interpretation. Staley also suggests that the 'agreeable upward journey' might refer to the two exits from Hades mentioned in *Aeneid* VI.894: the gate of horn and the gate of ivory. The former offers an easy way out for true shades; heroes such as Aeneas must take the return route through the gate of ivory. So Jung and Adler are shades afforded the unheroic route of the returning dead. Yet this seems strange: true dreams traditionally pass through the gate of horn and false, deceiving dreams through the gate of ivory.

Further, as Falconer notes, it is not so clear which journey really is the hardest, whatever the Sibyl says: the easy way to descend to Hades is by dying, but for the living the downward journey is tough; the return journey for mortals (or for Aeneas at least, if not all infernal travellers) is rarely made – but when it is, it is swift. Falconer also points out that '*sed revocare gradum*' can be translated either as 'but to retrace your step' or 'but to call to mind' (or 'remember') your step; both Staley and Mandelbaum catch this ambiguity in their translations by using the expression 'to recall' one's steps – which leaves open whether what is hard to remember is the route by which to ascend back out of the underworld – or rather the whole experience of loss and trauma implicated in the descent and return.[71] I suggest that the metaphor of *katabasis* in its application to psychological states entails a tension between similarity and difference – and a questioning of perspective and values – in which the appearance of difficulty may mask facility and vice versa. The descent may be hard in the sense of painful but easy in the sense of involuntary and swift.

Staley's notion of analytic work as *katabasis* is powerful and resonant.[72] It also enhances the irony of the 'agreeable upward journey' which Freud wishes to Jung and Adler: the Sibyl says the easy journey is the downward way – the hard yards are the return to daylight – but Freud suggests a comic inversion of this: those who leave the psychoanalytic fold have chosen a facile ascent which is really an unwitting (and easy) fall. Yet there is, I think, an interesting ambiguity here. Freud doesn't characterize the analytic work as an ascent from, but as a labour *staying within*, the depths. Is the true *opus* and *labor* the anabatic return from the depths bearing (in James Strachey's phrase) a 'mutative interpretation'?[73] Or is it the capacity to stay within the depths, as in (say) Bionian negative capability or Winnicottian play?[74] Is there a necessity which makes the depths the proper and permanent place of psychoanalysis? What is that necessity? I suggest that the core image here is strenuous, conflictual – staying within the depths is not a comfortable or fuzzy state; it resists the facile certainty of a destined return bearing analytic gold.

Furthermore, I suggest that the appropriation here is not only of Greek and Roman versions of the underworld but of Germanic myth; we may hear echoes of Richard Wagner's opera cycle *Der Ring des Nibelungen*. In Wagner's reworking of German and Norse texts, the home of the dwarves is Nibelheim, in the *Unterwelt*, and it is a place of hard labour, the mining and working of metals. The hero Siegfried belongs to the upper, human realm. Freud attended (and took, he said, 'a strange pleasure' in) a performance of Wagner's opera *Die Meistersinger von Nürnberg*,[75] but it is uncertain how familiar he was with Wagner's *Ring* cycle. Neil Cheshire, arguing against Cora Diaz de Chumaceiro, suggests that Freud knew the myths on which the cycle was based and would have had some exposure to Wagner's work from social acquaintance within his cultural milieu[76] but finds no evidence that he was familiar with either the libretto or the music of the *Ring*.

But such familiarity is not what I am postulating. ho 'labours in the depths' in mythology? A possible classical reference would be to Sisyphus, another prisoner of Tartarus, who was forced endlessly to roll repeatedly a boulder uphill until it rolled back down again, but it is unlikely that Freud would invoke that trickster, condemned to eternal, repetitive, and fruitless labour, as a model for psychoanalytic work. Hephaestus and Vulcan are craftsmen, labouring deities – but they are not chthonic, not of the depths.[77] Besides, Freud's reference here is to loyal psychoanalysts (plural), rather than a heroic self-identification. The labourers in Nibelheim, skilled craftsmen reviled by those who, lacking their talent, thought themselves superior, are a much more likely allusion: a Germanic analogue for the Vergilian defiance of the infernal forces against heavenly powers, or Freud and his acolytes against the establishment.

Wagner's antisemitism is well attested. Since Adorno's thorough and nuanced critique, critics have been divided as to whether it also infected his music dramas; for example, in the characterization of Beckmesser in *Meistersingers* or of Alberich, Mime, Hagen, and the chorus of dwarves in the *Ring*.[78] There are certainly very strong arguments for seeing these villainous figures as coded representatives of Jews: Wagner deploys obvious antisemitic tropes. Paul Roazen reports that Freud 'detested' Wagner[79]; yet, if that were so, Freud's feelings were clearly ambivalent (as evidenced by his 'strange pleasure' in the *Meistersingers*). He would certainly have detested Wagner for his antisemitism. We cannot be sure whether Freud himself or his associates would have associated Wagner's labourers in the depths with antisemitic stereotypes, but the metaphor may be read as Freud's defiant identification of the 'Jewish science' of psychoanalysis with the craftsmen of Nibelheim – in a context in which the leading non-Jewish analyst, Jung, had broken with him.

My reading of this passage resonates with Diane Jonte-Pace's reading of another Germanic myth reference in Freud – his likening of psychoanalytic dream interpretation to Hagen's recognition of the embroidered mark on Siegfried's cloak:

> If the first account given me by a patient of a dream is too hard to follow I ask him to repeat it. In doing so he rarely uses the same words. But the parts of the dream which he describes in different terms are by that fact revealed to me as the weak spot in the dream's disguise: they serve my purpose just as Hagen's was served by the embroidered mark on Siegfried's cloak.
>
> (*Interpretation of Dreams*, 515)

This treacherously placed 'mark' reveals the one vulnerable part of Siegfried's body; seeing it, Hagen is able to kill him. Jonte-Pace reads this as a reference to the opera which closes the *Ring* cycle, *Götterdämmerung*, and accordingly she draws on Marc Weiner's interpretation of the antisemitic currents in that work, particularly the depiction of the anti-hero, Hagen. She sees Freud as identifying with Hagen, the murderer of the Teutonic hero, Siegfried; the Jewish dream interpreter is thereby empowered in a reversal of Wagner's hegemonic values.[80] However, the detail of the embroidered mark occurs only in the medieval epic the *Nibelungenlied*, one of the sources of the opera, not the opera itself – in Wagner's telling, Siegfried's vulnerable spot is the whole of his back, which therefore needs no special marking: Wagner's Brünnhilde simply tells Hagen. Freud was therefore drawing on the medieval epic, which, according to Diaz de Chumaceiro, he had read by 1875 – and not on Wagner.[81] But in my view this does not weaken Jonte-Pace's argument. The detail may be from the historic literature, but the cultural milieu would have affected Freud's response to it – and encouraged him to identify with the anti-hero, the ultimately defeated representative of the outsider or Other. The anti-hero may not only be subversive of external powers (an outsider's defiance of the hegemonic figure of Siegfried) but of internal ones, too (Freud's own heroic ideals and values).

Armstrong notes Freud's strong identification with 'the Other of history'– Juno, Hannibal (a Semitic hero), the Jewish people, and another Vergilian (and Semitic) figure, Dido. (Juno would later champion Semitic Carthage, home to Dido and Hannibal, in its losing war with Rome.) I would now add the Nibelheim labourers (and, following Jonte-Pace, Hagen) to this list. But (Armstrong argues) Freud 'settles the issue of power in the end through a patriarchal teleology that returns herstory to the neverland of Acheron'.[82] Juno, as we have seen, grudgingly submits to Zeus's masculine authority. Armstrong presents this as a 'Juno principle' in contrast to Madelon Sprengnether's 'Penelope principle'. Sprengnether argues that unconscious elements of Freud's depiction of femininity subverted the thrust of his conscious, patriarchal arguments by threatening to unravel the work of analysis. Similarly, Jonte-Pace finds a counter-thesis in Freud's writing which disrupts the Oedipal paradigm and which she locates in the figure of Juno, in death anxieties, and misogynist fears that cannot be reductively dismissed as castration anxiety.[83] For all three scholars, there is a counterpoise to Freud's dominant narrative; the question is whether the rebellious counterforce represented (at least for Armstrong and Jonte-Pace) by Juno subverts or submits to that dominant, patriarchal power.

## Coincidentia Oppositorum

But perhaps this is a false choice? Elliot R. Wolfson speaks of 'the augmented capability of the dream to allow contradictory sensibilities to coexist, a notion that Freud links exegetically to' our Vergilian epigraph. Wolfson continues (again, linking insight to epigraph):

> Dreams license the coexistence of incompatible sensibilities, even to the point of generating monstrous combinations, an idea that can be traced

to ancient theories regarding the role of the dream imagination to create fantastic images by combining sense data that are ordinarily unrelated.[84]

He cites in support of this Freud's 1915 statement about the unconscious as a realm in which 'instinctual impulses are co-ordinate with one another, exist side by side without being influenced by one another, and are exempt from mutual contradiction'.[85] Wolfson connects this with the faculty of imagination – and metaphor – offering the following quotation from the political scientist John R. Wikse: 'Dreams speak the language of the imagination. They do so through images that do not obey the laws of noncontradiction, through metaphors which bring together and focus our emotional ambivalences'.[86] For Wolfson, 'it is not only the case that the dreamer can concomitantly bend heaven and arouse hell, but, even more profoundly, the bending of heaven is itself the arousing of hell'.[87]

Freud once confided to Fliess as follows:

My longing for Rome is, by the way, deeply neurotic. It is connected with my high school hero worship of the Semitic Hannibal, and this year in fact I did not reach Rome any more than he did from Lake Trasimeno.[88]

I suggest that Freud's identification with the Other of history is inseparable from his conquistador ambitions and that it is not so much that he wishes to visit Hannibal's home city of Carthage, as to enter Rome *as Hannibal*, to complete the conquest that Hannibal projected but never attained. Notions of heroism and defeat, conquistador and outsider, are inextricably linked.

Wolfson stresses both paradox in the *coincidentia oppositorum*, and the role of dream and metaphor in revealing by concealing and concealing by revealing. Ernst Simon also associates the Vergilian epigraph with concealment:

In Virgil, it [the epigraph] has a mythological meaning, in Lassalle a national and socialistic implication, and in Freud a psychological one. The factor common to all three is the realization that the part of the world which is hidden and covered is not less important than the visible part, or, as the *Talmud* puts it, 'blessing does not dwell but on that what is hidden from the eye.'[89]

(*Ta'anit* 8,b.)

Falconer notes that '*Hölle*' in German and 'hell' in English derive etymologically from the Old Norse '*hel*', from '*hehlen*' meaning 'to cover or conceal' and are related to the German '*Höhle*' meaning 'cave'.[90] (Freud knew the Divača Cave as the *Rudolfshöhle*.) They, like Hades, were originally morally neutral places, lands of the dead, not lands of the damned. What defined them was their hidden, cavernous, netherworld nature.

Thus concealed beneath Freud's heroic identification with Vergil the inter-
preter-guide and Aeneas the empire-builder is the disturbing and angry doubled presence of Juno/Allecto. Although Juno may finally be defeated by the
patriarchy, and Freud may attempt to contain untameable, unnameable
Allecto with the notion of castration anxiety, there's a sense in which both
goddesses break out of their bonds, asserting their deathly power. Freud, an
elective labourer in the very depths which Juno invoked and where Allecto
dwells, is of necessity of their realm – a realm of paradox and metaphor,
defined not by ethical judgment (despite normative social dictates) but by life
and death, concealment and excavation.

Schönau attributes to Ernest Jones another Vergilian association. He notes
that the epigraph to the second volume of Jones's Freud hagiography is from
Vergil's Second *Georgic*. Schönau quotes from the German edition, as
follows:

*Selig, wer es vermochte, das Wesenüder Welt zu ergründen,*
*Wer so all die Angst und das unerbittliche Schiksal,*
*Unter die Füße sich zwang und des gierigen Acheron Tosen!*[91]

(translated by Johannes Götte)

The third line refers to Acheron, again as a synecdoche for the underworld –
and therefore suggests a link to Freud's epigraph. Schönau reads this as a
kind of answer, a posthumous acknowledgement of Freud's heroic intention
to conquer the underworld, a hidden reference to the motto of the dream
book, whereby Jones congratulates his friend and master on his success,
on attaining his goal. But the original English edition of Jones's biography
in fact uses a shorter version of this motto, which omits any mention of
Acheron, stressing Freud's scientific pre-eminence and his triumph over emo-
tion and fate:

Happy is he who can search out the causes of things,
For thereby he masters all fear, and is throned above fate.
ALFRED NOYES AFTER VIRGIL[92]

I do not think that weakens Schönau's point, it just means that the hidden
reference to Acheron is still more concealed. For the original passage reads:

*felix qui potuit rerum cognoscere causas*
*atque metus omnis et inexorabile fatum*
*subiecit pedibus strepitumque Acherontis auari:*
*fortunatus et ille deos qui nouit agrestis*
*Panaque Siluanumque senem Nymphasque sorores.*

(Vergil, *Georgics*, II.490–494)

Rodman translates these lines:

> Happy is the one who's fit to trace the causes of things
> And who's trod down every fear, crushed pitiless fate
> And stifled the rattle of greedy Death:
> But blessed is the countryman who acknowledges his gods –
> The wild fields, the old woods, and the sisterhood of springs and streams.[93]

They evoke a heroic image of Freud as a man who knows how to trace the causal chain of origins, conquers underworld threats, and is at peace with nature (and nature's drives). We note that Jones edits out the references to death and nature – perhaps preferring to accentuate the scientist-hero than death and the gods of forest, field, and brook. Rodman suggests that Freud may have had this passage in mind when he wrote this famous description of *The Interpretation of Dreams* to Fliess (one of the passages in which, as we noted earlier, Hyman finds a landscape embodying the figure of the erotic mother):

> The whole thing is planned on the model of an imaginary walk. At the beginning, the dark forest of authors (who do not see the trees), hopelessly lost on wrong tracks. Then a concealed pass through which I lead the reader – my specimen dream with its peculiarities, details, indiscretions, bad jokes – and then suddenly the high ground and the view and the question: which way do you wish to go now?[94]

The very same images of a concealed pass, high ground, and the question of where to go next recur in Freud's dream book itself, immediately below a section heading which defines their centrality to the whole work – 'A Dream is the Fulfilment of a Wish':

> When, after passing through a narrow defile, we suddenly emerge upon a piece of high ground, where the path divides and the finest prospects open up on every side, we may pause for a moment and consider in which direction we shall first turn our steps.
>
> (*Interpretation of Dreams*, 122)

I want to try somehow to hold together, without choosing between this pastoral idyll of the scientific researcher, master of fate, reconciled with nature on the one hand, and on the other psychoanalysis as a dark, necessary labour in the deep caves of the underworld. But first, Freud's question, '[W]hich way do you wish to go now?' invites us to think about two metaphors of descent or access to the underworld: the *Via Regia* and the waters of Hades.

## The Road to Hell (Parts 1 and 2)

We began this chapter by noting the link between the Vergilian epigraph and Freud's statement that dream interpretation is the *Via Regia* to the knowledge of the unconscious in the inner life. Jonte-Pace stresses that the ancient royal roads were direct, secure, and efficient routes, in contrast to Freud's 'narrow defile' – 'The perilous journey stands in tension with the royal road'.[95] Noting the Dantescan echoes of Freud's dark wood metaphors, [96] she emphasizes the heroic dimension to Freud's quest – by mastering the royal road he is avenged for his father's humiliation when young Jacob Freud was forced off the pavement in Freiberg (modern-day Příbor) by a Christian antisemite.[97] She follows Freud's metaphoric trail (rightly, in my view) from the *Via Regia*, through the narrow defile, to the thickets of the *selva oscura*,[98] on to the navel of the dream via woven cloths and so to the mycelium of dream-wishes, and the path which ends in darkness – metaphors which mark a complex interplay between the direct, clear, secure, mainstream on one side (*Via Regia*, the umbilical cord as direct connection) and the hidden, perilous, descending, and ramifying on the other (weaving, mycelium, perhaps the omphalos itself); between, in a sense, imperial victors of the daylight way and outsider, subversive denizens of the dark. But let us stay a little while longer on the sunlit royal road.

Susan Sherwin-White persuasively argues that Freud's *Via Regia* is the ancient Persian (Achaemenid) system of royal roads, which run from modern-day Turkey east to India. It thereby evokes another ancient imperial conqueror, Alexander the Great, who took this route on his campaign against the Persians – and whom she adds to the list of Freud's formative military heroes. She also notes that Freud, in the third of his Clark University lectures delivered in 1909 at Worcester, Massachusetts, uses the same line about dream interpretation being the royal road to knowledge of the unconscious, and she comments on Freud's 'imperial tone here well suited to this momentous incursion of psychoanalysis to the New World'.[99] (Sterba suggests that Freud held America in low esteem due to Old World prejudice against its perceived lack of classical and humanist culture.[100])

It is worth stressing that the Achaemenid system was not only a military route – the *pirradazish* service, a postal relay system, was a crucial element of the Persian imperial bureaucracy, facilitating fast and accurate delivery of messages over vast distances and difficult terrain.[101] The royal road is, then, an imperial metaphor of both conquests – Hellenic appropriation of eastern 'barbarian' domains – *and* communication (between remote provinces and the centre). A key source of our knowledge of the Achaemenid road and postal system is Herodotus, whom Freud had studied at school in Greek and in whose work he maintained a lively interest through his maturity, reflected by many references in his writings.[102] It is, therefore, perfectly possible that this was the royal road which Freud had in mind.

Armstrong also notes Freud's admiration of Alexander the Great, focusing in particular on the analogy Freud makes between historical and psychoanalytic evidence (the historian is no more an eyewitness of Alexander's campaigns than the analyst is of his patient's early years, but both may be trusted).[103] Armstrong distinguishes Freud's heroes, Alexander from Hannibal – Hannibal presents 'dead-end oppositional strategies' in contrast to Alexander's *'inclusive*, imperialist Hellenism'*, the latter a model of cultural assimilation – and points out that Alexandria, the city the conqueror founded, became a centre of Hellenic Jewish culture.[104]

But, 'excavating the cultural unconscious of a set phrase', Armstrong makes a different connection to the *Via Regia*. Finding in it an echo of the road between Damascus and Aqaba mentioned in the biblical Book of Numbers (20:14-21), he traces its lineage through the Middle Platonist Hellenistic Jewish philosopher, Philo of Alexandria, to the Church Fathers, for whom it metaphorically represented the way of doctrinal truth and orthodoxy. In the biblical passage, the Edomites refused Moses and the Israelites use of the royal road, and their name thereafter became associated with obstructive Gentile culture. Freud's revisionist version of the *Via Regia* followed his Jewish precursor in finding truth in the father but challenged hegemonic beliefs by forcing us to face the fact of our underworld desires and the death of God the father, reclaiming the royal road from Edom.[105] Staley notes Armstrong's suggestion but counter-proposes that the *Via Regia* Freud had in mind was nearer home – the medieval imperial road crossing the Holy Roman Empire from the Rhineland-Palatinate in the west to Silesia in the East. He stresses the significance of this road in terms of speed and directness.[106]

One city through which this medieval imperial road passes is Breslau (Wroclaw) in Silesia. In the same letter in which Freud disclosed to Fliess his neurotic attachment to Rome and Hannibal, Freud wrote:

> Breslau also plays a role in my childhood memories. At the age of three years I passed through the station when we moved from Freiberg to Leipzig, and the gas flames which I saw for the first time reminded me of spirits burning in hell. I know a little of the connections. My travel anxiety, now overcome, also is bound up with this.
>
> (Masson, 285)

Some of the 'connections' he hints at had been touched on in earlier letters to Fliess – notably those of 3–4 October and 15 October 1897.[107] He had been taught about Christian hellfire by one of his nursemaids, 'an ugly, elderly, but clever woman, who told me a great deal about God Almighty and hell and who instilled in me a high opinion of my own capacities', but who was also his 'prime originator' (i.e., of his neuroses), his 'teacher in sexual matters', who had washed him in her own dirty bath water stained with her menstrual blood. She was dismissed by Freud's parents for theft when he was two and a half years old.[108]

Martin von Koppenfels links this childhood memory of the gas flames at Breslau station to the Vergilian epigraph and to Freud's account of his visit to the Divača and Škocjan caves. The connection, he argues, is Freud's association between the female body and death.[109] The epigraph enacts both the intention to rebel against repression and the submission to the punishment for that rebellion. (This resonates with, but does not encompass, Wolfson's dictum, quoted above: 'It is not only the case that the dreamer can concomitantly bend heaven and arouse hell, but, even more profoundly, the bending of heaven is itself the arousing of hell'). Freud's description of the Divača cave is preceded by a lively report of various Priapic items in the archaeological museum at Aquileia and is followed by the Tartarean Škocjan cave.[110] The three or four-year-old Freud's fantasy of hellfire at Breslau is likewise rooted in the shadow of punishment following sexual arousal. Freud links his travel phobia both to this incident and to an event when, aged nearly four, he saw his mother naked and his 'libido toward *matrem* was awakened'.[111]

Who knows which *Via Regia* Freud had in mind, or whether (consciously or not) associations with two or more of the three royal roads that I've mentioned (or any others I haven't) shaped his words? It is a metaphor rich in valence: does the *Via Regia* facilitate the conquest of the underworld of the unconscious, or is it a means of communication with that realm so arduous of access – or both? Where does it stand in relation to the counter-metaphor of the perilous journey? Perhaps its meaning is that, paradoxically, there is no royal road, no high-speed access: the only way is the hard, dark, and dangerous descent through the depths of the unconscious – the interstate highway a twisty, downhill dirt track. Perhaps, too, it speaks of the backward glance: the perilous journey may feel tortuous and uncertain, but in retrospect the pattern appears clear (whether through conscious analytic insight or unconscious symptom formation) – does that make it so?

*The Oxford Classical Dictionary* tells us that the Acheron is a river in north-western mainland Greece (Epirus). Flowing out from Hades, it emerges from an impenetrable gorge, crosses the Acherusian plain, to its estuary at Glycus Limen ('sweet harbour'). It features in the *nekyia* episode of the *Odyssey*. The Romans appropriated it for their underworld mythology; notably, it is mentioned six times in Vergil's *Aeneid*. First (at V.99), Aeneas honours the anniversary of the death of his father, Anchises, at his tomb in Sicily. A serpent appears, tastes the ritual feast, and returns to the tomb – Aeneas is unsure whether 'that serpent is the genius of the place / or the attendant spirit of Anchises' and he 'calls on great Anchises' / soul, on his Shade set free from Acheron' (Mandelbaum, 108). The second reference (VI.107) occurs when Aeneas consults the Cumaean Sibyl (an ecstatic oracle of Apollo) and asks about access to the underworld (at a site near modern-day Naples), 'since here is said to be / the gateway of the lower king and here/the marsh of overflowing Acheron [...]' (Mandelbaum, 136–137). Later in book 6, Vergil reports that the dead are ferried across Acheron by Charon on their entry into the underworld – and implies that its source lies in the depths of Tartarus (VI.295-326).

Acheron is mentioned three more times in book 7. First, King Latinus (husband of Amata, father of Lavinia) consults the incubation oracle of his own (divine) father, Faunus, at Albunea – and receives paternal advice not to wed his daughter to a local man but to a destined stranger (VII.81-102).[112] Second, at VII.312, we have Juno's familiar epigraph. Third (VII.569), Allecto returns to the underworld, having stirred up war at Juno's bidding, via Lake Amsanctus and 'a huge abyss/where Acheron erupts' (Mandelbaum, 181). The final reference in the *Aeneid* (XI.23) is to Aeneas's burial of his dead comrades – 'this, the only glory/deep Acheron can know' (Mandelbaum, 276).

If we ignore the second and third references in book 7 (Allecto's uprising and return), the river Acheron is not so much a route to the underworld, as a barrier or boundary, a liminal zone – a place to be crossed in Charon's boat and which Aeneas himself is able to cross alive (with Sibyl's guidance) having plucked the golden bough. But if we take those two references, it threatens incursion, a flooding surge: 'The repressions behave like dams against the pressure of water', Freud writes in 1937 – and with Juno the levee breaks.[113] Starobinski invites us to read '*Acheronta movebo*' not only metonymically but also literally: as Juno lifting up and moving the whole mythic river. The matched initial and final letters of the word 'Acheronta' imply, he says, circularity, recursion – and figure both the anabatic upthrust of infernal waters and their tumbling back into Lake Amsanctus, the rise and return of Allecto.[114] Vergil associates Acheron both with the female (the Sibyl, Juno, Allecto), and with the male (Anchises, Apollo, Charon, Faunus, Faunus's priest) – with mother and father, with Other and Master, with liminality and incursion, with descent and return.

Martin von Koppenfels notes that Freud's chapter on 'Affects in Dreams' (*Affektkapitel*) is marked by the use of underground river metaphors.[115] He associates them with 'the old hydraulic metaphor of the soul, which fits the rhetoric of the early hysteria studies better than the dream book'.[116] He draws attention to the following examples (my italics), commenting, 'Here, as usual, "depth" is a metaphor for life'[117]:

My present-day anger…received reinforcements from *sources in the depth* of my mind and thus *swelled into a current* of hostile feelings against persons of whom I was in reality fond. The *source* of this reinforcement *flowed* from my childhood.

(*Interpretation of Dreams*, 482–483)

This memory, or more probably phantasy [...] constituted an intermediate element in the dream-thoughts, which *gathered up the emotions raging in them as a well collects the water that flows into it.*

(*Interpretation of Dreams*, 484)

[…] other, unobjectionable trains of thought in connection with the same people found simultaneous satisfaction and screened with their affect the affect which *arose from the forbidden infantile source*.

(*Interpretation of Dreams*, 486)

I suggest that a possible source for all these fluvial metaphors is Plato.[118] In *Phaedo*, he describes how 'huge rivers of both hot and cold water thus flow beneath the earth eternally, much fire and large rivers of fire, and many of wet mud' (111e). At the centre of this flow of many rivers lies a huge chasm, Tartarus,

> into this chasm all the rivers flow together, and again flow out of it […]
> The reason for their flowing into and out of Tartarus is that this water
> has no bottom or solid base but it oscillates up and down in waves.

(112b)[119]

Tartarus is thus like a pump, both the source of every river and the place to which each returns – the beating heart of a vast hydraulic system. The Ocean, too, is a river and likewise flows out of and back into Tartarus. On this reading, Freud's 'great reservoir of the libido', the id, would metaphorically be represented as Tartarus, underworld source and final destination of rivers of water, fire, and mud.[120] *Katabasis* would then have something of the rhythm of systolic ascent and diastolic return, of the ebb and flow of object-libido and ego-libido, attachment and narcissism.

## Return to Juno

'Linear presentation', says Freud in a 1920 case study, 'is not a very adequate means of describing complicated mental processes going on in different layers of the mind'.[121] Two ways in which he seeks to address this problem of linearity are through metaphor and narrative. As Peter Brooks has noted, resemblance and difference lie at the heart of both metaphor and narrative.[122] The tensions between like and unlike, and between the simultaneity of metaphor on the one hand and narrative movement on the other, make for complex, bidirectional interactions between the two. The word 'transference' (used by Freud to describe the way that prior patterns of relating are repeated in the analytic relationship) etymologically refers to a 'carrying across' – as does the word 'metaphor'. The transference relationship is both a metaphor (the analyst as recapitulated parent or lover) and a narrative (the cyclical story of repeating relationships). Exploring sources of, intertextual references to, and commentary on some of Freud's core katabatic metaphors, we have encountered in this paper a variety of narratives: from classical mythology to Vergil's foundational story of Augustan Rome, from Freud's autobiographical accounts of travel and trauma to records of the reception of psychoanalysis, from Viennese politics to the history of empires.

Freud's 1926 paper *The Question of Lay Analysis* reveals, in a series of imaginary 'conversations with an impartial person' (a phrase from the paper's subtitle), something of his approach to theory-building. The dialogic form in which the author appears to converse with, or anticipate the objections of, an enlightened reader is a recurrent feature of Freud's writing throughout his career; a feature which places theory in an inherently dramatic (and thereby narrative) context. 'Science, as you know, is not a revelation;' he tells us, 'long after its beginnings it still lacks the attributes of definiteness, immutability and infallibility for which human thought so deeply longs. But such as it is, it is all that we can have'.[123] Here Freud associates 'definiteness, immutability and infallibility' with the deeply desired but illusory certainty of 'revelation'. By contrast, as a scientist, or more specifically as the founder of what he considers to be a new branch of science, he offers the modest and unlonged for possibilities of the indefinite, the mutable, perhaps even the fallible – for that 'is all that we can have'.

A few pages later he adds:

> In psychology we can only describe things by the help of analogies [*Vergleichungen*]. There is nothing peculiar in this; it is the case elsewhere as well. But we have constantly to keep changing these analogies, for none of them lasts us long enough.[124]

Here as elsewhere Freud is cautious and defensive about his use of comparison, analogy, metaphor – but also firmly insistent that they are essential, particularly in the early stages of scientific discovery. His emphasis on the need to change analogies – they have such short shelf lives, 'for none of them lasts us long enough'– is, I argue, central to his practice. This emphasis on change implies time, which is the matrix of narrative – a change in analogy represents not a causal progression in time, but an unfolding sequence of perspectives, a 'story' told from many different angles. What Freud seems to suggest is that the fixity and precision of literal language is aligned with the deceptive certitude of revelation – by contrast, a truly scientific discourse will be tentative, provisional, figurative – and especially given to shifting and unstable analogies which successively unfurl, fade, re-form, and emerge within a narrative dimension.

The metaphors we have been exploring are both constitutive and subversive of his theory-building – more, they are constitutive *because* they are subversive. They do not merely illustrate his theories but they are the workshop in which his theories are made and re-made. And this demands openness, paradox, and contradiction. Freud the conquistador, the founder of empires, is never far from Freud the outsider. And the outsider may embody fantasies of vengeance or communicative breakthrough. Freud's use of multiple metaphors embedded in multi-directional narrative patterns resists some of the dangers of bad metaphor use – namely, concretization and anthropomorphism: the drives are not simplified or reduced by their temporary identifications with Allecto, the Titans, or underground rivers – they are enriched.

In the same 1920 case study, Freud reflects on the development of his patient's condition as follows:

> So long as we trace the development from its final outcome backwards, the chain of events appears continuous, and we feel we have gained an insight which is completely satisfactory or even exhaustive. But if we proceed the reverse way, if we start from the premises inferred from the analysis and try to follow these up to the final result, then we no longer get the impression of an inevitable sequence of events which could not have been otherwise determined. We notice at once that there might have been another result, and that we might have been just as well able to understand and explain the latter. The synthesis is thus not so satisfactory as the analysis; in other words, from a knowledge of the premises we could not have foretold the nature of the result.[125]

Freud here faces the problem that psychoanalysis cannot offer falsifiable predictions about future events but may give a narrative explanation of present circumstances. Paul Roth writing about narrative explanations in history and evolutionary biology observes: '*Retrospection reveals truths about past times that can be known only retrospectively even though true at an earlier time*'[126] – a formulation which is, I propose, close to Freud's concept of *après-coup*. Freud famously confessed in 1893 that 'it still strikes me myself as strange that the case histories I write should read like short stories and that, as one might say, they lack the serious stamp of science', thereby expressing anxiety about the narrative form of the psychological case study.[127] By 1920, Freud has reached a narrative understanding of the aetiology of mental disorder which is perhaps closer to the world of evolutionary biology than that of thermodynamics – something which is, I suggest, reflected in the shift we have noted above in the move from hydraulic to fluvial metaphors.

Starobinski observes 'that Juno and the adversity she creates are the midwives of the narrative itself'. Juno may be defeated, but her strategy of deferral is central to the *Aeneid*, Vergil's foundation myth of Octavian's empire. She will ultimately become a friend to Rome – but that does not mean mere submission to Jupiter's will. Her actions have real effect and are a source of meaning. Without her, Aeneas would not be celebrated. For Starobinski, this reflects Freud's shift from the dominant explanatory myths of the late nineteenth century ('the short-acting causality of the reflex arc or organic excitation') to 'the narrativization of the psychological events considered necessary to an understanding of a "case"'.[128]

Juno's deferral means that the stories are never-ending. Old stories are renewed in their application to psychoanalytic theory, and new stories are implied in the shifts through progressive metaphor sequences – but closure is always postponed. It is in this sense that the *Via Regia* inevitably leads to the 'navel of the dream' and the 'mycelium of dream wishes': 'But as soon as we endeavour to penetrate more deeply into the mental process involved in dreaming, every path will end in darkness' (*Interpretation of Dreams*, 111, 525, 511).

## Notes

1 'If I cannot bend the Higher Powers, I will move the Infernal Regions', in James Strachey's translation of Freud, *The Interpretation of Dreams* [1900], in S. Freud, *Standard Edition of the Complete Psychological Works*, generals eds J. Strachey and A. Freud, 24 vols, London: Hogarth Press, 1953–1974, vol. 4, p.ix. Acheron is one of the five rivers of Hades in Greek mythology. Here (subject to my endnote 35 below) it is a synecdoche for the underworld as a whole.

2 'I am by temperament nothing but a conquistador – an adventurer, if you want it translated – with all the curiosity, daring, and tenacity characteristic of a man of this sort' (Freud, letter to Wilhelm Fliess of 1 February 1 1900). See J.M. Masson (tr. and ed.), *Complete Letters of Sigmund Freud to Wilhelm Fliess, 1887–1904*, Cambridge, MA, and London, England: Belknap Press of Harvard University Press, 1985, p. 398.

3 Freud, *Interpretation of Dreams*, p. 698. Freud uses the Latin expression '*Via Regia*' for royal road: '*Die Traumdeutung aber ist die Via regia zur Kenntnis des Unbewussten im Seelenleben*' (Freud, *Gesammelte Werke*, vol. 3, 613). An alternative (and closer) translation of Freud's German might be: 'The interpretation of dreams is the *Via Regia* to a knowledge of the unconscious in the inner (or soul) life.'

4 Letter from Freud to Fliess of 17 July 1899 (Masson, *Complete Letters*, p. 361).

5 E.L. Freud (ed.), *Letters of Sigmund Freud 1873–1939*, London: Hogarth Press, 1970. p. 375.

6 C.E. Schorske, *Fin-de-Siecle Vienna: Politics and Culture*, Cambridge: Cambridge University Press, 1981, p. 200; F. Lassalle, *Der italienische Krieg und die Aufgabe Preußens: Eine Stimme aus der Democratie*, Berlin: Duncker, 1859.

7 E. Jones, *Sigmund Freud: Life and Work*, vol. 1, *The Young Freud 1856–1900*, London: Hogarth Press, 1953, p. 22. Eva Laible identifies Freud's Latin translation passage for his *Matura* (high school diploma) examination as the Nisus and Euryalus episode from *Aeneid* IX.176-223 (E. Laible, 'Über Sigmund Freuds Gymnasialzeit, 125 Jahre Bg./B.R.G. Wien II', in *Festschrift Sigmund Freud, dem berühmtesten Schüler unseres Gymnasiums zur 50. Wiederkehr seines Todestages gewidmet*, Vienna: Festschrift Sigmund Freud, 1989, 19–30; cited by J. Rodman, 'Juno and the Symptom', in V. Zajko, V. and E. O'Gorman, (eds.), *Classical Myth and Psychoanalysis: Ancient and Modern Stories of the Self*, Oxford: Oxford University Press, 2013, pp. 134–147 [p. 135]). Jean Starobinski suggests that we can surmise, but not prove, that Freud read and remembered well the whole *Aeneid* (J. Starobinski, 'Acheronta Movebo' (tr. F. Meltzer), *Critical Inquiry*, 1987, vol. 13(2), 394–407).

8 J. Glenn, 'Freud, Vergil, and Aeneas: An Unnoticed Classical Influence on Freud', *American Journal of Psychoanalysis*, 1987, vol. 47(3), 279–281.

9 The '*sentimentale Goethe-Motto*' which Fliess rejected may have been the lines from the Dedication in Goethe's *Faust* which Freud cited feelingly in his letter to Fliess of 27 October 1897 (Masson, *Complete Letters*, p. 274). Freud in 1930 again quoted those lines, describing them as an evocation of 'the incomparable strength of the first affective ties of human creatures' expressed 'in words which we could repeat for each of our analyses' (Freud, 'The Goethe Prize: Address Delivered in the Goethe House at Frankfurt', *Standard Edition*, vol. 21, pp. 205–214 [p. 209]). See also the discussion in W. Schönau, *Sigmund Freuds Prosa: Literarische Elemente seines Stils*, Stuttgart: Metzler, 1968, pp. 73–76.

10  Letter to Fliess, see Masson, *Complete Letters*, p. 361; letter Achelis, see E.L. Freud, *Letters*, p. 375.
11  E.G. Schachtel, 'Notes on Freud's Personality and Style of Thought', *Contemporary Psychoanalysis*, 1965, vol. 1(2), 136–148, p. 143.
12  Quoted by Strachey in Freud, *Interpretation of Dreams*, p. 608 (n.1).
13  R.F. Sterba, 'The Psychoanalyst in a World of Change', *Psychoanalytic Quarterly*, 1969, vol. 38, 432–454.
14  H. Ellenberger, *The Discovery of the Unconscious: The History and Evolution of Dynamic Psychiatry*, New York: Basic Books, 1970, p. 452; P. Heller, 'Zur Biographie Freuds', *Merkur*, 1956, vol. 106(X), 1233–1239 (p. 1236): '[...] *ich kann die Götter der akademischen Hierarchie nicht beugen* [...]' (quoted by Schönau, *Sigmund Freuds Prosa*, p. 67); P. Gay, *Freud: A Life for Our Time*, New York and London: Norton, 1988, p.105; L. Shengold, 'The Metaphor of the Journey in *The Interpretation of Dreams*', *American Imago*, 1966, vol. 23(4), 316–331 (p. 320, n.1); and S. Frogel, 'The Will to Truth, the Death Drive and the Will to Power', *American Journal of Psychoanalysis*, 2020, vol. 80(1), 85–93.
15  J. Naiman, 'Freud's Quotation from Virgil', *Psychoanalytic Review*, 1991, vol. 78(3), 459–463; P. Bailey, *Sigmund the Unserene: A Tragedy in Three Acts*, Springfield, Illinois: Thomas, 1965, p. 85 (quoted in Schönau, *Sigmund Freuds Prosa*, p. 71); H.W. Puner, *Freud: His Life and Mind*, New York: Howell, Soskin, 1947, p. 90 (quoted in Schönau, *Sigmund Freuds Prosa*, p. 70).
16  Starobinski, 'Acheronta Movebo', pp. 399 and 395.
17  Starobinski offers his own literal translation of this passage: 'That which has been psychically pushed down (*das seelisch Underdrückte*) and which, in waking life, has been prevented from achieving expression by the antagonistic presence of contradictions, and has been cut off from internal perception – all of this will, in nocturnal life and under the aegis of compromise formations, find the ways and means to penetrate forcefully into consciousness' (Starobinski, 'Acheronta Movebo', p. 404). Starobinski's literal version is more explicitly katabatic than Strachey's – it emphasizes the diurnal downward push of repression and, under the nocturnal aegis of compromise formation, the upward penetration of consciousness in the return of the repressed.
18  'From heaven through the world to hell', from Goethe's *Faust*; see Masson, *Complete Letters*, p. 220.
19  Freud, *Three Essays on the Theory of Sexuality* [1905], in *Standard Edition*, vol. 7, pp. 123–246 (p. 162).
20  Freud reports Jacob's death to Fliess on 26 October 1896; in Masson, *Complete Letters*, p. 201.
21  D. Anzieu, *Freud's Self-Analysis*, London: Hogarth Press and Institute of Psycho-Analysis, 1986.
22  S.E. Hyman, *The Tangled Bank: Darwin, Marx, Frazer and Freud as Imaginative Writers*, New York: Atheneum, 1962, p. 336. The incident of Freud's father's prophecy occurred when Freud was seven or eight years old, as Freud recalls (*Interpretation of Dreams*, p. 216).
23  '*Ast ego magna Iovis coniunx* [...] *vincor ab Aenea*' (Vergil, *Aeneid* VII.8-10).
24  Anzieu, *Freud's Self-Analysis*; Naiman, 'Freud's Quotation from Virgil'.
25  Freud, *Interpretation of Dreams*, pp. 106–121 (and *passim*).
26  For Freud's later postulation of the death drive, see *Beyond the Pleasure Principle* [1920], in *Standard Edition*, vol. 18, pp. 1–64.
27  J.-B. Pontalis, 'On Death-work', in Pontalis, *Frontiers in Psychoanalysis: Between the Dream and Psychic Pain*, tr. C. and P. Cullen, London: Hogarth Press and Institute of Psycho-Analysis, 1981, pp. 184–193.
28  Hyman, *Tangled Bank*, p. 333.

29 Frogel, 'Will to Truth', p. 87.
30 I use *anabasis* in the sense of an upward or return journey. For a brief overview of *katabasis* and *anabasis* in Greek heroic mythology, see R. Georgiades, 'To Hell and Back: The Function of the Ancient Greek Hero's *Katabasis*', *Classicum*, 2017, vol. 43(2), 2–8.
31 Rodman, 'Juno and the Symptom', pp. 140–141.
32 See the entry on '*Erinyes*' in S. Hornblower, A. Spawforth, & E. Eidinow (eds.), *The Oxford Classical Dictionary*, 4th edn, Oxford: Oxford University Press, 2012.
33 A. Mandelbaum (tr.), *The Aeneid of Virgil*, New York: Bantam, 1981, p. 174.
34 Freud, 'Medusa's Head' [1922] in *Standard Edition*, vol. 18, pp. 273–274 (p. 274).
35 By synecdoche, Acheron stands for the 'Infernal Regions'; metonymically, it means Allecto. The chains of representation here are based on contiguity, not comparison (synecdoche and metonymy, not metaphor or simile) – which seems appropriate: here it implies an averted gaze or corner-of-the-eye glimpse rather than an imaginative, discriminating attunement to similarity and difference. Juno's intervention itself operates in a chain of contiguity: Juno, Acheron, Allecto, snake, poison, Amata. To follow Frazer's categorization of sympathetic magic, it follows the Law of Contact or Contagion rather than the Law of Sympathy (it is the magic of contact not resemblance or imitation) (J.G. Frazer, *The Golden Bough: A Study in Magic and Religion*, New York: Macmillan, 1922). Frazer's categorization is interestingly comparable to the distinction that Ella Freeman Sharpe made between the operation of Freud's mechanism of *displacement* in the dream-work by synecdoche and metonymy (contiguity, contact, contagion) as distinct from that of *condensation* by metaphor and simile (similarity, comparison, resemblance) (E.F. Sharpe, *Dream Analysis*, London: Hogarth, 1937). In contrast to her attack on Amata, Allecto stirs up Turnus by the Law of Sympathy (condensation, metaphor): she appears to him in a dream as Calybe, an old priestess, and in his dream flings a burning torch at his chest – thereby inflaming his soul to vengeance (*Aeneid*, VII.413-474; Mandelbaum, *Aeneid*, pp. 176–178).
36 H. Loewald, 'Ego and Reality' [1951], in *The Essential Loewald: Collected Papers and* Monographs, Hagerstown: University Publishing Group, 2000, pp. 3–20 (p. 9): 'Let him rejoice who breathes up here in the roseate light!' (Schiller, 'Der Taucher'); Strachey's translation. This is another *anabasis* following a *katabasis*: the eponymous diver ascends from suffocating depths to return to rose-perfumed daylight. See Freud, *Civilization and its Discontents* [1930] in *Standard Edition*, vol. 21, pp. 57–146 (p. 73).
37 Lassalle also appears in Freud's account of his '*Autodidasker*' dream (*Interpretation of Dreams*, pp. 298–299). Anzieu's commentary on that dream retells the story of Lassalle's fatal duel (*Freud's Self-Analysis*, p. 397).
38 D.L. Pike, *Passage Through Hell: Modernist Descents, Medieval Underworlds*, Ithaca and London: Cornell University Press, 1997, pp. xii and 19; W. Benjamin, 'On the Concept of History' [1940], in H. Eiland and M.W. Jennings (eds.), *Walter Benjamin: Selected Writings*, vol. 4, *1938–1940*, Cambridge, MA and London, England: Belknap Press of Harvard University Press, pp. 389–400 (p. 395).
39 Rodman, 'Juno and the Symptom', p. 135.
40 *Nachträglichkeit* or (in Strachey's translation) 'deferred action'. Freud relates the concept metaphorically to the re-writing of the past in the light of subsequent events: 'I am working on the assumption that our psychic mechanism has come into being by a process of stratification: the material present in the form of memory traces being subjected from time to time to a *rearrangement* in accordance with fresh circumstances – to a *retranscription*' (lett to Fliess of 6 December 1896; in Masson, *Complete Letters*, p. 207, original italics).

41   Starobinski, 'Acheronta Movebo.'
42   R.H. Armstrong, *A Compulsion for Antiquity: Freud and the Ancient World*, Ithaca and London: Cornell University Press, 2005.
43   *Interpretation of Dreams*, p. 249; cf. p. 553 (fn. 1).
44   Starobinski, 'Acheronta Movebo', p. 398.
45   Armstrong, *Compulsion for Antiquity*, p. 145.
46   Homer's *Iliad* 8:14ff. According to Hesiod (*Theogony*, 720–725), a bronze anvil dropped from heaven would reach earth ten days later; dropped from earth, it would reach Tartarus in the same period. Vergil (*Aeneid*, VI.577-579) says Tartarus is twice as deep as Olympus is high. It is the deepest point in the Greco-Roman underworld.
47   J. Breuer, 'Section III: Theoretical' [1893] in Breuer and Freud, *Studies on Hysteria*, in *Standard Edition*, vol. 2, pp. 183–251, p. 229.
48   Goethe, *Faust: Part One*, scene 4; see Strachey's n.2 to Breuer, 'Section III' (p. 229).
49   J. Dean, 'Psychoanalysis as a Philosophical Revolution: Freud's Divergence from the Philosophy of Kant, Schopenhauer, and Nietzsche', *Psychoanalytic Review*, 2016, vol. 103(4), 455–482. The quotations are from Nietzsche, *The Birth of Tragedy* [1872], in R. Geuss (ed.) and R. Speirs (ed. and tr.), *The Birth of Tragedy and Other Writings*, Cambridge: Cambridge University Press, 1999, p. 23.
50   A. Henrichs, '"Full of Gods": Nietzsche on Greek Polytheism and Culture', in P. Bishop (ed.), *Nietzsche and Antiquity: His Reaction and Response to the Classical Tradition*, Rochester, NY and Woodbridge: Camden House, 2004, pp. 114–137 (p. 127).
51   Starobinski, 'Acheronta Movebo', p. 405.
52   '*Die menschliche Kultur ruht auf zwei Stützen, die eine ist die Beherrschung der Naturkräfte, die andere die Beschränkung unserer Triebe. Gefesselte Sklaven tragen den Thron der Herrscherin*' (Freud, *Gesammelte Werke*, vol. 14, p. 106).
53   Freud, 'The Resistances to Psycho-Analysis' [1925], in *Standard Edition*, vol. 19, pp. 211–224 (p. 219).
54   On the Divača Cave and Gregor Žiberna, see HTTP https://www.showcaves. com/english/si/showcaves/Divaska.html and https://www.visitkras.info/en/the-divaca-cave (both retrieved 8 October 2020).
55   On the Škocjan Caves, see HTTP https://www.park-skocjanske-jame.si/en/ and https://www.visitkras.info/en/the-skocjan-caves-park?p=things-to-do/sights (both retrieved 8 October 2020).
56   Gay, *Freud: A Life*, p. 598.
57   P.J. Connolly, 'Karl Lueger: Mayor of Vienna', *Studies: An Irish Quarterly Review*, 1915, vol. 4(14), 226–249 (p. 226).
58   Schorske, *Fin-de-Siecle Vienna*, p. 134; H. von Hofmannsthal, *Buch der Freunder: Aufzeichnungen*, 1959, Frankfurt am Main: Fischer, 1959, p. 60.
59   S. Žižek, *The Indivisible Remainder: An Essay on Schelling and Related Matters*, London and New York: Verso, 1996, p. 1.
60   Charon ferries the dead across Acheron in return for a small fee; see L.Y. Rahmani, 'A Note on Charon's Obol', *'Atiqot*, 1993, vol. 22, 149–150.
61   R. Falconer, *Hell in Contemporary Literature: Western Descent Narratives since 1945*, Edinburgh: Edinburgh University Press, 2005, p.144.
62   M. Schur, *Freud: Living and Dying*, New York: International Universities Press, 1971.
63   Freud, *On the History of the Psycho-Analytic Movement* [1914], *Standard Edition*, vol. 14, pp. 1–66 (p. 66).
64   I.e., depth-psychology. Freud speaks of *Tiefenpsychologie* in his published works many times from 1913 onward, appropriating it from the Zurich school after his break with Jung.

65  P. Homans, 'We (Not so) Happy Few: Symbolic Loss and Mourning in Freud's Psychoanalytic Movement and the History of Psychoanalysis', *Psychoanalytic History*, 1999, vol. 1(1), 69–86.

66  E. Michaelis, *Die Menschheitsproblematik der Freudschen Psychoanalyse: Urbild und Maske: Eine grundsätzliche Untersuchung zur neueren Seelenforschung*, Leipzig: Barth, p. 65 (quoted in Schönau, *Sigmund Freuds Prosa*, p. 68).

67  G.A. Staley, 'Freud's Vergil', in V. Zajko and E. O'Gorman (eds.), *Classical Myth and Psychoanalysis: Ancient and Modern Stories of the Self*, Oxford: Oxford University Press, 2013, pp. 118–133 (p. 122).

68  C.G. Jung, 'Individual Dream Symbolism in Relation to Alchemy: A Study of the Unconscious Processes at Work in Dreams' [1935/1968], Jung, *Collected Works*, vol. 12, *Psychology and Alchemy*, pp. 39–223 (p. 39).

69  S. Shamdasani, 'Towards a Visionary Science: Jung's Notebooks of Transformation' in C.G. Jung, *The Black Books 1913–32*, ed. S. Shamdasani, New York: Norton, 2020, vol. 1, pp. 11–120 (pp.109–110). Jung used the expression 'confrontation with the unconscious' to describe his self-experiment (or spiritual crisis) recorded in *The Black Books*.

70  Freud, *New Introductory Lectures on Psycho-Analysis* [1933], in *Standard Edition*, vol. 22, pp. 1–182 (p. 80).

71  Falconer, *Hell in Contemporary Literature*, pp. 43 and 50–51; Staley, 'Freud's Vergil', p. 122; Mandelbaum, *Aeneid*, p. 137.

72  Robert D. Romanyshyn adopts this same Vergilian quotation in his post-Jungian study of soul work in academic research as the epigraph to a section titled 'Prologue: Falling Into the Work' (R.D. Romanyshyn, *The Wounded Researcher: Research with Soul in Mind*, New Orleans: Spring Journal Books, 2013, p. 1. Falconer, *Hell in Contemporary Literature*, explores recent katabatic memoirs of mental illness (pp. 113–143).

73  J. Strachey, 'The Nature of the Therapeutic Action of Psycho-Analysis', *International Journal of Psycho-Analysis*, 1934, vol. 15, 127–159.

74  See especially Giuseppe Civitarese on Bion's notion of negative capability – a major enrichment of Freud's 'evenly suspended attention' (*gleichschwebende Aufmerksamkeit*), the analyst's required receptive state (Freud, 'Recommendations to Physicians Practising Psycho-Analysis' [1912], *Standard Edition*, vol. 12, pp. 109–120 [p.111]; and G. Civitarese, 'On Bion's Concepts of Negative Capability and Faith', *Psychoanalytic Quarterly*, 2019, vol. 88(4), 751–783. According to Winnicott, 'psychotherapy of a deep-going kind may be done without interpretative work [...] the significant moment is that at which *the child surprises him- or herself*. It is not the moment of my clever interpretation that is significant' (Winnicott, 'Playing: Its Theoretical Status in the Clinical Situation', *International Journal of Psycho-Analysis*, 1968, vol. 49, 591–599 [p. 597]; original italics).

75  Letter to Fliess of 12 December 1897; in Masson, *Complete Letters*, p. 286.

76  N.M. Cheshire, 'The Empire of the Ear: Freud's Problem With Music', *International Journal of Psycho-Analysis*, 1996, vol. 77, 1127–1168; C.L. Diaz de Chumaceiro, 'Richard Wagner's life and music: What Freud knew', in S. Feder et al. (eds), *Psychoanalytic Explorations in Music*, Madison, CT: International University Press, 1993, pp. 249–278. As for Freud's musical milieu (as noted by Carpenter), Max Graf, the father of Freud's 'Little Hans', was a professor of music history, a prominent music critic and a member of Freud's Psychological Wednesday Society (the precursor to the Viennese Psychoanalytic Society) (A. Carpenter, 'Towards a History of Operatic Psychoanalysis', *Psychoanalytic History*, 2010, vol. 12(2), 173–194).

77  Although associated with volcanoes, Hephaestus and Vulcan are not chthonic – nor, in contrast to Hermes, Demeter, and Zeus, are they Olympian gods with chthonian aspects.

78  See, for example, Wagner's 1850 essay *Das Judentum in der Musik*; T.W. Adorno, *Versuch über Wagner*, in *In Search of Wagner*, tr. R Livingston, London and New York: Verso, 2005; and M.A. Weiner, *Richard Wagner and the Anti-Semitic Imagination*, Lincoln: University of Nebraska Press, 1995.

79  Quoted in Diaz de Chumaceiro, 'What Freud knew', p. 251.

80  D. Jonte-Pace, *Speaking the Unspeakable: Religion, Misogyny, and the Uncanny Mother in Freud's Cultural Texts*, Berkeley, Los Angeles, and London: University of California Press, 2001; and Weiner, *Richard Wagner and the Anti-Semitic Imagination*.

81  Diaz de Chumaceiro, 'What Freud knew'. Jonte-Pace refers to 'the Germanic *Nibelungenlied*, best known to Freud and his contemporaries in its Wagnerian form, with its great adversaries Siegfried and Hagen' (*Speaking the Unspeakable*, p. 26). In fact, Freud knew the ancient text rather better than the modern music drama. Cheshire, 'Empire of the Ear', gives other examples of scholars assuming that references by Freud to northern myth derive from Wagner when they actually derived from the older literary sources.

82  Armstrong, *Compulsion for Antiquity*, pp. 239–240.

83  M. Sprengnether, *The Spectral Mother: Freud, Feminism, and Psychoanalysis*, Ithaca and London: Cornell University Press 1990; Jonte-Pace, *Speaking the Unspeakable*.

84  E.R. Wolfson, *A Dream Interpreted Within a Dream: Oneiropoiesis and the Prism of Imagination*, New York: Zone Books, 2011, pp. 65 and 185.

85  Wolfson, *A Dream Interpreted*, p. 185; Freud, *The Unconscious* [1915], in *Standard Edition*, vol. 14, pp. 159–215 (p. 186).

86  Wolfson, *A Dream Interpreted*, p. 187; J.R. Wikse, 'Night Rule: Dreams as Social Intelligence', in M. Ullman and C. Limmer (eds.), *The Variety of Dream Experience: Expanding Our Ways of Working with Dreams*, 2nd edn, Albany: State University of New York Press, 1999, p. 145.

87  Wolfson, *A Dream Interpreted*, p. 65.

88  Freud to Fliess on 3 December 1897 (in Masson, *Complete Letters*, p. 285).

89  E. Simon, 'Sigmund Freud, the Jew', *The Leo Baeck Institute Year Book*, 1957, vol. 2(1), 270–305 (p. 301) (quoted in Schönau, *Sigmund Freuds Prosa*, p. 72).

90  Falconer, *Hell in Contemporary Literature*, pp. 18–19.

91  Schönau, *Sigmund Freuds Prosa*, p. 69.

92  E. Jones, *Sigmund Freud: Life and Work*, vol. 2, *The Years of Maturity 1900–1919*, London: Hogarth Press, 1955, title page.

93  Rodman, 'Juno and the Symptom', p. 147.

94  Freud to Fliess on 6 August 1899 (in Masson, *Complete Letters*, p. 365); see Rodman, 'Juno and the Symptom'; Hyman, *Tangled Bank*.

95  Jonte-Pace, *Speaking the Unspeakable*, p. 24.

96  Shengold, 'Metaphor of the Journey', also draws parallels between Freud's *Interpretation of Dreams* and Dante. Jones reports that Freud read (among many other authors) Dante during the period in which he wrote the dream book (*Sigmund Freud*, vol. 1, p. 380).

97  Freud himself tells the story (*Interpretation of Dreams*, p. 197).

98  Dante's 'dark wood' in which he finds himself at midlife in *Inferno* I.2.

99  S. Sherwin-White, 'Freud, the *Via Regia*, and Alexander the Great', *Psychoanalytic History*, 2003, vol. 5(2), 187–193 (p. 188). For Freud's Clark lecture reference to the 'royal road', see 'Five Lectures on Psycho-analysis' [1910], in *Standard Edition*, vol. 11, pp. 1–56 (p. 33).

100  Sterba, 'The Psychoanalyst in a World of Change'.

101  H.P. Colburn, "Connectivity and Communication in the Achaemenid Empire", *Journal of the Economic and Social History of the Orient*, 2013, vol. 56(1), 29–52.

102 J. Glenn, 'The Open-Air Closet', *American Journal of Psychoanalysis*, 1980, vol. 40(2), 165–168. See Herodotus, *Histories* V.52-54 and VIII.98, for his description of the *Via Regia* and the Persian imperial postal service.
103 Armstrong, *Compulsion for Antiquity*; Freud, *Introductory Lectures on Psycho-Analysis* [1916], in *Standard Edition*, vol. 15, pp. 1–240.
104 Armstrong, *Compulsion for Antiquity*, pp. 225 and 107 (original italics).
105 Armstrong, *Compulsion for Antiquity*, p. 250.
106 Neither Armstrong (*Compulsion*), nor Staley ('Freud's Vergil'), refers to Sherwin-White ('Freud, the Via Regia').
107 Masson, *Complete Letters*, pp. 268–271.
108 Masson, *Complete Letters*, pp. 268, 269, 271. It is unclear to what extent Freud's memories of his nursemaids are screen memories or are distorted by fantasy and/or splitting.
109 M. von Koppenfels, 'Ein Schloss am Meer: Freuds Traum vom "Frühstücksschiff" und das Affektkapitel der *Traumdeutung*', *Psyche*, 2012, vol. 66(9–10), 968–991.
110 Letter from Freud to Fliess of 14 April 1898; in Masson, *Complete Letters*, pp. 307–310.
111 Letter to Fliess of 3 October 3 1897; in Masson, *Complete Letters*, p. 268. Freud here reports that he was aged between two and two and a half when, travelling from Leipzig to Vienna and staying the night alone with his mother, he saw her nude. Gay points out that repression distorted his recollection: he was nearly four (*Freud: A Life*, p. 11).
112 Albunea is a sulphurous thermal spring. According to the *Oxford Classical Dictionary*, the oracle of Faunus is only mentioned by Vergil and Albunea's likely location is modern day Acque Albule at Tivoli, near Rome.
113 Freud, *Analysis Terminable and Interminable* [1937], in *Standard Edition*, vol. 23, pp. 209–254 (p. 226).
114 Starobinski, 'Acheronta Movebo.'
115 Von Koppenfels, 'Ein Schloss am Meer'. The Chapter on Affects (*Affektkapitel*) is Freud, *Interpretation of Dreams*, Section VI(H) (pp. 460–487). In this chapter, Freud even mentions his Easter 1898 trip, recalling Aquileia in particular, but not specifically the Slovenian caves (pp. 464, 466). As von Koppenfels observes, '*Unterirdische Flüsse spielen jedoch auch im Affektkapitel der Traumdeutung*' (p. 983).
116 '[…] *die alte hydraulische Metaphorik der Seele zurückgreift, die zur Rhetorik der frühen Hysteriestudien besser passt als zum Traumbuch*' (von Koppenfels, 'Ein Schloss am Meer', p. 983).
117 '[…] *»Tiefe« ist hier, wie üblich, eine Metapher für Lebenszeit*' (von Koppenfels, 'Ein Schloss am Meer', p. 983).
118 Hydraulic metaphors of brain and nerve function long preceded Freud – for example, Descartes' explanation of human reflexes by analogy with hydraulic automata then fashionable in royal gardens. Freud's hydraulic metaphors are primarily rooted in nineteenth-century engineering and thermodynamics – for example, 'blowing off steam' (Freud, 'Psychopathic Characters on the Stage' [1905 or 1906], in *Standard Edition*, vol. 7, pp. 303–310 [p. 305]). What is interesting about the examples von Koppenfels highlights is that they are geological – underground rivers, wells, springs, water currents – rather than mechanical. The unconscious influence of Freud's holiday memories of the Škocjan cave may, I think, have influenced Freud's *Affektkapitel* text. Freud's best-known Platonic metaphor is that of the rider in *The Ego and the Id* (Freud, *The Ego and the Id* [1923], in *Standard Edition*, vol. 19, pp. 1–66 [p. 25]). On Plato and Freud, see B. Simon, 'Plato and Freud – The Mind in Conflict and the Mind in Dialogue', *Psychoanalytic Quarterly*, 1973, vol. 42, 91–122; and J. Lear, *Open Minded: Working Out the Logic of the Soul*, Cambridge, MA and London, England: Harvard University Press, 1998.

119  *Phaedo*, tr. Grube, in Plato, *Complete Works*, ed. J.M. Cooper, Indianapolis and Cambridge: Hackett, 1997, p. 95.

120  On Freud's inconsistent use of the expression 'great reservoir of the libido', see J. Strachey, 'Appendix B: The Great Reservoir of Libido' [1961] in *Standard Edition*, vol. 19, pp. 63-66. Strachey notes that Freud sometimes identifies the ego and sometimes the id with that expression, and also the ambiguity of the term 'reservoir' which may imply a water storage tank or a water source. Freud, Strahcey observes, uses it in both senses, and the latter ambiguity is equally present in the Platonic image of Tartarus as both destination and source of all rivers.

121  Freud, 'The Psychogenesis of a Case of Homosexuality in a Woman' [1920], in *Standard Edition*, vol. 18, pp. 145–172 (p. 160).

122  P. Brooks, 'Freud's Masterplot', *Yale French Studies*, 1977, vol. 55/56, 280–300.

123  Freud, 'The Question of Lay Analysis' [1926], in *Standard Edition*, vol. 20, pp. 177–25 (p. 191).

124  Freud, 'The Question of Lay Analysis', p. 195.

125  Freud, 'Psychogenesis of a Case of Homosexuality in a Woman', p. 167.

126  P. A. Roth, 'Essentially narrative explanations', *Studies in History and Philosophy of Science*, 2017, vol. 62, 42–50.

127  Freud, 'Fräulein Elisabeth von R' [1893], one of the case histories from *Studies on Hysteria* in *Standard Edition*, vol. 2, pp. 135–181 (p. 160).

128  Starobinski, 'Acheronta Movebo', p. 406.

# Chapter 10

# Orestes, *Katabasis*, and Aggrieved Masculine Entitlement (in Athens, Rhegium, and Today)

*Kurt Lampe*

## Orestes: Insane Badness or Exemplary Mental Health?

The final scene of Euripides' *Orestes* is set six days after the protagonist has murdered his mother Clytemnestra and moments after Apollo has prevented him from murdering his aunt Helen. He has taken his cousin Hermione hostage and issues a breathtakingly nonchalant warning to his uncle: 'I'm going to kill your daughter, if you want to know' (*Or.* 1578).[1] When Menelaus suggests there has been enough killing, Orestes replies, 'I could never tire of killing bad women!' (1590). It is no wonder that this play is at the center of claims about 'the crisis of meaning in Euripides',[2] where the Athenian malaise of foreign wars, internecine violence, and the collapse of received values supposedly finds representation in a character who is 'not only bad, but unpleasantly, stupidly, insanely bad'.[3] Nor are claims about Orestes' 'insanity' limited to this specific tragedy. Psychoanalytic readers have associated all the portrayals of Orestes by Aeschylus, Sophocles, and Euripides with various kinds of mental illness.[4]

On the other hand, some Freudian readers have come to the opposite conclusion. They have found in Orestes, and especially in Aeschylus' trilogy the *Oresteia*, a paradigm of healthy psychological development.[5] Jungian readers generally agree with them. The most detailed and insightful is Ben Pestell's recent chapter, which claims that 'Orestes is the crucial figure in Greek tragedy for the healthy mind in general, and for individuation in particular', and that Orestes' acquittal on the charge of matricide 'signifies his release from divine compulsion and finds him safely on the path of individuation'.[6] In this Pestell agrees with some classicists, who recognize in Aeschylus' characters a progression toward greater lucidity, temperance, and harmonization with divine powers.[7]

How are we to account for this sharp difference of opinion? Part of the explanation undoubtedly lies in the evaluative frameworks applied by different readers: we would not expect a Freudian, a Jungian, and a historian of Greek ethics to analyze tragic texts in the same way. We should also recognize that there is considerable diversity in different tragedians' portrayals of Orestes. Finally, let us note that there *is* no stable truth about the psychology

DOI: 10.4324/9781003054139-14

of a fictional character, only readings with more or less power to enhance the significance of the text for a given community of interpreters. Yet it remains worthwhile, after we have acknowledged these provisos, to use stories about Orestes in order to think about recurring psychosocial patterns.

With this in mind, I suggest that Carl Jung's analysis of the *katabasis* motif can help us to arbitrate this dispute. Although it is not obvious at first glance, many elements of the *katabasis* scheme map onto the Orestes tradition. The first benefit of using this framework is that it presumes disintegration (psychosis) and integration (healthy psychological development) are complementary movements in a transformational process, not exclusive alternatives. The second benefit is that it helps us to articulate how thinking about Orestes can improve our understanding of today's psychosocial challenges. For this we will need to draw upon Helene Shulman's more recent theorization of crisis and creative renewal. The upshot, to put it simply, is that we should view Orestes neither as an instance of 'insane badness' nor as a paradigm for 'the healthy mind'. Rather, the variations in his story communicate both a promise and a warning for contemporary individuals and communities in need of transformation.

## Orestes and *Katabasis*

Let me begin by explaining what I mean by '*katabasis*' and how it relates to Orestes. I will use '*katabasis*' to designate any narrative in which a person, their family, or their community undergoes the following events:

1. a crisis of order, such as a threat to the organization or existence of the personality, family, or constitution;
2. a 'going down', whether spatially (into an underworld), psychologically (into the inner world, through madness or dreaming), or socially (into chaos, by suspending routines and removing everyday categories and boundaries);
3. creative reorganization of elements, energies, and relationships;
4. renewal or 'rebirth' of the psyche, family, or polity.

In *Symbols of Transformation*, Jung argues that the first element – crisis of order – is often symbolized by the Great Mother. This archetypal figure manifests not only as a woman but also as a sunset, ocean, abyss, serpent, dragon, or whale. There is a psychological explanation for this symbolism: when the ego, represented by the hero, is confronted by challenges for which it is poorly adapted, it must 'go down the sunset way' and 'be reborn' from the life-giving 'womb' of the unconscious.[8] In other words, the mother archetype appears due to her connection with gestation and life-giving. At the same time, this 'strange idea of becoming a child again, of returning to the parental shelter, and of entering into the mother in order to be reborn through her' triggers several kinds of fear: first, the ego hesitates to make this 'self-sacrifice', which is a kind of death for it; second, the image of 'entering into the mother' activates incest anxieties.[9] Jung adds that in many societies, 'ritual actions' have been used to guide this turbulent, dangerous, but crucial process.[10] Mircea Eliade collects and analyzes reports of such rituals in *Rites and Symbols of Initiation: The Mysteries of Birth and Rebirth*. Though he puts significantly less emphasis on maternal figures, he notes the importance of separation from the mother during coming of age ceremonies.[11] Moreover, he documents how initiands in many places are secluded in huts that represent the 'belly' or 'womb' of the monster that has devoured them, and from which they will be reborn. Curiously, in some cases they are reborn precisely as the monster that has killed them.[12]

A word is in order about how the unconscious renews the ego, hero, family, or community. For this I shall turn to Helene Shulman's *Living at the Edge of Chaos: Complex Systems in Culture and Psyche*.[13] Shulman explains that the psyche's unconscious screening and integration of internal and external information flows provide the ego with continuity, coherence, and 'a somewhat reliable interface with the environment'.[14] We experience this as meaning, purpose, and adjustment to 'reality'. When these cannot be integrated, a crisis occurs. Crucially, Shulman adds that analogous processes occur at multiple levels of organization, such as the family and the city. Disorder at any level is often connected with problems at other levels.

For example, the schizophrenic symptoms of Shulman's patient 'Edward Coe' were inseparable from his family history of neglect and abuse, his native American heritage of cultural and ecological devastation, the psychiatric system that isolated him with minimal therapeutic support, and the socioeconomic system that underpaid, under-educated, and antagonized the nurses who were his primary contacts.[15] From this perspective, it is not only Edward's psyche but the entire interlocking 'ecosystem' that needs to undergo descent, reorganization, and rebirth. The symptoms of crisis include not only Edward's dysfunctional affective, cognitive, and relational patterns but also the patterns of poverty and sickness in indigenous communities, the disappearance of flora and fauna, and the exploitation of a low-wage underclass. In theorizing how renewal can occur, Shulman once again takes inspiration from the cultural psychiatry and anthropology. For instance, the treatment for a young man diagnosed with schizophrenia in Chile's Mapuche community culminates with a collective ritual:

> The experience is intense and emotional, filled with numinous symbols, sweaty movement, and physical touching. [...] The whole group shares a homeopathic melting in a fragile and treasured ritual journey. The community moves deep into a chaotic region and [...] is led toward meaning and integration.[16]

Note that this experience involves the entire community in a descent or 'homeopathic melting [...] into a chaotic region'. The community's everyday logic and hierarchy, like the sufferer's ego, undergo a kind of 'death': both 'melt' in the strong emotions, kinetic and sensory experiences, and promiscuous bodily contact. This 'chaos' makes space for creative renewal through archetypal 'numinous' narratives and dramatic reenactments, from which the sufferer and the community are renewed and reborn.

Let us now turn to Orestes. In this section, I will permit myself to freely combine ancient Greek literary texts and testimonia about political and religious practices. It is important to acknowledge that each of these sources has its own external contexts and internal structure, which would require careful investigation if we aimed at grasping their meaning with any degree of nuance. However, there are also core elements in Orestes' narrative that manifest repeatedly throughout this tradition. For now, it is merely this schematic pattern I wish to illuminate.

Let me begin with the first component of *katabasis*, namely crisis of order. All the stories about Orestes involve overlapping personal, familial, political, and religious crises. In the core narrative (as told in Aeschylus' *Oresteia* and Sophocles' and Euripides' *Electra*s),[17] Orestes returns home on the cusp of adulthood and kills his mother Clytemnestra, who had herself killed his father Agamemnon, partly because the latter had sacrificed their daughter – Orestes' sister Iphigenia – to Artemis. The violent dysfunction here is not only familial but also political, since Orestes' family rules the polis and leads the pan-Hellenic war against Troy.

Other narratives project this multifactorial crisis to other stages of Orestes' life, beginning with his infancy. Many Greek vases depict a scene from Euripides' fragmentary *Telephus*, in which the titular hero holds his sword to the baby Orestes' throat while clinging to an altar. We know from Hyginus' summary that Clytemnestra advised Telephus to adopt this tactic in order to persuade Agamemnon to help him.[18] If we turn to events after the matricide, Euripides' *Iphigenia among the Taurians* sees Iphigenia nearly kill Orestes. We have already witnessed Orestes' attempt to kill his aunt and cousin in Euripides' *Orestes*; this compulsion to kill female relatives extends also to his half-sister Erigone, who – like his own sister, threatened by his father – was saved by Artemis.[19] It is obvious that all this violent mayhem exhibits the same kind of disorder we find in the core narrative. This is one reason why Artemis features throughout the stories. Because she is a goddess of liminal conditions and transitions, her appearance often signals release from personal, familial, and political structures. As both savior and punisher in these liminal conditions, she represents their ambivalent potency.[20]

It is evident from the foregoing that the Great Mother plays a key role in all of this: it is Clytemnestra who orchestrates Telephus' threat to the infant Orestes, kills Orestes' father, and occupies the throne that would otherwise pass to him. The homicidal antagonism between Orestes and his sister, half-sister, female cousin, and aunt replicates his fundamental tension with his mother.[21] Also noteworthy is that, in Aeschylus' *Libation Bearers*, Orestes repeatedly refers to his mother as a 'moray', 'viper', or 'dragon' (*muraina, ekhidna, drakō*, 994–6, 1046–7). As Eliade's research leads us to expect, the 'dragon' is a mobile signifier in this family: Clytemnestra dreams of both Agamemnon and Orestes as dragons,[22] and Orestes interprets the dream to mean 'I will turn into a dragon, and kill her' (*Cho.*, 549–50). A local tradition in Arcadia tells us that Orestes died there from a snake bite.[23]

Although the metaphor of 'going down' is subtle in Orestes' narratives, we find many allusions to descent into the underworld, into a deathlike torpor, and into initiatory incubation. In Aeschylus' *Kindly Ones*, the Erinyes threaten, 'I'll dry you out and drag you living below, where you'll pay for your matricidal crimes. [...] For mighty Hades is the arbiter of mortals beneath the earth' (267–74). In Euripides' *Iphigenia among the Taurians*, Iphigenia tells Orestes and Pylades, 'You've traveled a long way to this land, and long will be your stay away from home, below (μακρὸν δ' ἀπ' οἴκων χρόνον ἔσεσθε δὴ κατώ)' (480-1). In Euripides' *Orestes*, Electra reports that he has been bedridden since the murder'. 'I sit sleepless beside a wretched corpse', she laments, 'for with so little breath, he is a corpse' (84–9). According to the people in Troezen, when Orestes arrived, polluted with his mother's blood, he was secluded in a small hut until he could be purified. The Troezenians point to a 'Sacred Stone' in front of the temple of Apollo the Watcher, beside the Temple of Artemis of the Wolves, where nine men purified Orestes. Those men buried the offscourings nearby, and a laurel tree – sacred to Apollo – grew on that spot. People claiming descent from the nine purifiers dined in 'what was called the hut of Orestes' (Ὀρέστου καλούμενον σκηνή) on specified dates in Pausanias' own time (second century CE, Paus. 2.34.4, 8-9).

We have now seen how the Orestes tradition includes the katabatic stages of crisis and descent. The Troezenian rituals of purification point toward the third and fourth elements, creative reorganization, and rebirth. Perhaps more familiar to most readers is the resolution in Aeschylus' *Libation Bearers*, which we will examine further below. Both examples confront us with an unanticipated complication, to which psychological interpreters of myth have given far too little attention. The complication is that it is not only (and not even primarily) Orestes, his family, and his polis which are reorganized and reborn. Orestes' rebirth is usually narrated with amazingly little detail: few indications are given of how his psychical energies have been reorganized. More strikingly, we generally hear nothing at all about reorganization in his home community. The explanation for this is obvious: commemorating the madness, descent, and purification of Orestes aims to contribute to the creative renewal *of the communities which invoke him.* He is almost always represented as a polluted visitor, not a denizen of the community. This is why it is crucial to take account of the contexts in which myths are retold. In order to elucidate this suggestion, I need to turn to specific examples.

## Orestes at Rhegium

Let us first turn our attention to the Greek cities of Rhegium (modern Reggio di Calabria) and Messene (modern Messina), which faced each other across the strait between Sicily and Calabria. Thanks to excellent French and Italian scholarship,[24] we can roughly understand how these communities integrated versions of Orestes into their etiological myths and rituals in the early fifth century BCE. This will allow us not only to supplement the Athenocentric mainstream tradition but also to illustrate how the fulfilment of Orestes' *katabasis* belongs to the community that commemorates him.

We mostly owe our knowledge of this tradition to testimony preserved by a commentary on Vergil.[25] It begins with the author's own summary of the myth:

> Orestes, who was mad after killing his mother, was told by the oracle that he'd finally escape his madness if he brought back his sister Iphigenia and was cleansed in a stream that united seven rivers. After long suffering he rescued Iphigenia from Tauris and came to the territory of the Rhegians. There he found the river, was purified, and crossed to Sicily. Near Syracuse he established a temple and consecrated the idol of the goddess he had brought from Tauris, as he was instructed in a dream.
>
> (ibid., 325)

Slightly later, the author quotes two Latin works that are now lost:

> Varro mentions this river, in which Orestes was purified, in Book 11 of the *Human Antiquities*: "By Rhegium there are seven rivers close together [...] It's said that in these Orestes was purified from his mother's murder, and for a long time his bronze sword remained there. He built a temple to Apollo, from whose precinct the Rhegians, after a ceremony, would pluck laurel to take with them when setting out for Delphi." So too Cato, *Origins* Book 3: [...] in the territory <of the people of Taurianum> there are six rivers; the seventh divides Taurian and Rhegian land, and its name is the Pecolus. There they say Orestes came with Iphigenia and Pylades in order to expiate his mother's murder. It's remembered that not long ago you could see in a tree the sword that Orestes is said to have left behind as he departed."
>
> (ibid., 326)

Another surviving source, a Greek scholium to Theocritus' *Idylls*, is more cursory and provides no additional details.[26] We can sketch two ways in which this testimony relates to psychosocial transformations at Rhegium. The first is a ritualized transition from adolescence to adulthood. Varro claims that Orestes 'built a temple to Apollo, from whose precinct the Rhegians, after a ceremony (*re divina facta*), would pluck laurel to take with them when setting out for Delphi'. We heard earlier that at Troezen, a laurel tree marked the spot where the pollution washed from Orestes was buried. The motif of picking laurel for Apollo recalls better-known festivals at Thebes (the *Daphnēphoria*) and Delphi (the *Septērion*), both of which involve coming of age.[27] Pilgrimage to Delphi by choruses of young boys or girls has also been connected with transition to adulthood. 'One might want to see this as a sort of *rite de passage*', Ian Rutherford suggests, 'where the young men assert their identity as citizens of their polis for the first time'.[28] It is therefore noteworthy that the people of Messene had a custom of sending a chorus of boys with a trainer and *aulos*-player to Rhegium (Pausanias 5.25.2). As Felice Costabile argues, this probably relates to the very same festival. Taking all of this together, Costabile conjectures that the festival mentioned by Varro includes the following events (among many others, evidence for which has not survived): a chorus of Messenian boys sails to Rhegium; Rhegian and Messenian choruses perform somewhere in Rhegian territory; they take laurel from the precinct of the temple of Apollo in Rhegium; they depart as part of a sacred delegation to Apollo's center at Delphi; they return to Rhegium.[29]

Though we are missing most of the details, this already gives us enough to outline how Orestes' story furnishes a narrative and imaginal container for the boys' experience. This container conforms to the katabatic scheme described in the previous section. First, there is a crisis of order: mythically speaking, Orestes arrives in a state of madness, suffering, and pollution. This corresponds to the boys' separation from their previous familial, social, political, and religious status. Second, a going down: Orestes goes mad and receives instructions in dreams and oracles. This corresponds to the suspension of routine activities and boundaries during the festival. Third, creative reorganization: Orestes brings the idol of Artemis to southern Italy, bathes in the river, dedicates his polluted sword, founds the temple of Apollo at Rhegium and the temples of Artemis Phakelitis in Messenian and Rhegian territory. This corresponds to the ritualized activities of the chorus of boys, most of which are unknown to us. We know they picked laurel from the sanctuary of Apollo connected with Orestes. It is tempting to speculate that before that, the choruses also visited the other sites associated with Orestes: the river dividing Rhegian from Taurian land in the north, and the temple of Artemis Phakelitis at the Leukopetra peninsula in the south.[30] Visits to territorial peripheries are another common feature in coming of age procedures.[31] Finally, there is rebirth: Orestes is freed from madness. This corresponds to the social and religious reintegration of the chorus members in their new roles.

The second kind of transformation occurs through the same ritual cycle but concerns the entire community. In order to perceive this broader cultural logic, we need to take account of historical contexts. While our earliest source for Orestes at Rhegium is Cato (c. 170 BCE), Pausanias' testimony securely dates the festival to the early fifth century BCE.[32] Several events in this period

seem relevant. First, in 494 the tyrant Anaxilaus deposed Rhegium's oligarchy of one thousand citizens. Later, he conquered and renamed Messene
(hitherto Zancle), where he stabilized his rule partly by re-settling exiles from
the original Messene (in the Peloponnese).[33] Since Rhegians traced their
ancestry to a mixture of Ionians from Chalcis and Dorians from Messene,
this undoubtedly created ripples in the social hierarchy in Rhegium as well.[34]
Archeological evidence shows new walls were built at this time, which added
a substantial area to the polis. Epigraphical dedications to Apollo have been
discovered in the newly enclosed area, leading Emilia Andronico to speculate
that a temple of Apollo was built there.[35] Giulia Gasparro also notes that
Apollo began to feature prominently on Rhegian coins in the later fifth century BCE, having scarcely appeared on them before.[36] This architectural and
numismatic evidence tends to confirm Costabile's conjecture that it was
Anaxilaus who inaugurated the joint Messene-Rhegium choral celebrations
of Apollo and their associated myths as part of a larger cultural program.[37]

This allows us to postulate that the ritual cycle under examination, in addition to initiating young men, also aimed to stabilize and renew society more
broadly. By introducing a festival re-enacting Orestes' journey, the new regime
would effectively be establishing a new 'founding hero' for the polis. Though
the Rhegians had several myths associated with their historical foundations,[38]
the Orestes story projects the delimitation of their territory and establishment of their temples much further into the past. Foundation myths and
founder cults were both important to civic identity: by commemorating
where they came from and why the citizens celebrated who they were.

Orestes' story lends itself to foundation myths for the same reason as it
works for coming of age ceremonies. In Greek myth, the two are surprisingly
similar. Coming of age is narrativized as violent separation from previous
roles and transgression into a new social and cosmic space, which creates
danger, guilt, and the need for expiation.[39] So too colonization is represented
as forced emigration from the mother city, often due to impious violence, for
which the colonists atone through their divinely authorized expedition.[40] In
fact, murder is the most paradigmatic starting point for Greek colonial foundation myths: 'Within colonial discourse', Carol Dougherty writes, 'murder
is emblematic of civic crisis [...] as the impetus for colonization. [...] [M]urder
(and the purification it requires) describes colonization as the move from a
state of disordered chaos to an ordered city'.[41] This parallelism between coming of age and colonization coalesces in Apollo, who protects and guides
both adolescents and founders. He represents the creative dynamism that
connects crime and pollution with new order and purity, as is clearest in the
myths and cults associated with Delphi.[42] Orestes, the adolescent murderer
who establishes shrines and cities throughout the Greek world, may in fact be
a mortal doublet of Apollo.[43]

We can now outline how Orestes' story functions in Anaxilaus' attempted
re-foundation. First is a crisis of order: Orestes' murder and pollution correspond to Anaxilaus' coup d'état, displacement of the thousand-man

oligarchy, and the disruption that ensues. Next, there is a going down: Orestes' pollution and wandering correspond to the period of social, political, and cultural chaos as new governmental, spatial, and ritual structures are being devised. The community also re-enacts this period of chaos through the boys' commemoration of Orestes' visit during the festival. This leads to reorganization and renewal: Orestes' salvation corresponds to the moment when the boys pick laurel from the sanctuary legendarily founded by Orestes, but recently enclosed in the city walls and (re)built by Anaxilaus. They take this laurel to Delphic Apollo, whose divine power conjoins the pure and the impure, legitimating a new order that has emerged from crime. Orestes simply disappears from the scene, but the community – represented by its new citizens – is reborn. (That, at least, is the logic of the performance. Whether it succeeded is another question.)

## *Katabasis* in Aeschylus' *Oresteia*

The previous section illustrates my claim that we need to focus on the community that commemorates Orestes but the evidence is too scanty for us to fully explain its psychosocial significance. For that we must turn to Aeschylus' *Oresteia*. Since this well-known text has been exhaustively discussed by previous scholars, I will not go through it in detail. Rather, I will focus on making two arguments. First, I will affirm that it dramatizes a katabic renewal for both Athens and Orestes. Second, I will argue that Orestes' rebirth involves very limited psychological integration, while Athens' politico-religious integration, though genuine, is grounded in systemic misogyny. For this reason, we need to take care claiming that Orestes is a model for 'healthy integration' today.

Many critics have written insightfully about the resolution of crisis and creation of new order in the *Libation Bearers*. Richard Seaford in particular has illuminated how the *Oresteia* dramatizes oppositions between life and death, love and enmity, stillness and mobility, the masculine and the feminine, the old and the new, and the lower and upper worlds. These tensions drive a cycle of violence, which is resolved at the end of the trilogy through the inaugural trial at the Areopagus and the integration of the Erinyes into Athenian topography and cult.[44] Building on the work of both Seaford and Richard Trousdell, Ben Pestell adds that we can fruitfully view Athena's act of persuasion after this trial as a precursor to 'talking cures'; as the mediating speaker throughout the *Libation Bearers*, Athena brings the Erinyes' power into collective symbolic consciousness, and thus helps to integrate their old, underworldly, feminine, vengeful power into both Athenian religion and Orestes' psyche.[45] In fact, we should reiterate that pollution and violence are also central to Apollo's youthful masculine divinity, which likewise becomes more integrated in the course of the trilogy.[46]

Yet this integration does not establish parity between opposing terms; to the contrary, it subordinates the feminine to the masculine in the family, political community, and divine hierarchy. In her brilliant article, Froma Zeitlin shows that the logic of this subordination is not only 'sexist' and 'patriarchal',[47] but downright 'misogynistic'. Its implicit logic is familiar: feminine erotic, procreative, and maternal powers are represented as dangerous and in need of domestication by masculine governance.[48] That is why, even though the trilogy acknowledges Agamemnon's crime and Apollo's savagery, both of which are explicitly connected with spirits of vengeance,[49] the final play connects the female Erinyes exclusively with Clytemnestra's maternal wrath. Feminine anger becomes the most prominent cause of crisis for both Orestes and Athens. The Erinyes drive Orestes into solitude and madness and threaten the polis with sterility and childlessness. Their mollification and inclusion are orchestrated by Athena, a goddess who straightforwardly proclaims, 'I praise the male in all things, [...] with all my heart' (*Eum.* 737–8). This brings about a new order for Athens, as the Erinyes – now Eumenides (or 'Kindly Ones') – promise increased fertility rather than blight, foreign war rather than civil strife, and the temperance and justice of legal procedures rather than the excess and guilt of vendettas (*Eum.* 681–710, 902–1020).

Orestes too experiences a kind of rebirth, if we accept that he has been released from pollution and madness and can henceforth govern his household and kingdom at Argos (*Eum.* 754–7). But we should not hastily accept that he is on his way to healthy individuation in modern psychodynamic terms. It is important to note that Orestes' only (and very weak) expression of regret for his action is both preceded and followed by blaming his victim and defending himself. This is the closest he comes to remorse:

> I'm pained by what was done, by what was suffered, by this whole family,
> since I bear the unenviable pollution of this victory.
> (ἀλγῶ μὲν ἔργα καὶ πάθος γένος τε πᾶν,
> ἄζηλα νίκης τῆσδ᾽ ἔχων μιάσματα)
>
> (*Cho.* 900-2)

Both before and immediately after this vague admission, he justifies himself and blames the victim. First, he asks for the implements of his father's murder to be spread out,

> that the father may see--
> not my father, but the one who beholds all things--
> that he may some day be my witness in justice
> that I justly pursued my mother's doom.
>
> (*Cho.* 984–9)

Next, he expresses his loathing for his dead mother:

> What does she seem to be?
> If she were a moray or a viper [...][50]
> May I never have such a wife in my house:
> sooner let the gods kill me, childless!
>
> (*Cho.* 994–1006)

Finally, he recapitulates both his self-justification and his hatred for his mother:

> I proclaim to my friends
> that I killed my mother not without justice,
> since she was a father-slaying pollution and abomination to the gods!
>
> (*Cho.* 1026–8)

Nor has Orestes become remorseful by the time of the trial. When asked whether Apollo guided him to kill his mother, he testifies, 'And at no point up to the present have I found fault with what happened' (καὶ δεῦρό γ' ἀεὶ τὴν τύχην οὐ μέμφομαι, *Eum.* 596). Thus, there is considerable merit in Marie Delcourt's claim that Orestes never moves past his 'neurotic' mother complex.[51] His rebirth involves no change in his schizoid idealization of his father and loathing for his mother.

Setting the trilogy in its historical contexts helps to explain both Athens' systemic misogyny and Orestes' denigration of his female parent. We do not know whether Aeschylus composed this trilogy (in 458 BCE) in response to some perceived moral and/or political crisis. Certainly, the plays allude to Ephialtes' reforms of the Areopagus and an alliance between Athens and Argos, both of which can be dated to 462 BCE.[52] But it is safest to view the *Oresteia* as an abstract template for renewal more than a solution to specific problems. The key point for us is that this template was probably satisfying for the majority of its original audience. As David Cohen has shown, in ancient Athens the gender politics of honor, shame, and the division of public space generated recurrent anxiety and hostility toward women.[53] For this reason, crises of order were often mythologized as problems with mothers, stepmothers, wives, or other female subjects and objects of male sexual desire. In these myths, reorganization and renewal were represented as reintegration of feminine maternal and erotic powers. The *Oresteia* as a whole and Orestes individually conform to this pattern.

We live in a different era now, in which it is no longer acceptable to impute crises of order to the female volatility and immoderation. Yet misogyny still plays an enormous (and surprisingly under-acknowledged) role in recent socio-political trends. If we want to make claims about Orestes' significance for mental and political health today, we need to confront the disturbing analogies between his story and contemporary phenomena.

## Aggrieved Masculine Entitlement and the Need for *Katabasis*

I have borrowed the phrase 'aggrieved masculine entitlement' from Rachel Kalish and Michael Kimmel's seminal study of the perpetrators of school shootings. While some may find it jarring to link Orestes' mythical violence with real-world massacres, the similarities are unnerving. They sound an alarm about one way the 'Orestes complex' is playing out in large segments of many societies today.[54]

Kalish and Kimmel encapsulate 'aggrieved masculine entitlement' as follows:

> Feeling aggrieved, wronged by the world – these are typical adolescent feelings, common to many boys and girls. What transforms the aggrieved into mass murderers is also a sense of entitlement. [...] Aggrieved entitlement inspires revenge against those who have wronged you; it is the compensation for humiliation. Humiliation is emasculation: humiliate someone and you take away his manhood. For many men, humiliation must be avenged, or you cease to be a man. Aggrieved entitlement is a gendered emotion, a fusion of that humiliating loss of manhood and the moral obligation and entitlement to get it back.[55]

The authors go on to show that the three shooters they study express precisely these sentiments: (1) suffering and grievance in response to perceived wrongs; (2) the construal of those wrongs as emasculation; (3) the belief that when a man is wronged, he is entitled and even obliged to seek violent revenge. In fact, (4) this revenge is a restoration of self-worth, typically represented as an assertion of manliness.[56]

While mainstream culture has been reluctant to admit the connection between the proliferation of mass shootings in the last thirty years and masculine anxieties, the link is undeniable in the case of so-called 'incel' shootings. 'Incel', or 'involuntary celibate', is the preferred label of the most virulently misogynistic subculture of the online 'manosphere'. Incel ideology is elaborate, contradictory, and of course variable.[57] To simplify a great deal, incels view themselves as failing in terms of normative bodily masculinity (e.g., appearance, strength, and speed), hate women for supposedly preferring more masculine men, and hate 'effeminate' liberal society for permitting women to reject marriage or choose their own husbands. Their ideology reached a degree of popular awareness when Elliot Rodger killed six people and wounded thirteen others during his rampage in Isla Vista, California, in 2013. Rodger left behind a 137-page manifesto about his 'war on women', which vividly demonstrates the role of aggrieved masculine entitlement in his motivations.[58] Five years later, in 2018, Alek Minassian killed ten and injured sixteen in Toronto. Before his rampage, he posted a message on Facebook reading, 'the Incel Rebellion has already begun!'.[59] In November of that same year, Scott Beierle shot six people in a yoga studio in Tallahassee, Florida.[60] Both Minassian and Beierle cited their admiration for Rodgers. It is important to insist that incel misogyny is by no means reducible to 'sexual frustration'.[61] Their reactionary fantasy of 'returning' to a society in which all (heterosexual) men have access to women's bodies expresses their feeling that they have been deprived of an entitlement, which they must vindicate. Incel shooters not only enact in the most literal and violent form their moral right and duty to punish those who wrong them, they also illuminate an additional element of aggrieved masculine entitlement: (5) they blame women and 'effeminate' society for their emasculation.

It is obvious that Orestes is not an incel. However, elements of his story recall the core narrative of aggrieved masculine entitlement. This is clear even if we continue to focus on Aeschylus' *Oresteia* rather than Euripides' more dystopian *Orestes*. Aeschylus' Orestes repeatedly cites the loss of his inheritance as one of his motivations (*Cho.* 249–50, 301). He connects this perceived wrong with masculinity via his admiring identification with an idealized image of his father (*Eum.* 454–8). Reclaiming his 'paternal house' and 'paternal possessions' is the first thing on his mind after his acquittal is announced:

> Pallas, you have saved me and my house. I was deprived of my paternal land, but you have re-established me there. Some Greek will say, "This man is an Argive, and once again lives in his father's house, with his father's estate" (Ἀργεῖος ἀνὴρ αὖθις ἔν τε χρήμασιν οἰκεῖ πατρῴοις).
>
> (*Eum.* 755–58)

He expresses the same motivation when preparing to murder his mother: 'O Father', he prays, 'Your death was not kingly. Grant me power over your house' (*Cho.* 479–80). Orestes obviously believes both his father's wrongful death and his own wrongful deprivation entitle and oblige him to seek violent revenge, which will restore his rightful position as a man in his community. Addressing his absent mother, he declares, 'Your deed was wholly without honor, and you will pay for dishonoring my father – by the gods, and by my hands' (*Eum.* 434–349). The misogyny of this entitlement comes across most clearly in his loathing for his mother (see previous section) and refusal to take his father's crimes into consideration (*Ag.* 104–258, *Cho.* 904–30). But he also detests the idea of a woman and an effeminate man ruling in his place, which he cites as another of his motivations: 'that the most illustrious of mortal citizens, who overthrew Troy with their renowned courage, should not be subject to these two women!' (*Cho.* 302–4). To sum up, Aeschylus' Orestes expresses four of the five core features of aggrieved masculine entitlement, namely that (1) he is suffering through being wronged, (3) he is entitled and obliged to violently avenge this wrong, (4) this vengeance will restore his manly worth, and (5) a woman and an effeminate man are to blame. The final feature, (2) perceived emasculation, is not explicitly attested but may be implicit in Orestes' emphasis on his loss of paternal privileges and wealth.

The foregoing gives us reason to think that these mass murderers are acting out the same archetypal narrative as Orestes. However, despite these connections, there is an important difference. Orestes' grievance, murder, and madness form part of a *katabasis* arc: as we have seen, the crisis and descent he undergoes in Aeschylus' *Oresteia* are followed by reorganization and rebirth. This is possible because the transformational process is shared and supported by the psychosocial and spiritual ecosystem to which he belongs. As Helene Shulman writes, when such an ecosystem no longer provides opportunities for crises to be resolved by 'homeopathic melting' and reintegration, both individuals and societies become dysfunctional. Individuals may then project archetypal narratives such as 'slaying the dragon' in ways that are repetitive, insane, and criminal, fantasizing women as monsters and themselves as heroes.[62] (We see this in Euripides' *Orestes.*)

The incels are only the most extreme manifestation of this pattern, which is increasingly widespread today. Though centrist commentators hesitate to admit it, scholarship convincingly shows that aggrieved masculine entitlement plays a dominant role in so-called 'alt-right' and 'far-right' political movements (alongside aggrieved racial, ethnic, or sectarian entitlements).[63] This rapidly growing and evolving international phenomenon is arguably the greatest current threat to the world's political and ecological health. One way to understand it is as a dysfunctional response to a crisis that is simultaneously individual, social, economic, technological, and ecological. In katabatic terms, we might say that these movements represent an eruption of the underworld into the light of day. Rather than 'going down' and working creatively with the kind of atavistic fantasies that stir 'deep' in most of us, these people act them out. Thus, they support organizations that endorse their feelings of 'nostalgic deprivation' and channel their resentment against Terrible Mothers.[64] In America, major conservative outlets rail against 'man-hating' feminist leftists who have 'ruined everything' by turning men into 'pajama boys'.[65] At the same time, they idealize divisive authoritarian leaders ('strongmen') in ways that undermine democratic institutions, economic prosperity, the rule of law, the management of public health, and ecological policy. This is the same psychosocial pathology we find in incel ideology but with inestimably greater impact. Understanding, opposing, and 'healing' it undoubtedly requires the collaboration of numerous interpretive and practical approaches. Post-Jungian psychosocial theory and the study of ancient religions certainly cannot provide all the answers, but they can contribute to the diagnostic and therapeutic collaboration our situation demands. In this chapter, I have tried to take some steps in this direction by reflecting on Orestes' ambivalent potency in antiquity and today.

## Notes

1  All translations are my own unless otherwise noted.
2  K. Reinhardt, 'Die Sinneskrise bei Euripides', in *Tradition und Geist: Gesammelte Essays zur Dichtung*, ed. C. Becker, Göttingen: Vandenhoeck & Ruprecht, 1960, pp. 243–56.

3  P. Vellacott, *Ironic Drama: A Study of Euripides' Method and Meaning*, London: Cambridge University Press, 1975, p. 79. Compare N.A. Greenberg, 'Euripides' *Orestes*: An Interpretation', *Harvard Studies in Classical Philology*, 1962, vol. 66, 157–92; W. Arrowsmith, 'A Greek Theater of Ideas', *Arion*, 1963, 2.3, 32–57 (pp. 45–7); C. Wolff, 'Orestes', in *Oxford Readings in Greek Tragedy*, ed. E. Segal, Oxford: Oxford University Press, pp. 340–56; F. Zeitlin, 'The Closet of Masks: Role-Playing and Myth-Making in the *Orestes* of Euripides', in *Oxford Readings in Classical Studies: Euripides*, ed. J. Mossman, Oxford, 2003, pp. 310–41 (pp. 328–33).

4  F. Wertham, *Dark Legend: A Study in Murder*, London: Gollancz, 1947; L. Veszy-Wagner, 'Orestes the Delinquent: The Inevitability of Parricide', *American Imago*, 1961, vol. 18.4, 371–81; and A. Green, *The Tragic Effect: The Oedipus Complex in Tragedy*, tr. A. Sheridan, Cambridge University Press, pp. 35–87.

5  H. Fingarette, 'Orestes: Paradigm Hero and Central Motif of Contemorary Ego Psychology', *Psychoanalytic Review*, 1963, vol. 50.3, 437–61; M. Klein, 'Some Reflections on the *Oresteia*', in *Envy and Gratitude and Other Works 1946–1963*, London: Vintage, 1997, 175–99.

6  B. Pestell, 'Ecstatic Atoms: The Question of Oresteian Individuation', in *The Ecstatic and the Archaic: An Analytical Psychological Inquiry*, ed. P. Bishop and L. Gardner, London: Routledge, 2018, pp. 97–116 (pp. 98 and 107); cf. R. Trousdell, 'Tragedy and Transformation: The *Oresteia* of Aeschylus', *Jung Journal: Culture and Psyche*, 2010. vol. 2.3, 5–38.

7  See, for exampple, E.R. Dodds, 'Morals and Politics in the *Oresteia*', in *The Ancient Concept of Progress and Other Essays on Greek Literature and Belief*, Oxford University Press, 1972, pp. 45–63; N.R.E. Fisher, *Hybris: A Study in the Values of Honour and Shame in Ancient Greece*, Warminster: Aris & Phillips, pp. 270–97.

8  Jung, *Symbols of Transformation*, in *Collected Works*, vol. 5, tr. R.F.C. Hull, London: Routledge and Kegan Paul, 1956, §312–§313, §332, §351–§352, §365–§387, §395, §449, §473, §484, §553 and §611.

9  Jung, *Collected Works*, vol. 5, §332, §313, and §395. Jung's preoccupation with maternal incest at this date (1912) obviously belies his effort to assert his independence from Freud. Maternal symbols play much subtler roles in his own katabasis narrative in *The Red Book: Liber Novus, Reader's Edition*, ed. S. Shamdasani, tr. M. Kyburz, J. Peck, and S. Shamdasani, New York: Norton, 2009, and feature hardly at all in 'Concerning Rebirth', in *The Archetypes of the Collective Unconscious* [*Collected Works*, vol. 9/i], tr. R.F.C. Hull, 2nd edn, London: Routledge and Kegan Paul, 1968, §199–§258.

10  Jung, *Symbols of Transformation*, §450.

11  M. Eliade, *Rites and Symbols of Initiation: The Mysteries of Birth and Rebirth*, tr. W.R. Trask, New York: Harper, 1958, pp. 7–10.

12  Eliade, *Rites and Symbols of Initiation*, pp. 21–5, 30–7.

13  H. Shulman, *Living at the Edge of Chaos: Complex Systems in Culture and Psyche*, Einsiedeln: Daimon, 1997 [iBook]. Because I was not able to access this book in paginated format during the pandemic, I will cite it by chapter.

14  Shulman, *Living at the Edge of Chaos*, Introduction.

15  Shulman, *Living at the Edge of Chaos*, chapter 1. Like most subjects in clinical case studies, 'Edward Coe' has been anonymized.

16  Shulman, *Living at the Edge of Chaos*, chapter 4, referring to the anthropologist Ana Maria Oyarce (dir.), *Vida entre dos mundos*, Temuco, Chile: Grupo de Registro y Comunicacion Audiovisual, 1988.

17  For the previous literary tradition, see M. Delcourt, *Oreste et Alcméon. Étude sur la projection légendaire du matricide en Grèce*, Belles lettres: Paris, pp. 19–30.

18  Hyginus 101. Typical images are *Lexicon Iconographicum Mythologiae Graecae* [LIMC], https://www.weblimc.org. Accessed 27.04.2020, ID 8739, 8741, 8821, 8832.

19  Hyginus 122.
20  J.-P. Vernant, *Mortals and Immortals: Collected Essays*, ed. F.I. Zeitlin, Princeton: 1991, 195–243; P. Ellinger and M. Dennehy, *Artémis, déesse de tous les dangers*, Paris: Larousse, 2009, 39–104. On Artemis and Iphigeneia, see also H. Lloyd-Jones, 'Artemis and Iphigeneia; *Journal of Hellenic*, 1983, vol. 103, 87–102.
21  Delcourt, *Oreste*, pp. 81–2.
22  Stesichorus fr. 219, in M. Davies (ed.), *Poetarum Melicorum Graecorum Fragmenta*. Clarendon: Oxford, 1991; Aesch. *Cho.* 524–550.
23  Schol. in Eurip. Or. 1645: 'Asclepiades says that Orestes was killed in Arcadia by a snake (*ophis*) when he was 70 years old'; Apoll. *Ep.* 6.28: 'Orestes was bitten by a snake in Oresteion in Arcadia and died'.
24  I am particularly indebted to F. Costabile, 'Il culto di Apollo quale testimonianza della tradizione corale e religiosa di Reggio e Messana', *Mélanges de l'école française de Rome, Antiquité*, 1979, vol. 91.1, 525–45; J. Ducat, 'Les thèmes des récits du fondation de Rhégion', in *Mélanges hélleniques offerts à Georges Daux*, ed. G. Daux, Paris: Brocard, 1974, pp. 93–114; B. Gentili and A. Pinzone (eds), *Messine e Reggio nell' Antichità: Storia, Società, Cultura*, Messina: DiScaM, 2002.
25  It is wrongly attributed to Valerius Probus in the manuscripts. The text can be consulted in *Servii grammatici qui feruntur in Vergilli carmina commentarii*, vol. 3.2, *Appendix serviana*, ed. G. Thilo and H. Hagen, Cambridge: Cambridge University Press, 1902, pp. 323–90.
26  Quoted by Costabile, 'Il culto di Apollo, p. 529.
27  Costabile, 'Il culto di Apollo', pp. 531–5; A. Schachter, *Boiotia in Antiquity: Selected Papers*, Cambridge: Cambridge University Press, 2016, pp. 255–78; and W. Burkert, *Homo Necans: The Anthropology of Ancient Greek Sacrificial Ritual and Myth*, tr. P. Bing, Berkeley: University of California, 1983, pp. 116–30.
28  I. Rutherford, '(Xen. *Mem.* 3.3.12) Song-Dance and State Pilgrimmage at Athens', in *Music and the Muses: The Cult of Mousike in the Classical Athenian City*, ed. P. Murray and P. Wilson, Oxford: Oxford University Press, 2004, pp. 67–90 (p. 69).
29  Costabile, 'Il culto di Apollo', pp. 524–35.
30  For the location of the temple of Artemis, see E. Andronico, 'Topografia Archeologica di Reggio di Calabria', in *Messine e Reggio nell' Antichità: Storia, Società, Cultura*, ed. B. Gentili and A. Pinzone, Messina: DiScaM, 2002, pp. 197–238 (pp. 215–6). There appear to have been two temples of Artemis Phakelitis, one north of Messene and one south of Rhegium. Cf. Costabile, 'Il culto di Apollo', pp. 534–5.
31  P. Vidal-Naquet, *The Black Hunter: Forms of Thought and Forms of Society in the Greek World*, tr. Andrew Szegedy-Maszak, Baltimore: Johns Hopkins University Press, 1986, pp. 106–28; and Schachter, *Boiotia in Antiquity*, pp. 267–9.
32  Pausanias says the monument was sculpted by Calon of Elis (early fifth century BCE), to which an epigram by Hippias of Elis (late fifth century BCE) had later been added.
33  K. Meister, 'Anaxilaus', in *Brill's New Pauly*, ed. H. Cancik, H. Schneider, and C.F. Salazer. Available online HPP: http://dx.doi.org/10.1163/1574-9347_bnp_e120600, 2006. Accessed 20 May 2020.
34  Ducat, 'Les thèmes des récits', pp. 98–9.
35  Andronico, 'Topografia Archeologica', pp. 216–29.
36  G.S. Gasparro, 'Itinerari mitico-cultuali nell'area dello stretto', in *Messine e Reggio nell' Antichità*, ed. Gentili and Pinzone, pp. 329–50 (pp. 341–3).
37  Costabile, 'Il culto di Apollo', p. 526.
38  See Strabo, 6.1.6-7, 8.4.9; Paus., 4.4.1-3; with the other sources and analysis in Ducat, 'Les thèmes des récits', pp. 98–99.

39 Ellinger and Dennehy, *Artémis*, pp. 39–104; Eliade, *Rites*, pp. 1–40; Vidal-Naquet, *The Black Hunter*, pp. 106–28.

40 C. Dougherty, *The Poetics of Colonization in Ancient Greece*, New York: Oxford, 1993, pp. 31–44.

41 Dougheryy, *The Poetics of Colonization*, p. 26.

42 Pausanias 2.7.7-8; Plutarch, *Greek Questions*, 12, *The Obsolescence of Oracles*, 15; Aelian, *True Histories*, 3.1; Detienne, *Apollon*, pp. 175–234.

43 T. Zielinski, 'Die Orestessage und die Rechtfertigungsidee', *Neue Jahrbücher für das klassische Altertum*, 1989, vol. 2, 81–100 (pp. 87–90); Delcourt, *Oreste*, pp. 80–3 and 103–6; Detienne, *Apollon*, pp. 138–47, 205–6, and 212–7.

44 R. Seaford, 'Aeschylus and the Unity of Opposites', in *Tragedy, Ritual and Money in Ancient Greece: Selected Essays*, ed. R. Bostock, Cambridge: Cambridge University Press, 2018, pp. 111–42.

45 Pestell, 'Atoms', pp. 104–7; cf. Trousdell, 'Transformation', pp. 20–35.

46 This is clearest at *Cho.* 265–98, where Apollo explicitly threatens Orestes with 'Erinyes' attacks' (*prosbolas Erinuōn*) if he does not avenge his father.

47 These adjectives are Pestell's (in 'Atoms', p. 105).

48 F. Zeitlin, 'The Dynamics of Misogyny: Myth and Mythmaking in Aeschylus' *Oresteia*', in *Playing the Other: Gender and Society in Classical Greek Literature*, Chicago and London: University of Chicago, 1996, pp. 87–119 (pp. 98–111).

49 See note 46 above.

50 The following Greek line is probably corrupt.

51 Delcourt, *Oreste*, pp. 88–9, is criticizing Jung's student Erich Neumann; se E. Neumann, *The Origins and History of Consciousness*, tr. R.F.C. Hull, Princeotn, NJ: Princeton University Press, 2014, pp. 168–9.

52 C. Macleod, 'Politics and the *Oresteia*', in *Oxford Readings in Classical Studies: Aeschylus*, ed. M. Lloyd, Oxford: Oxford University Press, 2007, pp. 265–301.

53 D. Cohen, *Law, Sexuality, and Society: The Enforcement of Morals in Classical Athens*, Cambridge: Cambridge University Press, 1991, esp. 133–69.

54 Compare Wertham's attempt to inaugurate this diagnostic label in *Dark Legend*, pp. 95–6.

55 R. Kalish and M. Kimmel, 'Suicide by Mass Murder: Masculinity, Aggrieved Entitlement, and Rampage School Shootings', *Health Sociology Review*, 2020, vol. 19.2, 451–65 (p. 454).

56 Kalish and Kimmel, 'Suicide by Mass Murder', p. 463.

57 At the time of writing, there is surprisingly little academic research on this group, although there is some good journalism. In addition to Kalish and Kimmel's article (see note 55 above), see C. Vito, A. Admire, and E. Hughes, 'Masculinity, Aggrieved Entitlement, and Violence: Considering the Isla Vista Shooting', *Norma*, 2018, vol. 13.2, 2018, 86–102; J. Tolentino, 'The Rage of the Incels', *The New Yorker*, 15 May 2018 (available online HTTP: https://www.newyorker.com/culture/cultural-comment/the-rage-of-the-incels?fbclid=IwAR28RbzGRLZkm HrfxhuhqK8ORHu1KBVVimGo7JBpAI_-qbiCbWFiCEreQVc, accessed 13 September 2018); Z. Beauchamp, 'Our Incel Problem', *Vox*, 23 April 2019 (available online HTTP: https://www.vox.com/the-highlight/2019/4/16/18287446/incel-definition-reddit?fbclid=IwAR3Jrglcu3nNtMg3FlqAep0rHatBqRiZBj80 PcyTQy3hGvMZbKwGsLYqWh0, accessed 13 September 2019).

58 See Vito, Admire, and Hughes, 'Masculinity, Aggrieved Entitlement, and Violence' (see note 57).

59 D. Bilefsky and I. Austen, 'Toronto Van Attack Suspect Expressed Anger at Women', *New York Times*, 24 April 2018 (available online HTTP https://www.nytimes.com/2018/04/24/world/canada/toronto-van-rampage.html, accessed 13 September 2019).

60  M. Zaveri, J. Jacobs, and S. Mervosh, 'Gunman in Yoga Studio Recorded Misogynistic Videos and Faced Battery Charges', *New York Times*, 3 November 2018 (available online HTTP https://www.nytimes.com/2018/11/03/us/yoga-studio-shooting-florida.html?searchResultPosition=3, accessed 13 September 2019).

61  Tolentino is thus correct, though she over-simplifies their grievance: 'Incels aren't really looking for sex; they're looking for absolute male supremacy. Sex, defined to them as dominion over female bodies, is just their preferred sort of proof' ('The Rage of the Incels').

62  Shulman, *Chaos*, chapter 10, 'Altered States at the Edge of Chaos'.

63  See especially the impressive collection and analysis of survey evidence by P.S. Forscher and N.S. Kteily, 'A Psychological Profile of the Alt-Right', *Perspectives on Psychological Science*, 2020, vol. 15.1, 90–116 (especially pp. 106 and 111–2); cf. A. Kelly, 'The Alt-Right: Reactionary Rehabilitation for White Masculinity', *Soundings*, 2017, vol. 66, 68–78. For a case study of how alt-right politics are being appropriated around the world, see S. Thobani, 'Alt-Right with the Hindu-right: long-distance nationalism and the perfection of Hindutva', *Ethnic and Racial Studies*, 2019, vol. 42.5, 745–62. See also notes 64 and 65 below.

64  For the term 'nostalgic deprivation', see J. Gest, T. Reny, and J. Mayer, 'Roots of the Radical Right: Nostalgic Deprivation in the United States and Britain', *Comparative Political Studies*, 2018, vol. 51.13, 1694–1719.

65  This fantasy replays constantly on *The Daily Wire*, which claims to be 'the largest conservative news site in America'. See P. Bois, 'When Knights Surrender Their Swords, Beasts Shall Devour Maidens', 18 October 2017, available online HTTP https://www.dailywire.com/news/when-knights-surrender-their-swords-beasts-shall-paul-bois, accessed 13 September 2019; and [Staff], 'Watch: Shapiro Rips Radical Feminist in University of Buffalo Speech', 9 October 2018, available online HTTP https://www.dailywire.com/news/watch-shapiro-rips-radical-feminism-university-daily-wire, accessed 13 September 2019.

# Chapter 11

# Regression, *Nekyia*, and Involution in the Thought of Jung and Deleuze

*Christian McMillan*

In his *Deleuze and the Unconscious*, Christian Kerslake writes that '[t]he notion of a 'second birth', rebirth or renaissance is fundamental to the work of Gilles Deleuze from the beginning'.[1] Kerslake adds that

> large tracts of Jung's *Symbols and Transformations of the Libido* (*Symbole und Wandlungen der Libido*) (1911–1912) (the work to which Deleuze most frequently refers) are devoted to the myth of rebirth which Jung discovers in the background to the mythologies handed down by history.
> (p. 81)

The myth of the hero who enters on a 'night sea journey' (*Nekyia*, or the Journey into Hades) is one that preoccupied the work of Deleuze (1925–1995) and his collaborator Félix Guattari (1930–1992).

This chapter considers the extent to which the early conceptual affinities evident in Jung's influence on Deleuze persist through later works written by Deleuze and by Deleuze and Guattari. It is argued that the early conceptual affinities are exclusively psychological in character and gravitate around a common theme concerning symbolic death and rebirth. Jung's articulation of a 'night sea journey' (*Nekyia*) in *The Psychology of the Unconscious* (1916)[2] can be identified in Deleuze's 'From Sacher-Masoch to Masochism' (1961)[3] in which Sacher-Masoch is entranced and transformed by an encounter with the image of Venus in furs.[4] This is Deleuze's early notion of *katabasis* although he does not refer to psychological transformation by this term. Deleuze openly criticises Freud in his reading of Sacher-Masoch's transformation, and this criticism is informed by his reading of Jung's early work.

Building on the work of others, I argue that there is a clear evidence for a Deleuzian adoption of what one might call a 'Jungian reading' of Freud's death instinct and that this reading has strong resonances with Deleuze's concept of 'involution', which he will use in later works to describe transformation, not only in a psychological register but also in a biological-vitalistic context and even as a vital-materialist principle. Involution is a concept that Jung first refers to in *The Psychology of the Unconscious* when discussing the night sea journey, and I speculate that Deleuze might first have learned of

DOI: 10.4324/9781003054139-15

this concept from his close reading of this work in the early part of his academic career.

## Deleuze on Jung: Early Influences and Conceptual Affinities

In his 1961 commentary on Sacher-Masoch (1835–1895) and the nature of masochism Deleuze writes:

> As Jung demonstrated, incest signifies the second birth, that is to say a heroic birth, a parthenogenesis (entering a second time into the maternal breast in order to be born anew or to become a child again).
>
> (*SMM*, 129–130)

Although Deleuze scatters references to Jung throughout most of his core works, in this chapter I want to return to some of Deleuze's earliest work, work in which he is arguably at his most 'Jungian'.[5] In his article 'From Sacher-Masoch to Masochism', Deleuze demonstrates a very strong commitment to a number of Jung's ideas. Kerslake has translated Deleuze's article into English and he writes that in the article 'we find Deleuze entranced by Jung's labyrinthine 1912 book *Transformations and Symbols of the Libido*'.[6] Furthermore, he states that Deleuze's central thesis in the article 'is that masochism must be conceived as a *perverse realisation of the fantasy of incest* – on condition that incest is taken in its "more profound" significance as a symbol of rebirth, as Jung claims' (*SMM*, p. 135). In his article on masochism, Deleuze argues that Freud was unable to understand the role of the 'image' of the mother in masochism, preferring the interiorisation of the image of the Father following from its re-exteriorisation in the image of woman:

> Freudian psychoanalysis in general suffers from an inflation of the father. In the case of masochism in particular, we have to perform some astonishing gymnastics to explain how the image of the Father is first of all interiorised in the superego, and then re-exteriorised in an image of a woman. It is as if Freudian interpretations are often only able to reach the most superficial and most individualised levels of the unconscious. They do not enter into the profound dimensions where the image of the Mother reigns in its own terms, without owing anything to the influence of the father.
>
> (*SMM*, 128)

Deleuze claims that Jung valued the meaning and importance of the image of the mother, this in turn emerging from Jung's discovery and investigation of the role of a 'deeper unconscious':

> That there are very different levels of the unconscious, of unequal origin and value, arousing regressions which differ in nature, which have

relations of opposition, compensation and reorganisation going on between them: this principle dear to Jung was never recognised by Freud because the latter reduced the unconscious to the simple fact of desiring. So one ends up seeing alliances of consciousness with the superficial layers of the unconscious, while the deeper unconscious which encircles us in a tie of blood is held in check.

*(SMM, 128)*

Hence, there is a subjective relation to the maternal imago which operates at the deepest level of the unconscious. Deleuze follows Jung by referring to the relation with the 'deeper unconscious' as 'subjective' as opposed to 'objective'. Jung's distinction can be identified from *Two Essays on Analytical Psychology* (1928) where, with respect to dream interpretation, he states that 'interpretation on the subjective level is synthetic, because it detaches the underlying memory-complexes from their external causes, regards them as tendencies or components of the subject, and reunites them with that subject'.[7] In his affirmation of Jung's synthetic method, Deleuze distances himself from Freud's 'reductive' approach and permits the 'original Images' *(SMM*, 131) of the deeper unconscious to remain beyond all possible experience whilst also being the very condition of *real* experience; transcendent and immanent.[8] By 'real' experience Deleuze intends a kind of experience which does not presuppose a 'subject' in the phenomenological sense, one involving a transcendental unity of apperception.[9] Indeed, it is this very search for conditions of real experience (transcendental empiricism)[10] which drives much of Deleuze's philosophical experimentation, an experimentation in which the conditions of real experience are investigated in different registers relating to the unconscious, matter, and time.

A condition of real experience has a problematic structure and Deleuze's preoccupation in 'From Sacher-Masoch to Masochism' is the problematic structure of the image of the Mother, problematic because it is never fully exhausted by its expressions. This correlates with Jung's notion of the productive power of the symbol which is never reducible to or exhausted by one of its representations. In other words, the solution (representation/expression) is never adequate to the problem (symbol). With respect to the early work on masochism, Deleuze appears to view masochism as an exemplary instance of the manner in which a 'paradoxical' experience can initiate a regression that terminates in a 'symbol' or 'original Image' bearing no apparent relationship to the actual experiences of the affected individual. Such an image remains irreducible to reality, 'surreal'; and this is the source of its potentially 'revolutionary' value as manifest in Masoch's own fantasies, and of its therapeutic value if handled correctly, but also, finally, of its extraordinary danger for the subject, him or herself. The problem-solution dynamic is one Deleuze continues to explore in *Difference and Repetition* (1968) and *The Logic of Sense* (1969).

In *Proust and Signs* (1964), written four years before *Difference and Repetition*, Deleuze appears to broaden the Jungian notion of 'original image' to include encounters with empirical objects that occasion a paradoxical experience. A paradoxical object can now engender regression in what Deleuze, following Marcel Proust (1871–1922), refers to as an 'involuntary encounter'. Or as he claims:

> The real theme of a work [of art] is therefore not the subject the words designate, but the unconscious themes, the involuntary archetypes in which the words, but also the colours and the sounds, assume their meaning and their life. Art is a veritable transmutation of substance.[11]

Here the paradoxical object may be a work of art itself, one which has a destabilising influence and problematic structure which is generative of something radically new and transformative. A few years later in *Difference and Repetition* Deleuze recapitulates this point, suggesting:

> Something in the world forces us to think. This something is an object not of recognition but of a fundamental *encounter*. What is encountered may be Socrates, a temple or a demon. It may be grasped in range of affective tones: wonder, love, hatred, suffering. In whichever tone, its primary characteristic is that it can only be sensed. In this sense it is opposed to recognition. In recognition, the sensible is not at all that which can only be sensed, but that which bears directly upon the senses in an object which can be recalled, imagined, or conceived.
>
> (*DR*, 139)

Proust's encounter with the madeleine from his *In Search of Lost Time* (1913) would later become paradigmatic of such an experience in Deleuze's work, along with several Platonic examples tied to recollection, notably in the *Phaedo* and book 7 of the *Republic*. In this later theory, such paradoxical experiences can initiate a process within the psyche that terminates in something analogous to what Deleuze will call a 'transcendent exercise' of the faculties, that is, their exercise in relation to objects that they themselves synthesise. The transcendent exercise of the faculties – an individuation and process of transformation, an exercise which is forced – is wholly incompatible with the ordinary coordination of the faculties according to the rules of empirical 'common sense'. Kerslake suggests that 'the path of individuation necessarily involves a series of 'transcendent exercises' of the mind carried out beyond conceptual representation, in which unconscious Ideas emerge to shape and reshape the consciousness of the subject (who is both a thinking and passive subject)'.[12] Involution, another term for the journey that begins on the basis of a paradoxical encounter, gestures to the emergence of a symbiotic field, or what Deleuze would occasionally refer to in subsequent works as the 'transcendental field' that allows assignable relations between disparate things to come into play.

In 'From Sacher-Masoch to Masochism' Deleuze claims that only Jung was able to grasp the process of return or 'regression' as it functions in perversions and psychic disorders (*SMM*, 128). By 'perversion' Deleuze intends something quite different from its more common reduction to the abnormal or pathological. Kazarian has investigated Deleuze's use of perversion as it appears in *The Logic of Sense*. As he notes, '[T]he issue of perversion is not an issue to be addressed at the level of the subject but rather in terms of a conception of the unconscious and desire that is analogous to the "impersonal" transcendental field'.[13] In this instance, the transcendental field is a new register for what has appeared in 'From Sacher-Masoch to Masochism' as the 'deeper unconscious'. The perversion of the masochist in 'From Sacher-Masoch to Masochism' and the type of perversion discussed throughout *The Logic of Sense* are different only by degree. Deleuze articulates that

> perversion is not defined by the force of a certain desire in the system of drives, the pervert is not someone who desires, but someone who introduces desire into an entirely different system and makes it play, within this system, the role of an internal limit.
>
> (*SMM*, 304)[14]

The introduction of desire by Masoch into the problematic 'system' engendered by an encounter with the Image of the Mother (mediated by the image of Venus in furs)[15] will be transformative precisely because it destabilises the ego. Deleuze challenges the idea that the form of the 'I' is somehow innate, and he condemns the Kantian notion that at the heart of subjectivity there must be some seat of synthesis such as the transcendental unity of apperception which performs the function of synthesis presupposed as necessary for possible experience.[16] Masoch's encounter with the Image of the Mother entails that the ego/subject is brought into contact with the impersonal unconscious to encounter non-subjective forces which are transformative of the ego/subject. In very general terms, these forces can be aligned with conditions of *real* experience as opposed to conditions of possible experience, the latter presupposing some unified synthesising agency responsible for the world of representation and recognition. Furthermore, Deleuze's interpretation of perversion in 'From Sacher-Masoch to Masochism' involves the use of desire as an internal limit with which to confront constituted systems and habits, the elements of which are arranged in a sedentary and largely unchanging manner. Kazarian comments that it is '[t]he pervert's aim is to avoid fixity and completeness, stable and harmonious distributions as such'.[17]

Returning to the context of Sacher-Masoch's masochism, when Deleuze invokes the image of Venus in furs he argues that 'regression' to an Image refers to a transmutation, a kind of *katabasis* or rebirth (*SMM*, 130). This is a regression to the 'problem' of the Mother, a kind of perversion which is revolutionary because of its transformative effects. These effects concern the potential to overturn patriarchy and three characteristics of masochism are necessary for this end to be realised to some extent, as Deleuze interrogates it.[18] First, the aesthetic origins of the masochistic fantasy:

> It is when the senses take works of art for their objects that they become masochistic for the first time. It is through Renaissance paintings that the power and musculature of a woman wrapped in furs is revealed to Masoch.
>
> (*SMM*, 126)

Second the juridical forms by which the fantasy is realised and thirdly the mythological and historical contexts in which the first two characteristics find stability, involving, for example, 'allusions to an epoch of beautiful Nature, to an archaic world presided over by Venus Aphrodite, where the fleeting relationship between woman and man has pleasure between equal partners as its only law' (*SMM*, 127).

Of these characteristics, it is the second that appears most significant for Deleuze in terms of the role it might play in challenging the patriarchal order (and psychoanalytic discourses which privilege the Father).[19] This characteristic revolves around the role of the contract in masochism; 'the contract here expresses the material predominance of the woman and the superiority of the maternal principle' (*SMM*, 126). This contract is the 'subversive double of the [patriarchal] marriage contract'.[20] Under ordinary circumstances, claims Deleuze, the patriarchal marriage contract is 'made to express and even justify the notion that there is something non-material, spiritual or instituted in the relations of authority and association which are established between men, including between father and son' (*SMM*, 126). By contrast, the subversive contract of Masoch recapitulates the sense of dependence ('chthonic tie') between mother and child; it expresses 'the material predominance of the woman and the superiority of the maternal principle' (*SMM*, 126). The aim of this new contract, within the regressive fantasy of the masochist, is to restore gynocracy; for 'he who unearths the Anima enters on this regression: all the more terrible for being repressed, the Anima will know how to turn patriarchal structures to its own advantage and rediscover the power of the devouring Mother' (*SMM*, 127). On the basis of this Deleuze avers that the 'true man' will emerge from the 'ordeals of a restored gynocracy' (*SMM*, 127).[21]

Deleuze refers to Johann Jakob Bachofen's *Mother Right* (1861) and Pierre Gordon's *Sex and Religion* (1949) to offer speculative insights into a primal historical epoch regarding the existence of a gynocracy which gave way to patriarchy in the time of Rome and beyond.[22] The notion of a repressed matriarchal law, with its specific social forms and symbolic and ritual structures, is significant as a historical phenomenon, but Deleuze does not pursue this, preferring instead to read this as a 'speculative *historicisation* (a kind of transcendental illusion) extrapolated from tendencies at work within the temporal matrix of the Oedipal triangle', according to Kerslake.[23] It is the *regressive fantasy* itself which is of most significance, the means by which '[Sacher-] Masoch dreams of using patriarchy itself in order to restore gynocracy in order to restore primitive communism' (*SMM*, 127).

Some influences of Jung's *Psychology of the Unconscious* and *Symbols of Transformation* are evident in Deleuze's references to regressive fantasy and gynocracy in *SMM*. Notably, it is the theme of rebirth (and symbolic death) which accompany a 'night journey to the sea'[24] (or 'night sea journey', i.e., *Nekyia*)[25] that is of significance. Jung's use of the idea of the night sea journey (*die Nachtmeerfahrt*) can be attributed to the ethnologist Leo Frobenius (1873–1938), where he describes the journey in his book, *Das Zeitalter Des Sonnengottes* (*The Age of the Sun God*), first published in 1904.[26] Whether Deleuze was familiar with this text or not is unknown. Nonetheless, the influence of symbols of an archetypal Mother which are encountered on this journey and which involve rebirth is a theme which informs Deleuze's work well beyond his early, 'Jungian' phase as detailed in the *Sacher-Masoch to Masochism* essay. In what follows I turn to a concept that Deleuze introduces in some of his later works and which continues to exemplify the themes of rebirth that have been recounted thus far.

## *Nekyia* and Involution

At no point in the *Psychology of the Unconscious* does Jung employ the term *Nekyia* directly. Yet a comment from 'The Dual Mother Role' expresses what Jung will come to refer to as *Nekyia* in subsequent works. Jung relates that the place of *katabasis* is symbolic of the 'descent into the lower world'.[27] Somewhat later, in his monograph on 'Picasso' (first published in 1932 which accompanies his critical examination of James Joyce's *Ulysses*), Jung articulates *Nekyia* as a 'journey into Hades, the descent into the unconscious and the leave taking from the upper world'.[28] Furthermore, this *Nekyia* journey is 'no aimless and truly destructive fall into the abyss but a meaningful *katabasis*, a descent into the cave of initiation and secret knowledge'.[29] Evidently, the relationship between the night sea journey and a descent into the unconscious are closely related and involve a process of *katabasis*.

Having introduced these terms, I want to offer one more: involution. Appearing far less than the term *Nekyia* in the *Collected Works*, involution makes an appearance in the *Psychology of the Unconscious* in a crucial passage where Jung articulates the night sea journey with his customary literary flare and also in a diagrammatic form drawing from the work of Frobenius.[30] The stages of this journey are as follows: (1) the devouring of the hero by a water monster in the West, (2) the hero lights a fire in the belly of the beast and cuts part of its heart to quell hunger, (3) the sea-monster becomes beached on the shore, (4) the hero cuts free of the sea-monster and slides out, (5) the hero has lost his hair given the heat inside the sea-monster, and (6) the hero frees other captives devoured by the sea-monster. Jung indicates that there is a link between being devoured and the endurance of heat which, as we have seen, the hero suffers in the belly of the beast. To be devoured and endure heat in the context of psychological regression is captured by the term 'involution' to which I return momentarily.

Whilst considering the etymology of related terms in a passage from 'Symbolism of Mother and of Rebirth', it is worth recounting that Jung spends much of this chapter reflecting on maternal symbols as they occur in sun-myths and related religious myths. These symbols of the mother include the chest, the sea, water, the city, and the tree of life. The notion of entwining or being entwined is raised as a symbolic example of rebirth by Jung:

> There is an Indo-Germanic root, *vélu, vel-*, with the meaning of "encircling, surrounding, turning." From this is derived Sanskrit *val, valati* = to cover, to surround, to encircle, to encoil (symbol of the snake); *vallî* = creeping plant; *ûluta* = boa-constrictor = Latin *vulûtus*, Lithuanian *velù, velti* = wickeln (to roll up); Church Slavonian *vlina* = Old High German, *wella* = *Wella* (wave or billow). To the root *vélu* also belongs the root *vlvo*, with the meaning "cover, conum, womb (The serpent on account of its casting its skin is an excellent symbol of rebirth.) Sanskrit *ulva, ulba* has the same meaning, Latin *volva, volvula, vulva*. To *vélu* also belongs the root *ulvorâ*, with the meaning of "fruitful field, covering or husk of plants, sheath." Sanskrit *urvârâ* = sown field. Zend *urvara* = plant. (See the personification of the ploughed furrow.) The same root vel has also the meaning of "wallen" (to undulate). Sanskrit ulmuka = conflagration. ϝαλέα, ϝέλα, Gothic vulan = wallen (to undulate). Old High German and Middle High German *walm* = heat, glow. It is typical that in the state of "involution" the hair of the sun-hero always falls out from the heat. Further the root *vel* is found with the meaning "to sound, and to will, to wish" (libido!).[31]

Jung continues that the 'motif of entwining is a mother symbol'.[32] Venus wrapped in furs is an image which entrances Sacher-Masoch and, as Deleuze relates, 'furs have multiple meanings'. To reduce these meanings to a paternal image would be 'singularly devoid of foundation' [...] as 'fur is first of all a directly maternal symbol, indicating the refolding of the law in the feminine principle' (*SMM*, 127). Wrapped, entwined, encircled, Sacher-Masoch dreams of being devoured by 'the fur of the despotic and devouring mother who establishes the gynocratic order' (*SMM*, 127). Sacher-Masoch, the hero on a night sea journey towards rebirth; Sacher-Masoch, another version of the sun-hero?

Involution and libido are revisited by Jung in his *Symbols of Transformation*, when he links them directly in the following passage:

> It is as if the libido were not only a ceaseless forward movement, an unending will for life, evolution, creation, such as Schopenhauer envisaged in

his cosmic Will, where death is a mishap or fatality coming from outside; like the sun, the libido also wills its own descent, its own involution.[33]

Deleuze will make much of the notion of involution as a form of becoming. Like Jung, Deleuze regards involution as a descent or regression (*Nekyia*) but one which is anything but a return to a less differentiated state. Recalling the experience of Sacher-Masoch and his 'regression' Deleuze asserts:

> In masochism, *regression* to the mother is "like the pathological protest of a part of ourselves that has been wrecked by the law; but regression also conceals and contains possibilities for a compensating or normative *progression* of this same part, as one can glimpse in the masochistic fantasy of rebirth".
>
> (*SMM*, 131)

The endpoint of this kind of regression is symbolic death as rebirth and Deleuze is keen to point out that this kind of death must be distinguished from what he regards as Freud's assertion that the death instinct involves a return to a state of inanimate matter. In *SMM* he claims that Freud was right to recognise that the nature of instinct consists solely in regression and that the only difference between instincts of life and death for example lies in the terminus of the regression (*SMM*, 131). Yet, argues Deleuze, it 'was not left to him [Freud] to grasp the role of original Images', for it is these Images (symbols) which are the 'terminus of each regression' and '[i]nstincts are simply internal perceptions of original images'. Within this Jungian account of Freud's death instinct, Deleuze relates that death must be understood as symbolic death, and 'the return to matter as a return to the symbolic mother'.

Jung was an important catalyst for Freud's thinking on the death instinct, making certain moves in *The Psychology of the Unconscious* the effects of which would ripple through psychoanalysis. His inspiration for this thinking is arguably due to the influence of Sabina Spielrein (1885–1942). In *Symbols of Transformation* he comments that the terrible mother devours and destroys and symbolises death itself and that it was

> [t]his fact led my pupil Dr. Spielrein to develop her idea of the death-instinct, which was then taken up by Freud. In my opinion it is not so much a question of a death-instinct as of that "other" instinct (Goethe) which signifies spiritual life.[34]

Jung undertook what one might call a 'holistic approach' towards the instincts that would be taken up by Freud in his paper 'On Narcissism' (1914) and his rejection was necessary for the emergence of the split between the life and death instincts.[35] Jung abolishes the dualistic structure of the instincts that was necessary for psychoanalytic theory, and his genetic standpoint makes the multiplicity of instincts arise from a relative unity from the Ur-libido.

The recognition of such displaceable libidinal contributions was incompatible with the view that in the repressed the ego and the id, as two essentially different kinds of instinct, were at work. On a related note, in 'On the Psychology of the Unconscious' Jung writes that, '[s]ince the so-called destructive instinct is also a phenomenon of energy, it seems to me simpler to define libido as an inclusive term for psychic intensities, and consequently as sheer psychic energy'.[36]

Regression as symbolic death is not restricted in Deleuze's works to 'From Sacher-Masoch to Masochism', however. In his seminal work *Difference and Repetition*, written seven years later, he remarks that Freud 'strangely refused any other dimension to death, any prototype or any presentation of death in the unconscious, even though he conceded the existence of such prototypes for birth and castration' (*DR*, 111). In this instance, 'prototypes' are substituted for 'original images'. Nonetheless, the meaning remains largely unchanged between the two texts, and Deleuze restates his critical commentary on what he considered to be lacking in Freud's conceptualisation of the death instinct: 'Death does not appear in the objective model of an indifferent inanimate matter to which the living would "return"; it is present in the living in the form of a subjective and differenciated experience endowed with its own prototype' (*DR*, 112). The prototype that is 'death' is 'the last form of the problematic, the source of problems and questions, the sign of their persistence over and above every response' (*DR*, 112). As he makes these remarks, we can assume that Deleuze still has Jung in mind when elsewhere in *Difference and Repetition* he asks, 'Was not one of the most important points of Jung's theory already to be found here: the force of "questioning in the unconscious, the conception of the unconscious as an unconscious of "problems" and "tasks"?' (*DR*, 161).[37]

Regression is not a return to the inanimate, and involution must also not be confused with a movement towards the less differentiated. In *A Thousand Plateaus* (1980), a work Deleuze co-authored with Felix Guattari, the writer's comment on what involution entails when considered in relation to evolution:

> [...] Becoming is not an evolution, at least not an evolution by descent and filiation. Becoming produces nothing by filiation [...] It concerns alliance. If evolution includes any veritable becomings, it is in the domain of symbioses that bring into play beings of totally different scales and kingdoms, with no possible filiation. [...] Accordingly, the term we would prefer for this form of evolution between heterogeneous terms is "involution", on the condition that involution is in no way confused with regression. Becoming is involu-tionary, involution is creative. To regress is to move in the direction of something less differentiated. But to involve is to form a block that runs its own line "between" terms in play and beneath assignable relations.[38]

The nature of becoming as related by Deleuze and Guattari in this passage has much in common with Jung's assertion that libido 'wills its own descent'. The regression/involution which characterises this notion of descent is underpinned by a philosophy which Deleuze seeks to articulate in many registers (the psychological, the aesthetic, biological, and the material). Involution does not presuppose a differentiable totality from which one becomes less differentiated. Nor does it presuppose an original, organised unity which is then lost and to which a return is deemed essential.[39] In other words, the creative nature of involution concerns movement by alliance in a direction which cannot be determined in advance. Masoch becomes involutionary when he encounters an original image which prompts his descent and spiritual rebirth. For Deleuze, the resulting *katabasis* is one which enables a challenge to the patriarchal order itself and this challenge could not have been determined or even envisaged in advance. In Deleuze's Jungian reading of Masoch's *Venus in Furs*, the alliance which is formed between Masoch and the image of the Mother leads to a rebirth which is revolutionary in the sense that something genuinely new emerges, a novel alliance.

## Concluding Remarks

Whether libido is considered in the narrower psychological sense, libido as a vitalistic life principle,[40] or libido as a material-vitalism,[41] these different registers belie the same philosophical approaches within the work of Jung and Deleuze with respect to symbolic death and spiritual rebirth. The Nekyia journey of psychological regression and involution as a material vital principle in which there is a 'return' to a power to forge new alliances which cut across different phyletic lineages may be processes which occur in different registers, but the process of regression-involution remains the same. There is no 'return' to the inanimate because there is no *a priori* assumption that death is synonymous with an entropic state of lifelessness. This insight is given its fullest philosophical expression in Deleuze's *Difference and Repetition*, where he equates the notion of return with a form of repetition which can be defined by what it is not; a 'material, bare and brute repetition understood as the repetition of the same' (*DR*, 103). The Freudian conception of the death instinct understood as a return to the inanimate remains, says Deleuze, 'is inseparable from the positing of an ultimate term, the model of a material and bare repetition and the conflictual dualism of between life and death' (*DR*, 104).

From where did Deleuze derive this idea? As we have seen, its most likely source was Jung's *Psychology of the Unconscious* and it finds itself re-imagined in different registers and concepts throughout Deleuze's work, one of the most important of which was involution. It is also noteworthy that in some of his earliest and final works, Jung approaches the idea of symbolic death within the context of the quasi-vitalist notion of the 'psychoid'.[42] Whilst it is beyond the scope of this chapter to offer any insight into the relationship between the psychoid and involution, it is enough to suggest that further resonances may exist between these two concepts which can and should be subjected to further investigation.

## Notes

1 C. Kerslake, *Deleuze and the Unconscious*, London: Continuum, 2007, p. 81.
2 C.G. Jung, *The Psychology of the Unconscious* [1912/1916], tr. B.M. Hinkle, New York: Dodd, Mead, 1949.
3 G. Deleuze, 'From Sacher-Masoch to Masochism', tr. C. Kerslake, *Angelaki*, April 2004, vol. 9(1), 125–133. Originally published as 'De Sacher Masoch au masochisme' in *Arguments*, 1961, vol. 5 (21)/1, 40–46 (hereafter referred to as *SMM*).
4 *Venus in Furs* is also a novella by Ritter von Leopold Sacher-Masoch, first published in 1870.
5 Cf. C. Kerslake, 'Deleuze and the Jungian Unconscious' in C. Kerslake, *Deleuze and the Unconscious*. London: Continuum, 2007, p. 69.
6 C. Kerslake, 'Rebirth through incest', *Angelaki*, April 2005, vol. 9(1), 135–157 (p. 135).
7 C.G. Jung, 'The Relations between the Ego and the Unconscious' [1928], in *Two Essays on Analytical Psychology* [*Collected Works*, vol. 7, tr. R.F.C. Hull], 2nd edn, London: Routledge & Kegan Paul, 1966, pp. 113–169 (p. 130). Cf. G. Deleuze, 'From Sacher-Masoch to Masochism', p. 132, n. 13. Cf. E.P. Kazarian, 'The Revolutionary Unconscious: Deleuze and Masoch', *Substance*, 2010, vol. 39(2), 91–106 (p. 102).
8 G. Deleuze, *Difference and Repetition* [1968], tr. P. Patton, New York: Columbia University Press, 1994, p. 163 (hereafter referred to as *DR*). Cf. Kazarian, 'The Revolutionary Unconscious', p. 92.
9 Kazarian summarises as follows: 'To make "possible experience" is to subject experience to the conditions of self-identity, and to subject sensibility to the rigours of conceptual representation. Real experience, on the contrary, does not depend on the presence of a transcendental ego but upon a "virtual" transcendental field, equivalent to the unconscious', in 'Deleuze, Perversion and Politics', *International Journal of Philosophy*, 1998, vol. 30(1), 91–106 (p. 101).
10 For example, Deleuze comments as follows: 'Empiricism truly becomes transcendental, and aesthetics an apodictic discipline, only when we apprehend directly in the sensible that which can only be sensed, the very being *of* the sensible: difference, potential difference and difference in intensity as the reason behind qualitative diversity' (*DR*, 57).
11 G. Deleuze, *Proust and Signs* [1964], tr. R. Howard, Minneapolis: University of Minnesota Press, 2000, p. 47.
12 Kerslake, *Deleuze and the Unconscious*, p. 96.
13 Kazarian, 'Deleuze, Perversion and Politics', p. 96.
14 Cf. Kazarian, 'Deleuze, Perversion and Politics', p. 95.
15 On the symbolism of fur in which Venus is wrapped and by which Masoch is entranced, Deleuze states that 'fur is first of all a directly maternal symbol, indicating the refolding of the law in the feminine principle, the *mater Natura* threatened by the ambition of her sons' (*SMM*, 127).
16 See G. Deleuze, 'The Image of Thought', in Deleuze, *DR*, 129–167.
17 Kazarian, 'Deleuze, Perversion and Politics', p. 98.
18 See *SMM*, 126; cf. Kazarian, 'The Revolutionary Unconscious: Deleuze and Masoch', p. 92.
19 As Deleuze writes, '[I]t therefore seems very doubtful that the image of the Father in masochism has the role which Freud gives it. Freudian psychoanalysis in general suffers from an inflation of the father' (*SMM*, 128).

20  Kazarian, 'The Revolutionary Unconscious: Deleuze and Masoch', p. 97.
21  On the notion of the 'ordeal' in masochism, Deleuze writes that 'the castration of Attis or Osiris, being swallowed up by a whale-dragon or a gluttonous fish, being bitten by a serpent, being suspended from a maternal tree, all these symbols of return to the Mother signify the necessity of sacrificing the genital sexuality inherited from the father, in order to obtain the rebirth or renaissance which will equip us with a new and independent virility' (*SMM*, 130).
22  See *SMM*, 127. Cf. Kerslake, 'Rebirth through incest', p. 146; Kazarian, 'The Revolutionary Unconscious: Deleuze and Masoch', pp. 98–99.
23  Kerslake, 'Rebirth through incest', p. 146.
24  Jung, *Psychology of the Unconscious*, pp. 237, 240, 245, 267, 273, 277, 351, 384, 392.
25  C.G. Jung, *Symbols of Transformation* [1952] [*Collected Works*, vol. 5, tr. R.F.C. Hull], London: Routledge & Kegan Paul, 1956, pp. 210, 212, 218, 233, 236, 243, 316, 331, 350, 358, 371.
26  Cf. P. Bishop, *Analytical Psychology and German Classical Aesthetics: Goethe, Schiller and Jung*, vol. 1, *The Development of the Personality*, London and New York: Routledge, 2008, p. 34.
27  Jung, *Psychology of the Unconscious*, p. 399; cf. Jung, *Symbols of Transformation*, p. 365.
28  See C.G. Jung, 'Picasso' [1932] in *The Spirit in Man, Art and Literature* [*Collected Works*, vol. 15, tr. R.F.C. Hull], London: Routledge & Kegan Paul, 1966, pp. 135–141 (p. 138). Jung also says that 'Nekyia is therefore is an apt designation for the "journey to Hades," the descent into the land of the dead', in 'Individual Dream Symbolism in Relation to Alchemy' [1936] in *Psychology and Alchemy* [*Collected Works*, vol. 12, tr. R.F.C. Hull], 2nd edn, London: Routledge & Kegan Paul, 1968, pp. 41–223 (p. 53, n. 2). Jung goes on to say that his use of the term is derived from the work of Albrecht Dieterich (1866–1908) and his commentary on the Codex of Akhmim; see A. Dieterich, *Nekyia: Beiträge zur Erklärung der neuentdeckten Petrusapokalypse*, Leipzig and Berlin: Teubner, 1913.
29  Jung, 'Picasso', p. 139.
30  See Jung, *Psychology of the Unconscious*, p. 238.
31  Jung, *Psychology of the Unconscious*, p. 278; cf. Jung, *Symbols of Transformation*, p. 245.
32  Jung, *Symbols of Transformation*, p. 245.
33  Jung, *Symbols of Transformation*, p. 438.
34  Jung, *Symbols of Transformation*, p. 328, n. 38.
35  According to Fátima Caropreso, Sabina Spielrein was another who did not subscribe to this: 'Thus, [Spielrein] maintains the opposition between the ego drives and sexual drives and places the death instinct within these two. This latter instinct would not seek the annihilation of life, would not aim to completely eliminate stimulation, as Freud proposed in 1920, but would in fact attempt to destroy the Self; the transformation of *Self* into *Us*. The hypothesis of the inseparability between destruction and creation means that, for Spielrein, there is no purely negative drive, which is part of the Freudian theory', in 'The death drive according to Sabrina Spielrein', *Piscologia USP*, 2016, vol. 27(3), 414–419 (p. 418).
36  Jung, 'On the Psychology of the Unconscious' [1917/1926/1943] in *Two Essays on Analytical Psychology*, [*Collected Works*, vol. 7, tr. R.F.C. Hull], 2nd edn, London: Routledge & Kegan Paul, 1966, pp. 9–119 (p. 53, n. 6).
37  Cf. Kerslake, *Deleuze and the Unconscious*, pp. 96–97.
38  G. Deleuze, 'Becoming Intense, Becoming Animal' [1980], in G. Deleuze and F. Guattari, *A Thousand Plateaus: Capitalism and Schizophrenia*, tr. B. Massumi, Minneapolis: University of Minnesota Press, 1987, pp. 238–239.

39 A recurring theme throughout all of Deleuze's thought and when writing with Guattari concerns relations of the 'whole' (*tout*). Deleuze's persistent criticisms of a 'logical', 'organic unity'/'organic totality', and internal relations and relations of interiority (that Deleuze tends to identify with organic unity/totality) are situated across many different registers throughout his works (e.g., history, literature, art, cinema, politics, biology) and the notion of the 'whole' frequently appears with them. See G. Deleuze, *Proust and Signs*: pp. 113–116, 161, and 163; G. Deleuze, *Cinema I: The Movement-Image* [1983], tr. H. Tomlinson and B. Habberjam, Minneapolis: University of Minnesota, pp. 95–96, 322–323, and 326–327 (cf. 'closed' and 'open' whole/s, in G. Deleuze and F. Guattari, *What is Philosophy* [1991], tr. H. Tomlinson and G. Burchell, New York: Columbia University Press, 1994, p. 105); and G. Deleuze, *Cinema II: The Time-Image* [1985], tr. H. Tomlinson and R. Galeta, Minneapolis: University of Minnesota, 1989, pp. 9–11 and 16–20.

40 On related themes concerning vitalism in the work of Jung and Deleuze, see C. McMillan, 'Jung and Deleuze: Enchanted Openings to the Other: A Philosophical Contribution', *International Journal of Jungian Studies*, 2018, vol. 10(3), 184–198; and C. McMillan, 'Kant's influence on Jung's vitalism in the *Zofingia Lectures*', in C. McMillan, R. Main, and D. Henderson (eds), *Holism: Possibilities and Problems*, London and New York: Routledge, 2019, pp. 118–129.

41 Deleuze was an anti-foundational thinker, but he also refers to himself as a 'vitalist' and a 'metaphysician', highly critical of most branches of phenomenology which had emerged before and during his life-time', so that he could say: 'Everything I've written is vitalistic, at least I hope it is' (*Negotiations, 1972–1990*, tr. M. Joughin, New York: Columbia University Press, 1995, p. 143).

42 See M. Nagy, *Philosophical Issues in the Psychology of C.G. Jung*, Albany: State University of New York Press, p. 251; and A. Addison, 'Jung, vitalism and 'the psychoid': an historical reconstruction', *Journal of Analytical Psychology*, 2009, vol. 54(1), 123–142 (p. 128).

# Epilogue

## *Salon Noir*[1]

### Ruth Padel

When we went down into the cave
this summer     after her death
had opened the vein to a year of reckoning
across the whole family     everyone upset

    both of them dead within six hours on the same night
    a hundred miles apart     my mother and my aunt
    her sister-in-law
    our gentle     daring     painter
    whose children were rushing her in an ambulance
        from the room upstairs
        in the family house
        where I was born
    to a London hospital
    just when for us it was all over

we were each a little afraid.
Also unprepared. The young     apparently
were thinking of vampires. For me
it was breaking an ankle.

          *

Take nothing     said the guide     a girl
from the green hills of the Ariège
who knew every centimetre of the caves.

Leave behind
all bags and mobile phones.
You're not allowed to take pictures

and you'll need your hands.
The path is slippery
broken     rough

DOI: 10.4324/9781003054139-16

you have to crouch
you'll be carrying a heavy torch
but don't touch the walls

if you stumble. Even your breath
each in-and-out of oxygen
does a little destroying.

                    *

Our flashlights in the tunnel      showed
dangerous ridges underfoot.
Wild knobs of embryonic stalagmites
glistened like sea anemones. Beware
they said to our stout shoes      we have time
we *are* time      the texture itself.

The floor of the first
chamber swirled
    like quivers in the structure of a raga.
We were treading limestone waves
millennia of solid flood
breathing shallow as we could

then dark-blistered stone
and pure
        geological process
personal
inexorable
    closed in.

The walls swirled too      when I stopped
to play a beam on them in the dark.
Rough surfaces      map-shapes
of amber      russet      grey
and all around us      black.
No ceramics      no shards

of biscuity pottery
we might piece together into a cup
touched by their lips
fifteen thousand years ago.
This was origin. Way before any potter.
So many ways to begin.

I heard the hiss of time      like the swish of tyres
    on a wet road
as we faltered along      bowed our heads
felt the blowing of solar winds

and the need for fire
like the start cry of a race.

We slipped down a chimney of slime
a tunnel opened out to the *Salon Noir*
and we saw the first human trace
red stripes and black      vertical signs
like sleep-marks on skin
a key-shape      an arrow

we turned off our heavy torches
and laid them down in violet night on a bridge of rock
so our guide could shine her power lamp
of snowy halogen      alone
and we saw bison      flickering the black
circles of their eyes

rippling on cream
stone as if over a canvas of the mind.
I thought of Freud      how the unconscious
is constructed geologically by pressure      a kind
of archaeological layering under the soul
inaccessible except in dreams.

Horses appeared      the tissue of their manes      clear
against grey rock      every tuft erect
scribble-shaggy      bolshie      necks
stretched out      eyes closed      mealy-muzzled as an Exmoor
pony      a whole wall of horses on prehistoric limestone
like a page of Leonardo's sketch-book

whoever drew them had no idea
they would come to be our partners      change
    human work      ambition      history
but I felt at home. Here were the horses
my mum used to draw      for me
    till I could draw my own.

In that milk-flower ray of fluorine
these beasts      called down to the dark
from valleys above      seemed to move

as they must have done then
    for the very first time
in a pitch-flare held for the artist.

While we took it all in      the delicate expressions
the questioning back-turned nose of an ibex
the flaring nostril and lifted tail

of one bison challenging another
I felt my mother's greatest gift
to me was noticing.

She taught us to be curious     to wonder
at all animal life     however small
the territory fights of a chaffinch

fox cubs creeping out at night
their skirmishes with cats.
Snails     she murmured once

at a TV programme on invertebrates.
Who would have thought a snail
could be so tender?

                    *

The guide asked if anyone would sing.
The *Salon Noir*     she said     is only one
of many caves. We wonder
if the artists     over the centuries     chose
this chamber for the acoustic     resonant
as a cathedral. Try. I wondered if an echo

might set off an avalanche
and the whole cave-system   the cracked
mysterious mass of hollow stone
would crash     bury us under the mountain
but the notes when they came in that black air
were a flow of prayer     a thread

of unearthly melody like the deep-space vibrato
of a theremin     surely not from my throat.
Our guide followed my song upward with her torch
     a wing-bone of white light     floating into tiered
     pinnacles and funnels of jagged stone
as if lifting us on feathers of pure sound

to the point where all sound disappeared.
I imagined the voice of Orpheus
his aria to life and hope
     ringing out in the kingdom of the dead.
Here in deep earth     the black
blossom of mourning still sifting within me

I remembered that emerald was my birthstone
that an emerald
     mined in the dark

but lucent green
as leaves      returning
after a hundred thousand years of ice

green for awakening      for bringing life
back from the dead      renewal
in earth and of the earth
is a token of re-birth.
I pictured the attic room where I was born
in that enchanted house none of us will enter again

where my mother gave birth to me in May
      her first of five
six      if you count the baby that died. I heard
a trickle of water over rock like buried tears
and in this cave of making
      birth of transformation and of art      I understood

how anyone in darkness longs for green
      for the animal life which goes with green
and which      like faceted crystal
      light in stone      lets us see the impossible
      our own lives with their faults and wounds
in a different way

      and how the very idea of one gem for our birth
might make us try
      to say the story of ourselves with a whole heart

      to carry the true good burden of being known
even by animal eyes      and not alone
   like the singer      who drew
all life towards him and went down into the dark
      taking his art into the earth
and art takes him up to the light again      renewed.

We came back changed. We saw black rock
jagged round the entrance      the golden eye
of afternoon. Those who came before
      the dancers      the mothers      were gone into the hill.
But the mountains      rising one behind the other
were herds of green bison      drifting away into the sky.

## Note

1  From Emerald by Ruth Padel published by Chatto & Windus. Copyright © Ruth
   Padel 2018. Reproduced by permission of The Random House Group Ltd.

# Index

Page numbers followed by 'n' refer to notes.

For Product Safety Concerns and Information please contact our EU
representative GPSR@taylorandfrancis.com
Taylor & Francis Verlag GmbH, Kaufingerstraße 24, 80331 München, Germany

www.ingramcontent.com/pod-product-compliance
Lightning Source LLC
Chambersburg PA
CBHW050350270326
41926CB00016B/3671

9 780367 515010